Business Leaders Praise
Grown Up Digital: How the Net Generation is Changing Your World
By Don Tapscott

"Once again, Don Tapscott has captured a piece of the zeitgeist. *Grown Up Digital* demonstrates the world-changing power of the Net Generation and the way they are rethinking everything, from education to home life to citizen participation. If you want to understand their impact, read this book."

—Eric Schmidt, CEO, Google

"A decade ago Don Tapscott recognized that the kids growing up online were different, and that speaking digital as a first language was the key competitive skill of our age. Now that generation has grown up and Tapscott has followed them into the workplace and the world, where those skills are playing out in surprising ways. This is a rich and data-packed atlas of that generation."

—Chris Anderson, Editor in Chief, *Wired*

"To be sustainable, a knowledge economy needs highly educated, skilled workers. More than manpower, we need workers with mindpower. The no. 1 challenge we face as leaders in business, government, education, and the community is educating and engaging our kids. Tapscott makes a well-reasoned, persuasive case for how to harness the Net Gen. Every educator and manager should read this book."

—Jim Goodnight, CEO, SAS

"No one knows the digital generation and its impact on society better than Don Tapscott. *Grown Up Digital* is a fresh look at a global phenomenon that has been brewing for over 15 years. As a demographer, marketer, and social observer, Don brings the net generation to life and equips the reader with practical advice on how to cope with a world gone digital."

—Brian Fetherstonhaugh, Chairman & CEO, OgilvyOne Worldwide

"Only those who understand the new paradigms as described in the latest book by Don Tapscott will not be displaced as individuals or businesses in the world of tomorrow."   —Klaus Schwab, Founder & Executive Chairman,
World Economic Forum

"Don Tapscott is always relevant, always fresh. His new book, *Grown Up Digital*, adds depth and insight to an important issue impacting talent and leadership in the hyper-connected world of today, and tomorrow."

—Kevin Kelly, CEO, Heidrick& Struggles

"Don Tapscott delivers insights. As usually is the case, these insights reflect the world around us in ways we possibly should see but perhaps don't. As a business leader and as a father of young adults, I see *Grown Up Digital* as a collection of insights that contain tremendous value to understanding how this generation will impact the world and our future."

—Michael McCain, CEO, Maple Leaf Foods

"Don Tapscott offers compelling insight into how the Net Generation is changing the nature of work, culture, and government and what that means for anyone who wants to engage them. *Grown Up Digital* is both a comprehensive guide to understanding the world of Web 2.0 and to unleashing the power of Talent 2.0." —Tammy Johns, SVP, Global Workforce Strategy, Manpower Inc.

"Understanding the expectations and motivations of the next generation is a critical challenge for all businesses. Don Tapscott's latest book is fascinating and entertaining for parents and educators, but it is a must-read for business leaders who have much to gain from understanding this important and different demographic."

—Gordon Nixon, President & CEO, RBC Financial Group

"Don's book is like the firm nudge with a cold steel pointer from a teacher who catches you looking out the window. Tapscott explains that success is not about the control and authority we grant ourselves to "empower people"—it's all about genuine understanding and creating an environment where people can and will choose to motivate themselves."

—Bill McEwan, President & CEO, Sobeys Inc.

"For anyone leading a talent-based organization, *Grown Up Digital* is an essential read. The Net Generation is transforming the way we work, learn, play, and communicate and redefining how organizations recruit, train, motivate, collaborate, and innovate. A revolution in how we live and work is upon us. This generation is the one to watch and learn from."

—Bill Green, Chairman & CEO, Accenture

"Today's workforce is no longer one size that fits all, which leaves employers across all industries in a serious state of peril. Employers need to recognize and adapt to the rapidly changing world of work, channeling the motivations that different generations bring to their workforce. Don Tapscott has not only grasped the subject, but he is uniquely positioned to offer real advice on how to address these changes."

—Jeffrey A. Joerres, Chairman & CEO, Manpower Inc.

"Don Tapscott nails it. *Grown Up Digital* provides a guided tour of how the pioneering Net Generation is changing the way we all live, work, and play in a global creative economy. A must-read."

—Richard Florida, author, *Who's Your City?* and
The Rise of the Creative Class

FROM THE AUTHOR OF
Growing Up Digital

OTHER BOOKS BY DON TAPSCOTT

Wikinomics: How Mass Collaboration Changes Everything (2006)
with Anthony D. Williams

*The Naked Corporation: How the Age of Transparency
Will Revolutionize Business* (2003)
with David Ticoll

Digital Capital: Harnessing the Power of Business Webs (2000)
with David Ticoll and Alex Lowy

Creating Value in the Network Economy (1999)

Blueprint to the Digital Economy: Creating Wealth in the Era of E-Business (1999)
with David Ticoll and Alex Lowy

Growing Up Digital: The Rise of the Net Generation (1997)

The Digital Economy: Promise and Peril in the Age of Networked Intelligence (1996)

Who Knows: Safeguarding Your Privacy in a Networked World (1996)
with Ann Cavoukian

Paradigm Shift: The New Promise of Information Technology (1992)
with Art Caston

Planning for Integrated Office Systems: A Strategic Approach (1984)
with Del Henderson and Morley Greenberg

Office Automation: A User-Driven Method (1982)
with Del Henderson and Morley Greenberg

"Don Tapscott delivers an insightful and practical book for anyone seeking to better understand, appreciate, and unlock the full potential of today's youth. Backed by comprehensive research, *Grown Up Digital* debunks popular myths and reveals the norms and motivations of a generation poised to transform business, education, government, and society."
—James Quigley, CEO, Deloitte Touche Tohmatsu

"Don captures learnings and statistics about the Net Generation that are on target. Net Geners are coming into the world and workplace now. Moreover, as a parent, I read with recognition yet found it amazing that some of the things I've experienced were captured on a page. Don's realizations in *Grown Up Digital* are highly relevant and must be brought to a broader audience."
—Ann Purr, Second Vice President, Information Management, LOMA

"In *Grown Up Digital*, Tapscott tells us how the Net Generation is creating our future and why their opinions count. He uniquely shows how to harvest the big contributions this generation has to offer."
—Fred Smith, President & CEO, FedEx

"No one has been a more informed commentator on the transformative impact of the digital age than Don Tapscott. *Grown Up Digital* reveals the impact that youthful empowered employees, customers, and citizens are having and will have on our daily lives. It is profound."   —Brad Anderson, CEO, Best Buy

"In *Grown Up Digital*, Don Tapscott portrays eloquently and in rich color the massive impact that The Net Generation—those born between 1977 and 1997, 80 million in the U.S. alone—will have on the future of society and the economy. He accomplishes this with his usual acumen, deftness, depth, and good humor."   —Bill Dimma, former senior executive and director of 55 companies over 45 years

"Don Tapscott provides an exciting road map to surviving and thriving in the Connected Era."   —Michael Dell, CEO, Dell

"Ignore the deep insights in *Grown Up Digital* and you risk becoming an irrelevant leader for next generation employees. Tapscott's optimism for youth is infectious and inspirational."   —Kal Patel, Executive Vice President, Emerging Business, Best Buy

"*Grown Up Digital* is the first guide to the land of the Net Generation that should be read both by visitors and residents alike. Tapscott's latest work follows *Growing Up Digital* with lockstep obedience and shows all signs of being as prescient and relevant."   —Nicholas Negroponte, Founder & Chairman, One Laptop Per Child

the book's themes. All citations in the book that are not footnoted came from these interviews or from comments made in one of our online discussion groups.

We also endeavored to ensure that every presentation—especially newspaper and journal articles and research reports—that was available online would be easily accessible to the readers of this book. Given the state of the Web, we were partially successful—63 percent of all such citations are accompanied by a Web site where the information can be found and studied in more detail.

Thank you to the following people who provided insights to this research, usually through an interview or conversation: Monica Aguilar, Rhadeena De Alwis, Michele Azar, Linda Barker, Shannon and Chris Barry, Ann Bender, Steve Bendt, Zachary Best, Robbie Blinkoff, Danah Boyd, Louise Brandy, Michelle Brantley-Patterson, Amy Brinkman, John Seely Brown, Whitney Burton, Barry Campbell, Ron Canuel, Frances Cardinal, Briony Cayley, Matt Ceniceros, Matt Cohler, Jeffrey Connor, Barbara Coloroso, Ann Coster, Kelly Cox, Samia Cury, Victoria Davis, Rob Dean, Eriel Deranger, Bill and Janet Dreitlein, Matthew Dreitlein, Thomas Dreitlein, Barbara Dwyer, Matthew Dye, Robert Epstein, Allison Fetherstonhaugh, Brian Fetherstonhaugh, Michael Furdyk, Ed Gordon, Fernando Gonzalez, Jordan Grafman, C. Shawn Green, Matthew Hanwell, Idit Harel, Rahaf Harfoush, Dennis Harper, Chris Hughes, Yunan Jin, Kirsten Jordan, Joe Kalkman, Alan Kay, Fred and Evan Killeen, Gary Koelling, Cherrie Kong, Matthew Kutcher, Stan Kutcher, Tung Le, Jure Leskovec, Lawrence Lessig, Donald Leu, Julie Lindsay, Raymond Ling, Kaelyn Lowmaster, Alan Majer, Chris Manseri, Elliot Masie, Emily McCartan, Mollie Merry, David Meyer, Jerry Michalski, Sarah Antoinette Millican, Oscar Morales, Matthew Myers, Juan Niscimbene, Gregor Novak, Nigel Paine, Dan Oscar, Seymour Papert, Kevina Power Njoroge, Marc Prensky, Luis M. Proenza, Jim Quigley, Tahir and Aisha Rauf, Feroz Rauf, Jennifer Rock, Ahren Sadoff, Shay Sanders, Stephen Satris, Eric Schmidt, Stephen Seaward, Effie Seidberg, Dan Shea, Julian Sher, Andy Shimberg, Peggy Siegel, George Siemens, Lara Smith, Gregory Spencer, Trudy Steinfeld, Catherine Tamis-LeMonda, Bill Tapscott, Bob Tapscott, Katharine Tapscott, Mary Tapscott, Maria Terrell, David Thompson, Emma Thompson, Sherry Turkle, Jean Twenge, John Della Volpe, Kim Watterson, William D. Winn, Ben Way, Amy Welsman, John Wolf, Stanton Wortham, and Mark Zuckerberg.

Others quoted in the book, usually from Web discussions, include: Aditi Bakht, Yochai Benkler, Keenan Borde, Melissa Bowlby, Matt Ceniceros, Greg Curtis, Kevin DaSilva, Rebecca Dobrzynski, Nick Dubois, Phil Dumouchel, Ben Elron, John Geraci, Kevin Gessner, Charles Grantham, Aaron Hay, Danny

Wikinomics, contributed many of the big ideas in the program and became our executive editor for the second phase of the work. I hold each of these people in highest esteem. It is hard to imagine a better team for conducting a massive and complex program like this.

The Program Faculty

A number of thoughtful and disciplined researchers, consultants, authors, and academics conducted individual projects and/or wrote key research papers. These include: Paul Artiuch, Robert Barnard, Paul Barter, Pierre-Luc Bisaillon, Nick Bontis, Grant Buckler, Ann Cavoukian, Lisa Chen, Amy Cortese, Ian Da Silva, Tammy Erickson, Bill Gillies, Anastasia Goodstein, Denis Hancock, Nauman Haque, Janet Hardy, Dan Herman, Neil Howe, Mathew Ingram, Claudy Jules, Stan Kutcher, Rich Lauf, Victoria Luby, Alan Majer, Chuck Martin, Abby Miller, Sean Moffitt, Brendan Peat, Joe Pine, Deepak Ramachandran, Paul Regan, Bruce Rogow, Rob Salkowitz, Denise Schiffman, Bruce Sellery, David Singleton, Bruce Stewart, and William Strauss.

The Program Team

We assembled a great team of researchers, coordinators, and program administrators, many who work for nGenera Insight and others who subcontracted to the effort: Pat Atkinson, David Cameron, Fred Carter, Jeff DeChambeau, Thusenth Dhavaloganathan, Will Dick, Laura Dobrzynski, Karen Doktor, Dana Dramnitzke, Matthew Dreitlein, Jeff Fila, Hagai Fleiman, Rahaf Harfoush, Samir Khan, Karolina Kibis, Natalie Klym, Daniela Kortan, Matthew Kutcher, Ming Kwan, Erin Lemon, Caleb Love, Jason Papadimos, Nikki Papadopolous, Lauren Peer, Derek Pokora, Stanley Rodos, Antoinette Schatz, Corinne Shannon, Heather Shaw, Roberta Smith, Jocelyn Svengsouk, David Wilcox, and Daniel Williamson.

THE GROWN UP DIGITAL BOOK PROJECT
Research Methods

The book team conducted qualitative research. We created a community on Facebook of over 200 people (Grown Up Digital—Help Me Write the Book) to solicit views and stories and many Net Geners actively contributed to the effort. The global network of 140,000 Net Geners—TakingITGlobal (www.takingitglobal.org) also hosted a series of discussions over several months on our behalf.

Additionally, we interviewed dozens of authorities on various topics related to fielded the survey. We also conducted 30 deep-dive, ethnographic studies of Net Geners in their home settings.

Client Sponsors and Partners

I am very grateful to the thoughtful CEOs and other business executives who showed leadership in engaging their companies in this work: Sonia Baxendale, CIBC; Deborah Bothun, PricewaterhouseCoopers; Deb Capolarello, MetLife; Peter Cheese, Accenture; Cathy Cornish, MetLife; Judy Edge, FedEx; Karen Evans, OMB; Allan Falvey, Hershey's; Mike Fasulo, Sony; Brian Fetherston-haugh, OgilvyOne Worldwide; Dennis Folz, Sobeys; Joyce France, U.S. Department of Defense; Ian Gee, Nokia; Steve Hanna, GM; Matthew Hanwell, Nokia; Tammy Johns, Manpower; Barry Judge, Best Buy; Rod MacDonald, Service Canada; Walt Macnee, MasterCard; Pat McLean, BCE; Dominic Mercuri, TD Bank; Marilyn Mersereau, Cisco; John Newell, Scotiabank; Kal Patel, Best Buy; JP Rangaswami, BT; John Smith, Canada Post; Mike Turillo, Spencer Trask; Ken Wilson, Coril Holdings; Colette Wycech, Verizon.

Client Collaborators

The following people were among those who worked closely with the research team, providing insights, attending events, and working to ensure that their company benefited from the research. Michele Azar, Best Buy; Dessia Blank, FedEx; Logie Bruce-Lockhart, Sobeys; Warren Dodge, Accenture; Wendy Hartzell, GM; Darcy Lake, Accenture; Rob Leighton, Canada Post; Susan McVey, TD Bank; Sally Potts, PricewaterhouseCoopers; and Warren Tomlin, Canada Post.

The Program Management

A core team worked with me to manage the program. Joan Bigham headed up all client relationships, including recruiting program sponsors. Mike Dover acted as project manager, ensuring that hundreds of activities were effectively coordinated and marshaled to achieve our goals. John Geraci, one of the world's leading youth-market researchers, conceived many aspects of the program and as research director oversaw all the surveys and qualitative work conducted, including subcontracting pieces to research partners. Jody Stevens managed program finances and administration with her usual precision. My longtime collaborator and coauthor of two books David Ticoll ably took responsibility for all content—architecting client deliverables, working with research teams, and editing reports. Anthony D. Williams, coauthor of

RESEARCH METHODS, TEAMS, AND ACKNOWLEDGMENTS

Grown Up Digital was inspired by a $4 million research project, "The Net Generation: a Strategic Investigation," funded by large companies. The work began under the auspices of New Paradigm—the company I founded in 1993. New Paradigm was acquired by nGenera in 2007 and continues this work today. The nGenera executive team, lead by the CEO Steve Papermaster, has been enormously supportive of this research and for that I am very grateful.

My colleagues and I interviewed close to 10,000 people and produced over 40 reports, conducted several conferences, and held dozens of private executive briefings on program results and recommendations. The reports are proprietary to the research sponsors, but some of the high-level findings and main conclusions can now be shared publicly.

Once this work was complete, I launched the "Grown Up Digital" book project, and, with a core team of researchers, set out to understand the implications of this generation's experience with digital technology for the rest of society and to address the many issues raised in the book.

So, in all, thousands of people contributed to the creation of this book. However, the opinions expressed in this book are mine and I take full responsibility for the content and views contained herein.

THE NET GENERATION: A STRATEGIC INVESTIGATION
Research Methods
As part of the pilot phase of the program we interviewed 1,750 young people, 13 to 20 years old, in the United States and Canada. Beginning May 3, 2007, we interviewed 5,935 Net Geners aged 16 to 29 in 12 countries (the United States, Canada, the United Kingdom, Germany, France, Spain, Mexico, Brazil, Russia, China, Japan, and India). In addition, a benchmark sample of Gen Xers, aged 30 to 41, and baby boomers, aged 42 to 61, was gathered in the United States and Canada (approximately n = 400 of each group in each country). The total Net Gen sample is 7,685, and, adding in the Gen Xers and boomers we have interviewed, the total is 9,442 people. The sample was composed of randomly selected Internet users, stratified to avoid any gender or socioeconomic biases. Interviews were done through an online questionnaire. Crux Research

CONTENTS

Acknowledgments/xi

PART ONE: **MEET THE NET GEN**

INTRODUCTION 1

CHAPTER 1 The Net Generation Comes of Age 9

CHAPTER 2 A Generation Bathed in Bits 39

CHAPTER 3 The Eight Net Gen Norms: Characteristics of a Generation 73

CHAPTER 4 The Net Generation Brain 97

PART TWO: **TRANSFORMING INSTITUTIONS**

CHAPTER 5 The Net Generation as Learners: Rethinking Education 121

CHAPTER 6 The Net Generation in the Workforce: Rethinking Talent
and Management 149

CHAPTER 7 The Net Generation as Consumers: N-Fluence Networks
and the Prosumer Revolution 185

CHAPTER 8 The Net Generation and the Family: No Place Like the
New Home 219

PART THREE: **TRANSFORMING SOCIETY**

CHAPTER 9 The Net Generation and Democracy: Obama,
Social Networks, and Citizen Engagement 243

CHAPTER 10 Making the World a Better Place—at Ground Level 269

CHAPTER 11 In Defense of the Future 289

Appendix/313
Notes/319
Bibliography/345
Index/361

For Niki, Alex, and Ana

grown up digital

HOW THE NET GENERATION IS CHANGING YOUR WORLD

DON TAPSCOTT

NEW YORK   CHICAGO   SAN FRANCISCO
LISBON   LONDON   MADRID   MEXICO CITY   MILAN
NEW DELHI   SAN JUAN   SEOUL   SINGAPORE
SYDNEY   TORONTO

ISBN: 978-0-07-150863-6
MHID: 0-07-150863-5

This publication is designed to provide accurate and authoritative information in regard to the subject matter covered. It is sold with the understanding that neither the author nor the publisher is engaged in rendering legal, accounting, or other professional service. If legal advice or other expert assistance is required, the services of a competent professional person should be sought.

> —From a Declaration of Principles jointly adopted
> by a Committee of the American Bar
> Association and a Committee of Publishers

McGraw-Hill books are available at special quantity discounts to use as premiums and sales promotions, or for use in corporate training programs. For more information, please write to the Director of Special Sales, Professional Publishing, McGraw-Hill, Two Penn Plaza, New York, NY 10121-2298. Or contact your local bookstore.

This book is printed on acid-free paper.

Herbst, Henry Jenkins, Savannah Jones, Mike Kanert, Vanessa Kenalty, Melissa Kenninger, Moritz Kettler, Cherrie Kong, Mike Lazear, Nate Lewin, Erin Lewis, Austin Locke, Del McLean, Bobbi Munroe, Rod Paige, Eric Potter, Boca Raton, Rin, Erik Rubadeau, Alex Salzillo, Jen Shaw, Karen Shim, Graham Smith, Tina Sturgeon, Jocelyn Svengsouk, Eva Szymanski, Anita Tang, Katie Tinkham, John Della Volpe, Martin Westwell, Daniel Williamson, and Jonathan Wolf.

The Book Team

Psychology-trained researcher Lisa Chen, who was one of the principal authors of the Net Generation project along with my longtime research associate Bill Gillies, ably conducted the preliminary research throughout the latter half of 2007. They spent many hours with me architecting the book and helping me formulate the main messages, assisted by a great student team of Laura Dobrzynski, Karen Doktor, and Jocelyn Svengsouk. Rahaf Harfoush, an independent consultant who has worked with me since she graduated in 2006, contributed critical thinking and ideas at several junctures. Recent SUNY political science graduate Matthew Dreitlein worked for many months digging up a wealth of important information and completing the painstaking work of documenting and fact checking the book. In the spirit of full disclosure, Matthew's and Rahaf's personal stories were so insightful I have included them in the book. Mike Dover, who heads nGenera's Talent 2.0 work, gave the manuscript a thoughtful, detailed critique.

From the beginning, I wanted this book to be completely accessible to any reader of nonfiction, not just the cognoscenti. I believe I have achieved this, and much of the credit goes to the brilliant writer and editor, Sarah Scott. In the last six months she and I became a two-person team, refining the core concepts, restructuring and reworking the material, and cutting the manuscript in half. We had a thoroughly enjoyable and enormously productive collaboration.

I'm also thankful to the folks at McGraw-Hill, who published *Growing Up Digital* many years ago. Phil Ruppel, the vice president and group publisher of McGraw-Hill Professional, had been encouraging me to write the sequel for many years and I'm thankful for his support. He and Herb Schaffner, the publisher at McGraw-Hill Professional, assigned Leah Spiro, one of their most senior, most experienced (and toughest) editors, to work with me. Having to set aside my pride of authorship was humbling but ultimately good for you as a reader.

Terry Deal, a thoughtful and thorough editor, managed the entire editing and production process and made many important editorial suggestions that I heartily adopted. The marketing and publicity team was also first-rate—my sincere thanks to Amy Morse, Laura Friedman, Ann Pryor, and Gaya Vinay from McGraw-Hill, and our own team coordinated by Kasi Bruno—Jessie Brumfiel, Ian Da Silva, Ming Kwan, Derek Pokora, and Scott Waddell. Happily, my Executive Assistant of 15 years, Antoinette Schatz, was, as always, involved in everything.

Overall, my family was my most important influence. My wife, Ana Lopes, has always been a tough critic and has kept me grounded. We have discussed these ideas at length, both as parents and as collaborators in my writing.

Niki and Alex Tapscott, who are now young adults, have been my inspiration and most important source of insights over the years on this topic. In a sense, they are my coauthors. I am enormously thankful and blessed.

INTRODUCTION

It's amazing to think how far the kids have come in the dozen or so years since I wrote *Growing Up Digital*. The inspiration for that book came from watching my two children use complex technologies like computers, video games, and VCRs with seemingly no effort. By 1993, my son Alex, then 7, played sophisticated games, typed class assignments on a Mac, and sent an e-mail to Santa Claus at Christmas. That same year, my 10-year-old daughter Nicole figured out how to communicate with friends on computer chat lines. She was always pushing the envelope on technology in our home, even more so than her brother. When the first browser, Mosaic, brought the World Wide Web onto the scene, they took to it like ducks to water, becoming more proficient surfers than either me or my wife Ana. When a new technology came into the house, we would often turn to the kids to figure it out.

I thought they were prodigies. Then I noticed that all their friends were just as talented. So to find out what was going on, the company I founded, now called nGenera, launched a project to study the impact of the Internet on youth in an effort to understand this unique generation. I initially assembled a team to interview 300 young people aged 20 or under, and I spent a lot of time trying to understand my own kids and their friends, especially regarding how they interacted with technology and how that might be changing the ways in which they learned, played, communicated, and even thought. In the end, Niki and Alex weren't just subjects of my research, they became partners of sorts—even though they were still children.

THE FIRST GENERATION TO COME OF AGE IN THE DIGITAL AGE

I came to the conclusion that the defining characteristic of an entire generation was that they were the first to be "growing up digital." In the book of the same title, written between 1996 and 1997, I named them the Net Generation. "The baby boom has an echo and it's even louder than the original," I wrote. They outnumbered the boomer adults, I noted, and they were different from any other generation because they were the first to grow up surrounded by digital media. "Today's kids are so bathed in bits that they think it's all part of the natural landscape."

They related to technology in a different way than we boomers did. "To them the digital technology is no more intimidating than a VCR or toaster," I said. "For the first time in history, children are more comfortable, knowledgeable, and literate than their parents with an innovation central to society. And it is through the use of the digital media that the Net Generation will develop and superimpose its culture on the rest of society. Boomers, stand back. Already these kids are learning, playing, communicating, working, and creating communities very differently than their parents. They are a force for social transformation."

When I wrote those words, the Web had only just arrived. Technology was relatively primitive. We were still using a low-speed dial-up connection to the Internet. Although I was always first on my block to get the fastest connection possible, it was so slow you had time to get a cup of coffee while you were waiting for information to pop up. If my kids had to deal with a slow connection like that today, they'd go crazy.

It was a different world in 1997, digitally speaking. There was no Google, no Facebook, no Twitter, and no BlackBerrys. YouTube didn't exist; you had to watch a music video on TV. I could, nonetheless, see the potential of this incredible new technology, so I speculated on the impact of the new media on youth.

People listened. *Growing Up Digital* was, for a while, the bestselling nonfiction book on Amazon.com and won the first ever Amazon.com bestseller award in the nonfiction category. It was translated into two dozen languages, and I shared the conclusions I had set forth in the book with literally hundreds of audiences around the world and with many millions of people through radio, television, and the print media. Many educators, as well as business and government leaders, told us that the book changed the way they manage their organizations and how they relate to youth.

Flash forward a decade—to the high-speed, interactive world that grown-up Net Geners live in. The speed of delivery on the Internet is far faster, as high-speed broadband Internet access is now common. What's more, you can tap into a world of knowledge from far more places—from your BlackBerry, for example, or your mobile phone, which can surf the Internet, capture GPS coordinates, take photos, and swap text messages. Just about every kid has an iPod and a personal profile on social networking sites such as Facebook, which lets Net Geners monitor their friends' every twitch—all the time.

The Net Generation has *come of age.* In 2008, the eldest of the generation turned 31. The youngest turned 11. Around the world the generation is flooding into the workplace, marketplace, and every niche of society. They are bringing their demographic muscle, media smarts, purchasing power, new models of collaborating and parenting, entrepreneurship, and political power into the world.

THE DARK SIDE

But there are plenty of concerns and criticisms of this generation that are voiced by everyone from parents to frustrated employers. Many academics, journalists, and pundits present skeptical, negative, even cynical views of the Net Generation. The top 10 issues are:

- *They're dumber than we were at their age.* You hear different variations of this popular theme. They don't know anything, writes Mark Bauerlein in *The Dumbest Generation: How the Digital Age Stupefies Young Americans and Jeopardizes Our Future.* According to Bauerlein, Net Geners are a "portrait of vigorous, indiscriminate ignorance."[1] All these gadgets can even give some people, including Net Geners, symptoms that look like attention deficit disorder, psychiatrist Edward Hallowell suggests in his book *CrazyBusy.* The result: a shallow, distracted generation that can't focus on anything. Then there's the full frontal attack that comes from novelist Robert Bly: "Today we are lying to ourselves about the renaissance the computer will bring. It will bring nothing. What it means is that the neo-cortex is finally eating itself."[2] They don't read and are poor communicators. All this time online is reflected in the schools and universities where they perform badly on tests.
- *They're screenagers, Net addicted, losing their social skills, and they have no time for sports or healthy activities.* Time spent online could have been devoted to sports and face-to-face conversation; the result is a generation of awkward, fat people. And when they get addicted to video games, some say, the results can be worse. Mothers Against Videogame Addiction and Violence (MAVAV), for example, describes video games as "the world's fastest growing addiction and the most reckless endangerment of children today—comparable to drug and alcohol abuse."

- *They have no shame.* "It is pretty routine these days for girls to post provocative pictures of themselves online," warns M. Gigi Durham, the thoughtful author of *The Lolita Effect*.[3] Young people, unaware that it may come back to haunt them, merrily give out all sorts of personal information online, whether it's to a college recruiter, a future employer, or to a manipulative marketer, cyberbully, or predator. Parents, educators, and employers are amazed when they see what kinds of digital displays of affection are posted online for the entire world to see. Kids don't understand what the problem is!

- *Because their parents have coddled them, they are adrift in the world and afraid to choose a path.* That's why so many of them move home after college. They really can't cope with the independence. Parents are often delighted, but the neighbors raise their eyebrows. Why aren't they setting off on their own? Are they going to be coddled all their lives by helicopter parents who hover over their university professors and even their employers? According to William Damon, author of *The Path to Purpose*, "Youth are so afraid of commitment that many of them may never marry, and they're so uncertain about picking a career that they may wind up living at home forever."[4] Seminars like *Spoiled Rotten: Today's Children and How to Change Them*, by former telecommunications salesman Fred Gosman, advise parents to impose stricter codes of discipline.

- *They steal.* They violate intellectual property rights, downloading music, swapping songs, and sharing anything they can on peer-to-peer networks with no respect for the rights of the creators or owners. "When you go online and download songs without permission, you are stealing," the Recording Industry Association of America says on its Web site. It should be a criminal offense, the recording industry says. That's why they feel justified in suing children. The ease with which the Net Gen uses the Internet has also made them masters of plagiarism.

- *They're bullying friends online.* Witness the eight teens, six of them girls, who beat up a teenager in April 2008 and put it on YouTube. Here is the explanation from Glenn Beck, the controversial TV host: "Teens are living in virtual reality and a voyeuristic culture of violence and humiliation, and it's all for fame and fortune."

- *They're violent.* Just look at the two youths who committed mass murder in 1999 at Columbine High School near Denver, Colorado. "Absent the combination of extremely violent video games and these boys' incredibly deep involvement, use of, and addiction to these games, and the boys' basic personalities, these murders and this massacre would not have occurred," claims a lawsuit against computer makers lodged by the victims. According to MAVAV, the video game industry promotes "hatred, racism, sexism, and the most disturbing trend: clans and guilds, an underground video game phenomenon which closely resembles gangs."

- *They have no work ethic and will be bad employees.* William Damon, in *The Path to Purpose*, says that students today are drifting aimlessly, with no clue as to what they want to do or become in the future.[5] They are "slackers"[6] who have a sense of entitlement, and as they enter the workforce they are placing all kinds of unrealistic demands on employers for everything from sophisticated technology to new approaches to management. Many companies and governments have banned social networks like Facebook because youth "love to waste their time." "They're woefully ill-prepared for the demands of today's (and tomorrow's) workplace," according to a consortium led by the Conference Board.

- *This is the latest narcissistic "me" generation.* "They are far more narcissistic than students were 25 years ago," says Jean Twenge, the professor who reviewed college students' responses to the Narcissistic Personality Inventory between the early 1980s and 2006. "Current technology fuels an increase in narcissism," she said. "By its very name, MySpace encourages attention-seeking, as does YouTube."

- *They don't give a damn.* They have no values and they don't care about anyone else. Their only interests are popular culture, celebrities, and their friends. They don't read newspapers or watch television news. They get their news from *The Daily Show with Jon Stewart* on Comedy Central. They don't vote and are not involved in civil society. When they become adults, they will be bad citizens.

Professor Bauerlein sums it up well: "The twenty-first-century teen, connected and multitasked, autonomous yet peer-mindful, makes no great leap forward in human intelligence, global thinking, or netizen-ship. Young users have learned a thousand new things, no doubt. They upload and download, surf and chat, post and design, but they haven't learned to analyze a complex text, store facts in their heads, comprehend a foreign policy decision, take lessons from history, or spell correctly. Never having recognized their responsibility to the past, they have opened a fissure in our civic foundations, and it shows in their halting passage into adulthood and citizenship."[7]

We should look closely at the criticisms. They're not coming from some crazy zealots or from hardened ideologues. Robert Bly, for instance, is a mainstream, well-known, bestselling author and social commentator. While there are some interesting ideas in his writings, his hostility is so over-the-top it should cause us all to listen up.

WHAT IS THE TRUTH?

It's a pretty depressing picture of this generation! And if accurate, the future is surely bleak.

To find out the truth about this generation, my company set out to conduct the most comprehensive investigation of them ever done. This $4 million research project, funded by large organizations, was conducted between 2006 and 2008. My colleagues and I have interviewed nearly 6,000 Net Geners from around the world, and while most of the research, described in over 40 reports, is proprietary to the research sponsors, I'm going to share some of the findings and main conclusions throughout this book.

I then put together a core team that could help me take this work to the next level by creating an accessible book that I hope will have mass appeal. I've spoken to hundreds of members of the Net Generation, from the kids in my neighborhood to some of the generation's biggest stars, like Facebook founder Mark Zuckerberg and Michael Furdyk, who made his first million in the dot-com age in high school, and then launched a network called TakingITGlobal.org, comprised of over 100,000 digital activists from around the world. We created communities on Facebook and TakingITGlobal.org that would give me answers to dozens of difficult questions. We also interviewed academics, scientists, and business, education, and government leaders who have unique experiences and insights.

Not surprisingly, my two most important collaborators were my children, Niki and Alex, who spent many hours with me brainstorming, reviewing ideas, and often setting me straight. In a sense they are my coauthors, and you will read many of their insights and comments throughout the course of this book, supplementing all the hard data, case reports, and interviews.

THE NET GENERATION HAS ARRIVED

In this book you'll learn that the Net Generation *has* arrived. And while there are many concerns, overall the kids are more than alright.

The story that emerges from the research is an inspiring one, and it should bring us all great hope. As the first global generation ever, the Net Geners are smarter, quicker, and more tolerant of diversity than their predecessors. They care strongly about justice and the problems faced by their society and are typically engaged in some kind of civic activity at school, at work, or in their communities. Recently in the United States, hundreds of thousands of them have been inspired by Barack Obama's run for the presidency and have gotten involved in politics for the first time. This generation is engaging politically and sees democracy and government as key tools for improving the world.

With their reflexes tuned to speed and freedom, these empowered young people are beginning to transform every institution of modern life. From the workplace to the marketplace, from politics to education to the basic unit of any society, the family, they are replacing a culture of control with a culture of enablement.

Eight characteristics, or norms, describe the typical Net Gener and differentiate them from their boomer parents. They prize freedom and freedom of choice. They want to customize things, make them their own. They're natural collaborators, who enjoy a conversation, not a lecture. They'll scrutinize you and your organization. They insist on integrity. They want to have fun, even at work and at school. Speed is normal. Innovation is part of life.

CONQUERING FEAR WITH KNOWLEDGE

Why the apparent hostility toward the youth culture and its media? People become defensive when threatened by something new and which they don't understand. Historic innovations and shifts in thinking are often received with coolness, even mockery. Vested interests fight change. Just as the proponents of Newtonian physics argued against Einstein's general theory of relativity, so the leaders of traditional media are typically skeptical, at best, toward the new. Both film and print media showed considerable unease with television.

Baby boomers set a precedent of being a major generational threat to their elders. Previous generations didn't have the luxury of a prolonged adolescence; after a brief childhood, kids went straight into the workforce. But baby boomers grew up in a time of relative prosperity and attended school for many more years than did their parents. They had time to develop their own youth culture. Rock 'n' roll, long hair, protest movements, weird clothes, and new lifestyles made their parents uneasy. They also had a new medium through which to communicate their culture—television.

Now it's the boomers' turn to feel uneasy. A new generation has emerged, with new values, and it understands the new media much better than the boomers do. The situation that has developed is a classic generation gap. No wonder you see so much confusion and insecurity being shown by the boomers, not to mention all the nasty books, articles, and TV shows targeting today's youth and the Net Generation's culture and new media.

I think that, overall, the Internet has been good for them, and they will be good for us. Of all my concerns, one big one stands out. Net Geners are making a serious mistake, and most of them don't realize it. They're giving away their personal information on social networks and elsewhere and in doing so are undermining their future privacy. They tell me they don't care; it's all about sharing. But here I must speak with the voice of experience. Some day that party picture is going to bite them when they seek a senior corporate job or public office. I think they should wake up, now, and become aware of the extent to which they're sharing parts of themselves that one day they may wish they had kept private. You will also read that other concerns are more complicated and require a thoughtful response on our part, rather than the cynical and popular sport of attacking and ridiculing youth.

Most of the criticisms are founded on suspicion and fear, usually on the part of older people. Those fears are perhaps understandable. The New Web, in the hands of a technologically savvy and community-minded Net Generation, has the power to shake up society and topple authorities in many walks of life. Once information flows freely and the people have the tools to share it effectively and use it to organize themselves, life as we know it will be different. Schools, universities, stores, businesses, even politics will have to adapt to this generation's style of doing things , and in my view, that will be good. Families will have new challenges too, as their kids explore the world out there online. Life, in other words, will change, and many people find change hard.

It's only natural to fear what we don't understand.

LEARN FROM THEM AND ACT

It is my hope that this book will dispel some of the myths about this generation, revealing what they're really like and how we can learn from them in order to change our institutions and society for the better. Perhaps employers will consider changing their HR and management practices once they see the value of tapping into the typical Net Gener's extraordinary collaborative orientation, which has become so critical for twenty-first-century business. I hope that educators will consider altering their traditional sage-on-the-stage approach to instruction once they see how inappropriate it is for Net Gen learners. I'm pretty sure that politicians will take careful note of the novel ways that the Obama campaign has used the Internet to rally young people. I hope parents who come to my speeches because they wonder what is going on with their kids will read this book and understand their children a little better. I hope this book will reassure them and help them to realize that the digital immersion is a good thing for their kids.

What an extraordinary period in human history this is—for the first time the next generation coming of age can teach us how to ready our world for the future. The digital tools of their childhood and youth are more powerful than what exists in much of corporate America. I believe that if we listen to them and engage them, their culture of interaction, collaboration, and enablement will drive economic and social development and prepare this shrinking planet for a more secure, fair, and prosperous future. We *can* learn how to avoid and manage the dark side—a predictable thing with any new communications medium—more effectively.

Learn from them and you will see the new culture of high-performance work, the twenty-first-century school and college, the innovative corporation, a more open family, a democracy where citizens are engaged, and perhaps even the new, networked society.

THE NET GENERATION COMES OF AGE

Chances are you know a young person aged 11–31. You may be a parent, aunt, teacher, or manager. You've seen these young people multitasking five activities at once. You see the way they interact with the various media—say, watching movies on two-inch screens. They use their mobile phones differently. You talk on the phone and check your e-mail; to them, e-mail is old-school. They use the phone to text incessantly, surf the Web, find directions, take pictures and make videos, and collaborate. They seem to be on Facebook every chance they get, including at work. Instant messaging or Skype is always running in the background. And what's with those video games? How can someone play World of Warcraft for five hours straight?

Sure, you're as cyber-sophisticated as the next person—you shop online, use Wikipedia, and do the BlackBerry prayer throughout the day. But young people have a natural affinity for technology that seems uncanny. They instinctively turn first to the Net to communicate, understand, learn, find, and do many things. To sell a car or rent an apartment, you use the classifieds; they go to Craigslist. A good night to see a movie? You look to the newspaper to see what's playing; they go online. You watch the television news; they have RSS feeds to their favorite sources or get their news by stumbling upon it as they travel the Web. Sometimes you enjoy music; their iPods are always playing.

You consume content on the Web, but they seem to be constantly creating or changing online content. You visit YouTube to check out a video you've heard about; they go to YouTube throughout the day to find out what's new. You buy a new gadget and get out the manual. They buy a new gadget and just use it. You talk to other passengers in the car, but your kids in the back are texting each other. They seem to feast on technology and have an aptitude for all things digital that is sometimes mind-boggling.

But it's not just about how they use technology. They seem to behave, and even to *be*, different. As a manager, you notice that new recruits collaborate very differently than you do. They seem to have new motivations and don't have the same concept of a career that you do. As a marketer, you notice that television advertising is for the most part ineffective with young people, who seem to have mature BS detectors. As a teacher or professor, you are finding that young people seem to lack long attention spans, at least when it comes to listening to your lectures. Indeed, they show signs of learning differently, and the best of them make yesterday's cream of the crop look dull. As a parent, you see your children becoming adults and doing things you never would have dreamed of, like wanting to live at home after graduation. As a politician, you've noticed for some time that they are not interested in the political process, yet you marvel at how Barack Obama was able to engage them and ride their energy to become a presidential candidate.

You're reminded of the old Bob Dylan line "There's something happening here but you don't know what it is."

There *is* something happening here. The Net Generation has come of age. Growing up digital has had a profound impact on the way this generation thinks, even changing the way their brains are wired. And although this digital immersion presents significant challenges for young people—such as dealing with a vast amount of incoming information or ensuring balance between the digital and physical worlds—their immersion has not hurt them overall. It has been positive. The generation is more tolerant of racial diversity, and is smarter and quicker than their predecessors. These young people are remaking every institution of modern life, from the workplace to the marketplace, from politics to education, and down to the basic structure of the family. Here are some of the ways in which this is occurring.

- As employees and managers, the Net Generation is approaching work collaboratively, collapsing the rigid hierarchy and forcing organizations to rethink how they recruit, compensate, develop, and supervise talent. I believe that the very idea of management is changing, with the exodus from corporations to start-ups just beginning.

- As consumers, they want to be "prosumers"—co-innovating products and services with producers. The concept of a brand is in the process of changing forever because of them.

- In education, they are forcing a change in the model of pedagogy, from a teacher-focused approach based on instruction to a student-focused model based on collaboration.

- Within the family, they have already changed the relationship between parents and children, since they are experts in something really important—the Internet.

- As citizens, the Net Generation is in the early days of transforming how government services are conceived and delivered and how we understand and decide what the basic imperatives of citizenship and democracy should be. For the growing numbers trying to achieve social change, there is a sea of change under way, ranging from civic activities to political engagement. The Net Gen is bringing political action to life more than in any previous generation.

- And in society as a whole, empowered by the global reach of the Internet, their civic activity is becoming a new, more powerful kind of social activism.

The bottom line is this: if you understand the Net Generation, you will understand the future. You will also understand how our institutions and society need to change today.

BOOM, BUST, ECHO

To begin our journey, it's important to understand some earthshaking demographic facts.

The Net Generation is a distinct generation. It is made up of the children of the post–World War II generation, called the baby boomers in the United States. This proverbial baby-boom "echo" generation, in the United States alone, is the biggest generation. Around the world there has been an even greater demographic explosion with 81 million members.

The Baby Boom (1946–64)

Anyone born between 1946 and 1964 is considered a baby boomer, and the boom was heard loudest in the United States, Canada, and Australia. Many families postponed having children until after the war, for obvious reasons. Hundreds of thousands of young men were serving overseas and were not available for fathering. When the war was over, the men came back into the workforce and the pictures of "Rosie the Riveter" that had appeared in *Life* magazine were replaced with photos of cheery women in their shiny kitchens waiting for hubby to come home from work. I saw this with my own mother. She worked in a steel mill during the war, and right afterward married my dad and had me.

> It is 1976. The first member of the post–World War II baby boom is 30 years old. She awakes to news reports on her clock radio about the presidential election and wonders whether she'll vote for Jimmy Carter, or the man who pardoned President Richard Nixon just two years earlier. Turning the dial, she eases into Paul McCartney's new hit, "Silly Love Songs." On her way to work as a teacher (one of the best jobs available to women in the mid-1970s), in her made-in-America car, she notices that she has a special $2 Bicentennial bill in her wallet as she pays for her gas, which cost 60 cents a gallon. After work, she decides to see why everyone is so terrified by that new blockbuster movie, *Jaws*. Still shaking as she walks out of the movie, she wonders why she isn't married yet—most of her friends are.[1]

The economy was very strong after the war, giving families the confidence to have lots of kids. It is hard to imagine today, but by 1957 American families had an average of 3.7 children.[2] It was a time of great hope and optimism because the Allies had won the war and there was finally peace, and prosperity was taking hold. Immigrants flooded into the United States, contributing to the population boom, and, as their children, in great numbers, matured, they grew into a powerful cultural, social, and political force. (See Figures 1.1 and 1.2.)

FIGURE 1.1   BOOM, BUST, ECHO: NUMBER OF BIRTHS PER YEAR (JANUARY 1, 1945–DECEMBER 31, 1997)

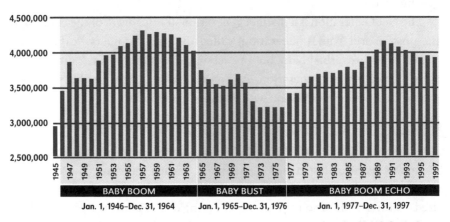

Source: U.S. Census Bureau

FIGURE 1.2   SCHOOL ENROLLMENT IN THE UNITED STATES

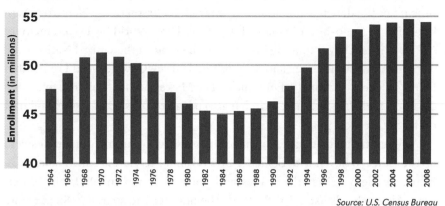

Source: U.S. Census Bureau

The Baby Boom Became the TV Generation

The boomers could be called the "Cold War Generation," the "Growth Economy Generation," or any other name that linked them to their era. It was really the impact of a communications revolution, however—led by the rise of television—that shaped this generation more than anything else. To say that television transformed the world around the boomers is a cliché, but it's also a vast understatement of the impact of the ubiquitous "boob tube." Imagine— or think back if you can—to the world before television. My family used to gather around the rather large piece of furniture, that was a radio, to listen to news programs and *The Lux Radio Theater.* Our own imaginations conjured up mental images of the announcers, actors, and their environments. My mother remembers that when TVs became popular, our family just had to get one. "This was the innovation of the century," she says. "It was so exciting to think that you could not only hear people who were far away, but actually see them."

In early 1953 when our first set was installed in our living room, the chairs and sofa were moved from their place near the radio and clustered around the TV. I have vivid memories of Queen Elizabeth II's coronation, which was televised on June 2, 1953, and of my mother explaining to us that the tears on Her Majesty's face were due to the emotional pressure and also the physical strain of a heavy crown and the rigor of the procession and events. I saw my parents and other adult relatives react in horror as rumors that Elvis would shake his pelvis on *The Ed Sullivan Show* were spread, and then it didn't happen. I remember my uncle, a music teacher, howling at Kate Smith, saying that she couldn't carry a tune if her life depended on it. I remember Don Larson of the New York Yankees pitching a no-hitter in Game Five of the 1956 World Series. I remember Nikita Khrushchev thumping his shoe on the table at the United Nations and watching, in real time, the shooting of Lee Harvey Oswald. And I remember falling in love with Annette Funicello of *The Mickey Mouse Club*. The television created a real-time alternate world. It also began to consume a significant part of the day for most people.

A generation introduced to its medium grew with a momentum that swept up the Chicago Seven with *Bonanza*, Bob Dylan, JFK, *Harold and Maude,* marijuana, the Vietnam War, the Beatles, and Abbie Hoffman. In 1950, only 12 percent of households had a TV. By 1958, the number had soared to 83 percent.[3] The medium had quickly become the most powerful communication technology available, unseating radio and Hollywood films and newsreels. When the American civil rights movement made its demands known, it was television that served as the messenger and the mobilizer. When the boomers marched in the streets against the Vietnam War, television chronicled and amplified their presence. Television was there to record and broadcast the movements of a massive generation. Right in front of the baby boomers' eyes, television turned youth itself into an event.

> It is 1976. The last member of the Boomer Generation has just turned 12 years old. He wakes up and scrambles downstairs to the television set. He changes the rotary dial to PBS, which is playing *Sesame Street*. He eats the breakfast Mom prepares for him and rides his bike helmetless across the neighborhood to class. After school he rides home, lets himself into the house with the key hidden in the garage, and waits for his mom to get home from work. He and his friends play pickup baseball in the backyard, making up rules as they go along.[4]

Gen X—The Baby Bust (1965–76)

In the 10 years following the boom, birth rates declined dramatically with 15 percent fewer babies born. Hence the name: the Baby Bust. But the term never caught on. Instead, they're called Generation X, after the title of a novel by Douglas Coupland. The X refers to a group that feels excluded from society and entered the labor force only to find that their older brothers and sisters had filled all the positions.

Gen Xers are among the best-educated group in history. They faced some of the highest rates of American unemployment, peaking at 10.8 percent in November–December 1982, although the later Gen-Xers saw unemployment decline much lower. They also saw some of the lowest relative starting salaries of any group since those entering the workforce during the 1930s Depression era.

Gen X—now adults between the ages of 32 and 43—are aggressive communicators who are extremely media-centered. They are the oldest segment of the population whose computer and Internet habits resemble those of Net Geners and provide the closest adult experience from which we can begin to predict how Net Geners will master the digital universe. Like Net Geners, Gen Xers view radio, TV, film, and the Internet as nonspecialist media, available for everyone's use to package information and put forward their perspective.

The Echo of the Baby Boom—Net Generation, Gen Y, or Millennials (1977–97)
The boomers started having children in greater numbers after 1978. By 1997, there were almost as many 5- to 9-year-olds (19,854,000) as there were 30- to 34-year-olds (20,775,000).[5] See Figure 1.3.

FIGURE 1.3   DEMOGRAPHIC BREAKDOWN OF U.S. POPULATION BY GENERATION

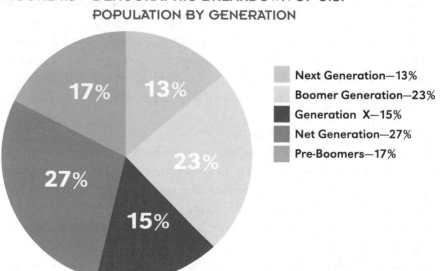

Next Generation—13%
Boomer Generation—23%
Generation X—15%
Net Generation—27%
Pre-Boomers—17%

Source: U.S. Census Data

Four Generations: From 1946 to Present*

1. **The Baby Boom Generation**
    January 1946 to December 1964—19 years, producing 77.2 million children or
    23 percent of the U.S. population**.

2. **Generation X**
    January 1965 to December 1976—12 years, producing 44.9 million children or
    15 percent of the U.S. population. Also called the Baby Bust.

3. **The Net Generation**
    January 1977 to December 1997—21 years, producing approximately 81.1
    million children or 27 percent of the U.S. population. Also called the Millennials
    or Generation Y.

4. **Generation Next**
    January 1998 to present—10 years, producing 40.1 million children or 13.4
    percent of the U.S. population. Also called Generation Z.

One of the key reasons why the Net Gen has lasted so long is the number of
baby-boom women who have put off having children until their thirties or forties. Relatively few boomers became parents in their early twenties, the typical
age for beginning the process of marriage and child rearing. Many boomers
were prolonging youth. In fact, I am a perfect example of this trend. I spent
most of the first decade after college organizing various social movements, pursuing postgraduate studies, learning about computing, writing music, researching various issues, and in general trying to fathom and change the world.
Planning for a family and a career was the last thing on my mind. I knew that
when it was time to think about such issues, I would be just fine. Self-confidence
grew from prosperous times and a rich social background.

THE ECHO BECOMES THE NET GENERATION
Each generation is exposed to a unique set of events that defines their place in
history and shapes their outlook. The Echo Boomers (the Net Gen) have grown
up with such defining moments as the O.J. Simpson trial, the Columbine school
shootings, the *Exxon Valdez* oil spill, and the Gulf War. Then there is September 11, the war in Iraq, AIDS, Band Aid, and Live Aid. Influential figures are
Tiger Woods, Bono, Lance Armstrong, Princess Diana, Bill and Hillary Clinton, George Bush, and Al Gore—first as the man who would be president and

*U.S. Population—301,621,157 (2008)
**268.9 million by the end of 1997

then as the campaigner against global warming and champion of environmental protection.

When researching *Growing Up Digital*, I decided to name the echo generation by their defining characteristic. Today some people call them the millennials, but the advent of the year 2000 didn't really alter the experience of the young people of that time. I suppose we could call them "Generation Y," but naming them as an afterthought to the smaller Gen X diminishes their importance in the big scheme of things.

If you look back over the last 20 years, clearly the most significant change affecting youth is the rise of the computer, the Internet, and other digital technologies. This is why I call the people who have grown up during this time the Net Generation, the first generation to be bathed in bits.

Broadband Internet access is now ubiquitous: iPods are everywhere; mobile phones can surf the Internet, capture GPS coordinates, take photos, and swap text messages; and social networking sites such as Facebook let Net Geners monitor their friends' every twitch.

In 1983, only 7 percent of households owned computers.[6] By 2004, the number had grown to 44 percent and a whopping 60 percent of those households had children. In 1996, only 15 percent of all households in the United States had access to the Internet and World Wide Web, but during the same period 1 in 10 Internet users worldwide was reported to be under 16 years of age. In 1994, 35 percent of schools provided access to the Internet in their schools.

Flash forward to today. Now, 100 percent of American schools provide Internet access, and it is estimated that there is a computer for every four schoolchildren in America.[7] Three-quarters (75 percent) of teenagers between 15 and 17 now have mobile phones,[8] and about 73 percent of young people aged 12 through 17 use the Internet.[9] Broadband connections are bringing the Internet to millions of Americans every day, with 37 percent of Americans using some sort of broadband connection in 2004.[10] Yet this progress has not closed the digital divide between those who have Internet access and those who do not. It is still an important problem. I believe it is the right of every young person to grow up digital, which is why the One Laptop Per Child campaign, launched by MIT media technology professor Nicholas Negroponte, is so wonderful and important. It deserves support from corporations, governments, foundations, and other institutions.

When I wrote *Growing Up Digital*, most people were using a very primitive Internet. It was low speed, often dial-up, and it was based on a programming language called HTML—a platform for the presentation of content. This is why everyone talked about Web sites, getting lots of "eyeballs," stickiness, clicks, and page views. The Internet was about viewing content. You could visit a site and observe its information, but you couldn't modify or interact with it or with others.

Today's Web is based on something called XML. Rather than a standard for presenting content, it is a standard for programmability—call it the "program-mable Web." And every time you use it, you change it, in a sense programming a global computer. Facebook is simply one of thousands of XML-based applica-tions that enable people to collaborate. The old Web was something you surfed for content. The new Web is a communications medium that enables people to create their own content, collaborate with others, and build communities. It has become a tool for self-organization.

We got a prophetic glimpse into the future of the Web itself. While adults were using the Internet to view Web pages, the youngsters we studied were using the Web to communicate with their friends. Their online experiences were the core of what would become the Web 2.0—a totally new and revolu-tionary platform for communication.

Technology Is Like the Air

While Net Gen children assimilated technology because they grew up with it, as adults we have had to accommodate it—a different and much more difficult type of learning process. With assimilation, kids came to view technology as just another part of their environment, and they soaked it up along with every-thing else. For many kids, using the new technology is as natural as breathing. As Andy Putschoegl is quoted as saying in *Growing Up Digital*, "I was born using an Apple computer."

It's much harder to teach old dogs new tricks. Learning a whole new way of communicating, accessing information, and entertaining oneself is hard work, and our established patterns of thinking must change to accommodate the new technology.

Today, most of us oldsters have a pretty good facility with technology, but you may not remember what the initial adjustment was like. When PCs first arrived, the stories about our difficulties using them proliferated; there were so many bizarre narratives, in fact, that some may have been hoaxes. One help desk reported that someone thought the mouse was a foot pedal and couldn't get it to work. Somewhere else a secretary was asked to copy a disk and came back with a photocopy. Another person "hit" the keyboard so hard, he broke it. When asked by a support line if she had Windows, one woman apparently replied, "No, we have air-conditioning." One person was said to be found trying to delete files on a disk using Wite-Out. There were hundreds of such stories. A friend of mine tried using a mouse to point at the computer screen as if it was a TV remote. What can we learn from this? Are adults just stupid?

While laughable, the actions of these adults made sense. Boomers were familiar with TV remotes, foot pedals, photocopiers, windows, Wite-Out, and doors. Each of these artifacts had decades of meaning and behaviors associated with it. Net Geners had a cleaner slate. Absorbing the digital media was easy.

Computer visionary Alan Kay said that technology is "technology only for people who are born before it was invented." In agreement is the pioneer of learning and technology, Seymour Papert, who said: "That's why we don't argue about whether the piano is corrupting music with technology."[11]

Technology has been completely transparent to the Net Gen. "It doesn't exist. It's like the air," said Coco Conn, cofounder of the Web-based Cityspace project. MIT's Dr. Idit Harel, a professor of epistemology, agreed: "For the kids, it's like using a pencil. Parents don't talk about pencils, they talk about writing. And kids don't talk about technology—they talk about playing, building a Web site, writing a friend, about the rain forest."[12]

Net Gen kids growing up looked at computers in the same way boomers look at TV. Boomers don't marvel at the technology or wonder how television transfers video and audio through thin air, we simply watch the screen. TV is a fact of life. So it has been with Net Geners and computers. And as technology relentlessly advances each month, young people just breathe it in, like improvements in the atmosphere.

Some personal experiences with my own children made this clear to me. In early 1997, I spent an hour as a guest on a Canadian television program called *Pamela Wallin Live*, helping to demonstrate how to surf the Web. The point of the show was to illustrate to the viewers the wealth of material available on the Net. When I returned home, my wife Ana, my most trusted critic, told me she thought the show was good, but that our son Alex, who was 12 at the time, thought the whole idea of the program was dumb.

Ana said to him: "Hey Alex, Dad's going to be on TV live for an hour. Let's go watch."

"Cool, what's the show about?" Alex replied.

"Dad's going to use the Internet on TV—surf the Web," Ana said.

"That's the dumbest TV show I've ever heard of. Why would anyone want to watch Dad use the Internet?" Alex asked.

"Everyone is interested in this new technology, how to use it, and how it works. It's a technology revolution," said Ana.

"Mom, this is so embarrassing. All my friends are going to see this. You don't need to show people how to use Internet," said Alex.

The next day over breakfast, to hear it for myself, I asked him why he didn't want to watch the show.

"Dad, no offense, but I think you adults are obsessed with technology. You call this a technology revolution and you are so fascinated by how the technology works. Imagine some other technology, Dad." At this point I sensed he was going to use an analogy, and sure enough he pointed to the television. "The television—is that technology to you, Dad? Imagine a TV show where people watch you surf television! Wow! Let's see if my dad can find a football game on television! Now my dad is going to try and find a sitcom!"

At this point his 13-year-old sister Niki came to his support (a rare thing), embellishing a point from a previous conversation.

"Yeah Dad, how about the refrigerator. Remember, it's technology too. Why don't we have a TV show where we can all watch you surf the fridge?" To rub it in, she said, "Check this out, my dad has found some meatloaf. This is just fascinating television!"

In another incident, Alex, then about 14, asked me to come to his room to see what he'd found. On the screen, he had a beautiful, high-resolution, full-screen color photo of Mars. It was beautiful. I told him it was spectacular and asked where he got it. "Dad, I'm looking through this thing called the Hubble Telescope." At this point I'm thinking how incredible that my son from his bedroom is accessing one of the most sophisticated pieces of technology ever invented by humankind.

But he's thinking something different: "Isn't Mars amazing?"

To them, technology *is* like the air.

The Net Gen Media Diet

Compared with their boomer parents, time online is not time that could have been spent hanging out with their friends, playing soccer, learning the piano, or doing any of dozens of other things. More than anything, time online is time that would probably have been spent watching TV. At their age, their baby-boomer parents watched an average of 22.4 hours of television each week.[13] They were passive viewers; they took what they were given, and when the commercials came, they might even have watched them.

Net Geners watch less television than their parents do, and they watch it differently. A Net Gener is more likely to turn on the computer and simultaneously interact in several different windows, talk on the telephone, listen to music, do homework, read a magazine, and watch television. TV has become like background Muzak for them.

The Net Geners don't just take what they are given either. They are the active initiators, collaborators, organizers, readers, writers, authenticators, and even strategists, as in the case of video games. They do not just observe; they participate. They inquire, discuss, argue, play, shop, critique, investigate, ridicule, fantasize, seek, and inform.

> It is 2007. The last member of the Net Generation has just turned 10 years old. After his mom wakes him up, he turns on the bedroom computer to find the latest "cheat code" for his favorite Xbox 360 game. He scrambles downstairs, where the TV is on, but he pays no attention to it, grabbing his Portable Play Station instead. The school bus, which stops at the end of every driveway, takes him the two blocks to school. After school his mother arrives in a hybrid SUV and whisks him off to a fast-food restaurant for a snack and then to his soccer game. He's barely out of the car before his mother has sprayed a fresh coat of sunscreen on him. Dad shows up at the game at about halftime, but seems distracted by his BlackBerry. After dinner, he sits down to do homework on his laptop, while checking up on his friends via instant messaging and Facebook.

The print media company and the TV network are hierarchical organizations that reflect the values of their owners. New media, on the other hand, give control to all users. The distinction between bottom-up and top-down organizational structure is at the heart of the new generation. For the first time ever, young people have taken control of critical elements of a communications revolution.

On the Net, children have had to search for, rather than simply look at, information. This forces them to develop thinking and investigative skills—and much more. They must become critics. Which Web sites are good? How can I tell what is real and what is fictitious—whether in a data source or in the teenage movie star in a chat session?

The Net Generation is in many ways the antithesis of the TV generation. This shift from one-way broadcast media to interactive media has had a profound effect on the Net Gen.

THE FIRST GLOBAL GENERATION

The global picture is even more startling. There was no baby boom in Western Europe or Japan. The generation that survived the war produced a relatively small number of offspring and today there are proportionally fewer young people aged 11–31 in these countries. This is emerging as a huge social problem, as, among other things, a major crisis is in the making owing to the shortage of talent.

Other parts of the world, however, are experiencing a youth explosion. There are nearly as many Net Geners in China and India as there are in the United

FIGURE 1.4   THE WORLD ACCORDING TO LANDMASS

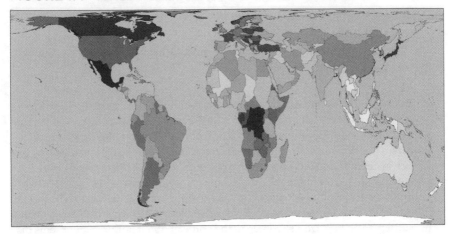

Source: www.worldmapper.org

States and Canada. The percentage of each country's population represented by Net Geners varies considerably from country to country. Many developed economies, for example, have large older generations whose life expectancy is climbing; while in many developing nations, life expectancy is shorter and the average age of the population is quite young. As a result, youth population is expanding more rapidly in countries like India and Brazil, and declining in nations like Japan and Spain. (See Figures 1.4, 1.5, and 1.6.)

FIGURE 1.5   THE WORLD ACCORDING TO POPULATION: AGE 15 TO 30

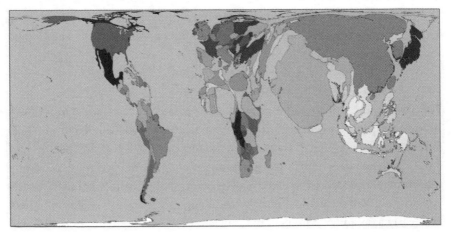

Source: www.worldmapper.org

FIGURE 1.6   THE WORLD ACCORDING TO INTERNET USERS
                    IN 2008

Source: www.worldmapper.org

To be sure, many of the young people in this demographic tidal wave do not have access to the Web. When I wrote *Growing Up Digital*, hundreds of millions more didn't even have power. We were looking at a digital divide between information haves and have-nots.[14] However, since then a whopping 1.3 billion people have begun using the Net, hundreds of millions of them children and young people. The global growth rate from 2000 to 2008 was 290 percent,[15] meaning that across the world the number of people using the Internet has more than tripled! And those gains have been worldwide: there are more people on the Web in China, for example, than there are in the United States. The Net Generation has gone global. See the population pyramids for the countries with the most explosive populations in Figures 1.7–1.16.

There are surprising similarities among Net Geners in the 12 countries we studied.

Measured by communications and cultural trends, today's youth inhabit a flattening world. Digital technologies make it as easy to send an instant message to an acquaintance thousands of miles away as to a next-door neighbor. The technical infrastructure is rapidly shrinking the world.

"For the first time ever, we can speak of a worldwide youth generation."
—JOHN GERACI, PROJECT MANAGER,
THE NET GENERATION RESEARCH

What makes the Net Gen unique? More than anything else, the Internet and its global reach. A true global generation of youth is emerging. Technical barriers are falling, which is "flattening"

FIGURE 1.7   U.S. 2009 POPULATION PYRAMID

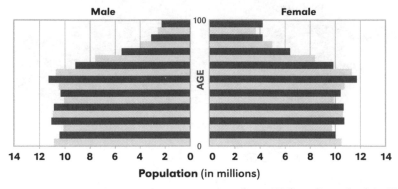

Source: U.S. Census Bureau, Population Division

FIGURE 1.8   UNITED KINGDOM 2009 POPULATION PYRAMID

Source: U.S. Census Bureau, Population Division

FIGURE 1.9   CHINA 2009 POPULATION PYRAMID

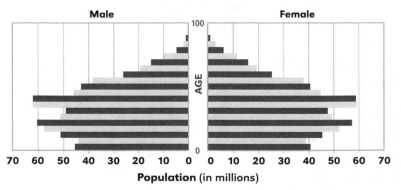

Source: U.S. Census Bureau, Population Division

FIGURE 1.10   INDIA 2009 POPULATION PYRAMID

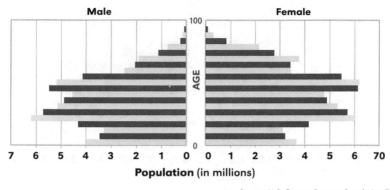

Population (in millions)

Source: U.S. Census Bureau, Population Division

FIGURE 1.11   RUSSIA 2009 POPULATION PYRAMID

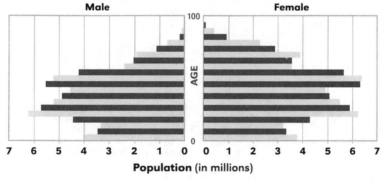

Population (in millions)

Source: U.S. Census Bureau, Population Division

FIGURE 1.12   BRAZIL 2009 POPULATION PYRAMID

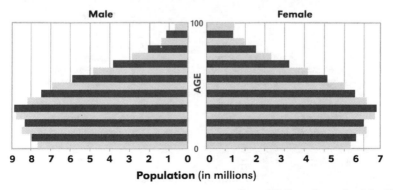

Population (in millions)

Source: U.S. Census Bureau, Population Division

FIGURE 1.13   ITALY 2009 POPULATION PYRAMID

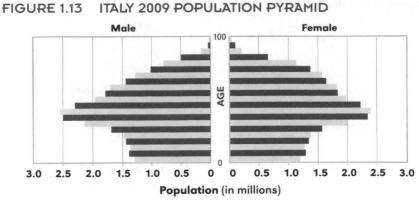

Source: U.S. Census Bureau, Population Division

FIGURE 1.14   IRAN 2009 POPULATION PYRAMID

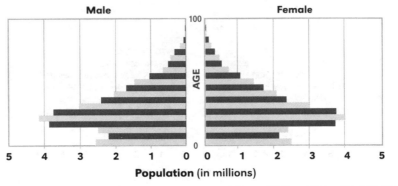

Source: U.S. Census Bureau, Population Division

FIGURE 1.15   JAPAN 2009 POPULATION PYRAMID

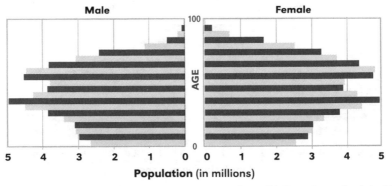

Source: U.S. Census Bureau, Population Division

FIGURE 1.16   CANADA 2009 POPULATION PYRAMID

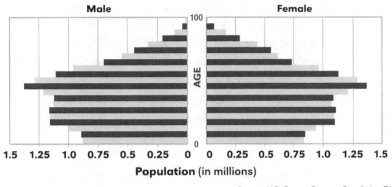

Source: U.S. Census Bureau, Population Division

the world, as *New York Times* columnist Thomas Friedman puts it, enabling global communication like never before. With the rise of the Internet, the distinct localized characteristics specific to young people are somehow fading. Yes, countries and regions will still have unique cultures and independent features, but increasingly young people around the world are becoming very much alike. As you will see, they have similar generational attitudes, norms, and behaviors.

To be sure, we're in the early days of such a global generation. Technologies are not distributed equally or equitably, and digital divides are quite pronounced

FIGURE 1.17   POPULATION UNDER 30 BY COUNTRY

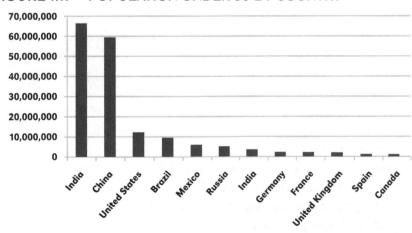

Source: Population Division of the Department of Economic and Social Affairs of the United Nations Secretariat,
World Population Prospects: The 2006 Revision and World Urbanization Prospects:
The 2005 Revision; http://esa.un.org/unpp

in many countries. The Western reverence for the young that has emerged over the past half century is not necessarily shared in the East, which tends to revere its older generations. Growth in the youth population and economic opportunity are most apparent in the East (see Figure 1.17). However, pop culture remains America's most efficient export. And Western pop culture is driven by the needs of the Western Net Gen, and technology is more and more a part of it. So, although the demographic epicenter of the global Net Gen is in Asia, the driving forces that influence the generation, worldwide, reside in the West.

The Generation Lap Revisited

In the 1960s and '70s, there were big differences between boomer kids and parents over values, lifestyle, and ideas. But now, boomers get along pretty well with their kids. Just look at your iPod and your Net Geners' iPods—there is big overlap in music. When I was young, hardly any parents liked the Beatles, let alone the Doors. Today, instead of a gap, there is a "generation lap"—kids are outpacing and overtaking adults on the technology track, "lapping" them in many areas of daily life.

> "For once in our civilization, children are educating older people. Adults are looking to children for information and help with computers and other computer-related stuff."
> —AUSTIN LOCKE, 15

"This is a unique period in history in that the role of the child in the home is changing," said John Seely Brown, director emeritus at Xerox PARC and a visiting scholar at The Annenberg Center at University of South California. In the past, the parents were the authority figures when it came to anything of real value. The notion that the child might be able to do anything new, novel, or really useful for the parent was considered bogus. "So for the first time there are things that parents want to be able to know about and do, where the kids are, in fact, the authority," Brown says.

Society has never before experienced en masse this phenomenon of the knowledge hierarchy being so effectively flipped on its head. But it is definitely happening, and the situation has magnified over the years with the appearance of each new technology—such as mobile devices and social networks.

The implications are huge. In some families, members have begun to respect each other as the authorities they actually are. This has created a more engaged dynamic within families. If managed well by the parents, this dynamic can create a more open, consensual, and effective family unit.

This diffusion of parental authority has spread beyond the family home. Consider the changing relationship between students and teachers in Finland. The government has chosen 5,000 Net Geners to train the country's teachers in how to use computers. For the first time ever, in one domain, the students will be the teachers and the teachers will be the students. The power dynamic between students and teachers will be forever altered.

Imagine what will happen when this tech-savvy generation moves into the workforce, where many

> "Each one of us is, in some way, an authority in some domains and a student in other domains. We must be prepared to learn major things from our subordinates and vice versa."
>
> —*JOHN SEELY BROWN*

managers, especially in Europe and Japan, make little personal use of the Internet. Will Net Geners be satisfied with the old hierarchical model of the enterprise? The successful companies will be those that recognize that networked structures work more effectively than old-fashioned hierarchies. Peer collaboration drives innovation and new approaches to management and government.

Generational versus Life-Stage Differences

In *Growing Up Digital*, I made a number of hypotheses—arguing that spending time online rather than being the passive recipients of television was probably affecting the brain development of Net Geners. In the last dozen years, we have learned more about this complex topic, and I have come to the conclusion that Net Geners' brains have indeed developed differently than those of their parents.

Some pundits have criticized my work with young people on the grounds that the differences I have observed between the Net Generation and their parents are *life-stage*, not *generational* differences. At first blush, their argument may seem like a convincing one: "Hey, the boomers were different from their parents. They protested war and then grew up and voted for George W. Bush." Won't the same thing happen to the Net Geners?

There are many reasons to believe that what we are seeing is the first case of a generation that is growing up with brains that are wired differently from those of the previous generation. Evidence is mounting that Net Geners process information and behave differently because they have indeed developed brains that are functionally different than those of their parents. They're quicker, for example, to process fast-moving images than their parents are. This view is not one I developed as a layperson (although a little-known fact is that I began my career many years ago as a psychologist). It comes from research done for my company by two of the smartest brain scientists I know—Stanley Kutcher and his son Matthew. The Kutchers describe how time spent with digital technologies may be changing the physical structure and functioning of their developing brains. There are two critical periods of brain development during which our brains get wired and developed. The first is early childhood, say from birth to three years old. It's likely that Net Geners got more stimulation during this period than did their boomer parents. The boomers had more children, and each probably received less attention. Nannies were less popular in the '50s and early '60s when the boomers were babies, and there was less emphasis on early childhood education.

The second critical period of brain development occurs roughly during the adolescent and teenage years. During that period the boomers as kids were watching a lot of television—between 20 and 30 hours a week. Contrast this with Net Geners, who spend an equivalent amount of time as active users of media rather than as passive viewers. It's logical to hypothesize that this affects brain development, because how one spends one's time during this period shapes one's brain. In the chapters that follow, you will read about a number of different ways in which Net Geners input data from the world, process information, learn, think, and communicate—but suffice to say here that pretty much all of this is positive.

Consider the impact of their rich, interactive media environment. When I was a kid growing up in a small town, there were three television stations, a small-town library, one newspaper, and a couple of magazines that interested me. Today's youth in the United States have access to 200-plus cable television networks, 5,500 magazines, 10,500 radio stations, and 40 billion Web pages. In addition, there are 22,000 books published every year; 240 million television sets are in operation throughout the country, and there are even 2 million TV sets in bathrooms. This generation has been flooded with information, and learning to access, sort, categorize, and remember it all has enhanced their intelligence.

The Smartest Generation

The evidence is strong that they are the smartest generation ever. More students are challenging themselves: the number of students taking AP exams has more than doubled between 1997 and 2005.[16] Raw IQ scores are climbing too, by three points a decade since World War II, and they have been increasing across racial, income, and regional boundaries.[17]

This generation even thinks it's cool to be smart, and they see themselves as an essential part of the world's future success. Teens rank "scientists" and "young people" as the two groups that will cause the "most changes for the better in the future."[18] When we asked our global sample of thousands of Net Geners, "Which would you rather be, smart or good-looking," 7 out of 10 chose having smarts.

A New Family Org Chart

The Net Gen's values were shaped not only by technology but by their parents. In the United States, the boomers' parents believed in the old maxim "Spare the rod and spoil the child," and as a young person there was nothing I dreaded more than being strapped by a parent or teacher. If there had been a family "organizational chart" like those that most companies have today, it would have indicated that boomer kids reported to their mother who reported to their father. But when the boomers had kids, they created a different kind of org chart with the child at the center. Many Net Geners were raised in kind and supportive families, where kids and parents got along well. The pejorative term for this is "being coddled," and it's true that sometimes it went too far—think of the "helicopter parents," who hover like a Sikorsky Blackhawk over their children, even at the university.

In fairness to the boomers, you can understand why they're hyped about their kids' education. Not only is education their children's key to the future in a knowledge economy; sending a child to school is expensive. In addition to the tens of thousands of dollars a year in tuition, some parents also invest up to $40,000 on university prep courses. One New Jersey father of two paid $30,000 to a college counselor for advice on everything from course selection to summer planning.[19] Including school expenses, the average American receives $38,000 a year from her or his parents between the ages of 18 and 34.[20]

Some Sikorsky parents have even helicoptered their way into their children's job interviews and performance reviews. Smart companies are trying to determine strategies to deal with helicopter parents without alienating their Net Gen children.

Family is a big deal for today's youth—much more so than for their boomer parents. They listen to their parents' opinions on everything from college selection to financial planning, and banks like Citibank have taken note, waiving all fees on accounts that parents open for their children.[21] My parents didn't even know what universities I was applying to. But both my children sought out my opinion when they were debating what schools they should apply to. Net Gen teens and young adults travel more with their parents than boomers did, and after college even choose to live at home for a while. To anyone in my generation, moving back in with your parents once you had left home would have been unthinkable. But now, most young people and their parents get along well.

Generational Values

When I wrote *Growing Up Digital*, I analyzed books and articles about the young generation. It was a sad tale. Young people were said to be self-centered and obsessed with short-term gratification. One analyst wrote: " . . . many baby boomer parents are so concerned with building youngsters' self-esteem, protecting them from stress, and making them partners in the family that they are raising a generation of selfish, ill-mannered, troubled children."[22] Books like *Spoiled Rotten: Today's Children and How to Change Them*, by Fred Gosman, advised parents to impose stricter codes of discipline. Youth crime was said to be rampant, and the generation's so-called material-ism and impulsiveness entered into experts' analysis of youth crime. Charles Ewing, a juvenile-crime expert at the University of Buffalo, said: "Juveniles have little impulse control, and a gun is an impulsive weapon."[23, 24] They were alleged to be greedy, self-centered, intolerant, and narcissistic; to have an inflated sense of self, a sense of entitlement, and unrealistic expectations; and to be concerned only about their own possessions and financial success.[25]

At the time, I argued that the data did not support these views. Flash forward to today—it still doesn't. While there are important differences across cultures, nations, genders, and classes, the evidence is strong that this is a positive gener-ation, with strong values. Take young people in North America—they care about the world. They are open, tolerant, and the least prejudiced generation ever. And, not surprisingly, when asked if they felt that young people were too negatively portrayed in the media, a majority—in the United States two-thirds—agreed.

These varied experiences have shaped the early lives of Net Geners, and 9 in 10 Net Geners in the United States describe themselves as "happy," "confi-dent," and "positive."[26] An increasing number of Net Geners believe growing up is easier for them than it was for their parents. A rapidly shrinking group worries about violence, sex, and drugs. Teen suicide rates have been generally falling since the 1990s.[27] Over the last 10 to 20 years, rates of homicide, violent crime, abortion, and pregnancy among U.S. teens have all plummeted.[28] Drug use and alcohol use by teens has been dropping pretty much for a decade.[29] The stereotype on crime is wrong, too. A teen is less likely today to be a victim of a serious violent crime than at any time since the late 1960s.

Net Geners display considerable tolerance compared with previous genera-tions. The world around them has changed. (See Figure 1.18.)

When I was a teenager, my closest friends were all white males who were of exactly the same age. Today, males aged 18–21 in the United States report that

FIGURE 1.18   PERCENT OF U.S. CHILDREN BY RACE

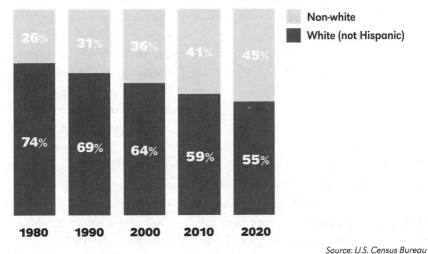

Source: U.S. Census Bureau

20 percent of their best friends are more than two years younger; 33 percent, more than two years older; 49 percent, from a different racial and/or ethnic background; and 60 percent, from the opposite sex.[30] What a stunning transformation!

Waves of immigration have created an increasingly multiracial American population, and "the younger the age group, the more diverse the population," says Gregory Spencer, who heads the Census Bureau's Population Projections Branch. A disproportionate number of mixed-race Americans are young: census results show that those under 18 are twice as likely as adults to be classified as multiracial.[31] The ease with which young people of different races and ethnicities mingle and marry also differentiates Net Gen from earlier generations: 91 percent of Net Gen respondents agree that interracial dating is acceptable, compared with 50 percent of the G.I. Generation (which reached adulthood during World War II), who express this view.[32]

It is 2008. The first member of the Net Generation is 31 years old. She awakes to news reports of the war in Iraq and wonders how President Bush's proposed immigration policy will affect the employment status of her Hispanic friends. On her iPod, she plays her "morning mix," which contains songs from 10 different music genres. On her way to work as a marketing manager in her Japanese-made hybrid, she wonders if this will be the day that gas hits $5 a gallon. U.S. Census Population counts for 2006 put the population of those Americans over 80 to be approximately 4 percent of the population, or about 12 million people.

Of course the story is not completely positive. As with any generation, there are troubling issues. Is being totally immersed in the online world a good thing for everyone? What about balance in a young person's life, and do some kids spend too much time online and multitasking? Are too many of them stressed out from heavy workloads and college application processes? Does the Internet make it easier to plagiarize or cheat in other ways at school? Are their attitudes and norms positive as they enter the workforce, marketplace, society? Until recently they have not been voting in elections, so what does this mean for the future of democracy? What about privacy? They spill their guts online and sometimes seem oblivious to how this could come back to haunt them. These issues will all be discussed throughout the book.

> "What piece of wisdom can I impart to you about my journey that will somehow ease your transition from college back to your parents' basement?"[33]
>
> —JON STEWART, COMEDIAN

THE EIGHT NET GENERATION NORMS

If Wonder bread builds strong bodies in 12 ways, this generation is different from its parents in 8 ways. We call these 8 differentiating characteristics the Net Generation Norms. Each norm is a cluster of attitudes and behaviors that define the generation. These norms are central to understanding how this generation is changing work, markets, learning, the family, and society. You'll read about them throughout the book.

- They want *freedom* in everything they do, from freedom of choice to freedom of expression. We all love freedom, but not like this generation. Choice is like oxygen to them. While older generations feel overwhelmed by the proliferation of sales channels, product types, and brands, the Net Gen takes it for granted. Net Geners leverage technology to cut through the clutter and find the marketing message that fits their needs. They also expect to choose where and when they work. They use technology to escape traditional office constraints and integrate their work lives with their home and social lives. Net Geners seek the freedom to change jobs, freedom to take their own path, and to express themselves.

- They love to *customize*, personalize. When I was a kid, I never got to customize *The Mickey Mouse Club*. Today's youth can change the media world around them—their desktop, Web site, ring tone, handle, screen saver, news sources, and entertainment. They have grown up getting what media they want, when they want it, and being able to change it. Millions around the world don't just access the Web, they are creating it by creating online content. Now the need to customize is extending beyond the digital world to just about everything they touch. Forget standard job descriptions and only one variety of product. As for government portals, they want "my government" customized online.

- **They are the new** *scrutinizers.* When I was young, a picture was a picture. No more. Transparency, namely stakeholder access to pertinent information about companies and their offerings,[34] just seems natural to the Net Gen. While older generations marvel at the consumer research available on the Internet, the Net Gen expects it. As they grow older, their online engagement increases. Businesses targeting the Net Gen should expect and welcome intense scrutiny of its products, promotional efforts, and corporate practices. The Net Gen knows that their market power allows them to demand more of companies, which goes for employers as well.

- **They look for** *corporate integrity and openness* **when deciding what to buy and where to work.** The Internet, and other information and communication technologies, strip away the barriers between companies and their various constituencies, including consumers, activists, and shareholders. Whether consumers are exposing a flawed viral marketing campaign or researching a future employer, Net Geners make sure company values align with their own.

- **The Net Gen wants** *entertainment and play* **in their work, education, and social life.** This generation brings a playful mentality to work. From their experience in the latest video game, they know that there's always more than one way to achieve a goal. This outside-the-box thinking results from 82 percent of American children aged 2 to 17 having regular access to video games. It's a fast-growing industry: in the United States, video game sales were $8.4 billion in 2005, with worldwide sales expected to hit $46.5 billion by 2010.[35] This is a generation that has been bred on interactive experiences. Brand recognition alone is no longer enough, something leading companies recognize.

- **They are the** *collaboration and relationship* **generation.** Today, youth collaborate on Facebook, play multiuser video games; text each other incessantly; and share files for school, work, or just for fun. As evidenced by sites such as Yub.com, they also engage in relationship-oriented purchasing. Nine out of ten young people we interviewed said that if a best friend recommends a product, they are likely to buy it. They influence each other through what we call N-fluence Networks—online networks of Net Geners who, among other things, discuss brands, companies, products, and services.

- **The Net Gen has a need for** *speed*—**and not just in video games.** Real-time chats with a database of global contacts have made rapid communication the new norm for the Net Generation. In a world where speed characterizes the flow of information among vast networks of people, communication with friends, colleagues, and superiors takes place faster than ever. And marketers and employers should realize that Net Geners expect the same quick communication from others—every instant message should draw an instant response.

- **They are the *innovators*.** When I was young, the pace of innovation was glacial. Today it's on hyperdrive. A twentysomething in the workforce wants the new BlackBerry, Palm, or iPhone not because the old one is no longer cool, but because the new one does so much more. They seek innovative companies as employers and are constantly looking for innovative ways to collaborate, entertain themselves, learn, and work.

Creating the Future

The famous communications philosopher Marshall McLuhan viewed language assembled into a book as a probe. He said, "When information is brushed against information the results are startling and effective."[36] Which is why I love writing books and why I was so excited when *Growing Up Digital* was published. It probed the idea that for the first time in history, we can learn what we must do from children. The experience of the last dozen years has, in my view, shown this to be true.

As talent, the Net Generation is already transforming the workforce. The biggest generation ever is flooding into a talent vortex being created by the expansion of the global economy, the mobility of labor, and the fastest and biggest generational retirement ever. They are bringing new approaches to collaboration, knowledge sharing, and innovation in businesses and governments around the world. There is strong evidence that the organizations that embrace these new ways of working experience better performance, growth, and success. To win the battle for talent, organizations need to rethink many aspects of how they recruit, compensate, develop, collaborate with, and supervise talent. I believe the very idea of management is changing.

As consumers, the Net Geners are transforming markets and marketing, not just because they have huge purchasing power and influence. They also value different characteristics of products and services, and they want companies to create rich experiences. They influence each other and other generations in new ways, and traditional media are ineffective in reaching them. Only 2 percent of our sample indicated high trust in the ad campaigns of marketers. The old saw, "Half my ads are effective; I just don't know which half," isn't real any more, as a majority of ads on television are deleted and never appear to growing millions of young people around the world. Instead of consumers, they want to be prosumers—co-innovating products and services with producers. The concept of a brand is forever changing because of them. Companies can now understand how to redesign a total customer experience for the twenty-first century from R&D through to customer support, by learning from them.

Until recently, they have been disengaged from formal politics, preferring to be involved in civic activity in their communities, or in working behind the scenes to solve global problems. But 2008 was the year they entered formal political life, and exercised their power by launching Barak Obama as the Democratic contender for the U.S. presidency. I believe the Net Geners' experience in this election campaign will not stop on Election Day. They won't settle for a passive role in politics or in government.

> "During the time when most members of our generation became politically aware, our government was spiraling out of control . . . this will all change with time. We are, after all, still young."
> —PHIL DUMOUCHEL, *20, ROCHESTER, NEW YORK*

They are already placing demands on our political institutions in order to engage them. I believe they will insist on changes to the way governments are run, too. They see that checking into a hotel or renting a car can be done in 30 seconds, and wonder why it takes governments weeks to do a similar activity. Broadcast democracy was fine for the TV generation. Not for them.

Will their civic activity around the world become a new kind of activism? Will they rise to the challenges of deepening problems that my generation is handing to them? Never has there been a time of greater promise or peril. The challenge of achieving that promise and in so doing saving our fragile planet will rest with the Net Generation. Our responsibility to them is to give them the tools and opportunity to fulfill their destiny.

The Net Generation, the biggest ever, is coming of age. As they go to college and begin jobs, Net Geners are beginning to use remarkable digital tools that give individuals the power that in the past was reserved for the authorities. They're the first global generation, and around the world they share many of the eight norms that we presented here—the Net Generation Norms. We have an unparalleled opportunity to learn from them. Increasingly the people, companies, and nations that are succeeding today are those who are listening to the new generation. We can listen to their views on the world. We can learn from their effortless mastery and application of new tools, ways of working, and methods of collaboration. I believe, by listening, we can envision and enact the new institutional models required for the twenty-first century.

Read on.

A GENERATION
BATHED IN BITS

In January 2004, Mark Zuckerberg had a real-life version of a common nightmare. He was facing his first round of exams at Harvard and he hadn't studied or read anything the professor had assigned for a first-year art history course called Rome of Augustus. Zuckerberg hadn't even gone to class during the term. He was too busy creating a cool computer program called Facebook that would help students get to know one another and share information. Now, a few days before the exam, Zuckerberg was, in his words, "just completely screwed."

But he had an idea, straight out of twenty-first-century computer science. He created a Web site and put pictures from the course on it, with a little discussion beside each picture. Maybe the other students could help out by filling in the blanks. Within 24 hours, Zuckerberg's classmates helped out alright, with notes so cogent that everyone, Zuckerberg included, passed the test with flying colors. And according to Zuckerberg, the professor didn't see it as cheating. Instead, he was "really pleased" to see the students collaborate in such a creative fashion.

After acing his art history test, Zuckerberg returned to his school project, Facebook, which has since become one of the most ubiquitous social networking sites in the world; on it, friends and acquaintances keep up with each other's news. Now, with more than 70 million active users and a market value estimated at a couple of billion dollars or more, Facebook is a great example of how this generation uses and revolutionizes technology. As we'll see in this chapter, this is a generation that likes to share information. They want to be connected with friends and family all the time, and they use technology—from mobile phones to social networks—to do it. So when the TV is on, they don't sit and watch, as their parents did. TV is background Muzak for them, to which they listen while they check out information or talk to friends online or via text message. Their mobile phones aren't just useful communication devices; they're a vital connection to friends. And now that the "phones" are increasingly connected to the Internet, the Net Geners can stay connected with friends online wherever they go. In this chapter, we'll look at this small-screen revolution in the United States, and, as an indication of where it might be headed, in Japan.

The Net Generation uses digital technology in a very different way than boomers do. The Net Geners have developed different reflexes and behaviors, which they use when they are on their mobile phones or are surfing the Internet. But the differences don't stop there.

This generation is revolutionizing the very nature of the Internet itself. Zuckerberg's Facebook is just one example of the popular social networking sites that are turning the Internet into a place to share and connect, a kind of cyber community center. Net Geners are transforming the Internet from a place where you mainly find information to a place where you share information, collaborate on projects of mutual interest, and create new ways to solve some of our most pressing problems.

One way that they are doing this is by creating content—in the form of their own blogs, or in combination with other people's content. In this way, the Net Generation is democratizing the creation of content, and this new paradigm of communication will have a revolutionary impact on everything it touches— from music and movies, to political life, business, and education.

They might just be the generation to activate that slogan that we boomers chanted in our youth—Power to the People. It can happen now because the Web 2.0 makes it easier for ordinary people to organize themselves, instead of having to do so under the control of hierarchical, often authoritarian, organizations. Instead of being just small cogs in a large and impersonal machine, they now may be finding the power to become autonomous entities unto themselves.

But this sunny story may have a dark cloud hanging over it, one that few Net Geners have yet seen. They are sharing intimate details about themselves, lavishly illustrated by pictures that might come back to haunt them once they are seeking public office, or a high-ranking job in a public corporation. We'll explore this issue toward the end of this chapter. This generation is giving up its privacy, not only because of the social networks, but because they are happily answering questions from the corporate world about their private lives. George Orwell, as it turns out, was only partly right when he wrote *1984*. It's not Big Brother who is watching you just yet; it is Little Brother—your friendly marketer. And this is only the beginning. We appear to be moving into a world in which you will be connected to everyone all the time wherever you go, from the little device in the palm of your hand. Will that finally signal the end of privacy?

THEY USE TECHNOLOGY DIFFERENTLY THAN BOOMERS

To this generation, the Internet is like the fridge. They don't belabor the nuts and bolts of its operation; it's just part of life. "Kids think money comes from a wall," says Internet authority Jerry Michalski, referring to an ATM machine, "and music comes from computers."

Consider how Matt Ceniceros, a 26-year-old and father of two, begins his day in Memphis with his BlackBerry. "I use it as my alarm clock, night-light, watch, and a phone," he says. Like most Net Geners, he doesn't bother with a home phone. "I wake up and check e-mail that comes in from overseas throughout the night and from the early starters in my work group and start planning out my day. It's much easier to look at my BlackBerry than it is to fire up my laptop and fight with the Virtual Private Network. Plus as more sites are optimized for mobile phone users and the wireless networks get better, using my BlackBerry as a Web browser becomes easier and easier. On trips it becomes a makeshift GPS device."

On the way to work, Matt doesn't listen to top 40 songs or the news on the car radio. He plugs his iPod into the car and listens to his own selection. For morning news, he checks the NewsGator RSS aggregator, and then checks up on the blogs in Bloglines, the Google Blog search tool, and Technorati.

In the evening he doesn't settle into the sitcom routine. Instead, he talks to friends on Skype (an Internet-based telephone service that lets you make long-distance calls for pennies an hour) and shares photos on Facebook, plays on his Nintendo Wii, and checks the latest on YouTube while his two-year-old son watches videos of sharks and airplanes. He barely mentions TV.

TV—the New Background Muzak

Net Geners have completely different media habits than their boomer parents did at their age. When my generation, the boomers, watched TV as teenagers, we just watched, about 22.4 hours a week; we didn't talk back. When we read newspapers or listened to top 40 hits on the radio, we were mostly passive consumers. It was the great, distant powers-that-be in the news and entertainment industry decided what news was fit to print, what songs were worth hearing, and what movies would be in the movie theaters—not us.[1]

The Net Generation watches a lot less TV than boomers did at their age—only 17.4 hours a week.[2] But of course they spend more time on the Internet—anywhere from 8 to 33 hours a week, depending on the survey. Older Americans, in contrast, watch more TV and spend less time on the Internet.[3] Estimates of the Net Gen's online use vary as widely as the Net Geners themselves do. Serious game players might spend even more time online; people who do not have Internet access at home would probably spend less. (About 9 in 10 American Net Geners have Internet access and their own computer at home.)[4]

But when Net Geners watch TV, they treat it like background Muzak as they hunt for information and chat with friends online or on the phone. Multitasking is natural for this generation. While they're online, 53 percent listen to MP3s, 40 percent talk on the phone, 39 percent watch TV, and 24 percent do their homework, according to a survey by Harris Interactive. When they're talking to their friends, they don't hog the family phone either—telephone use has dropped significantly for this demographic. Instead, kids text-message, or type out a comment on Facebook, Skype, GTalk, or AIM.[5]

But if you ask them which medium they can do without—Internet or TV—TV is the loser in all 12 countries we surveyed. (See Figure 2.1.)

Everywhere you look, TV is suffering as the leaders of the first global generation turn their backs on it. The 2008 Grammy Awards tell the story. Most award shows have been suffering a viewer decline over the last few years, but the 2008 Grammies were hit especially hard—particularly by the teen demographic. The awards ceremony, which aired on CBS, had a 3.8 percent viewer rating among teens aged 12–17, down from 9.7 percent in 2004.[6]

To be sure, teens are still interested in the Grammy performances, the award winners, and red-carpet fashions. They just don't want to sit through an entire broadcast to see the interesting bits. Instead, many headed to YouTube, where four- to six-minute highlights were available. Teens also headed to the various celebrity and fashion blogs covering the event. The same teen behavior was also seen with respect to the 2008 Academy Awards.

The Net Geners want to see it with their friends—not in the same room necessarily, but online. When they watch red-carpet fashions online, they want to critique the fashions with their friends, online. They often experience the communal aspect of watching large award shows without actually watching the entire show as older generations do. Instead, they join the real-time polling,

FIGURE 2.1   NET GENERS ANSWER THE QUESTION: WOULD YOU RATHER LIVE WITHOUT TV OR INTERNET?

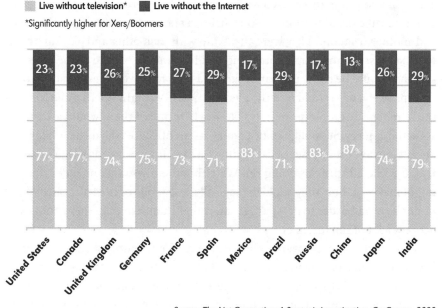

Source: The Net Generation: A Strategic Investigation, © nGenera, 2008

live chats, and lively discussion boards on sites such as Popsugar.com and GoFugyourself.com, which posted images of celebrity outfits complete with discussion and analysis.

When they do watch TV, Net Geners prefer downloading the TV shows they follow onto their computer, or prerecording them on TiVo, which lets them take their content wherever they go and watch it whenever they want. My Time replaces Prime Time.[7]

The TV they do watch is very different from the TV their boomer parents watched as kids. There are now hundreds of channels. Because of the greater choice there is more nonvacuous content: TV is a distribution channel for good movies, documentaries, sports events, music, comedy, interviews, and news. As a teenager, Alex's favorite channel was the History Channel. Many television sets have multiple windows by means of which you can read sports scores while watching a game, or that enable you to watch a few games or shows simultaneously. When they do watch TV, they do so through these multiple lenses.

> "Why watch cable when I can download my favorite shows—in HD and without commercials—whenever I want?"
>
> —JESSE MORGAN, 27

One day, when I was visiting my son Alex at Amherst College, in Massachusetts, I learned how he and his friends "watch" television. Five of them were sitting in a common room, each with a laptop. They were watching three television sets, all closed-captioned—one airing a sports show; another, the news; and another, a sitcom. They were all talking with each other and playing a game they had just dreamed up. Something would come up on one of the three TV sets that would be the source of debate and then they would each race to their laptops to see who could find the answer. One TV might say that the Mafia is the number one employer in Italy? No way! Or one of them would assert that something Jerry Seinfeld had just said was an obscure Shakespearean reference. No way! Of course, occasionally, one would use a cell phone or text a friend while all this was going on. Watching the boys, anyone older than 40 might marvel at how they could manage all these kinds of media at once. What might be even harder to grasp was that, rather than stressing them out, it was actually a lot of fun for them.

The writing is on the wall for broadcasters. We're witnessing a classic market disruption, a profound disturbance that acts like a devastating earthquake, with the potential to level every structure in sight. Back in 2007, I was asked to give the opening speech at a conference of national broadcasters. The conference was aptly titled "The Transformation of Broadcasting," and I told them that their theme was a good one, perhaps better than even they realized. In the years to come, broadcasting wouldn't be broad, I said, and it wouldn't be casting. They could no longer count on reaching a wide spectrum of the public. And it wouldn't be one-way communication either. The dominance of one-way, passive media consumption was over. This fact has profound implications for this generation, and for the major media players, as we'll see later in this book.

Natural Inquirers

The Net Generation isn't content to wait until 6 p.m. for the nightly news—or 8 p.m. for their favorite TV show. They want it where and when they want it.

> "I don't read newspapers but I'm informed. If information is important, it will find me."
>
> —BEN RATTRAY, 27, SAN FRANCISCO, FOUNDER AND CEO OF CHANGE.ORG

Most Net Geners get their news online, from official news sources and blogs.[8] Take 24-year-old Rahaf Harfoush. In 2008, I introduced her at a meeting of executives from the media and telecommunications industry, and during a panel discussion I asked her why she doesn't read newspapers. "Why would you?" she replied. "They come out once a day, they don't have hot links and they're not multimedia.

Besides, who needs that black gunk all over your fingers?" Rahaf has created her own digital newspaper, featuring a sophisticated, personalized set of information gathering tools. They provide her with real-time, on-demand access to dozens of information sources. "The news is no longer a one-stop trip," she told me later. "I think the changing nature of the story, and the constant updating of the Internet, make it possible to sample a wide variety of opinions and perspectives. I rely on all these different pieces to triangulate the issues I care about and kind of get to the heart of things."

The New Content Creators

When they search for information or entertainment, they expect it to turn into a conversation. Nearly 80 percent of Net Geners under age 28 regularly visit blogs, the most popular way to create and share content. These collections of personal thoughts, opinions, and interests—or even artwork, photos, stories, or videos—represent unfiltered self-expression. Some 40 percent of teens and young adults have their own blogs, according to the Pew Research Center. They're contributing more content, too. Some 64 percent of the Net Generation engaged in some form of content creation in 2007, compared with 57 percent in 2006.[9] That amounts to half of all teens aged 12–17, or about 12 million young people, in the United States alone, and this number looks likely to grow year after year.

Mashups—mixing other people's content—is also popular. One in four Internet-using teens remixes content online to create some form of artistic expression.[10] Over the past few years, for example, fans of the artists represented by the label Wind-up Records have spent at least a quarter of a million hours producing and sharing more than 3,000 music videos, says Stanford professor Lawrence Lessig. But these are not your garden-variety music videos.

Fans—primarily kids—use their PCs to synchronize Japanese anime art with popular music tracks to create an entirely new art form called anime music videos. According to Lessig, the 3,000 anime music videos relating to Wind-up Records represent just 5 percent of the total Net-generated creations circulating on one popular site. AnimeMusicVideos.org is one such Web site, with over 900,000

> "There's something exhilarating about it, everyone wants to feel like they're part of something."
> —MELISSA BOWLBY, 17, KITCHENER, ONTARIO

registered users and close to a million posts (900,000). But, as Lessig indicated, this is only the tip of the iceberg. Half a million users frequent this site and close to 30,000 music and anime enthusiasts contribute to it.[11]

The Small Screen Revolution: The Age of the Mobile Phone

However, this is not about use of PCs. There is a small screen revolution and this generation is taking it to the streets. For Net Geners, the mobile phone is becoming the tool of choice to access the Web. Most kids in the United States have them. By the middle of 2007, 72 percent of 13- to 17-year-olds in the United States had mobile phones. Teens, along with their 8-to 12-year-old younger siblings, are the fastest-growing segment of the mobile phone market, according to the Yankee Group. Their parents are buying them because they see mobile phones as a security device. A survey released in December 2007 showed that 78 percent of parents considering mobile phones as a holiday gift for their child were motivated by safety, and not entertainment.[12] With a mobile phone, kids can call home in an emergency, while parents can call to remind them of a curfew—or even check their whereabouts.

Kids naturally see the phones differently, as an indispensable social tool—like having a friend in their pocket. Think of what the typical teenage girl does as she exits high school in the afternoon. She flips open her mobile phone—even if friends surround her. Teens are being serious when they tell their parents that without a mobile phone they're a nobody, says Robbie Blinkoff, principal anthropologist at Context, a Baltimore research company that studies consumer trends.

"I don't use my phone for voice because I have a cheaper data plan."

—KATIE TINKHAM, 16,
RIVER FOREST, ILLINOIS

They use mobile phones differently than their parents do. While most boomers still are likely to use the phone to call family and friends, teens are more likely to text message their friends and call their parents.

> ## E-mail: So Yesterday
>
> For Net Geners, e-mail is so yesterday. It's what you use when you write a polite thank-you letter to a friend's parent. We asked respondents in an nGenera study to describe various means of communication, including face-to-face, e-mail, texting, social networking, telephone conversations, and instant messaging.[13] I was amused to see that 48 percent of respondents considered e-mail professional, while another 31 percent considered it boring. It was also seen as a more formal method of communication. "I use e-mail for business type [sic] of things," said one respondent. "I don't say to my friends 'e-mail me later.'"

Without their mobile phones, Net Geners get anxious in a hurry. Teens that are used to having unfettered access to a mobile phone begin to feel real anxiety and a sense of "deprivation" when separated from the gadget for longer than 24 hours, according to Context. In the UK, they even have a word for it—"no-mo-phobia." Some teenagers do not turn off their phones, and sleep with their prized possession beside them on their pillow, in case someone texts them after midnight with dramatic news.[14] Part of the research that we did was qualitative, allowing Net Geners to create a collage describing how they would feel under different circumstances. Opinions were gathered from the west coast of the United States to South Africa. Some of the most revealing collages were seen when Net Geners were asked to describe how they would feel if they were disconnected from their technology for an entire month. The collages shown below and on page 48 are representative of the submitted responses.[15]

HOW WOULD YOU FEEL WITHOUT ACCESS TO COMMUNICATIONS TECHNOLOGY?

Source: The Net Generation: A Strategic Investigation, © nGenera, 2008

HOW WOULD YOU FEEL WITHOUT ACCESS TO COMMUNICATIONS TECHNOLOGY?

Source: The Net Generation: A Strategic Investigation, © nGenera, 2008

Phone or Digital Copilot?

Today's phones are sleek digital Swiss Army Knives that do a lot more than make a phone call. Now, as mobile phones are being linked to the Internet, they're turning into something completely different. Already the word *mobile phone* is a misnomer. Manufacturers are piling on features, turning these devices into small, powerful computers that are part voice communication, part BlackBerry, part iPod, part Web browser, part texting device, part digital camera, part video camera, part voice recorder, and part GPS compass. They will have a persistent connection to the Internet, so you will always be online.

We'll have to call them something else—a buddy or even a digital copilot—because all of us, young and old, will rely on them heavily to get through our day. Apple's hugely popular iPhone, with its 16 applications, hints at the versatility of tomorrow's devices. Apple also released details of the iPhone's operating system to encourage other companies to dream up new uses for the phone. Google is doing the same thing with its so-called Android initiative. The search-engine giant has partnered with dozens of phone makers, networks, and software companies to make it as easy as possible to develop new uses for tomorrow's copilots.

To get an idea of what the future will look like in the United States and Canada, look at the way Net Geners use mobile phones outside North America. Mobile phone usage worldwide is skyrocketing, from 11 million mobile subscribers in 1990 to 2.2 billion in 2005, according to the UN Millennial Goals Report. In many countries, access to desktop or laptop computers with a broadband Internet connection is limited, and the mobile phone with high-speed connection to the Internet is the preferred method to go online. Connecting to the Internet with a mobile phone is cheaper than connecting by computer, which is why they're growing so fast in Africa, where mobiles outnumber landlines in every country. More than 50 million Africans had a mobile subscription by the end of 2005, representing 5 percent of Africa's population.[16] In Asia, up to 90 percent of consumers in some Asian countries subscribe to wireless data plans, versus just over half in the United States. And while Americans mostly use basic data features such as mobile text messaging, Asians are already using their phones for many other purposes, such as watching movies, buying food at vending machines, and using them as train passes.[17]

Japanese youth, who are bellwethers for the future, love their mobile phones. In Japan, about one-third of primary school students aged 7–12 years old use mobile phones, and in high school this figure jumps to 96 percent, according to a government survey released in late 2007. Japanese youth use their phones extensively—an average of 124 minutes a day for high school girls and 92 minutes for boys—to listen to music, chat with friends, surf the Internet, and even read books.

Mobile phone novels in Japan are a huge hit. Of last year's 10 bestselling novels, 5 began as mobile phone novels.[18] Here's how it works: Each day the author uploads snippets of text to mobile phone novel Web sites, and readers download the text to their phones. One author, a 21-year-old woman named Rin, wrote *If You* over a six-month stretch while attending high school.[19] She attracted 20 million readers. Her story of tragic love between two childhood friends was turned into a 142-page hardcover that was the fifth-best-selling novel in Japan in 2007.[20]

> "My mother didn't even know that I was writing a novel. So when I told her, I'm coming out with a novel, she was like, what? She didn't believe it until it appeared in bookstores."
>
> —RIN, JAPANESE NOVELIST

FIGURE 2.2 GLOBAL INTERNET USAGE NOW SURPASSES PERSONAL COMPUTER USAGE

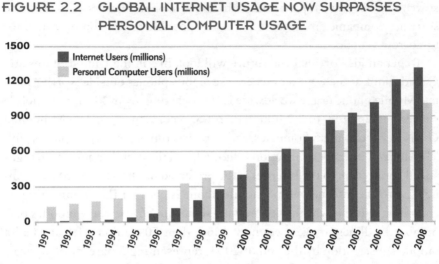

Source: The Net Generation: A Strategic Investigation, © nGenera, 2008

Mobile Phones Overtake PCs

No wonder Internet usage surpassed personal computer usage back in 2002. But, then again, I've always thought the term *personal computer* was an oxymoron, like jumbo shrimp, military music, or plastic glasses. The whole purpose of computing is not personal. It's not a private activity—it is about connecting and collaborating and engaging with the world. Net Geners are proving me right. (See Figures 2.2, 2.3, and 2.4.)

FIGURE 2.3 PERCENTAGE OF NET GENERS WHO OWN A PHONE OR HAVE ONE FOR PERSONAL USE

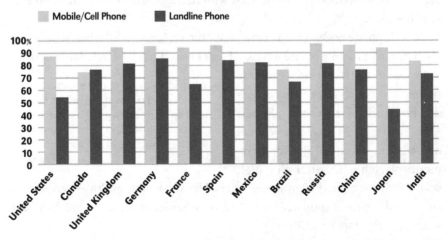

Source: The Net Generation: A Strategic Investigation, © nGenera, 2008

FIGURE 2.4   PERCENTAGE OF NET GENERS WHO TEXT
            MESSAGED, E-MAILED ON MOBILE/CELL PHONE
            IN THE PAST MONTH

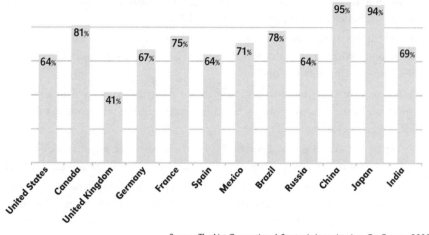

Source: The Net Generation: A Strategic Investigation, © nGenera, 2008

DIGITAL TECHNOLOGY IS CHANGING THEIR BEHAVIOR:
A DAY IN THE LIFE

How is the digital technology influencing the Net Geners' behavior? We asked
the members of the *GrownUpDigital* community on Facebook to describe a day
in their life. Here's one from Rahaf, the 24-year-old I interviewed in front of
executives—which provides an extraordinary glimpse into the future. She left
her job at a leading-edge market research company this year to become an independent new-media strategist. She travels a lot, mainly in North America and
bills clients for about 50 hours a week. Business is great, she says. Just compare
her digital day with the kind of technology that a boomer uses in, say, corporate
America. She works out of her apartment in Toronto.

> 10:00 a.m. Wake up, shower, change, have breakfast. I'm so glad I make my own
> hours, because 10:00 a.m. is the earliest I think anyone should be up. I much pre-
> fer the night!!
>
> 10:30 a.m. Log on to my MacBook. Sandy (<http://www.iwantsandy.com>
> www.iwantsandy.com) is my online virtual assistant who manages my day to day
> tasks/appointments. She sends me an overview of what I have planned each day
> as well as reminders. I use Google blog reader to check out what's happening on
> the blogosphere (I read over 55 blogs in a week) and Google News to get cus-
> tomized news relevant to my interests, and related to some of the projects I'm
> working on. I'm subscribed to customized RSS feeds to get news that's espe-
> cially relevant to me.

11:00 a.m. Start working on client projects. Log on to private client Wiki that I set up to see what has been added night before. (Client in different time zone.) Make some changes and input. Add new milestones to time lines. Use Google notebook to grab various pages for different research projects. MSN with friends. Check out some funny YouTube videos.

12:00 Skype Sister, she's in London. We hang out via videoconference while we're both working. I watch her make amazing roast chicken sandwich for lunch. My own cooking network online.

1:30 p.m. Use SkypeOut to dial grandparents in Syria. So cheap. Amazing. They are doing well. Talk with my uncle via video chat in Dubai. Promise to upload more pictures on our family site.

2:00 p.m. Head to the gym. Load up iPod with latest podcasts, and usually one or two episodes of the Colbert Report/Daily Show to entertain me on the treadmill.

3:00 p.m. On my way home, I get a text from my older sister, reminding me it's mom's birthday dinner on Saturday. I write Sandy an email from my BB and she adds it automatically to my Google calendar which wirelessly syncs with my BlackBerry calendar. Ping boyfriend via BlackBerry voice note, and tell him not to forget to pick up a movie. Ask Sandy to send him a list of tagged videos we previously thought we'd want to see.

3:30 p.m. Client meeting. Head on over, use BlackBerry GPS to navigate to an unfamiliar part of the city. Chat with friends on BB messenger & Google chat while taking a cab.

5:00 p.m. Back at my desk. I see my friends have scheduled us for a movie night via our shared events calendar on Google. I check out a preview online and check Rottentomatoes.com for a review. Looks good. Listen to iTunes, while working or to SeeqPod.com (Live streaming music search engine). My dad Skypes me (He's north of the city). We video chat and make plans for me to come on the weekend. He subscribes to one of my calendar feeds, so he knows when I'm free.

6:00 p.m. Dinner. Use<http://www.cookthink.com> to find a recipe that matches the ingredients in my fridge AND my mood. Yummy, stuffed peppers. I use iMovie and take a mini clip to send to sis. Stuffed peppers trump roasted chickensandwich!

7:00 p.m. Online errands. Pay bills, buy mom's birthday gift off of amazon, check Facebook. Get photo text messages from sister. Should she buy the blue shirt or the red shirt. Look at both pictures. Recommend red shirt. It's a nicer color and fits her better.

8:00 p.m.-10:00 p.m. Hanging out. Check out Oprah that I'd PVR'd earlier that day. I love fast forwarding through commercials. Watch some TV on my computer via Joost.com. Discuss latest Lost Episode on forum. Glad to see I'm not the only one going crazy with all the mystery this season. Discuss some good theories with the hard core viewers.

10:00 p.m.-1:30a.m. Finish up client work.

2:00 a.m. Play some X-box live with some friends in the city. I suck so bad at Halo three they always sneak up behind me and take me out.

2:30 a.m. Update my Shelfari.com site with the latest book I just finished. I rated it, and discussed it with some other people online who have read it. Compare what my friends are planning to read, and order some of their favorite picks off of Amazon.

2:45 a.m. Check my "Daily Digest" sent by Sandy with tomorrow's meetings and to do's. Prioritize important tasks and get ready for bed.

When I interviewed Rahaf in front of the business executives, I asked why she left her job to become an entrepreneur. She paused for a moment to reflect. The first thing she said was "I'm not a morning person."

THEY ARE CHANGING THE TECHNOLOGY: IT'S NOT YOUR DADDY'S INTERNET

Technology is influencing the way kids think and behave, but it's a two-way street—the way kids think and behave is influencing and shaping the Internet itself. In the twenty-first century, knowledge is flowing more freely than ever, thanks to the Internet, but the Internet's true potential was not realized until the young people started using computers. Now they're helping to transform it into something new—Web 2.0, the living Web, the Hypernet, the active web, the read-write Web. Call it what you like—this ain't your daddy's Internet. It's become a global, active, networked computer that allows everyone not only to contribute but to change the very nature of the beast.

Wikipedia, the global encyclopedia written and edited by tens of thousands of contributors worldwide, is a classic example of this new Web of collaboration. The Net Gen is driving the transformation in lots of ways. They're putting 100 million blogs online, all searchable by Technorati—a company that monitors blog usage. They're having fun with online, multiplayer games, which are projected to top $44 billion in revenue by 2011[21]—making collaboration entertainment bigger than Hollywood. They're sharing movies and songs online with tens of millions of people through peer-to-peer file sharing tools, such as Kazaa, BitTorrent, and LimeWire.

It is getting easier all the time to join the global conversation. A couple of years ago, sending a video clip to YouTube was a complicated process. You had to record, upload, and convert. But now it has been simplified to a few clicks. Casio recently announced two low-cost point-and-shoot digital cameras that could also be set to record short videos in a YouTube-type format.[22] No computer manipulation required; just shoot your video and upload it for the world to see. The Casio camera is important for this generation because it makes it easy for them to collaborate and create online. For the Net Gen, and the rest of us who can adapt, this is a chance to see ourselves, in living color, as part of the global conversation.

The graph in Figure 2.5 shows the percentage of our global Net Generation sample who say that they "regularly add or change things online," such as posting a comment on a blog, correcting a Wikipedia listing, writing a movie review, or uploading a YouTube video.

Social Networks: The Net Gen Version of a Global Community Center

Just as the Web was beginning to change into a platform to contribute and collaborate, Mark Zuckerberg entered Harvard University. A few weeks after passing his exam on Augustus in Rome, Zuckerberg launched Facebook from his college dorm. He moved to California that summer, intending to return to Harvard to complete his degree in computer science. Instead, he dropped out to become full-time CEO of Facebook, the archetypal social network for

FIGURE 2.5   PERCENT OF NET GENERS WHO REGULARLY ADD OR CHANGE THINGS ONLINE

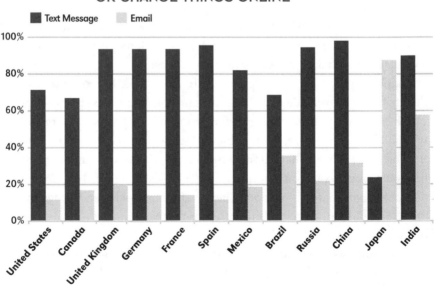

Source: The Net Generation: A Strategic Investigation, © nGenera, 2008

friends. It wasn't a public space like MySpace, where you can connect with 1,000 of your "best friends." Nor was it a chat room, where you were supposed to be interested in conversing with an anonymous person called Mooselips or Cyberchick.

This was a place where you could be yourself, a real person, and feel free to talk with your close friends or your wider circle of friends. You could show them pictures, tell jokes, make plans, and do many of the things that friends do together. Facebook allowed you to create an online community for friends. You could also shut out people you didn't know, or didn't want to have in your circle of friends. It's a community independent of time and space. You can contribute whenever you can, from wherever you are.

In a conversation I had with Zuckerberg in spring 2008, he explained the sudden popularity of Facebook this way: "In order for us to be successful in this century, we're going to need to be more connected and we're going to need to have a better sense of understanding of where other people are coming from and just greater sense of like, we're all connected."

Or, as Erin Lewis put it: "My high school reunion happens on Facebook. All day. Every day."[23]

A Place to Hang Out: New Private Spaces Online

For today's teens, spending time on MySpace or Facebook is about reclaiming private space, says dana boyd, a University of Berkeley–based social scientist. "Adults control the home, the school, and most activity spaces," she said in a recent talk to the American Association for the Advancement of Science. "Teens are told where to be, what to do, and how to do it. They lack control at home, and many teens don't see home as their private space."

They're finding new private spaces online, where young people gather en masse, network with peers and make shared spaces of their own. Online spaces are becoming more appealing as the physical world becomes less welcoming. "Classic 1950s hang-out locations like the roller rink and burger joint are disappearing, while malls and 7-Elevens are banning teens, unless accompanied by their parents. . . . Hanging out around the neighborhood or in the woods has been deemed unsafe for fear of predators, drug dealers, and abductors," says boyd.

The personal profiles on social networks are what she calls "public displays of identity." In virtual spaces, teens are increasingly free to shape their own identities and manage their networks. Comments from friends provide a channel for feedback and affection. Though many of these relationships are shallow, boyd argues, the process plays an important role in how teens learn the rules of social life and cope with issues such as status, respect, gossip, and trust.

What They Mean: A Potent Organizing Tool for Communities

We're still in the early days of understanding how social networks will be used and for what purposes. The picture is not clear yet, which is not surprising. "People tend to frame the new in terms of the old," notes Alan Majer, executive analyst at nGenera. "When automobiles arrived, for instance," he says, "they were seen as 'horseless carriages.' It wasn't immediately obvious that drivers could share the interior with their passengers. And when 'moving pictures' were invented, it also took a while for studios to tap all the new possibilities the medium offered. Similarly, next-generation social networking platforms will unlock entirely new possibilities but it will not be immediately obvious what all of them are, or how they should be tapped."

Clearly, social networks are a phenomenal way to spread information. When you put a photo on your personal profile page, you don't have to e-mail friends or call them to tell them about it. The news about your photo is instantly transmitted to the "news feed" on their Facebook profile pages. You don't have to do anything; communication is instant and automatic. Friends can spread news to outsiders too, and the news can spread like wildfire. If you have 20 friends and they find something interesting, they might tell other people. If each of your friends sends the news to two other people, and they do the same, you can understand why some bits of information "go viral," as they say these days. But that's only the beginning of the deep impact that social networks will have on our lives.

People Can Self-Organize on the Internet Rather than Following the Leader

For several years, I have been studying social networks and how they affect this generation and the world. But I continue to learn from observing how young people use them in spontaneous and creative ways. On Christmas Day 2006, I got a wake-up call, Net Gen style. I had given my son Alex, then 20 and a college junior, as one of his Christmas presents under the tree, an advance copy of my new book *Wikinomics*. He thanked me and a couple of hours later let me know, "Hey Dad, this is a good book. I think I'll create a community on Facebook." I watched and 15 minutes later he had created the "Wikinomists of the World Unite" (WWU) community on Facebook. Fifteen minutes later he had six members. By the time we were eating turkey on the same evening, he had 130 members in seven countries; seven regional coordinators; a president (Alex), a secretary, and a chief information officer (to deal with the technical challenges facing the community)! He sent out a PDF of the first two chapters of the book, and before Christmas Day had ended, interesting things were happening. "I found an error in Mr. Tapscott's book," said one response. "Exactly how will Mr. Tapscott be contributing to *our* community?" said another—appearing to be placing demands on me!

The WWU community has drifted off to do other things; no one has posted anything for months. Yet it reminded me of how the Internet, in particular social networking, can give power to a new force. People have organized themselves—without guidance from authorities—throughout human history. Language was a product of self-organization. There was no central committee of the English language that said a book will be called a "book." The word *book* just happened. Science was initially a product of self-organization as was the early period of the arts, education, and government. But what used to take centuries or years can now happen in months or on a single Christmas Day. When I was 20, I could have never created a community with 130 people in seven countries, no matter what I did.

And because social networks are being driven by youth, young people are driving the resurgence of new collaborative models that are now shaking the windows and rattling the walls of every institution.

They started with things that young people do—playing games online, listening to music, watching TV, and going to the movies. Now, as the first Net Geners enter their thirties, they're making an impact on civic life, and in politics. And in the next few years, I believe, social networking will become the basis for doing business in other spheres of adult life.

THE PLAY'S THE THING: GAMES, MOVIES, AND CIVICS
Gaming Together

There is also something big happening in the world of video games—they are moving online. Through their multiplayer collaboration, young people are changing gaming and even the nature of entertainment. Forget about the loner game player who is playing only with the quick reflexes of his or her fingers. In this new world, you have to cooperate and learn from experience. The online game World of Warcraft, for example, now has an astonishing 10 million subscribers around the world. Within the game, people create an Avatar they use to explore the vast virtual world, completing quests, improving their skills, and battling monsters. As they succeed, players earn virtual money and other items, improve their experience, and add to their reputation. As they go through the game, their Avatar increases in strength and power. Many players choose to join guilds, a group of players who form a group and regularly play together.

Game players can even get exercise. Have you heard of the "massively multi-player online dance games"? The new genre represents an evolution in the gaming community; it has proven to be very popular in India and is quickly gaining traction around the world. One popular game is called Dance Mela,[24] created by Kreeda, an Indian-based game company. Dance Mela is one of the very first multiplayer games produced in India. Users create Avatars to explore the Kreeda world and dance along to popular Bollywood hits. Players can "dance" in one of two ways. They can dance just with their fingers, using their keyboard to press the appropriate keys or they can dance with their feet. They purchase a dance mat, attach it to their computer, and step on the corresponding patterns on the mat. Those with two left feet can even join the in-world virtual dance class taught by Saroj Khan, one of India's leading choreographers, to learn the basics.

They don't have to dance alone either. Dancers can create private dance rooms and invite their friends, or frequent one of the world's many public dance halls and meet new friends. The game is aimed at the Net Generation, with an emphasis on staying fit: if you don't dance for a few days, your Avatar is likely to put on a few pounds!

Music and Movies: The Online Audience Chooses the New Stars

While online dancing is fun, social networking sites are far more influential and they're used for much more than merely staying current with your friends' travels or love lives. Their true value lies in the ability of sites like MySpace and Facebook to unite people around their various interests, from politics to music. Social networks are now becoming the conduits through which new trends in music, fashion, technology, and other aspects of youth culture are flowing.

Take Ourstage.com, a venture started in 2006 by a group of Emory University students in Atlanta, Georgia, in an effort to promote the next generation of musicians and filmmakers. "The Internet was supposed to help artists go around record labels and studios to reach their fans," says Alyssa Hale, an OurStage representative. "It didn't work out that way," adds Quinn Strassel, another employee, "because tens of millions of people showed up at the Internet party at the same time, with no way to sort the quality from the noise—until now."

To deal with this overflow, they created Ourstage.com. Filmmakers and musicians can upload a five-minute movie they've produced or a song they've written onto the OurStage Web site. Artists have a variety of both music and film genres they can compete in. Users compare two entries side by side, selecting the entry they think is better (and by how much) and a complex algorithm accumulates data and eventually selects the top contenders, who then compete in quarter, semi, and final rounds.

Viewers use their mobile phones to choose the winner once the finalists have been selected. Prizes include cash, gadgets (iPods), and the opportunity to perform at a live event. Contestants can promote their work by downloading unique banners or badges that they can then embed into their blogs, sites, or e-mails directing people to watch and vote for their work. Songwriters also have the option of uploading their songs to the site, where users can download them for $0.99 a song, with all profit going to the artist. OurStage does not take a cut, nor do they charge any processing fees.

But it was getting onto the Facebook grid that really caused OurStage to explode. They started out with about 140,000 unique users, a community that they built by responding to the needs of their users over the course of three months. After they started reaching out to Facebook and MySpace, their exposure went viral, and in just one month they experienced the same amount of traffic on their site that they had in the past three. Just one year after its launch, OurStage has grown to a community of over 1.5 million unique users, making it the largest music site on the Web![25]

These online communities, like Facebook, are global, and they offer a virtual microphone or movie screen to unknown musicians and moviemakers with talent, yearning for their 15 minutes of fame. You don't need to be a large corporation or someone famous to be heard. You do, however, need to be innovative to get noticed. This is exactly what Without Tomorrow, a California band, did to promote its music.[26]

There's a surplus of unsigned indie bands with a MySpace presence, so it takes creativity and a good strategy to catch the eyes and ears of fans and record labels. Without Tomorrow came up with an innovative use of the social networking site: a free concert at their local boardwalk in Sacramento, broadcast live on the Internet. The reason for the live show? Celebrating a million song plays on their MySpace page. To overcome the high cost of the bandwidth necessary to support the Internet traffic, Jeremy Unruh, the band's drummer and cofounder, turned to the Network Foundation Technologies proprietary software. This software uses peer-to-peer file sharing, while live streaming can reduce the bandwidth by up to 50 percent. The more people with access to the video stream, the more people share the load. This allowed the band to use their large fan base to their advantage. Fans from all over the world were able to tune in to the live concert, and the band got its name out there. And, as the band grows in popularity, their concert and other revenues grow as well. [27]

Film 2.0: The Audience Helps Create Them

The Net Generation are starting to shake up the world of movies. For the last two years, the Berlin Film Festival has invited filmmakers to something they call the Berlinale Keynotes. At the 2008 festival, in my opening speech, I argued that just as MP3 and the Internet have turned the music industry upside down, even more dramatic changes are in store for movies. After I spoke, several young movie and video game entrepreneurs presented their projects. I have to say, I was blown away, and the audience was as well.

The film industry is being transformed by the combination of the Net Generation, the Web 2.0, and the game industry. The current paradigm of film viewing—two hours in a dark theater with popcorn—won't disappear, but it will become just a small piece of the bigger market I call Film 2.0. Movies, video games, digital effects, and networking will all mesh to change where and how we watch films, and how films are created, distributed, and funded.

By looking at Net Geners' interaction with video content, we can see that tomorrow's films will be more varied in length. Short films will be increasingly popular, watched not only on laptops but by young people on tiny screens. The three-minute movie already dominates YouTube. There will be frequent viewer participation in the plot. Today's video games show the direction in which we're headed.

Jade Raymond, a brilliant, stylish video game industry rock star, spoke after me. Jade started developing software at the age of 14; as a 29-year-old she became project director for Assassin's Creed, a game released in November 2007 on the PlayStation 3 and Xbox 360 video game consoles. The game features highly detailed and interactive environments from the time of the Third Crusade—the game's developers were diligent to ensure that these environments are historically accurate. The game, as it is played, acts as a sort of subliminal history lesson. The game sold 2.7 million copies in its first four weeks of distribution. When Jade demonstrated the game, the person sitting next to me whispered, "These games are really starting to look like a movie." Hollywood, look out!

Also, as this century unfolds, look for movie equivalents of such open-source Internet projects as Linux and Wikipedia. Next up at the Berlinale was Ton Roosendaal, who presented *Elephants Dream*, the culmination of the

Orange Open Movie Project, produced by the Blender Foundation and the Netherlands Media Art Institute. It is the world's first open movie, made entirely with open-source graphics software, such as Blender, and with all production files freely available for use by whomever it pleases. One of the world's first full-length open-source movies, *The Boy Who Never Slept*, tells the story of an insomniac writer meeting a teenage girl online. Their friendship develops into an unlikely love story wrapped in a harsh reality. The total cost of making the film: $200; number of online viewers so far: 4 million.

Matt Hanson discussed A Swarm of Angels, which aims to create a $2 million feature film and give it away. The concept calls on a global community of "angels," who each pay £25 in exchange for creative input on all aspects of the project. From the site: "A Swarm of Angels is a third way between the top-down approach of traditional filmmaking and the bottom-up nature of user-generated content. A way for anyone to influence the creation of a professional £1 million+ feature film."

The Tracey Fragments is a new film starring teenage Canadian actress Ellen Page. All of the footage shot for the film is available for wannabe filmmakers to download and edit into music videos or trailers, or to recut the entire movie. A challenge was issued for the best use of footage with judging currently underway. The winning video will be included with the bonus features of the DVD.

How will viewers know what films are worth watching? For sure, many of these filmmakers won't be taking out large newspaper ads. Understanding their young audience, they will rely on Web sites such as RottenTomatoes.com. This site is a wake-up call to the traditional "plan and push" model of marketing a film. Rotten Tomatoes uses the wisdom of crowds to rate movies and has become a leading source for online movie reviews. Anyone can be a critic. The site lets users, in addition to professional movie critics, contribute reviews. Users can also select which critics they want to hear from, and which ones they don't. For both my kids, Rotten Tomatoes is the film bible.

Self-Organization Hits the Streets

College students, when they are not studying or listening to music, often engage in civic causes, as I did in my student days. They're now starting to realize that social networking gives them extraordinary power to work outside the boundaries of political establishments in order to affect serious change. We will explore this topic in the final chapter of this book, but here it's worth leaving you with a story. When the Revolutionary Armed Forces of Colombia, the nation's largest rebel group, killed 11 lawmakers after taking them hostage in

2007, Colombians all over the world were outraged. Colombia has the unfortunate designation of being the kidnapping capital of the world, and it is estimated
that some 3,000 people are currently being held captive there for one reason or
another. FARC, the group named above, is responsible for many of the violent
crimes in the country.

Oscar Morales, a young engineer from Colombia, wanted to protest, and so
he went to Facebook. Enraged by the latest violence, he started a group titled A
Million Voices against the FARC, which grew to over 260,000 members within
the first few weeks.

Morales used the combined efforts of group members to organize mass
protests both in Colombia and around the world. "We expected the idea to
resound with a lot of people, but no so much and not so quickly," says Morales.
On Feburary 4, 2008, there were simultaneous protests in 27 cities in Colombia and 104 major cities around the world as millions of Colombians took to the
streets chanting, "No more deaths! No more kidnappings! No more FARC!"
There were protests across Europe, Asia, and the United States. In Colombia,
an estimated 4.8 million people took part in more than 360 marches in
the country.[28]

While many people are skeptical about the power of Facebook users to do
something serious, I think this protest is significant. It demonstrates how social
networking sites can be used to bypass mainstream organizations. Previous
protests in Colombia were always organized by various political parties, which
means that a certain level of control was usually exercised over the protesters.
The FARC protests allowed the Net Generation to unite under the banner of a
relevant issue and not be swayed by politics. They were able to remotely coordi-
nate the logistics of hundreds of protests and communicate across time zones,
languages, and borders. They used Facebook to become empowered to take
action. In the hands of the Net Gen, social networks can be a potent force for
change, as we'll explore in the final chapter of this book.

HELLO OFFICER, PLEASE SMILE FOR THE CAMERA

The Net Generation is driving the democratization of content creation as
young people generate online photos, music, and copy, from movie reviews to
commentaries on everything from products to politicians. This is leading to a
power shift from authorities to ordinary individuals—a topic that will be discussed throughout the book. People can participate in the economy in ways that
were previously unthinkable—creating television news clips that rival those
seen currently on TV, writing an encyclopedia like Wikipedia, or selling goods

in e-markets like Craigslist. As knowledge expands, power is becoming more widely distributed as well.

Consider the ability of young people today to scrutinize the authorities. In the summer of 2007, three 14-year-old boys were skateboarding in Baltimore's Inner Harbor, an activity that is prohibited by law. Police officer Salvatore Rivieri spotted the boys and told them to vacate the premises, which they did. But that's not the end of the story. Officer Rivieri was physically and verbally aggressive to one of the boys, putting him in a headlock and pushing him to the ground. Rivieri yelled at the teen, "You hear me? I'm not your father. You give that attitude to your father. You give it to me, I'll smack you upside the head. . . . Shut your mouth, I'm talking." Unfortunately for Rivieri, one of the boys was secretly taping the entire incident using his cell phone's video camera. The video was uploaded to YouTube.com in February 2008. It has been viewed more than 1.9 million times, and the story of Officer Rivieri—now dubbed "Baltimore Cop"—has garnered international media attention. It would be easy to blame the kids, as some have done, for showing lack of respect for the policeman, but the fact of the matter remains that they were illegally assaulted.

The Baltimore Police Department announced it would investigate the incident, and that Rivieri was suspended with pay. The video has sparked many comments on the behavior of the police and on the role of YouTube in the incident. One user put it this way: "Yeah, it's disappointing he is still getting paid, but keep in mind his reputation as an asshole is now world famous. He has embarrassed his name, his family, and the Baltimore PD. That amount of shame isn't worth his paycheck. Also, if he doesn't get fired he has probably at least ruined any shot of being promoted. Thanks to YouTube, JUSTICE IS SERVED."

To add to Rivieri's discomfort, a second video has been uploaded to YouTube.com showing him hassling another teen, this time an art student. The student was videotaping people's reaction to a shoebox he was moving with a remote controlled car. Rivieri is seen yelling at the teen to leave the public space and kicking both the box and the car. For many who didn't like Rivieri's behavior, the second video was icing on the cake.

A NEW SOCIAL UTILITY

By the time I flew to Davos last January, Facebook's membership had ballooned to 70 million or so active users. It had become a meeting place not just for college kids but for people of all ages. Although it was still number two in the social networking world, after Rupert Murdoch's MySpace, it was the network of choice for the Net Generation. Zuckerberg was famous and in demand, so I was a bit surprised when a Facebook assistant e-mailed me to say Zuckerberg and his 30-year-old (now former) strategy chief, Matt Cohler, wanted to meet me.

At the appointed hour, Zuckerberg and Cohler turned up in the busy lobby at the Davos convention center, which was teeming with famous names in business. They were polite and eager, even deferential, as if they were talking to a friend's parent. To my surprise, they even asked me to sign a copy of *Wikinomics*, the book I coauthored. I couldn't help but marvel at the moment. I had simply written a book that had sold a few hundred thousand copies, not a huge feat. They, however, had created a social network of tens of millions of humans that was changing the world. I asked them what Facebook would be in the future. Facebook, they explained, wasn't just going to be a social network for friends. It would be a social utility, like a power grid. It might seem like a grandiose claim for a site that has a "fun wall," a venue where their idea of fun is to poke someone, or throw a digital snowball.

But Facebook is, in fact, a prime example of the mass collaboration we were describing in *Wikinomics*. In the book, we wrote that "winning companies today have open and porous boundaries and compete by reaching outside their walls to harness external knowledge, resources and capabilities." Facebook is doing just that. As of the spring of 2007, they have allowed outsiders to create new services called "applications" that Facebook members can use. These applications can be anything from the popular photo sharing device that allows you to tag, or write a note about something in the photo and share it with your friends, to a gadget that lets you dedicate a favorite song to a significant other, or a device that facilitates an informal survey of your friends' political views so you can see where you fit in. If users like these applications, they can put them on their personal profile pages. The makers of these applications hand them out for free, but can make money by selling sponsorships, posting ads, or selling other things.

The Hidden Side of Social Networks: Are You Sharing Too Much of Yourself?

This new wave of applications for Facebook is growing fast, with 140 new ones added every day. But most Net Geners do not realize that these applications give the marketing world a new way to peep into the Net Gener's private life. Once you install one of these applications, it can see everything you see. According to Facebook's "Platform Application Terms of Use," application developers can potentially find out "your name, your profile picture, your gender, your birthday, your hometown location (city/state/country), your current location (city/state/country)."

In addition, application makers can see "your political view, your activities, your interests, your musical preferences, television shows in which you are interested, movies in which you are interested, books in which you are interested, your favorite quotes."

They can learn personal details about you—"the text of your 'About Me' section, your relationship status, your dating interests, your relationship interests, your summer plans, your Facebook user network affiliations."

They can delve into "your education history, your work history, your course information." And of course they can see "copies of photos in your Facebook Site photo albums" as well as "metadata associated with your Facebook Site photo albums (e.g., time of upload, album name, comments on your photos, etc.), the total number of messages sent and/or received by you, the total number of unread messages in your Facebook inbox, the total number of "pokes" you have sent and/or received, the total number of wall posts on your Wall,™ a list of user IDs mapped to your Facebook friends, your social timeline, and events associated with your Facebook profile."

In other words, they can learn a lot about you. Facebook, of course, was not the first to give marketers a window onto the Net Gener world. As Kathryn Montgomery tells us in her new book, *Generation Digital*, marketers have been using digital technology to probe the minds and behaviors of Net Geners for years: "Digital technologies make it possible to track every move, online and off, compiling elaborate personal profiles that combine behavioral, psychological, and social information on individuals."

But Facebook has become the lightning rod for what I think will become a huge issue: privacy. It is a major issue both for Facebook and other social networking sites, and for individual Net Geners. With all this sharing going on, I'm concerned that Net Geners are setting themselves up for the destruction of a basic right to be left alone.

THE DARK SIDE OF SOCIAL NETWORKING: IS PRIVACY OVER?
The Typical Net Gener Still Doesn't Get It

The Net Generation is opening up to a degree that astounds their parents. Many Facebook enthusiasts post any scrap of information they have about themselves and others online, for all their friends to see—from digital displays of affection to revealing pictures. Most are not motivated by malice; they simply want to share what they consider happy or fun events with others. Net Geners clearly don't understand why privacy is important. A 2007 Carnegie Mellon study showed that 40 percent of those who expressed the highest possible concern about protecting their class schedule still posted it on Facebook, and 47 percent of those concerned about political views still provided them. [29]

But They May Be Sorry

They should wake up, now. Lives have been shattered thanks to unsuspecting people flinging open their kimonos in the seeming intimacy of their Web sites. The Internet has a long memory. In Texas, for example, a driver involved in a fatal accident found his MySpace postings ("I'm not an alcoholic, I'm a drunkaholic") part of the prosecution's case. Stories are legion of social network site users losing their jobs or being turned down for new jobs because of what they have posted online. A Florida sheriff's deputy found himself unemployed when his bosses read his MySpace pages, which discussed his heavy drinking and fascination with female breasts. A Las Vegas Catholic school teacher was fired after he declared himself gay online. Colleges and schools are monitoring MySpace and Facebook pages for what they deem to be "inappropriate" content, and some kids are being severely disciplined or even expelled as a result.

A survey in the UK showed that 62 percent of British employers now check the social networking postings of applicants, and that a quarter have rejected candidates as a result. Reasons given by employers include concerns about alcohol abuse, ethics, and a disrespectful attitude.[30] My son Alex thinks employers should relax: "If there is a photo of me drinking a beer at a party what does that say about me—that I'm a bad potential hire who abuses alcohol, or alternatively that I'm a social person who likes to enjoy life, with friends and a good network?"

OK, a picture of someone drinking a beer at a party may not be a problem, but what if it's a more revealing picture—the kind that many Net Geners post on their sites these days? I think that, on this point, Alex and the Net Geners are wrong. The Net Generation may have lapped the boomers in the use of technology, but this is one area where the Net Generation has not lapped people my age. By now, we know that the late-night activities of our youth might not look so good in the sober light of our forties. But most Net Geners, as young people, aren't thinking that far ahead.

In my discussions with teens and young adults, it's clear that awareness is growing among Net Geners that inappropriate postings can do irreparable damage to a person's job prospects or career. I've been told that it is now quite common to have a "no-picture-tagging" policy when out with friends. This means that if a friend uploads a picture with you in it, they won't label that person as you, keeping you safe from Facebook's search engines and news feeds. In fact, many young people I've spoken with have told me there are parties where guests are asked to check their cameras at the door.

They may be starting to get it, but I still don't think they realize to what extent they are compromising their privacy on these social networking sites.

I Know What You're Buying

Back in 2007, Facebook users could show one face to their "friends"—and let them see those fun party pictures—and another face to everyone else in the world, who would presumably be shown pictures more suitable for public viewing. Many Net Geners didn't even bother using these privacy features. Only 20 percent of Facebook used any form of privacy on Facebook.[31] The rest are letting the whole world see their private life on Facebook.

Then Facebook whipped up a storm of controversy when it introduced features that would make users share more with their "friends" than they might want. In November 2007, Facebook announced that whenever you buy something at a participating retailer, your friends will be informed. For retailers this would give a personal endorsement to a product, which was supposed to be better than a conventional ad for this demographic. This type of social marketing could potentially give Facebook tremendous commercial power. But Facebook users revolted. What if the book they bought was a Christmas surprise, or about a sensitive topic like how to manage your bipolar child? Zuckerberg apologized, and changed the system so that users had to opt in to the system, as opposed to opt out of it. As Facebook found out, such marketing programs need to be implemented with extreme sensitivity to protect the privacy of everyone involved.

New Privacy Controls: Different Categories of Friends

By early in 2008, Zuckerberg clearly realized that privacy was a core issue, and that Facebook's privacy controls (friends versus outsiders) were inadequate. In March 2008, Facebook took steps to let users discriminate among different kinds of friends. So friends A, D, and E could see those bikini pictures, while friends X, Y, and Z could only see your work history. "We're giving people tools so that they can share information with exactly who they want," Zuckerberg told me just after introducing the new privacy measures. The new privacy measures, he added, did not reduce the amount of information that people share on Facebook. On the contrary, they encourage people to share more. Twenty percent of Facebook users, for instance, are sharing their cell phone number with their friends, secure in the knowledge that the 70-million-strong Facebook universe won't see it.

But That Doesn't Solve the Problem

I'm still worried, though, and I'm not alone. According to Adrienne Felt, the coauthor of a 2007 study on social networking privacy, the new measures do not fix a key problem. You can decide which of your friends can see what on your profile, and you can stop the applications that your friends install from peering into your Facebook world. But, if *you* install an application—say, a photo editing application that lets you put Angelina Jolie's hairdo on your best friend's high school graduation picture—the maker of that application can see anything you put on your profile, like your dating interests, your summer plans, your political views, your photos, the works. The only way to stop the application developers from peeping into your own Facebook world, Felt says, is to not put any applications on your personal profile. The vast majority of applications don't need your private data to do their thing, she notes, and yet all of them have access to whatever you can see.[32]

Information about Me Is Mine

Facebook and other social networks must address this privacy question if they want social networks to be the operating system for the Internet. The core principle is this: information about me should be mine to give away or sell. Companies like Facebook that want to share information they gather about me should give me explicit notice, and obtain my explicit consent. They should only collect what they actually need, and keep it only as long as required. I should know what they know about me. This is not a new issue, of course. People have been handing over details of their consumer lives when they sign up for loyalty programs. But now in the digital world it's a bigger issue, because people are disclosing far more information to far more people. And because Net Geners are the most active social network users, they are on the cutting edge of this issue. It's not just companies that bear the responsibility of protecting their customers' privacy. Each individual in the Net Generation has a responsibility to make sure he or she controls the information that goes out to the public. (This caveat applies to me too. Even though I have written a book on privacy in the digital age, I didn't shield my own Facebook profile from the scrutiny of business contacts until a few months ago.)

Matt Cohler, Facebook's former strategy chief, says the solution may spring from a redefining of what privacy is in a digital age: "In the past, privacy basically meant something was either visible to everybody or hidden from everybody," he told me. "Private meant it's a secret, or it's something that I don't share with other people. And I think what privacy is coming to mean today—for this generation that's kind of always plugged into this grid, and as more and more people in older generations also get plugged into the grid, I think the definition changed for them too—is less about kind of totally public versus totally hidden, and more about giving people the ability to control what information they're sharing with whom."

Cohler's solution to the privacy dilemma is to give each person control over what information he or she shares, and with whom: "My definition of the ultimate privacy setting would be if every person on Facebook had specified completely what information they wanted to share with what people, and what information they want to receive from what people. And if every user did that we would have sort of a perfect equilibrium of information sharing, and that would be sort of nirvana and utopia from our perspective. When I think of the ultimate privacy settings, I don't think everything is hidden from everybody, for everybody. I think everything is perfectly configured by each individual person for everybody else." Wise words. Such capabilities would go a long way to help, but people still need to use the privacy controls. That raises the question: what is the responsibility of social networks and other companies to help educate their users and customers on this issue?

A Broad-Based Invasion of Privacy

Facebook and the social networks are, of course, only part of the challenge. As the Net becomes the basis for commerce, work, the media, entertainment, healthcare, learning, and most forms of human discourse, our private lives are becoming a lot less private. When we buy books or music online, those purchases are recorded and entered into giant databases. When we buy drugs or groceries at the store, and we swipe our credit cards to pay, a record is made and kept. A child's research for a school project, the card reader at the parking lot, your car's conversations with a database via satellite, the online publications you read, the shirt you purchase in a department store with your store card, the prescription drugs you buy, and the hundreds of other network transactions in a typical week: all this information is recorded in various databases. Computers can inexpensively link and cross-reference such databases to slice, dice, and then recompile information about individuals in hundreds of different ways. They can create a profile of you, based on what you buy and what you do online.

Now let's take this discussion a step further. Imagine what your world will be like once the power of social networking is sitting in the palm of your hand—in your mobile phone, or whatever you want to call it. The future is not far away. The mobile phone already knows where you are. Thanks to the Enhanced 911 mandate imposed by the Federal Communications Commission, all mobile phone companies had to introduce technology that determines the precise location of mobile handsets. This helps emergency personnel pinpoint a caller's whereabouts for 911 emergency calls.

And the mobile phone that always knows its location vastly increases its usefulness. A mobile phone that's linked to the Internet can give you directions to your meeting, the closest ATM, or coffee shop. It can give you the local weather forecast because it knows where you are and what time it is. It can give you a list of local vegan restaurants, plus the reviews of people who have recently dined there. It can even suggest where you can go to the bathroom. If you sign up with Loopt.com, you'll know where your friends are. And in the not too distant future, it will let you know about a traffic accident clogging the roads on your way to the airport—and even call the airline to rebook the flight!

This privacy may evaporate once our digital copilots get up to speed—and start keeping a 24/7/365 record of our lives. They will record our conversations and photograph people we meet; using tricks such as face-recognition software to save us the hassle of having to tag all the photos. So ubiquitous audio and video recording will soon be a fact of life. Most of the technology already exists. Cameras can fit into a shirt button or the frame of a pair of eyeglasses. The biggest stumbling block is data storage, but that will soon be solved. Clever scientists are already fine-tuning an experimental storage device the size of a sugar cube that will hold a week's worth of video.[33]

CONCLUSION

As we have seen in this chapter, the Net Generation treats technology differently than their parents do. While TV was the signature medium of the boomer generation, the Net Generation doesn't just watch TV; they listen to it while they're chatting with friends and navigating the Web.

Now they're transforming the Internet into a place where people can communicate and collaborate and create together, and soon you will be able to access it all from the palm of your hand. We've looked at the rise of social networking sites. As we have seen, this could be the new grid for the Internet. It could have a significant impact on everything the Net Generation touches, from games to music to global civic action. The Net Geners are just starting to use the tremendous power of this digital tool, and I believe they have the power to realize the dream that many boomers had, to give power to the people.

Yet this great new opportunity also raises a significant new challenge—for privacy, the right to be left alone. Facebook is beginning to grapple with this challenge, but I don't think the Net Geners fully understand the long-term consequences of sharing intimate information about themselves with the world. But in other respects, I believe that the young people who have grown up immersed in these very technologies that are presenting such a challenge are especially equipped to navigate this new terrain. There is strong evidence, as we will see in the next chapters, that as their mastery of the Internet evolves, they will be able to adjust and handle whatever comes along.

THE EIGHT NET GEN NORMS

When *Growing Up Digital* was published in 1997, my daughter Niki had just turned 14. She did her homework on the computer in her room and, like most girls her age, she loved to talk with friends on the phone. We had a phone curfew of 10 p.m., and after a while we noticed she wasn't talking on the phone anymore. That seemed like a good thing, until we discovered that Niki was talking to her friends on the Internet via ICQ—one of the early instant messaging systems—from the moment she walked into her bedroom until she turned out the light. As her parents, our first reaction was to feel like she had tricked us, and the issue of ICQ became a sore spot for us all. But my wife and I were torn, because she was getting very good grades, and it was clear that all her friends were connected this way.

Since I was in the business of observing the impact of the Internet, I started pestering Niki with questions at the dinner table about what she was doing online. She was checking her horoscope, downloading music, researching for her homework, playing games, checking the movie schedule, and, of course, talking with friends. Niki tried to put an end to it, with a plea: "Can we have a normal conversation at the dinner table?"

For Niki, her link to the Internet was a sweet taste of freedom. She could talk to whom she wanted, find

"This is my world."

—*NIKI TAPSCOTT*

out whatever she wanted, and be who she wanted to be, without interference from her parents or other adults.

We all want that sense of freedom, but this generation has learned to expect it. They expect it because growing up digital gave kids like Niki the opportunity to explore the world, find out things, talk to strangers, and question the official story from companies and governments. When teenagers in my era did a geography project, they might have cut out some pictures from their parents' *National Geographic* and included some information sent by the PR department of the foreign country's local consulate. Niki, on the other hand, could find significantly more interesting information just by tapping her fingers on her computer in her bedroom.

Niki and her younger brother Alex, who started playing games and drawing pictures on the Internet at age seven, were the inspiration for *Growing Up Digital*. It seemed that every week they would do something amazing with technology or through technology that I had not seen before. Through my experience with them and the 300 other youngsters we studied, I concluded that these kids were very different than their boomer parents. I refer to these differences as "norms"—distinctive attitudinal and behavioral characteristics that differentiate this generation from their baby-boom parents and other generations. These norms were tested in the nGenera survey of 6,000 Net Geners around the world. The list stood up pretty well.

The eight norms are: 1) freedom; 2) customization; 3) scrutiny; 4) integrity; 5) collaboration; 6) entertainment; 7) speed; and 8) innovation.

These eight norms are rooted in the different experience of today's youth—especially with regard to their media diet. They have grown up being the actors, initiators, creators, players, and collaborators. It has made them who they are—young people who are different in many ways than their parents and grandparents were at their age. The Internet has been good for this generation. And I believe that even the skeptics will see that these *Grown Up Digital* kids will be good for us.

FREEDOM

When my generation graduated from college, we were grateful for that first job. We hung onto it like a life preserver. But times have changed. Kids see no reason to commit, at least not to the first job. High performers are on their fifth job by the time they are 27 and their average tenure at a job is 2.6 years.[1] They revel in the freedom. My son Alex, for instance, is thinking about getting an MBA or a law degree. But when I asked him about his immediate plans for a job, he put it this way: "A commitment of three years or more would make me hesitate. I don't want to get locked in to something I may not enjoy 10 years down the road. I want the freedom to try new and different things. If I like what I'm doing, if it challenges me and engages me and is fun, then I would definitely commit to it, I guess. I think about the time I reach age 30, I would settle on something. I view my twenties as a period of self-discovery and self-realization."

Alex is typical of his generation. The Internet has given them the freedom to choose what to buy, where to work, when to do things like buy a book or talk to friends, and even who they want to be. Politicians like Barack Obama have tapped into it. Obama's iconic line, "Yes we can," has spawned a music video by will.i.am of the Black Eyed Peas, plus the spoofs—proof positive that it went viral. These three words speak volumes about the Net Gen's belief that they can do anything, that no one can tell them not to. "Yes we can" was perfectly tuned to this generation, just as the peace sign was for mine. They're on a quest for freedom, and it's setting up expectations that may surprise and infuriate their elders.

Our research suggests that they expect to choose where and when they work; they use technology to escape traditional office space and hours; and they integrate their home and social lives with work life. More than half of the Net Geners we surveyed online in North America say they want to be able to work in places other than an office. This is particularly true of

> "I can work from home whenever I want. I just plug into my virtual private network and I have access to my e-mail, files. I'm just as productive at home as I would be at the office."
> —*MORITZ KETTLER*

white- and some gray-collar workers. An almost equal number say they want their job to have flexible hours, again with some differences among the various employee types.[2]

Alex doesn't buy the line that young people expect their first employers to accommodate them with flexible hours and telecommuting. "It makes young people look childish. We're not going to start making demands about hours." Alex says he and his friends want to work hard, be productive, and succeed. "I'm not sure it's a young–old thing."

Yet, in my research and in my work as a consultant to major corporations and governmental institutions, I see signs of a generational trend. They prefer flexible hours and compensation that is based on their performance and market value—not based on face time in the office. And they're not afraid to leave a great job if they find another one that offers more money, more challenging work, the chance to travel, or just a change. As one 26-year-old woman who answered our online survey put it: "We're given the technology that allows us to be mobile, so I don't understand why we need to be restricted to a desk; it feels like you're being micromanaged."

Intel gets it. Many of its employees telework, while other staffers take advantage of flextime, compressed workweeks, part-time hours, and job shares. All the company's major work sites offer employees great amenities, such as fitness centers, locker rooms, basketball and volleyball courts, dry cleaning, sundries, and food court–style cafes with menus that change daily.[3] Studies repeatedly show that perks such as those offered by Intel boost employee satisfaction and performance.[4]

So does Google. Its engineers are asked to spend 20 percent of their workplace time on projects that are of personal interest to them. Google says it has a strong business case for making such an offer. If Google's employees are the best and brightest available—and Google believes they are—then whatever piques their personal interest could open new avenues of business for the company.

While flexible work hours and workplace amenities are routine practice at many high-tech firms, the flexible workplace philosophy is making inroads in other sectors. Best Buy, America's leading electronics retailer, is trying to revamp its corporate culture to make its workplace more appealing to young employees. The endeavor, called ROWE, for results-only work environment, lets corporate employees do their work anytime, anywhere, as long as they get their work done. "This is like TiVo for your work," says the program's cofounder, Jody Thompson.[5] By June of 2008, 3,200 of Best Buy's 4,000 corporate staffers are participating in the ROWE program. The company plans to introduce the program into its stores, something no retailer has tried before.[6]

There are even signs that more Net Geners will seek to own their own business, especially after they worked for a traditional bureaucratic company for a while. The appeal is having more creative control, more freedom, and no boss to answer to. In recent years, YouTube, Facebook, and Digg have emerged as outstandingly successful examples of organizations started by individuals under the age of 25. Such stories inspire other youthful entrepreneurs to pursue their dreams.

Young people insist on freedom of choice. It's a basic feature of their media diet. Instead of listening to the top 10 hits on the radio, Net Geners compose iPod playlists of thousands of songs chosen from the millions of tunes available. So when they go shopping, they assume they'll have a world of choice. Curious whether the African Pygmy hedgehog makes a good pet for a pre-teen? Google offers more than 25,000 links to for "African Pygmy Hedge-hog," to help the Net Gener decide. Interested in buying a book? Amazon offers millions of choices. Search for a digital camera on Froogle, Google's shopping search engine, and more than 900,000 pages appear. The number is even greater in Asia, which has far more choice in consumer electronics than North America.

Baby boomers often find variety burdensome, but the Net Geners love it. When faced with thousands of choices, they show no signs of anxiety, from what we could see in our online survey of 1,750 North American kids. Only 13 percent strongly agree with the statement, "There is so much to choose from that when I buy something, I tend to wonder if I have made the right decision."

Typical Net Gen shoppers know what they are going to buy before they leave the house. They've already checked out all the choices online, and they are well informed and confident in their decisions—83 percent say they usually know what they want before they go to buy a product.[7] With the proliferation of media, sales channels, product types, and brands, Net Geners use digital tech-nologies to cut through the clutter and find the product that fits their needs. And if it turns out to be the wrong choice, Net Geners want to be able to change their mind. They are attracted to companies that make it easy to exchange the product for something different or get their money back.

The search for freedom is transforming education as well. At their fingertips they have access to much of the world's knowledge. Learning for them should take place where and when they want it. So attending a lecture at a specific time and place, given by a mediocre professor in a room where they are passive recip-ients, seems oddly old-fashioned, if not completely inappropriate. The same is true for politics. They have grown up with choice. Will a model of democracy that gives them only two choices and relegates them, between elections, to four years of listening to politicians endlessly repeating the same speeches actually meet their needs?

CUSTOMIZATION

Last year, someone sent me an iTouch PDA. It was sitting in a box on my desk at home when Niki and her boyfriend spied it. They were astonished I hadn't opened it up, so Moritz opened the box, and then hacked into the iTouch so he could give it some special features—lots of widgets, some of my favorite movies, like *The Departed*, plus some music from my computer, including a couple of great tunes pounded out by my band, Men In Suits, with Niki singing lead vocals and me on the keyboard. They kindly left the hotrod PDA on my desk, with a little note. It sat there for months, until someone took it away. It's not that I wasn't grateful. I just wanted the PDA to work. I didn't need it to work *for* me. That's the difference between me and the Net Gen.

As a typical boomer, I took what I got and hoped it would work. Net Geners get something, and customize it to make it theirs. This is the generation that has grown up with personalized mobile phones, TiVo, Slingbox, and podcasts. They've grown up getting what they want, when they want it, and where, and they make it fit their personal needs and desires.

Half of them tell us they modify products to reflect who they are.[8] Niki, for example, has a phone with white-and-orange swirly "wallpaper" on the screen, plus a ringtone that sings out a techno version of "Taking Care of Business."

> "My phone is an extension of me. It's an extension of who I am. It's like a nice handbag. It's a display of your personality."
>
> —NIKI TAPSCOTT

My son Alex has a special mouse for his laptop. Now, most of us have a mouse with two or three buttons. Alex has five. "My mouse is called the Mighty Mouse," he tells me. "Each of those buttons does a separate thing, according to my interests and what I need to use it for. My left button clicks on something. The right button opens up a window, just like a regular one. The middle button is a track wheel so if I'm on a Web page or a window in my operating system I can scroll 360 degrees. On the side, if I click on one button every single window that's open on my computer will shrink down so I can choose individually. On the other side is a button that opens up my dashboard, basically, which shows me different widgets—a news widget, a wiki widget, a sports widget, a weather widget, a time zone widget, and a widget that monitors the health and productivity of my computer." See what I mean? "It's funny," Alex notes. "I'm actually in the middle to the low end of technological advancement in my peer group."

Today, the "tuner" car-customization industry, largely fueled by Net Geners, is worth more than $3 billion in North America. The trend snuck in under the radar of the big auto companies. At least one auto company, Toyota, is trying to pounce on it by introducing the Scion niche brand back in 2003. Company research shows owners spend $1,000–$3,000 on customization and accessories, from paint jobs to XM satellite radios with Bazooka subwoofers. These are kids in their twenties, and they "have changed every category they have touched so far," says Jim Farley, VP of Scion. "It's the most diverse generation ever seen."[9]

Our research at nGenera also shows that the *potential* to personalize a product is important to the Net Generation, even if the individual decides not to make any changes. The desire is about personalizing and accessorizing—it is more aesthetic than functional. Personalized online space is now almost obligatory; witness the popularity of sites such as MySpace and Facebook. Net Geners also customize their media. Two-thirds of early technology adopters say they watch their favorite TV shows when they want to rather than at the time of broadcast. With YouTube, television networks run the risk of becoming quaint relics. The industry will still produce programming, but where and when the programming is watched will be up to the viewer.

At work, the Net Geners will want to customize their jobs. In our online survey of 1,750 kids in North America, more than half of Net Geners said they liked working offsite.[10] They enjoyed the change of scenery, they said, and their ability to work outside the office showed their employer they could be trusted to get the job done. They may even want to customize their job descriptions, although they still welcome some structure and want to know what is expected of them. Ideally, companies will replace job descriptions with work goals, and give Net Geners the tools, latitude, and guidance to get the job done. They may not do it on day one, though. "Demanding to customize a job description is a bit brash if you've only just started a job," Alex told me. "But after a while, I think it's fine to make suggestions on how the job could be changed or improved."

SCRUTINY

On April Fool's Day 2005, I decided to play a bit of a gag on my employees and associates. I asked my executive assistant to send them the following e-mail:

> Through Don's connections at the World Economic Forum, Angelina Jolie (she's an actress who has become involved in social responsibility), who attended the last Forum meetings, is interested in Don's work and wants to come to Toronto for a meeting to discuss transparency in the global economy.
>
> This has been arranged for Thursday, May 26th.
>
> Don will be having a private lunch with her and will come to the office afterwards so she can meet others here and continue the discussions. The day will end with a cocktail party at Verity.
>
> She'll bring some of her friends.
>
> Please confirm your attendance.
>
> Thanks,
>
> Antoinette

In my dreams. Anyway, not a single young member of my staff fell for the joke. I would get responses like "Nice try" and "You and Angelina. Right."

However, associates my age reacted in a completely different manner. They were falling over themselves to join the afternoon discussions and attend the cocktail party. I believe the expression is they fell for it hook, line, and sinker. And they were not happy to find out that Angelina was not going to appear.

Net Geners are the new scrutinizers. Given the large number of information sources on the Web, not to mention unreliable information—spam, phishers, inaccuracies, hoaxes, scams, and misrepresentations—today's youth have the ability to distinguish between fact and fiction. They appear to have high awareness about the world around them and want to know more about what is happening. They use digital technologies to find out what's really going on. Imagine if Orson Welles had directed the radio version of *War of the Worlds* today, instead of in 1938, when it caused widespread panic as many listeners believed the Martians had actually landed. In a couple of clicks, Net Geners would figure out it was a play, not a news broadcast. No one would have had to flee their homes!

The Net Generation knows to be skeptical whenever they're online.[11] When baby boomers were young, a picture was a picture; it documented reality. Not so today. "Trust but verify" would be an apt motto for today's youth. They accept few claims at face value. No wonder the 74-second "Evolution" video was such a big hit when it was posted on YouTube in October 2006. The video showed an ordinary attractive girl—the director's girlfriend, in fact—being transformed into a billboard model—with considerable help from Photoshop, which lengthened her neck, reshaped her head, and widened her eyes. You could see, before your very eyes, how fake the image of beauty is in magazines and billboards. The video was made for Dove soap by a young Australian working for the Ogilvy & Mather ad agency in Toronto. It instantly struck a chord among Net Geners worldwide. Unilever, the British conglomerate that owns Dove, estimates it was seen by at least 18.5 million people worldwide on the Net,[12] not including how many saw it on TV, where it was prominently featured on morning talk shows. Not bad for a video that cost only $135,000 to make.

But the story didn't end so well for Dove's parent Unilever. Very quickly, some young consumers took note that Unilever was also the maker of Axe, a men's cologne with a campaign of ads featuring highly sexual and exploitative photos of women. The theme was that if you bought Axe, women would be dying to strip and submit to you. As fast as you can say "mockumentary," videos began appearing on YouTube pointing out the contradiction. One, "A message from Unilever, the makers of Axe and Dove," ends with the tagline "Tell your daughters before Unilever gets to them."

Students Provide Correct Facts to Teachers

Lawrence Douglas is a professor of law, jurisprudence, and social thought at Amherst College. One day he was giving a lecture to students on the logistics of informing and training every cop in the United States about Miranda rights. "It is hard to even fathom how many officers there are in this country, at the federal, state, county, municipal, and collegiate levels," he said. "I have the number here, if you give me a second." Douglas began rummaging through his notes, trying to find this stat he scribbled down moments earlier in his office. After 30 unsuccessful seconds, he opened up his briefcase to test his luck again. No need. By the time he had pulled the first crumpled page from the bag, help was at hand—from sophomore Adam Shniderman. He had accessed the Internet on his BlackBerry and had found the U.S. Justice Department's Bureau of Justice Statistics page. There are, it turns out, 17,876 police departments in the United States, with over 800,000 full-time sworn-in officers. The professor thanked Adam and continued on with his lecture, which was, according to student reports, fascinating.

For anyone wanting to reach this age group, the best strategy is candor. They should provide Net Geners with ample product information that is easy to access. The more they have scrutinized a product, the better they feel about purchases, especially ones requiring a large financial or emotional investment.

Boomers marvel at the consumer research available online; Net Geners expect it. When they go shopping, almost two-thirds of Net Geners tell us, they search for information about products that interest them before they buy.[13] They compare and contrast product information online, and look for the cheapest price without sacrificing value. They read blogs, forums, and reviews. They're skeptical about online reviews. Instead, they consult their friends. They can be very picky. Our survey found that 69 percent of the "Bleeding Edge" (first adopters) said they "wouldn't buy a product unless it has the exact features I want." Only 46 percent of Luddites (technophobes) felt that way.[14] It's easy to be a smart shopper in the digital world, and it's about to get easier. As Niki tells me, "You'll be able to scan the barcode of a product on the store shelf and up will pop information on what the product costs at other stores." Barcodes that can hold that amount of information are already registered with the patent office.[15] It's only a matter of time.

Since companies are increasingly naked, they better be buff.[16] Corporate strategies should be built on good products, good prices, and good values. The

Progressive Group of Insurance Companies Web site is ideally suited to the Net Generation. It provides potential customers with an online insurance quote, and calculates how much the company's competitors would charge for the same package. Progressive believes it offers the best value in most cases, and backs its belief with facts.

Companies should expect employee scrutiny. Two-thirds of the Bleeding Edge say that they've searched a great deal for online information about the organization they are currently working for or about people working in their organization. Sixty percent of the same subgroup say they would thoroughly research an employer before accepting a job offer. Respondents say they want to prepare for a job interview, learn about corporate culture, and ensure that the company and job fit their needs and desired lifestyle.

> "Now that I am a lawyer and I have clients, I have to be careful what I put on my MySpace page. I have actually taken things off of my page just to be safe."
>
> — ANONYMOUS

Scrutiny, as we have seen, can go the other way too. Many Net Geners still don't realize that the private information they disclose on social networking sites like Facebook may come back to bite them when they're applying for a big job or public office.

INTEGRITY

Recently, Niki received an alarming message from one of her high school friends. The young woman, who was volunteering in Ecuador, reported that she had seen the horrible conditions of people working in the fields of roses—the dreadful chemicals sprayed on the flowers, the long hours, the child labor. Niki instantly sent the message to all her friends on her Facebook network. Now, whenever she buys roses, Niki asks questions about where they come from. She won't buy flowers from a company that sprays poisonous chemicals on plants that children pick. It's a small, but telling, example of the values Niki shares with her generation.

The stereotype that this generation doesn't give a damn is not supported by the facts. Net Geners care about integrity—being honest, considerate, transparent, and abiding by their commitments. This is also a generation with profound tolerance. Alex had an experience that drove this home for me. I asked him to describe it.

My junior year, I decided to study abroad in London, England. I will always remember what one of my fellow students said the very first day. Before we began, he stood up in front of an auditorium of 250 students, faculty, and program coordinators and made this announcement:

"Hi everyone, my name is Steve, I am from St. Louis, Missouri, and, like the rest of you, I am really excited about being in London. But perhaps unlike the rest of you, I have Tourette Syndrome. So if you think you hear a donkey or a sheep in the back of the classroom, don't hide your lunches because it is just me. Sometimes I can't help making animal noises. Also, don't be distracted if you hear any swear words or grunting either, because that's me too. Thanks for hearing me out."

With that, most people in the class just shrugged their shoulders and began making small talk with the people around them. Sure enough, the head of the program was barely able to get out a "Welcome to London" before Steve started *BAAAA*ing away. At first, some people did seem distracted. I personally was fascinated with him, both for his peculiar problem, and with his ballsy move at the beginning of class. I was impressed with his confidence and how honest and direct he could be about his illness, and I think everyone else was too. After a couple of minutes, it was like his illness wasn't even there (even though his grunting and cursing still was).

Alex's story made me flash back to when I was a kid. There would have been no student in my class with Tourette's syndrome. More likely, he would have never made it to any university, or worse, would have been locked up in a mental institution. If he had gotten into our class, how would we have reacted to such a seemingly bizarre thing? Would we even have known about psychiatric conditions like this? Would we have just shrugged it off as Alex and his 250 classmates did? Would we have had such tolerance for diversity and such instant compassion for someone with an illness like this? Or would the stigma of mental illness have gotten the better of us? And would we have had Alex's admiration for the courage and determination his fellow student showed?

Generation Me?

Psychology Professor Jean Twenge calls them Generation Me, "the most narcissistic generation in history." Narcissists have a positive and inflated view of themselves, she says. They think they are more powerful and more important than they really are. It affects their personal relationships: "Generation Me often lacks other basic human requirements: stable close relationships, a sense of community, a feeling of safety, a simple path to adulthood and the workplace,"[17] she writes. Narcissists can even be dangerous, Twenge's research suggests. They can abuse drugs and alcohol, make risky decisions, gamble in a pathological way, and even assault people. So all that praise from parents and teachers has done them a real disservice: "We may be training a little army of narcissists instead of raising kids' self-esteem."[18]

But is this generation really the most narcissistic ever? Twenge's claim is based on 16,000 college students who took a first-year psychology course and responded to a Narcissistic Personality Inventory.[19] This NPA asked college students to score themselves against statements such as "I think I am a special person" or "I can live my life any way I want to." (It's a measure of personality traits, not of a disorder.)

Her study reports that in the early 1980s, students answered 15 out of 40 statements in a narcissistic way. By 2006 the average score went up to 17. What's more, the percentage of students with what Twenge calls an elevated level of narcissism (a score of 22 out of 40) has gone up from one in seven students in 1982 to 1 in 4 in 2006.

This study has been widely quoted and criticized. One research group, led by a psychologist from the University of Western Ontario, challenged Twenge's findings head-on, saying there was "no evidence" that narcissism was rising in college.[20] Another study of over 400,000 high school students found no sign of an increase of narcissism either.

We could debate her methods—are the high-scorers narcissistic or just confident? It turns out, for example, that Twenge saw a noticeable increase in narcissism in women, but not in men (based an analysis of about half the participants).[21] Couldn't that just be a welcome sign that women were gaining confidence in themselves during that period? We could also debate her claims that the high-scorers have antisocial behaviors; other studies find that low self-esteem is the problem, not high self-esteem.

The bottom line is not what kids in a first-year psychology course write on a survey. It's what they do.

As you can see from the charts, their actions do not portray a self-centered generation with no sense of community who display antisocial behavior. It's just the opposite. As the charts show, risky behavior—like smoking and drinking and teen pregnancy—has gone down. Youth crime has gone down. Volunteering has gone up. This isn't a "little army of narcissists," it's a peace corps.

Their actions show that they are confident and self-assured, with qualities that are normally attributed to leaders.

It's not surprising that Net Geners display such tolerance and even wisdom, compared with previous generations. They have been exposed to a ton of scientific, medical, and other pertinent information that wasn't available to their parents. The world around them has changed, too. So it's not surprising that they

FIGURE 3.1   YOUTH RISK BEHAVIORS

YOUTH RISK BEHAVIOR	CURRENT RATE	RATE CHANGED SINCE 1990
Used seat belt	90%	+16%
Rode with someone who had been drinking	29%	-11%
Carried a weapon	19%	-8%
Was in a physical fight	36%	-7%
Used a condom	63%	+17%

Source: U.S. Center for Disease Control and Prevention

care about honesty. Among other things, they have seen the giants of corporate corruption, the CEOs of Enron and other major companies, being led away in handcuffs, convicted, and sent to jail. It's far easier for Net Geners than it was for boomers to tell whether a company president is doing one thing and saying another. They can use the Internet to find out, and then use social communities like Facebook to tell all their friends.

They expect other people to have integrity, too. They do not want to work for, or buy a product from, an organization that is dishonest. They also expect companies to be considerate of their customers, employees, and the communities in which they operate. Net Geners are also more aware of their world than ever before, due to the abundance of information on the Internet.

This astuteness of the Net Generation has big implications for companies that want to sell things to Net Geners, or employ them. At a time of uncertainty, young people look for companies they can trust. They have a low tolerance for companies that lie when they're trying to sell something, and they can find out pretty quickly if that's the case.

In a crowded marketplace, a company's integrity becomes an important point of difference. Net Geners don't like to be misled or hit with costly surprises, whether measured in money, time, quality, or function. Seventy-seven percent agreed with the statement "If a company makes untrue promises in their advertising, I'll tell my friends not to buy their products."[23] They get angry when they feel they were wronged: "Blockbuster says no late fees. It is all a lie!"

said one 15-year-old boy. "After a week you have to pay $1.25 and then you have to buy the movie after two weeks. They trick you!"

Although Net Geners are quick to condemn, they are also quick to forgive if they see signs that the company is truly sorry for an error. Seventy-one percent said they would continue to do business with a company if it corrected a mistake honestly and quickly.[24]

Integrity, to the Net Gener, primarily means telling the truth and living up to your commitments. Does it also mean doing good? Would Net Geners shun a company that pollutes on a massive scale or mistreats its employees? The survey data is not clear. Our research suggests that only a quarter take into account a company's policies on social responsibility or the environment when making a big purchase. About 40 percent would abandon a product they love if they discovered that the company has suspect social practices.[25]

Yet my interviews with Net Geners suggest that significant numbers of them think about values before they buy. It's not because they're necessarily better human beings. It's because they can easily find out how a product is made, and what's in it. Knowledge leads to action. When you can scrutinize the environmental and labor practices of a company as readily as Net Geners like Niki can, you can make decisions on the basis of what that company is doing—not just what it's saying.

Integrity swings both ways though. You can find plenty of Net Geners who judge companies by a very strict ethical standard, and yet they are downloading music for free—which the music industry regards as stealing. A third of iPod owners are downloading illegally, according to a study by Jupiter Research.[26] My research suggests that's an underestimation. According to nGenera research, 77 percent of Net Geners have downloaded music, software, games, or movies without paying for them.[27] What's more, 72 percent of file-sharers age 18–29 say they don't care about the copyright status of the files they share, according to a Pew Internet and American Life Project.[28] Most don't view it as stealing, or if they do, they justify it in different ways. They see the music industry as a big business that deserves what it gets, or they think the idea of owning music is over. Some even think they're doing small bands a favor.

Do You Steal Music?

We asked Net Geners: "Do you steal music? If you download from free sites, do you view this as stealing? If not, why not?"

Tony, 25, Systems Analyst: Yes I download music from the Internet without payment or borrow tunes from friends—however, I do purchase music using iTunes on occasion. This does constitute stealing because you are taking something you do not have the right to. I'm completely detached from the "victim"—in this case, massive corporations in the music industry. Does that make it right? No. That is why nowadays I make the utmost effort to pay for all digital media that I feel is of high quality and worthy of payment.

Morris, 23, Marketing Manager: Yes. I'm a thief. And so is everyone else I know. I do believe however that the definition of music ownership (and the transfer of ownership) is outdated. It just doesn't fit for our generation. I guess when we come to power we'll redefine what theft is. Hopefully we'll also come up with a new model so songwriters, artists, and others that actually create some value get properly compensated.

Graham, 24, Management Consultant: The manner in which the industry generates revenue from customers needs to better incorporate value derived from concert tours, merchandise, and placement in mediums such as ads, ringtones, television, movies, or video games. The channels through which people discover, obtain, appreciate, and consume music has shifted from the past; yet the music industry has been slow to react and adapt.

Carolina, 27, Consultant: I don't feel that it constitutes stealing to download music without payment or to borrow tunes from friends. If anything, I believe that this promotes new types of music that I wouldn't have otherwise been exposed to. If I am introduced to an artist that I really enjoy I will go out and buy the CD or download the album. I feel extremely lucky to have grown up in a time when Napster was first available to flood my computer with free music.

Alex, 22, Student: I don't have moral certainty about this issue. I pay for music on iTunes but I go onto LimeWire to download remixes and other things I can't find on iTunes. In the end, though, price matters to me. I can't afford to download 100 to 200 songs a month from iTunes' music store.

Alan, 23, Risk Analyst: I am completely comfortable stealing music. I believe this stems primarily from my early experiences with Napster, and the complete disconnect between the joy I felt downloading (and listening) to music, and any sense (or perceived existence) of downside risk. The rules may be clearer now, but my view of music downloading gestated when there was no transparent and consistent approach to intellectual-property laws and enforcement.

Morgan, 23, Video Games Developer: No, I do not download directly from the Internet without paying, mainly because I got sick of dealing with bad downloads and viruses embedded in the programs. I do however "borrow" music from friends. I do not think it is stealing because if they got it why can't they share it with others; same deal with letting a friend watch a video you rented, reading a book you bought, or eating half your lunch.

Joanna, 24, Publicist: No. There has to be some form of payment for the music. Whether it means that you buy a concert ticket to the artist's show, pick up a T-shirt, etc., it doesn't really matter so long as something is being given back so that the creative process can continue. Music is many artists' livelihood and if they aren't monetizing from that livelihood in one way or another then we are robbing them of their trade and ourselves of some potentially kickass art.

Graham, 24, Management Consultant: Yes. As for why, I'll start with the observation that a 160GB iPod, sadly, does not fill itself. I think that downloading without payment, and "borrowing" from friends, has become such second nature that in the minds of many it is likely viewed as the legal equivalent of exceeding the speed limit or crossing against a light on an empty street.

Zakir, 24, IT Analyst: Yes. I also buy bootleg DVDs. Why would I pay $5 to rent a movie from Blockbuster when I can just as easily own the movie forever for $5? Maybe we are a screwed-up generation because I know I am not the only one who thinks this way.

Brandon, 26, Consultant: Yes. However I don't consider this stealing. Buying CDs and paying for downloads is more beneficial to the record companies, not the artists themselves. Downloading is a preview—if I like the music, I will pay for a concert ticket to see the band.

There's one clear sign that Net Geners value the act of doing good: a record number of Net Geners, as we'll see in Chapter 11, are volunteering for civic causes. One of them even launched a magazine, aptly called *GOOD* magazine. Niki says 70 percent of her crowd is volunteering, and she's an enthusiastic example. This winter, she helped organize a big fundraiser for Toronto's Centre for Addiction and Mental Health. "We want to end the stigma against mental illness," says Niki. Her friends have taken a big step in this direction. "A lot of my friends have anorexia or depression and like most I've got mental illness in my own extended family. It's time to take a stand. We can talk about it. It's not swept under the carpet."

Integrity is driving their behavior in other institutions as well. They want their universities, schools, governments, and politicians to be honest, considerate of their interests, accountable, and open. As parents, the early evidence suggests, they want to run their families based on such values. This is such a hopeful finding—the biggest generation ever is demanding that companies and other institutions behave with integrity. What a powerful force for a better world.

COLLABORATION

At most companies, employees chat over coffee, in front of the fax machine, or by the water cooler. But at Best Buy, Net Gen store employees—some as young as 19—helped to create an entirely new kind of digital chat zone. It's The Watercooler, a mass-communication and dialogue tool for all employees at all levels. It's part of Best Buy's big effort to tap the unique skills of its Net Gen employees, especially in using digital technology to get the front-line staff to contribute ideas. "The Watercooler fills a huge hole we've had," said Best Buy's senior manager of communications, Jennifer Rock. It's "a direct line between employees in stores and all locations to talk about business topics directly with corporate leaders, teams, and with each other. In the first three months, we've gained 85,000 active users."

The Watercooler is the best place for employees to get answers to their questions about things like best practices for home theater installation, or why they do not sell Dell products in their stores. It gives the company a way to mine the knowledge and experience of the entire employee population for input on weighty business decisions. "Being that Best Buy, like most companies, has traditionally communicated *at* employees instead of *with* them, we didn't forecast how quickly The Watercooler would become this business communication tool," said Rock. "But our employees were obviously ready."

Net Geners are natural collaborators. This is the relationship generation. As much as I thought that I, as a 10-year-old, had a relationship with the fabulous teenager Annette Funicello on *The Mickey Mouse Club*, it wasn't so. (She did eventually answer my letters, but today I wonder if they were really her answers.)

They collaborate online in chat groups, play multiuser video games, use e-mail, and share files for school, work, or just for fun. They influence each other through what I call N-Fluence networks, where they discuss brands, companies, products, and services. They bring a culture of collaboration with them to work and the marketplace and are comfortable using new online tools to communicate. They like to be in touch with their friends on their BlackBerrys or cell phones wherever they are—on the street, in the store, or at work. It gives them a sense of virtual community all day long. It makes them feel like they have a friend in their pocket.

Their eagerness to collaborate can be a bonus for companies. Net Geners want to work hand-in-hand with companies to create better goods and services, something their parents never dreamed of. Companies never thought of it either: without the Internet for a free two-way dialogue with customers, they conceived new products in secret.

Today, Net Geners are helping companies develop advertising campaigns. In one early experiment in advertising collaboration, GM invited consumers to a newly built Web site that offered video clips and simple editing tools they could use to create ads for the Chevy Tahoe SUV. The site gained online fame after environmentalists hijacked the site's tools to build and post ads on the site condemning the Tahoe as an eco-unfriendly gas-guzzler. GM didn't take the ads down, which caused even more online buzz. Some pundits said GM was being foolhardy, but the numbers proved otherwise. The Web site quickly attracted more than 620,000 visitors, two-thirds of whom went on to visit Chevy.com. For three weeks running, the new site funneled more people to the Chevy site than either Google or Yahoo did. Most important, sales of the Tahoe soared.[29] To be sure, concern for the environment did not impede the young car enthusiasts from purchasing the Tahoe. For them, the competing norms resolved in GM's favor.

Many Net Geners are happy to help with product design. They believe they offer useful insights and like to feel part of a knowledgeable and exclusive group. They are willing to test product prototypes and answer survey questions. Half of Net Geners are willing to tell companies the details of their lives if the result is a product that better fits their needs. This number rises to 61 percent of Early Adopters and 74 percent of the Bleeding Edge. However, they hesitate to share the data if they feel a company might misuse the information, sell it to other companies, or inundate them with junk mail and spam.[30]

Now, Net Gen consumers are taking the next step and becoming producers, cocreating products and services with companies. Alvin Toffler coined the term *prosumer*, in his 1970s book *Future Shock*,[31] I called it *prosumption* a decade ago.[32] I can see it happening now, as the Internet transforms itself from a platform for presenting information to a place where you can collaborate and where individuals can organize themselves into new communities. In the Web 2.0, new communities are being formed in social networks such as Facebook and MySpace, and these communities are starting to go into production. People are making things together. So prosumption was an idea waiting to happen, waiting for a generation who had a natural instinct to collaborate and co-innovate.

Collaboration extends to other aspects of the Net Geners' lives. At work, they want to feel that their opinion counts. While they acknowledge their lack of experience, they feel they have relevant insights—especially about technology and the Internet—and they want the opportunity to influence decisions and change work processes to make them more efficient. Making this happen requires a receptive corporate culture and the work tools, such as blogs and wikis, that encourage collaboration.

The new collaboration is not traditional teamwork at all. The difference today is that individual efforts can be harnessed on a large scale to achieve collective outcomes, like Wikipedia, the online encyclopedia written by 75,000 active volunteers and continually edited by hundreds of thousands of readers around the world who perform millions of edits per month. That would have been impossible to achieve without a new generation of collaboration tools.

These tools make collaboration on an international scale so easy, as my daughter Niki found last year while working for an international consulting company. She'd cook up an idea for a widget that might be useful for a client, and at the end of the day she'd send a message to a team of four computer developers in the Czech Republic. The next morning, there it was: a new widget ready for her to check out. "There's an old saying that two heads are better than one," she says. "Well, I say that 10,000 heads are better than 2. There are lots of smart people out there, and we should be using new technologies to tap into their talents."

Net Geners are collaborators in every part of their lives. As civic activists, they're tapping into the collaborative characteristic with aplomb. The Net Gen wants to help. They'll help companies make better products and services. They're volunteering in record numbers, in part because the Internet offers so many ways, big and small, to help out.

Educators should take note. The current model of pedagogy is teacher focused, one-way, one size fits all. It isolates the student in the learning process. Many Net Geners learn more by collaborating—both with their teacher and with each other. They'll respond to the new model of education that's beginning to surface—student-focused and multiway, which is customized and collaborative.

ENTERTAINMENT

In the high-tech world, where employers put a premium on attracting the brightest Net Geners they can find, some work sites look like playgrounds. You can play foosball at Microsoft's Redmond campus—or baseball on the company diamond or soccer or volleyball. There's even a private lake. You can take your pick of the 25 cafeterias on campus, along with the requisite Starbucks stands. Xbox consoles are stashed in alcoves. Nearly 3,000 works of art hang on the walls. You can even go on whale-watching excursions. Over at Google, there's a rock-climbing wall on the premises, along with a company pool, a beach volleyball pit, a gym, plus pool tables. You'll feel like you're right back in college. You can even bring your pet.

These employers know that for Net Geners, work should be fun. Net Geners see no clear dividing line between the two. This may be anathema to corporate types who enjoy the grind. The old paradigm was that there was a time of day when one worked and a time of day when one relaxed and had fun. These two modes have now become merged in the same activity because Net Geners believe in enjoying what they do for a living. Net Geners expect their work to be intrinsically satisfying. They expect to be emotionally fulfilled by their work. They also see nothing

> "It is pretty useless to try to draw borders around different spheres of life for them. It's better to let them shift among them as long as the work gets done."[33]
>
> —CHARLES GRANTHAM,
> A PRINCIPAL AT FUTURE OF WORK

wrong with taking time off from work to check their profile on Facebook or play an online game. Eighty-one percent of teens play online games—and once they get jobs, they're likely to play online games at work to blow off steam.

Employers often growl when they see Net Geners goofing off online at work. But I think that employers should cool it. What's wrong with spending 20 minutes playing an online game at work? Why is that any worse than what my generation did—amble downstairs for a coffee, a smoke, and a shared complaint, usually about management? Immersion in digital technology has taught this generation to switch very quickly between one line of thought and another. Switching off for a few minutes by playing a game can generate fresh ways to solve problems. It's arguably more productive than hunkering down and spinning your wheels for hours on end.

The Internet gives them plenty of opportunity to amuse themselves online. The Web is the fun tool of choice with which to catch up on news headlines, Google, check e-mail, and IM with friends. There's entertainment from around the world from Web sites, chatting with "Net pals," and online gaming. There's niche entertainment that caters to their interests, such as HollywoodStockExchange.com for movie buffs, or StyleDiary.net for fashionistas. Many Net Geners maximize their interactions by engaging in multiple "netivities" simultaneously, such as chatting with friends on MSN while listening to their media player and surfing the Net. YouTube raises the bar for interactive entertainment. Users upload hundreds of thousands of videos daily, either snippets of television programs they like or content they've created. Users vote and comment on the submissions.

To be sure, employers who allow Net Geners to amuse themselves online or wear headphones, need proper work design and policies to maximize productivity. In some situations, listening to music on headphones at work is fine, while in other situations it might not be. Notwithstanding the Net Gen ability to multitask, it's best to minimize distractions, including online ones, for work that requires deep thinking.

Net Geners' love of entertainment also has important implications for companies that want to sell things to them. Nearly three-quarters of Net Geners agreed with the following statement: "Having fun while using a product is just as important as the product doing what it is supposed to do." Net Geners value the experience of using the product beyond its primary function. They find amusement in accessory options and playing with tactile features, particularly younger males. Net Geners become bored easily, so playing with their tech devices keeps them interested.[34]

Still, making a product fun as well as useful presents a challenge to companies targeting the generation. How, for instance, do you make a mortgage fun? Well, take a look at what MtvU, the national network for college students, is doing as part of its campaign to help Darfur. On the site, the network launched an audacious game that asked players to put themselves in the shoes of a teenager in Darfur faced with a terrible decision of whether to go and get water before the bloodthirsty militia roll in. Millions of kids have played the game online—a testament to the power of the "games for change movement."

SPEED

When I began working with computers, I used a 360-bits-per-second dial-up modem to write my first book from my home office. Fifteen years later, when I wrote *Growing Up Digital*, the typical access rate was 9,600 bits per second. Many young people today access the Web at between 5 million bits per second and 65 million bytes per second!

Having grown up digital, they expect speed—and not just in video games. They're used to instant response, 24/7. Video games give them instant feedback; Google answers their inquiries within nanoseconds. So they assume that everyone else in their world will respond quickly too. Every instant message should draw an instant response. If a member of their peer group doesn't respond instantly, they become irritated and worried. They fear it may be a negative comment on their status and a personal slight. "IM has made this worse, because if someone sees you online and you don't answer, they *know* you are ignoring them," a 28-year-old man said in our online survey.

Net Geners also expect to receive an item they have purchased within a matter of days. They are no longer willing to wait four to six weeks to receive their secret decoder ring after sending in their cereal box tops. Corporations that are quick to respond to inquiries are praised and viewed as trustworthy, while long wait times are criticized. Needless to say, Net Geners do not like being put on hold.

When they e-mail a company, 80 percent expect an answer back quickly. But when they talk to their friends, e-mail is too slow for this generation, too cumbersome. They prefer the speed of instant messaging. They're impatient, and they know it. When we asked them what they thought of the following statement—"I have little patience and I can't stand waiting for things"—56 percent agreed.[35]

It makes working in the conventional office hard. "Working in a typical company can really sap one's energy because things happen so slowly," said Net Gener Moritz Kettler. "A lot of my friends tell me they are frustrated with the glacial pace of decision making. There is a lack of urgency. There's no 'let's get this done.' There is a big culture clash in the workplace with my generation and the bosses, who can often be much older."

The pressure of living in an instantaneous environment can overwhelm some Net Geners. They know others are expecting an immediate response from them, and many experience feelings of saturation, craziness, and never having a moment of peace. Some wish they could disconnect by turning off their cell phones and logging off their computer, but they're reluctant to do this because they fear missing an important message and don't want to feel detached from their social environment.

E-mail is faster than talking, which is why Net Geners often prefer to communicate with people at work via electronic means rather than meeting them— unless it's a first-time meeting or an important negotiation.

Many Net Geners would like their careers to progress at the same fast pace as the rest of their lives. They appreciate continual performance feedback from employers. It helps them gauge their progress and enhances their professional self-esteem and sense of career momentum. Loyalty is strengthened when Net Geners regularly receive feedback that helps them feel "on track" to being successful at the company. Conversely, loyalty may weaken if requests for regular feedback are not acknowledged in a short time frame. This alone may not cause them to switch jobs, but they will feel less emotionally satisfied at work.

INNOVATION

When I was a kid, the pace of innovation was glacial. I remember when the transistor radio came on the scene. I got one and took it to summer camp. We all had one. It was a wonderful innovation. And that radio and its predecessors didn't really change for years. I also remember our first television. That thing lasted for many years as well, until a new innovation—color—appeared on the scene.

This generation, on the other hand, has been raised in a culture of invention. Innovation takes place in real time. Compare my transistor radio that lasted for years with today's mobile devices that improve, sometimes dramatically, every few weeks. Today my kids want the new mobile device every few months, because the current one doesn't have the capability of the new one. And as for televisions, flat panel technology is an engine of innovation, dropping in price significantly every 18 months or so.

For marketers, there is no doubt that Net Geners want the latest and greatest product available—in ways that supersede the needs of their parents. The Net Geners live to stay current, whether it's with their cell phone, iPod, or game console. The latest product makes their friends envious and contributes to their social status and their positive self-image.

Motorola came out three years ago with the RAZR, its ultrathin cell phone with built-in camera and music player. Samsung Group answered within a year with the Blade. Motorola responded with its SLVR, a phone even sleeker than its predecessor. "It's like having a popular nightclub. You have to keep opening new ones. To stay cool, you have to speed up," says Michael Greeson, president of market researcher The Diffusion Group.[36]

For Niki, her latest innovation is the Nike+ iPod Sport Kit. The Sport Kit allows a Nike+ shoe to talk to an iPod nano. The sensor uses a sensitive accelerometer to measure a runner's activity; then it wirelessly transfers this data to the receiver on the runner's iPod nano. As Apple's Web site says: "You don't just take iPod nano on your run. You let it take you. Music is your motivation. But what if you want to go further? Thanks to a unique partnership between Nike and Apple, your iPod nano becomes your coach. Your personal trainer. Your favorite workout companion." As you run, iPod nano tells you your time, distance, pace, and calories burned via voice feedback that adjusts music volume as it plays. In addition to progress reports, voice feedback congratulates you when you've reached a personal best—your fastest pace, longest distance and time, or most calories burned. Voice feedback occurs automatically, according to predetermined intervals that vary by workout type. Niki loves her Nikes and nano: it helps keep her fit.

In the workplace, innovation means rejecting the traditional command-and-control hierarchy and devising work processes that encourage collaboration and creativity. Former chairman and chief mentor N. R. Narayana Murthy at the Bangalore-based Infosys Technologies introduced the company's "voice of youth" program eight years ago. Each year, nine top-performing young employees—all under 30—participate in eight senior management council meetings, presenting and discussing their ideas with the top leadership team. "We believe these young ideas need the senior-most attention for them to be identified and fostered," says Sanjay Purohit, associate vice president and head of corporate planning. Infosys CEO Nandan M. Nilekani concurs: "If an organization becomes too hierarchical, ideas that bubble up from younger people [aren't going to be heard]."[37]

Infosys is on the right track. Net Geners don't want to toil in the same old bureaucracies as their parents. They've grown up in an era of constant innovation and change, and want the workplace to be equally innovative and creative. Net Geners told us an innovative work environment is perceived to be leading edge, dynamic, creative, and efficient. Not surprisingly, an innovative workplace is expected to have leading-edge technology.

These are the eight norms of the Net Generation. They value freedom— freedom to be who they are, freedom of choice. They want to customize everything, even their jobs. They learn to be skeptical, to scrutinize what they see and read in the media, including the Internet. They value integrity—being honest, considerate, transparent, and abiding by their commitments. They're great collaborators, with friends online and at work. They thrive on speed. They love to innovate. This is the Net Generation, and in the next few chapters, we will explore how those characteristics are displayed in different spheres of the Net Gen life and how, if you understand these norms, you can change your company, school or university, government, or family for the twenty-first century.

THE NET GENERATION BRAIN

When he was a premed student at the University of Rochester, C. Shawn Green used to stay up late on a lot of nights to play Counter-Strike. It's an action-packed video game that pits a team of counterterrorists against a team of terrorists. One morning in September 2000, Green sat down in front of his computer, not to return to the game, but to work on an experiment being conducted by the university's Brain and Vision Lab.

Something was wrong. The experiment was supposed to test whether deaf people had quicker visual reflexes than people with hearing. Participants had to identify an image flashing quickly on a computer screen that was filled with visual clutter. If the average Joe could pick out the target 50 percent of the time, would deaf people do better? But when Green took the test himself, he scored 100 percent. It must be a programming mistake, he thought, so he dragged his best friend into the lab. His buddy scored 100 percent too. Now Green was pretty sure there must be a programming error. So he brought a second friend into the lab. This one scored only 50 percent, just as expected.

What was happening? Then the light went on. Green and his best friend played video action games all night, while the other guy didn't. He was too busy being a resident advisor, helping out the younger students on his dormitory floor. It may not sound like an insight that ends up in the pages of the world's leading scientific journals, but it was. Green had stumbled onto concrete evidence that interactive technology—in this case, action video games—can change the brain, and in particular, the way we perceive things. As Green and his mentor, Daphne Bavelier, described it in a seminal article in *Nature*, these games can make you notice more in your field of vision and speed up your processing of visual information.[1]

When you consider the powerful evidence scientists have built over the past 20 years showing that brains change and evolve throughout a lifetime, Green's study is not as surprising as you might think. Everything we do, they've discovered, leaves a physical imprint on our brains. Scientists have found that parts of the brains of the best-informed London cabbies are larger than those of other drivers. The brain is particularly adaptable to outside influences in the first three years of life and then during teenage and early adult years, which is just when most Net Geners are immersing themselves in interactive digital technology 20 to 30 hours per week.

While there is much controversy, the early evidence suggests that the digital immersion has a tangible, positive impact. Not only do video game players notice more, but they have more highly developed spatial skills that are useful for architects, engineers, and surgeons. What's more, I can see from my own observations that the average Net Gener is quicker at switching tasks than I am, and quicker to find what they're looking for on the Internet. Although the research is in its early days, and not completely conclusive, the evidence in support of this is mounting. The Net Gen mind seems to be incredibly flexible, adaptable, and multimedia savvy.

I believe that we will see that being immersed in an interactive digital environment has made them smarter than your average TV-watching couch potato. They may read fewer works of literature, but they devote a lot of time to reading and writing online. As we will learn, that activity can be intellectually challenging. Instead of just numbly receiving information, they are gathering it from around the globe with lightning speed. Instead of just trusting a TV announcer to tell us the truth, there are assessing and scrutinizing the jumble of facts that are often contradictory or ambiguous. When they write to their blog or contribute a video, they have an opportunity to synthesize and come up with a new formulation, which leads to a giant opportunity for them. The Net Generation has been given the opportunity to fulfill their inherent human intellectual potential as no other generation.

Now I know that some people don't agree with me. English professor Mark Bauerlein thinks that young people today are "the dumbest generation." "Dumb," the Merriam-Webster online dictionary tells us, is an old English word that means "lacking the power of speech." It can also mean lacking intelligence, as in stupidity, or "not having the capability to process data." Is that the case? We will see, later in this chapter, just how wrong the professor is.

THE BRAIN CAN CHANGE, EVEN AFTER CHILDHOOD

Back when I was a teenager, most scientists thought that the human brain had nowhere to go but down. For 400 years, as psychiatrist Norman Doidge tells us in his brilliant book, *The Brain That Changes Itself*, "mainstream medicine and science believed that brain anatomy was fixed. The common wisdom was that after childhood, the brain changed only when it began the long process of decline; that when brain cells failed to develop properly, or were injured or died, they could not be replaced."[2] This theory of the unchanging brain held that the brain was like a "glorious machine," Doidge writes. "And while machines do many extraordinary things, they don't change and grow."[3]

Modern scientists have now disproved this theory. The brain, Doidge and other scientists tell us, does change and grow throughout a person's life. The study that examined the greater memory capacity of London taxi drivers involved the scanning of those drivers' brains, which produced some amazing results. It turned out that the hippocampus, which is associated with memory function, was larger in these taxi drivers than it was in all other categories of drivers of the same age. Similarly, research conducted using musicians who played stringed instruments revealed that, even among those who started learning the violin, cello, or guitar as adults, the musicians' frequent repetition of their finger exercises led to a different brain structure than that of nonmusicians.[4] Both these studies support the idea that continual and intense use of a particular brain region can lead it to respond like a muscle, increasing its size and presumably its efficiency.[5]

It might not take that long to train the brain to function differently either. Researchers already know that when blind people use their fingers to read, information from their fingers is processed through the visual cortex. In other words, they're using their fingers to "see." But what happens if sighted people are blindfolded? A series of studies exploring this very question showed that sighted people can improve tactile (Braille character) discrimination. What's more, after only five days of being blindfolded, their visual cortexes had heightened responses to touch and sound. Another study showed that mentally rehearsing a move can produce changes in the motor cortex as big as those induced by physical movement. One group of participants were asked to play a simple five-finger exercise on the piano while another group were asked to think about playing the same "song" in their heads using the same finger movements, one note at a time. Both groups showed a change in their brain functioning, with differences among the group who mentally rehearsed the song as great as those who physically played the piano.[6]

The research shows, in other words, that the brain can change throughout life as it responds to environmental influences. Children's brains can change

> "Anytime you engage in immersion over long periods of time, it's going to reflect brain structures."
>
> —JOHN SEELY BROWN, DIRECTOR EMERITUS OF XEROX PARC AND A VISITING SCHOLAR AT USC

to a greater degree than adult ones can, but the adult brain can and does change. "Neuroscience has shown that, in the most literal sense, the events of our lives get etched in the very physical structure and the activities of the brain," states Dr. Stan Kutcher, an internationally renowned expert on adolescent mental health, who with his son Matthew, a Net Gen neuroscientist, conducted a study measuring the effect of digital technology on human brain development for the nGenera research program.[7]

THE ADOLESCENT BRAIN: A WORK IN PROGRESS

By the time Net Generation kids reach their twenties, the typical Net Gener has spent over 20,000 hours on the Internet and over 10,000 hours playing video games of some kind.[8] This immersion is taking place at a time when their brains are particularly sensitive to outside influences—adolescence and their teenage years. Recent studies show that although total brain volume is largely unchanged after age 6, the brain continues to undergo significant structural remodeling throughout the adolescent years and into early adult life. The studies show that brain regions associated with attention, evaluation of rewards, emotional intelligence, impulse control, and goal-directed behavior all change significantly between age 12 and 24. These neurological changes during adolescence may explain, in part, why many teenagers appear to be disorganized, have poor impulse control, and have difficulty making long-term plans.

Research done at the National Institute of Mental Health (NIMH) documented some of the physical changes that take place in the brain between the ages of 4 and 20. It turns out that the volume of nerve cells in the frontal and parietal lobes, which are thought to be responsible for goal-directed behavior and other higher functions, peaks at age 12.[9] How can that be? NIMH researchers suggest that after age 12, the brain starts pruning, reducing connections among brain cells. Say, for example, you learned a language from your mother but stopped using it when you started speaking English. The pathways needed to speak your mother's language will die off, while the other neural pathways associated with speaking English will get stronger. In other words, you use it or you lose it. This pruning period lasts until about age 20.

Some studies suggest that the teen brain processes, operates, and functions differently than the adult one. Sarah-Jayne Blakemore of University College London conducted a series of studies in which participants were asked to answer hypothetical questions while their brain activity was monitored by MRI imaging. When the question was an impersonal one, the teens, whose average age was 15, used the same parts of their brain to answer as did the 28-year-old adults. But when they were asked a question like "You are at the cinema and have trouble seeing the screen. Do you move to another seat?" the teens used different parts of their brain to answer.[10] As this evidence suggests, the teen brain itself—not just our understanding of it—is still a work in progress.

DIGITAL IMMERSION: DOES IT AFFECT THE TEEN BRAIN?

Gamers Notice More: They Process Visual Information More Quickly

Can growing up digital affect the physical structure or the activities of the teenage brain? If so, how? One significant clue comes from the study by Green and Bavelier referred to above, which was conducted using keen action game players, aged 18 to 23, who played action games like Grand Theft Auto III and Crazy Taxi for at least one hour a day. The researchers set up five experiments to test whether playing action video games affects what you notice in a jumble of visual information. As researchers who study visual attention can tell you, what you notice is quite different from what you see. If you happen to be reading these words at your computer, for example, you might not be paying attention to other things in your field of vision, like the coffee cup sitting on the side of your desk. That's because your brain has a mechanism directing it to pay attention to some things in your visual field, and to pay less attention to the rest. In other words, it's not what you can see that really matters; it's what you notice.

Green and Bavelier's experiment compared hard-core action game players with non-video-game players on a standard test—with the usual array of squares, diamonds, and circles flashing on a computer screen. The idea was to evaluate how much each group noticed outside the target they were focusing on. The experiment showed that experienced video game players noticed more. Then the researchers looked at whether video game players could process rapid-fire visual information more effectively than could nonplayers. Once again, the video game players were better at this. You might think it's because the action game players had greater natural abilities; that's why they were attracted to the games in the first place. But it turned out, as Green and Bavelier showed in a third experiment, you could learn to speed up your visual processing after only 10 consecutive days playing Medal of Honor!

"Although video game playing may seem to be rather mindless, it is capable of altering visual attentional processing," Green and Bavelier concluded. In other words, people who play a lot of video games can track more objects at one time than people who don't. Second, they are better at monitoring a cluttered world; they can more quickly identify a target briefly presented in a field of clutter. And third, the experienced game players are better at processing a rapid stream of visual information. "We saw really big differences between the groups with the people who played the action games far outperforming the people who didn't," said Green and Bavelier. Yet, "the most important thing that we did in that paper was that we took a group of non-game-playing people, trained them on an action game, and saw similar improvements. This showed us the act of playing games can drive this improvement; it's not necessarily a population bias that the people who actually played the action games also naturally had better vision."

Gamers Develop Other Skills Too—Skills that Are Useful for Surgeons

Green and Bavelier's finding builds on other research showing other ways that video game playing affects the brain. It improves hand-eye coordination, quickens reaction times, and benefits peripheral vision. It improves spatial skills, the ability to mentally manipulate a 3-D object, which is helpful for architects, sculptors and engineers, and might be associated with improved results in some fields of mathematics. It can even prove useful in the training of surgeons. Laparoscopic surgery is a minimally invasive technique in which a camera and operating instruments are inserted in the body via miniscule incisions of about a centimeter. Laparoscopic surgeons conduct their operations only by seeing the images from the tiny internal camera. In a 2004 study, it was observed that younger doctors who were video game players being trained in laparoscopic techniques learned the skills more quickly and made fewer errors than did non-game-playing counterparts.[11] In fact, the researchers found that a surgeon's game-playing experience was a better predictor of his or her future success at laparoscopic surgery than was years of experience!

Video games also teach young people to work in teams. As Generation X came of age, the arcade video games available to them were largely about competition: scores were kept, and there tended to be a winner for every loser. In contrast, popular video games today highlight adventure and exploring what is around the corner, often in real time. They place extraordinary demands on multidimensional visual-spatial skills; enhance abilities for divided attention;[12] and encourage players to discover rules through observation, trial and error, and hypothesis testing.[13] They often require cooperation with opponents to defeat a common enemy offering problems to be solved collaboratively and creatively, and acting in a global community—signifying the movement of the game-playing experience to being social rather than a solitary activity.

Playing online games is good for your mind, according to Steven Johnson, writing in *Everything Bad Is Good for You:* "Games force you to decide, to choose, to prioritize."[14] Some of the world's leading thinkers in this field agree. When James Gee, a teacher and theoretical linguist, started playing video games at age 60, he realized he had to think in a new way. To excel at a video game you have to learn skills that are crucial for any learning experience, such as understanding design principles, making choices, practicing, and discovering.[15]

Matthew Myers, for instance, is a 21-year-old student at Southern Methodist University. He's the captain of his wrestling team, a church youth leader, and president of his dorm. He's also second-in-command in his guild, and every week he spends a few hours playing World of Warcraft. "I'm taking a class on managing people and strategy," he says. "I can take all the lessons that I learn in class and apply them to my guild." He continues to note that managing a group of 40-plus players is a complex job. There are new players to recruit and current guild members who need help raising their skill levels as they pursue quests and run raids.

Gaming: A Lesson in Trial and Error

To SMU student Matthew, the vast landscape of the game is the perfect Net Generation classroom. It's interactive, fun, and challenging. He gets to apply his knowledge in a game environment. I'll bet it beats having to listen to a boring lecture any day. John Seely Brown, director emeritus at Xerox PARC and a visiting scholar at USC, argues that games like World of Warcraft have a positive impact on learning. "Unlike education acquired through textbooks, lectures, and classroom instruction, what takes place in massively multiplayer online games is what we call accidental learning," he says. "It's learning to *be*— a natural by-product of adjusting to a new culture—as opposed to learning *about*. Where traditional learning is based on the execution of carefully graded challenges, accidental learning relies on failure. Virtual environments are safe platforms for trial and error. The chance of failure is high, but the cost is low and the lessons learned are immediate." Says Jerry Michalski, "Look at what it takes to run a guild raid in World of Warcraft. There is an immense amount of coordination, data management, and strategy." Gamers are not a bunch of loners, he says. "We're all bemoaning the so-called decline of social interaction. But kids are growing up with very deep social skills. They still hang out and when playing games or using the Web, they are interacting socially."

INTERNET SCREEN TIME: DOES IT AFFECT THE WAY NET GENERS ABSORB INFORMATION?

What about the overall effect of spending so much time in front of a screen—not a TV but an interactive screen? Does the medium affect the way we absorb the information? Back in the 1950s, Marshall McLuhan argued that it does. The way we receive information—by reading a book, watching a movie, or listening to someone on the telephone—has a big impact on the brain, and that impact is even more important than the actual content of the message. In other words, McLuhan said in his famous but somewhat oblique line, "the medium is the message."

The great Toronto thinker did not, of course, have the benefit of modern brain scans. So Erica Michael and Marcel Just of Carnegie Mellon University did a brain scan to test McLuhan's hypothesis. It turned out that he was right: the brain constructs the message differently for reading and listening. "Listening to an audio book leaves a different set of memories than reading does," say Michael and Just. "A newscast heard on the radio is processed differently from the same words read in a newspaper."

You'd expect, then, that information absorbed on the Internet would have a different impact than information obtained by reading the newspaper. A 2006 study of Net Geners certainly suggests it does. Researchers played the same newscast in four different ways—as a traditional radio newscast, as an online newscast played with one click, as an interactive Webcast where you click to get each news item, and as a Webcast that included links for details. Net Geners remembered less from the traditional newscasts—told from beginning to end—than they did from the interactive versions that gave them a chance to click to hear the news or learn more details.[16]

Net Geners Don't Always Start at the Beginning

The boomers typically go from beginning to end—whether it's writing an essay, watching *The Ed Sullivan Show*, or reading the instructions before working the remote control. That's how boomers, who were raised before Web sites, learned to absorb information. The Net Gener doesn't operate in this sequential way. Using tools like keywords in Google, hypertext, and "clicking, cutting, and pasting," today's young person can search for and organize information containing links to other information.[17] William D. Winn, director of the

Learning Center at the University of Washington's Human Interface Technology Laboratory, put it this way: children "think differently from the rest of us. They develop hypertext minds. They leap around. It's as though their cognitive structures were parallel, not sequential."[18] This is one way that digital immersion has literally rewired brains under 40, Marc Prensky argues in his book *Digital Game-Based Learning*.[19]

For example, when faced with a novel software package or video game, young people tend to explore first, and then ask for help by consulting a social network when stuck later. "I know that when people start playing video games, kids especially, they jump right in and they start playing it; then if they don't understand something, then they read the instructions to see what in the world they don't understand," says researcher Green. "Whereas, from my experience, older adults start by reading the instruction manual and then start playing the game, which is a real difference in kind of thinking about the problem."

Net Geners Look at It Differently

The differences between Net Geners and boomers even show up in the way their eyes move around the screen. Try this out: Take a look at my Web site for *Wikinomics*. If you're a boomer, I bet you'll start looking at the top left corner as you search for the text to tell you what this is all about. Your eyes will probably move from left to right, from top to bottom. You've been trained to read that way.[20]

FIGURE 4.1   THE *WIKINOMICS* WEB SITE

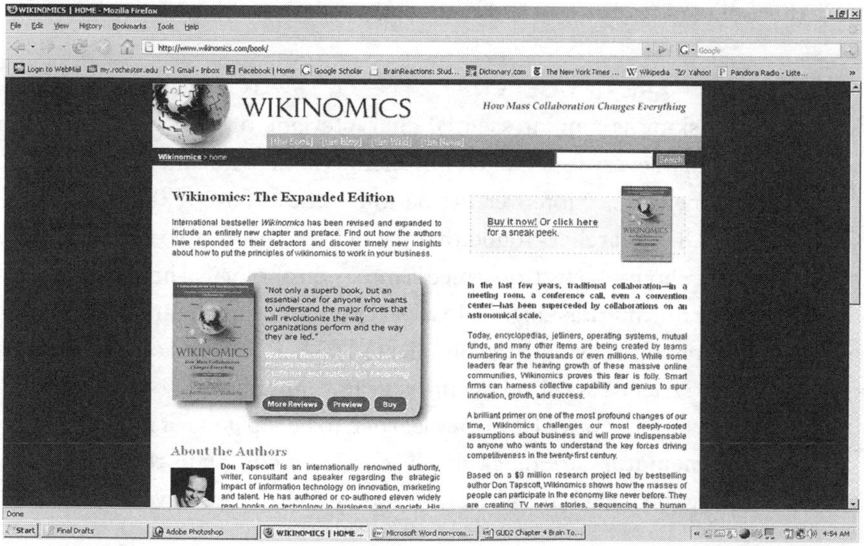

If you are a member of the Net Generation, on the other hand, you'll probably view it differently. I would guess that you started with the image of the book cover jacket. Then you moved on to the colored call-out box and text that explains what *Wikinomics* is about, "how mass collaboration changes everything," and that I am soliciting your help in making the Wikinomics Playbook. Then you likely turned to the body text to confirm your initial assumptions about the Web page. You see it this way because you've grown up digital and you've been trained to understand the meaning of a number of recognizable icons or images that quickly give you information at a glance. From your preschool days navigating on SesameStreet.com, you probably learned that size and color are cues signaling the importance of that piece of information.

Visual Experts

Net Geners who have grown up digital have learned how to read images, like pictures, graphs, and icons. They may be more visual than their parents are.[21] A study of Net Gen college students showed that they learned much better from visual images than from text-based ones. Students of a Library 1010 class at California State University (Hayward) tended to ignore lengthy step-by-step text instructions for their homework assignments, until the instructors switched their teaching methods to incorporate more images. The results were dramatic: students' scores increased by 11 to 16 percent.[22]

The early evidence suggests, as we discussed earlier in this chapter, that digital immersion may alter Net Geners' visual systems, especially the speed of their visual reflexes. It may also alter the way they like to take in information and what they remember. But does it also affect the way they think?

MULTITASKING: ARE NET GENERS BETTER AT SWITCHING ATTENTION?

Media multitasking is a quintessential characteristic of the Net Generation brain. Three out of every four Net Gen students claim to instant message while doing their homework.[23] Moreover, in a national study of over 2,000 young people, aged 8 to 18, researchers found that participants were able to squeeze the equivalent of 8.5 hours of electronic media into 6 chronological hours because of their penchant for multitasking.[24] Most parents can't understand it. Boomers usually have trouble focusing on a complicated task if the TV is on, the music is cranked up, and friends are checking in every few minutes. Are Net Geners any better at it than boomers are? Have they learned to be top guns of multitasking?

Many commentators are quick to say no. They complain that the digital world is cutting the Net Geners' attention span. "Most kids have the attention span of a gnat," complains one observer. They're "screenagers," said another,[25] or even "The ADD [attention deficit disorder] Generation."[26]

Most researchers take a dim view of multitasking. Psychological research has shown that our ability to do two things at once is limited. We can obviously walk and talk, but that's because walking and talking tap into two different mental channels, and one of those activities, walking, is automatic for adults. But if we try to think of two things that tap into the same channel, like a verbal one, we run into trouble. We're more likely to make mistakes. We slow down. Our brains cope with the overload of capacity by switching from one task to another, and unlike computers we don't switch very efficiently. The result, according to University of Michigan psychologist David Meyer, is that multitasking might double the time it takes to do two tasks, compared with doing them one at a time. There's little evidence that teens are any better than adults, he said. "To think that you're invulnerable because of age, it's delusional," he told one of my colleagues. "It's a myth."[27]

> "It is a part of human nature to be bored and not pay attention a lot of times. But the occasional or frequent daydreaming and boredom aren't ADD, damn it!"
>
> —REBECCA DOBRZYNSKI, 20, PHILADELPHIA, PENNSYLVANIA

To see whether young people really can multitask more effectively than older people, the Oxford Future of the Mind Institute conducted a study comparing Net Geners, aged 18 to 21 years, with people age 35 to 39. Net Geners performed 10 percent better on intensive problem-solving exercises without disruption than those aged 35 to 39 years. However, interruptions from communication-based messages (phone call, cell text message, or IM) caused the Net Geners to lose their cognitive advantage over their older counterparts. In other words, the thirtysomethings caught up in speed and accuracy.[28] So even though the Net Geners "think" more quickly, they are less effective at recovering from disruption when faced with a complex cognitive task.

Yet I see a different picture when I observe young Net Geners outside the laboratory—and the way they handle a multitude of streams of information coming in on their laptops or the tiny screens on their BlackBerrys and mobile phones. Is it possible the lab research is not yet sophisticated enough to measure the complexity of what occurs in the real world? My daughter Niki is a great example of this hyperconnected generation. She prefers to work at our kitchen table when she's not traveling on a work assignment, even though she has a killer office set up in her bedroom. She says she'd rather "be where the action is"—working while dealing with the dog, having her parents come in and out (rooting around the refrigerator), window for work documents open, multiple

Internet windows open for research, IM and Facebook windows open for communication, and ear buds in for music. Still she was a straight A student and is a rising star at the consulting company where she now works. I don't know how she does it. I simply can't work and listen to music at the same time. Geez, to me, my kids seem like air traffic controllers, constantly monitoring all those open windows on their computers.

When I look at my own children, their friends, and legions of other Net Geners, this is what I see: They're faster than I am at switching tasks, and better than I am at blocking out background noise. They can work effectively with music playing and news coming in from Facebook. They can keep up their social networks while they concentrate on work; they seem to need this to feel comfortable. I think they've learned to live in a world where they're bombarded with information, so that they can block out the TV or other distractions while they focus on the task at hand.

"People will often ask me, 'Are kids today different than kids 20 years ago?' Well, yes, they are. Because the world is different, their brains have wired up in a different way."
—MARTIN WESTWELL, OXFORD

So why do some Net Geners seem to have attention deficit disorder in class? Isn't it possible that the answer is because they're bored—both with the slow pace and with the content of the lecture? Author Marc Prensky agrees. "Their attention spans are not short for games, for example, or for music, or rollerblading, or for spending time on the Internet, or anything else that actually interests them," he writes. "It isn't that they can't pay attention, they just choose not to."[29]

They May Be Faster Switchers, but Can They Think?

Jordan Grafman leads the cognitive neuroscience section at the National Institute of Neurological Disorders and Stroke (NINDS). He acknowledges that the experience of growing up digital may make this generation quicker to switch from one thought to another. "If you're multitasking a lot as a kid, the likelihood is that your brain will develop around your adaptive behavior," he says. "Would it change the brain to optimize multitasking? The answer might be yes." But then he asks the core question: "Does optimizing for multitasking result in better functioning—that is, creativity, inventiveness, productiveness? The answer is, in more cases than not, no." While Net Geners may learn to switch focus on more quickly than their parents do, he says, that doesn't mean they'll be able to think more creatively or more deeply about a complicated issue. "The more you multitask," he says, "the less deliberative you become;

the less you're able to think and reason out a problem and the more you're will-ing to rely on stereotypical solutions." Meyer agrees. "You can't think deeply about a subject, analyze it, or develop a creative idea if you're constantly dis-tracted by an e-mail message, a new site, or a cell phone call," he says. Boomers can't do it; kids can't either.

A Critique from the House of Lords

The question these eminent scientists raise was eloquently expressed by Baroness Susan Greenfield, the glamorous and iconoclastic neurobiologist who sits in England's House of Lords, England's unelected upper house in the British government. I think it is worth exploring her argument, because she reflects the views of so many critics of digital immersion. On April 20, 2006, the baroness rose in the august chamber. Her fellow peers had just witnessed a scene that could be straight out of Monty Python, when the eleventh Baron Monson stood up to suggest that ordinary people might not realize that if you change the time on the country's clocks and watches so that the sun sets later at night, it will also rise later in the morning.

Greenfield, a pharmacology professor at Oxford, asked the unelected upper house a pertinent question: "Could this screen and multimedia culture impact our thinking and learning?"[30] She answered it with her trademark panache. "When we of the twentieth century read a book, most usually the author takes you by the hand, and you travel from the beginning to the middle to the end in a continuous narrative series of interconnected steps," she said.

"We then, of course, compare one narrative with another. In doing so, we start to build up a conceptual framework that enables us to evaluate further journeys, which in turn will influence our individualized framework. One might argue that this is the basis of education—education as we know it. It is the building up of a personalized conceptual framework, where we can relate incoming information to what we know already. We can place an isolated fact in a context that gives it significance. Traditional education has enabled us, if you like, to turn information into knowledge.

"Now imagine that there is no robust conceptual framework. Imagine you are sitting in front of a multimedia presentation where you are unable, because you have not had the experience of many different intellectual journeys, to evaluate what is flashing up on the screen. The most immediate reaction instead would be to place a premium on the most obvious feature, the immedi-ate sensory content—we could call it the 'yuk' or 'wow' factor. You would be having an experience rather than learning. Here sounds and sights of a fast-

FIGURE 4.2   IQ SCORES ARE ON THE RISE[32]*

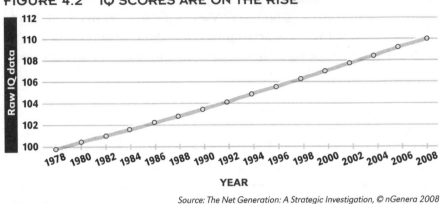

Source: The Net Generation: A Strategic Investigation, © nGenera 2008

*Data is from the U.S.

paced, fast-moving multimedia presentation would displace any time for reflection or any idiosyncratic or imaginative connections that we might make as we turn the pages and then stare at the wall to reflect."

Greenfield called for more study to see just how new technology is affecting the developing brain. Of course we need to study this; so much is unknown. But are the Baroness and her fellow critics right? Is screen time turning young people into a generation who just say "wow" and "yuk" instead of thinking about what they're reading? Mildly alarmed, I read the rest of the Baroness's speech to see what evidence she had amassed to back up her concern. Greenfield's argument led with a complaint that children are using the Internet without the benefit of how-to lessons, presumably from adults. That's when I started to chuckle. Just imagine: she wants the teachers to show the Net Geners how to use the Internet! I think, as my daughter Niki might put it, that's an LOL, or an OMG (or, for the benefit of the Baroness, that's "laugh out loud" or "oh my God").

And where was the proof that they fail to develop the intellectual skills to evaluate what they were reading? Even Baroness Greenfield had to acknowledge that there is, according to the National Literacy Trust, "no conclusive evidence that reading standards are deteriorating."[31] According to the Literacy Trust, she told her peers, reading from a screen is just as good as reading from a book.

TECHNOLOGY AND THINKING

In the fall of 2007, the National Endowment for the Arts in the United States released a report with a disturbing title: *Reading at Risk*. It revealed that only one-third of 13-year-old kids in the United States are daily readers of literature—down 14 percent from two decades ago. And nearly 1 in 5 17-year-old kids don't read literature at all, double the number of non-literature readers there were 20 years earlier. The survey did not, however, show that young people are reading less. They read more online than offline, and that's usually non-fiction, which was not included in the survey of literature.[33]

Now, as the writer of 12 books, I would never argue that kids should stop reading and buying books and just pick up bits of info on the Internet. I can only encourage young people to read more to expand their horizons and formulate the conceptual framework that the Baroness thinks is so crucial for the intelligent reader. Reading books of fiction and nonfiction is obviously important. Kids emulate their parents' reading habits, and if their parents read to them as youngsters, they'll probably love to read too. My wife reads a novel a week, and Niki and Alex have followed in her footsteps. Both are voracious readers of books, including plenty of fiction. So if you're a parent and you think your kids should love reading, read to them as kids and show them the love of reading by your own behavior.

Yet the real question is whether screen time discourages kids from developing the critical thinking skills that the Baroness mentioned in her speech. I do not share the Baroness's suspicions. Far from anesthetizing young brains, digital immersion can, in my opinion, help them to develop critical thinking skills, the ones you need to navigate in today's fast-paced information-saturated world.

You Need Those Key Mental Skills to Read and Search

Back in 1992, P. David Pearson, a comprehension theorist at the University of Illinois, set forth the skills that a good reader uses to understand a text. The good reader activates prior knowledge, makes sure she understands what she's reading and reads it again if necessary, makes inferences, and synthesizes or summarizes what she's learned—which is what you need to do to develop the intellectual framework that Baroness Greenfield mentioned in her speech. It turns out that searching for information on the Internet requires those same skills—and then some—according to a study in the September 2003 issue of the *Journal of Adolescent and Adult Literacy.*[34]

Searching for information on the Internet is obviously a different exercise than reading a book. You read or scan until you have found what you wanted, and then you click on a key word to hunt for more information. Unlike the journey you take when you read a book, no one is holding your hand or serving as your guide. You're on your own. But it requires the same skills you need to read a book—plus the ability to scan, navigate, analyze whether information is pertinent, synthesize, and remember what question you're trying to answer as you

FIGURE 4.3   MORE STUDENTS TAKING SAT BUT SCORES REMAINED STABLE OR UP*

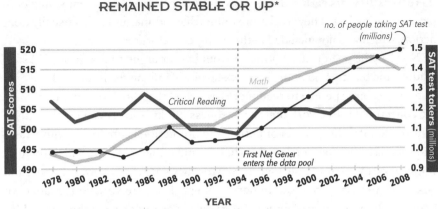

Source: The College Board[37]

*Large numbers of students take the SAT, not just the elite, top students, as was the case in the past. These data points correspond to both the restructuring of the SAT to include a written section and a decrease in the amount of people taking the test more than once. The rate of students who take the test only once increased to 49 percent from 44 percent, and the rate of students who took the test three times dropped to less than 13 percent from about 15 percent the previous year.

click on the links. The RAND Reading Study Group put it this way in 2002: "Accessing the Internet makes large demands on the individuals' literacy skills; in some cases, this new technology requires readers to have novel literacy skills."[35]

In some ways, searching on the Internet is more demanding than reading in the conventional way, according to Donald Leu, codirector of the New Literacies Research Team at the University of Connecticut and a member of the International Reading Association's International Hall of Fame. The online reader must not only read the text and understand it, but create his own mental journey as he clicks on the links to search for information. Because the reader is doing these two things at the same time, "online reading comprehension becomes by definition more complex."[36] Leu believes we need to redefine literacy to include "literacy skills necessary for individuals, groups, and societies to access the best information in the shortest time to identify and solve the most important problems and then communicate this information." Reading online, in other words, is not necessarily any less intellectually challenging than reading a book. It's just different, and it requires different skills.

Making Sense of the Mass of Information

As boomers, we spent a lot of time hunting for information. We couldn't always find it—maybe the library was closed on the night we had to finish that essay—so we grew up with a lot less information at hand than the Net Generation has. It made life easier in some ways. It's easier to jump to a conclusion when you don't have a lot of information to analyze. The Net Generation has the opposite problem—an avalanche of information coming from an astounding diversity of sources. This presents a real intellectual challenge. You have to make sense of different kinds of information that may be contradictory or ambiguous or just plain confusing. You have to really think about it to come up with an original view. You have to integrate that information into an argument or a solution, says author Prensky. That encourages what he calls "problem-based learning." If you practice it a lot, you may get better at it and improve your critical thinking skills. Now, of course there is a big if in that sentence. It may not work out that way. As Kutcher, the expert in adolescent mental health, points out, we tend to pay attention to the information we already think is true. People tend to look for information that confirms their belief and reject information that contradicts it. Even academics do this, Kutcher says: "That's the problem with the digital age. You can find stuff you like and ignore the rest."

But let's talk about the potential. The availability of vast amounts of information—when and where you want it—could help Net Geners develop the conceptual frame of reference needed to interpret incoming information, which is so crucial for the sophisticated reader. After all, they're not just clicking. They're reading a wider array of material than I did at school. They may even find that their frame of reference is challenged by new information, and will evolve. That to me is one of the characteristics of intelligence. So I believe the challenges of the Internet can actually provoke the Net Gener to do the hard thinking to make sense of a broader scope of information than the one that would have been available to the boomer. In fact, according to the Kutchers, "there is emerging evidence suggesting that exposure to new technologies may push the Net Gen brain past conventional 'capacity limitations.'" They argue the Net Gen brain may be able to execute certain perceptual tasks more rapidly, and may maintain more items in working memory.[38]

Scanning Helps

In order to deal with all that incoming information, you have to be a great scanner. Digital immersion has given the Net Generation the visual skills that make them superior scanners. They've learned to develop the filters they need to sort out what's important from what's not. But—and this is a big but—the outcome turns on the filter they choose, Stan Kutcher explains. If they are simply swayed by visual clues, they could easily be misguided by savvy designers. If, on the other hand, they learn to override the visual clues and zoom in on key words of importance, then they have developed a huge skill for dealing with the massive information inflow in this media-saturated world.

A New Form of Intelligence: "Distributed Cognition"

Digital immersion may encourage a new form of intelligence, according to Henry Jenkins, director of the Comparative Media Studies Program at the Massachusetts Institute of Technology.[39] Jenkins notes that more than half of teens create media content, while about one-third share content. "In this 'participatory culture,' the ability to interact with both people and computers can expand our mental capabilities," he contends. That may be surprising, because we usually think of intelligence as something an individual possesses, or not, but Jenkins argues that video game playing may help people tap into a collective form of intelligence—"distributed cognition." This means that intelligence is heightened through collaboration with other people and with machines.

Does the Internet Squelch Creativity?

What about creativity? The Baroness is worried: "Surely we are at risk of losing our imagination, that mysterious and special cognitive achievement that until now has always made the book so very much better than the film." Her evidence? Because they're sitting in front of a computer, kids are spending less time playing, letting their imaginations "roam free." Obviously kids need to play (and so do adults), but should we blame the Internet for the decline of unstructured playtime? Or should we point the finger at parents who structure every minute of their children's day with organized activities? Contrary to what the Baroness says, I think the Internet is great for creative young minds. Remember that the vast majority of teens play video games, and, as Jenkins notes, play for them is not a giddy childlike activity. They enjoy the "fun of engaging attention," he writes. This kind of play is deeply creative. It involves trial and error, learning by experiment, role playing, failure, and many other aspects of creative thinking.

It's certainly a lot more creative to check out things on the Internet than it is to sit in front of a TV. It's a boon for young writers, like 13-year-old Zöe Knowles, who lives a few blocks from me in Toronto. She has been writing her first novel, and she also contributes stories to a Web site called FicWad. These are little stories that might play off of a TV show, a film, or a comic, or they can be original pieces. One of her stories has been read by over 1,400 kids; she gets lots of feedback from the readers too. Think of what that response means for the creative youngster. Isn't that better than writing on paper and hoping that some day it might get published?

Is Memory Fading?

Memory of specific facts, the Baroness notes, may no longer be as important now that you can check the date of the Battle of Hastings with a click or two. Now here I agree with her. Why should we spend agonizing hours in school memorizing long passages or historical facts when you can look them up in an instant?

It makes me think of a brilliant twentysomething guy who worked for nGenera right out of college before becoming a star in the strategy practice at Deloitte. He's off the chart with his GMAT score and a really bright star in his organization, but he admits that he has no knowledge at all of the geography of the United States. He says he can Google it, and furthermore, if he were to be tested on the geography of the United States, he can memorize it in an hour, so why should he bother keeping that information? He'd rather concentrate on higher-ordered thinking tasks.

Now I'm not arguing here that you don't need to remember or know about geography. The fact that almost half of all 18- to 24-year-olds think it is not important or necessary to know where countries in the news are located and that about three-quarters of all college-educated young people can't identify Iraq, Iran, Saudi Arabia, and Israel on a map is a travesty.[40] You still need to know that events like the Battle of Hastings happened if you want to look them up on Wikipedia. But you might not have to stress about the details—those you can check.

What's more, Net Geners do learn memory skills while they're immersed in the Internet, and they certainly need more memory skills to surf the Web than they do to watch TV. Watching TV doesn't demand anything in the way of memory skills (as long as you can remember how to work the remote control). A young person today doesn't just sit and watch TV, as we have seen. He or she uses TV as background music while surfing the Web. In doing so, the Net Gener must remember dozens, perhaps hundreds, of applications. They access hundreds, perhaps thousands, of sites. Many require IDs and passwords and, given the dismal state of identity management, a typical teen needs to keep track of dozens of them. A video game may have dozens or hundreds of characters. They need to organize and file information and remember how to access it. Then there are your 100 to 700 Facebook friends—now who is the guy in the red hat again?—not to mention learning a new language of acronyms, like OMG and LOL; the names of dozens of bloggers; and a thousand Web sites. So Net Geners still need memory skills, but for different reasons.

Focus Is Important

Yet many Boomers still suspect that the Internet is weakening their power of concentration. "I'm not thinking the way I used to think," Nicholas Carr, the former executive editor of *Harvard Business Review*, wrote in an article called "Is Google Making Us Stupid?" which appeared in the summer issue of *Atlantic Monthly*. "I can feel it most strongly when I'm reading. Immersing myself in a book or a lengthy article used to be easy. My mind would get caught up in the narrative or the turns of the argument, and I'd spend hours strolling through long stretches of prose. That's rarely the case anymore. Now my concentration often starts to drift after two or three pages. I get fidgety, lose the thread, begin looking for something else to do. I feel as if I'm always dragging my wayward brain back to the text. The deep reading that used to come naturally has become a struggle." The Internet, Carr argues, is shaping the way he thinks: "It's chipping away my capacity for concentration and contemplation. My mind now expects to take in information the way the Net distributes it: in a swiftly moving stream of particles. Once I was a scuba diver in the sea of words. Now I zip along the surface like a guy on a Jet Ski."

The Internet, Carr notes, is extraordinarily helpful for a writer, but he's concerned that it will fill up those quiet spaces where you could read deeply, "not just for the knowledge we acquire from the author's words but for the intellectual vibrations those words set off within our own minds."

It is an eloquent, thoughtful article full of fascinating historical information on the impact of new technology on human thinking, which suggests that Carr managed to overcome his distraction to find a quiet space to write and think. But what about the rest of us, and Net Geners in particular? Have we lost that quiet space as we zip around on the Internet? There is no question that you need to block out distractions to think clearly or to imagine something. And when you are standing in a teeming marketplace of ideas, it is challenging to focus. But it can be done (try meditating), and I believe that the benefits of that huge inflow of information far outweigh the challenges.

What's more, I think the Net Gener is better able than the typical boomer to handle it. I can see from my own children that they know when they have to focus, block out the distractions, and seek a quiet mental place when they need to think deeply. Some of us go for a walk, or sit in front of a fire, or get in the bath to think. It doesn't matter where you do it, as long as you can let your mind work. Personally, when I'm writing I have four tools working and that's it: my word processor, e-mail for communicating with various sources, a wiki for sharing and coediting content with colleagues, and a browser—Google—for finding information. No social networks, no instant messaging, no iTunes, no television, no radio, no games. I'd recommend to any Net Gener that deep thinking is best done using only the tools and information sources that are pertinent. And for breaks I take a walk, resisting my natural temptation to eat something or fire off a few messages on my BlackBerry.

Mental Breaks Are Important, Too

When you're thinking deeply, mental breaks can be productive. We boomers shouldn't kid ourselves: we took lots of breaks at work or at school, coffee breaks or that slow walk to the water cooler. Net Geners take breaks too, Facebook breaks, and I would suggest that's better for you than a shot of caffeine, or certainly a quick cigarette. I think it's better for productivity, much like the way elite athletes must take a break from intense training to rest their muscles on the road to ultimately achieving their best performance.

> "If you're no longer working effectively, a distraction such as Wikipedia or YouTube can help you return to the task with a fresh perspective."
>
> —KEVIN DASILVA, 26, CAMBRIDGE, ONTARIO, CANADA

So I don't believe that multitasking—or more properly, quick switching—is necessarily bad for Net Geners' brains. It may help them. If they can learn to feed off of more sources of information in real time, while they are writing an essay or tackling a complicated problem, I think they're more productive than I was at their age, when I sat down with some textbooks and tried to make sense of them and come up with a novel idea. I think the kids have got it right. Allowing yourself to absorb new bits of information while you're working is not necessarily a distraction. Working this way certainly helps me to develop the capability to think profoundly. Real creative thinking and problem solving just can't be captured in a lab. Our brains are far too complicated and mysterious for that.

CONCLUSION: THE KIDS ARE ALL RIGHT

Over my career, I have listened to thousands of people make dire predictions about what technology will do to young brains. TV was supposed to melt their minds. Video games would turn them into zombies. It hasn't happened. Now I hear people express firm opinions that digital immersion is making kids stupid, without any convincing evidence.

Take Mark Bauerlein, the English professor who wrote *The Dumbest Generation: How the Digital Age Stupefies Young Americans and Jeopardizes Our Future.* The premise of his book is that youth today are stupider than any preceding generation because they spend so much time immersed in digital technology, especially the Internet. But are they really the dumbest generation? Even

Bauerlein has to admit that raw IQ scores have been going up three points a decade since World War II, and that screentime's ability to improve certain visual processing skills may have played a role in the rise in recent years.[41] After noting that inconvenient fact, the professor acknowledges that Net Geners may be "mentally agile" but says they are "culturally ignorant." They don't read the great works of literature, he complains, and their general knowledge is poor—they suffer from what he calls "vigorous indiscriminate ignorance." So now he's arguing that they're not mentally slow, just ignorant. But are Net Geners any more ignorant than boomers were at their age? Apparently not.

The professor hunts for more evidence to support the grandstanding title of his book from school test scores. Yet far from doing worse, American students—at least in grades four through eight—are doing better in math and reading than they did a few years ago.[42] The average scores of seniors haven't changed much for most courses. It seems the professor cannot prove that Net Geners are dumber than earlier generations, so he tries one more time. "No cohort in human history has opened such a fissure between its material conditions and its intellectual attainments," he thunders. "None has experienced so many technological enhancements and yielded so little mental progress."[43] In other words, they should be doing better, presumably because of the Internet. So which is it? The Internet is a force for stupefication or enlightenment?

He didn't convince me. This generation is not dumber. Far from it. Many of the Net Geners are using technology to become smarter than their parents ever could be. As we've seen in this chapter, growing up digital has equipped these Net Geners with the mental skills, such as scanning and quick mental switching, that they'll need to deal with today's overflow of information. I believe they know when they have to focus, just as the most intelligent members of my generation did. They may think and process information in a different way than most boomers do, but that doesn't stop them from coming up with brilliant insights, or new models of doing business and winning an election.

Yet the picture, as we'll see in the next chapter, is a lot more complex. The evidence suggests that the top students are reading more and performing spectacularly well in school. The bottom ones are failing and falling behind—for reasons that have little to do with the Internet and more to do with a failing educational system, problems with the family, poverty, and other social causes.

They would be doing better if the educational system changed to embrace the way they learn, think, and process information. As you'll see in Chapter 5, some educators are changing, but the system is still stuck in the old lecturing mode. I believe that if Net Geners are given the tools to handle the overflow of information available today on the Internet—as some Net Geners already are—they have the potential to be the smartest generation ever. Some are already entering adulthood with the intellectual skills to handle the demands and the opportunities provided by the Internet. Is the whole generation ready? Of course not. But we shouldn't blame technology.

"Technology provides me with the resources to pull in all the loose ends, connect the dots, and learn in the most haphazard and nonlinear fashion imaginable."
—ERIK RUBADEAU, 26, TORONTO

SEVEN GUIDELINES FOR A SHARPER MIND

(1) Work on your wiring—play a new instrument, learn a second language, or pick up a taxi route. You can do it; you have lifelong neuroplasticity on your side.

(2) Work on your wiring the Net Gen way—get fluent with the technology by immersing yourself. Try speed text messaging on your mobile phone (not while driving, of course), using IM and MySpace at the same time, or playing action video games.

(3) Multitask wisely. Don't answer every e-mail instantly; check it in chunks, ideally a few hours apart.

(4) Know when it's best to concentrate on just one task. Deep thought, reflection, critical thinking, innovation, and creativity are fostered best using a single-task focus.

(5) In today's fast-paced, stressed-out world, take a cue from Net Geners and get in the right rhythm of serial focusing. Ramp up to peak performance, then give your brain a break and cool down before ramping up again. It's as simple as: rinse, lather, repeat.

(6) Practice scanning. Instead of trying to read the whole article, or even scanning it in the traditional way, try looking for key words to see whether it's worth even a quick read.

(7) Study how you learn the best. See environments, learning tools (online courses, language immersion programs), and professors, teachers, and mentors who best fit your approach to learning for your specific needs. Customize to maximize your learning capabilities and potential.

⑤

RETHINKING EDUCATION

THE NET GENERATION AS LEARNERS

The video is called *A Vision of Students Today*. One of the hottest hits on YouTube in early 2008, it begins in a gray, empty classroom. The stark room suggests that nothing much has changed since the early nineteenth century, when the blackboard was introduced as a brilliant new way to help students visualize information. But this was made in 2007, and suddenly we see, in full color, the room fill up with students who look bored. One after another, they hold up signs that reflect the views of the 200 students who collaborated on the project, via the Net, at their schools. In less than five minutes, they deliver a stinging indictment of the education system:

"My class size is 115."

"Eighteen percent of my teachers know my name."

"I complete 49 percent of the readings assigned to me."

"I buy $100 textbooks I never open."

"I will read eight books this year, 2,300 Web pages, and 1,281 Facebook profiles."

"I will write 42 pages for class this semester and over 500 pages of e-mails."

"When I graduate, I probably will have a job that doesn't exist today."

Then a student holds up a multiple-choice test form along with a sign: "Filling this out won't get me there."

No kidding.

This remarkable video, created by Kansas State University cultural anthropologist Michael Wesch and 200 student collaborators, points to one of the most profound problems in education today. The Net Geners have grown up digital and they're living in the twenty-first century, but the education system in many places is lagging at least 100 years behind. The model of education that still prevails today was designed for the Industrial Age. It revolves around the teacher who delivers a one-size-fits-all, one-way lecture. The student, working alone, is expected to absorb the content delivered by the teacher. This might have been good for the mass production economy, but it doesn't deliver for challenges of the digital economy, or for the Net Gen mind.

No wonder so many students are spurning it.

As we'll see in this chapter, although this generation is going to college in unprecedented numbers, the United States has a massive dropout problem, both in high school and in college. The consequences are disastrous: high school dropouts are more likely to be unemployed, poor, sick, and alone.[1]

The causes of the dropout disaster are obviously complex, but I believe we can help this generation live up to their potential in this digital world by dumping the Industrial Age model of education and replacing it with a new one.

Instead of focusing on the teacher, the education system should focus on the student.

Instead of lecturing, teachers should interact with students and help them discover for themselves.

Instead of delivering a one-size-fits-all form of education, schools should customize the education to fit each child's individual way of learning.

Instead of isolating students, the schools should encourage them to collaborate.

This can be done. We'll look at some of the teachers who are doing this brilliantly, such as Chris Dede, creator of the River City multiuser visual environment, as well as forward-looking schools in Memphis and in Toronto. These Net Gen–friendly schools that put the student at the center of the learning process are a source of inspiration for all the students out there who are turned off by the classroom. We'll also look at the results so far of putting computers in the schools. And we will report on the move by some of the world's most advanced educators away from broadcast education to a more customized model. We'll end by offering educators some tips on how they can engage their students and start bringing their classrooms into the twenty-first century. If educators follow this advice, I believe they will not only engage students in the classroom (and outside of it) but they will also prepare them for the challenges of the digital economy, which requires different thinking skills than those needed for the Industrial Age.

TWO GENERATIONS: ONE THRIVING, ONE FAILING

This is the story of two generations, both of the same age. On one hand, the Net Generation is poised to become the most educated generation of Americans ever. The percentage of young people enrolling in college rose 50 percent from 1970 to 2003, while the percentage of 25- to 29-year-old Americans with a college degree doubled.[2] In 2006, 35 percent of Americans aged 18–24 were enrolled in a post-secondary school, which ranks the United States fifth in a survey of participating developed (OECD) countries.[3] The Net Generation is the largest, most ethnically diverse, and most female dominant college population to date.[4] They care about their education: the vast majority thinks that having a college degree is more important today than it was for their parents' generation.[5] For a minority who gets into the best universities, school is a wonderful experience. They have access to great professors, small classes, state-of-the-art tools and information resources, and they graduate at a rate close to 100 percent.

This dream ends in disappointment for too many of them—especially kids who are black, Hispanic, or Native American. Nearly half of the young people who enroll in college with high hopes for the future—and often with a big student loan—drop out of college or fail to finish within six years.[6] It's even more depressing when you look at what's happening in schools. One-third of all Americans drop out before finishing high school.[7] According to some analysts, the dropout problem is getting worse.[8]

Yet the kids who are dropping out are only the most visible part of the problem. So many others are not reaching their potential—or arrive at college without the skills they need to succeed. National testing in the United States suggests that over the last decade or so, students have improved in math and other subjects, especially at the Grade 4 and 8 levels. Meanwhile, Grade 12 students have either stayed the same or improved slightly in writing, civics, and history. (The average senior's score declined in science in the last decade, though.) Yet those scores, from the National Assessment of Educational Progress, do not look so good when you compare them with other OECD countries. The average American 15-year-old ranks in the bottom third in math, and at the midpoint in science. The comparison also reveals that the gap between the top students and the most challenged is bigger in the United States than in other OECD countries.[10] What's more, the test scores do not show

FIGURE 5.1   GRADUATES AND DROPOUTS: BOTH ON THE RISE

INCREASING NUMBER OF DROPOUT FACTORIES*

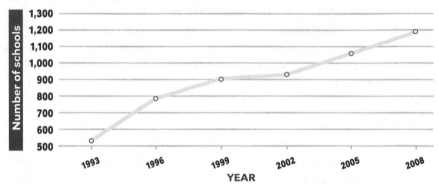

Source: Center for Research on the Education of Students Placed at Risk (CRESPAR)
*Regular or vocational schools with 300 kids or more and at least a 50 percent dropout rate.

INCREASING NUMBER OF COLLEGE GRADUATES*

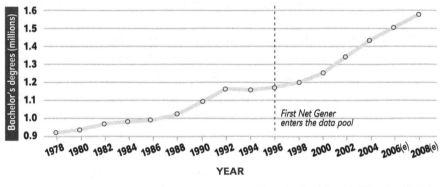

Source: National Center for Educational Statistics
*No. of bachelor's degrees conferred nationally per year in the United States.

whether they can write well enough to succeed in college. About one in five college students had to take remedial reading or writing in college.[11]

Two generations: one thriving, the other failing. This was the theme of a blistering speech I heard on the day my son Alex graduated from one of America's greatest liberal arts institutions, Amherst College. The university's president, Anthony W. Marx, delivered his speech to a couple thousand parents and students as we sat on a magnificent lawn surrounded by nineteenth-century red brick buildings. This was the best education America could offer, but Marx, the author of several books on nation building, chose this occasion to talk about the

education that was given to the other side of America: "Our nation's school system today has reduced itself to Darwinian principles: Make it if you can, those
already advantaged stand first in line, and we will accept widespread failure of
basic opportunities as collateral damage," he said. "American public schools do
not get enough funding to do their job. It is as simple and as embarrassing as
that. Granted, money alone isn't enough and some is surely ill spent. But our
classes are way too big, our teachers are severely underpaid, and the innovators
among them go without additional reward. This is a crime we commit against
ourselves. As a result of this catastrophe, fully half of our public school teachers
quit the profession within just five years of starting out.

"The funding for our K through 12 system is by design regressive. We base it
on property taxes. Schools nearest the wealthy get far more resources than
those in poorer neighborhoods, which instead often need more, not less, to
bring their students up to speed. In America today we spend six times as much
per student in the best funded schools as in the least. This is an astonishing
indictment and a violation of Rawls'[12] and America's ideals."

His conclusion was biting: "The result is that America today is seeing a drop
in educational quality," he said. "Graduation from high schools is down. Our
schools have re-segregated by race, class, and outcomes."

His timing was impeccable. Only a few weeks earlier, a research group led by
Christopher Swanson had issued a devastating report, "Cities in Crisis: A Special
Analytic Report on Graduation." The first chart in the report clearly showed the

FIGURE 5.2   HIGH SCHOOL GRADUATION GAPS

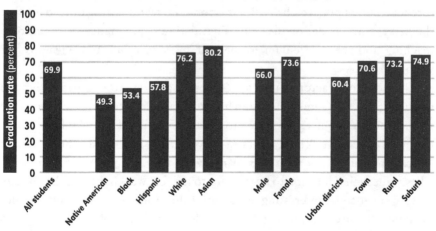

Source: EPE Research Center

difference between growing up in a mostly white suburb and a mostly black or Hispanic inner city.[13] In 2003–2004, the graduation rate was 15 percentage points higher among students living in the suburbs than it was for those in the cities. Over 76 percent of whites graduated, but only 53.4 percent of blacks and 57.8 percent of Hispanics did. Shockingly, fewer than half of Native Americans graduated that year.[14] "If three out of every ten students in the nation failing to graduate is reason for concern, then the fact that just half of those educated in America's largest cities are finishing high school truly raises cause for alarm," Swanson's report concluded. "And the much higher rates of high school completion among their suburban counterparts—who may literally live and attend school right around the corner—place in a particularly harsh and unflattering light the deep undercurrents of inequity that plague American public education."

They're Not Buying the Old Broadcast Learning Product

These deep divisions between rich and poor are a profound, complex and wide-ranging issue. But one thing is clear: You can't blame the kids for dropping out or underperforming, and you certainly can't blame the Internet for any part of this devastating failure. As President Marx points out, underpaid teachers and large class sizes are major culprits. You can also place at a big part of the blame on the model of education that is been foisted on Net Geners. The sad truth, according to a 2006 report by the Gates Foundation, is that most dropouts could have made it. Nearly half who dropped out said classes were either not interesting or just plain boring. Seven out of ten said they weren't motivated to work hard. Of course, there are significant socioeconomic factors: one-third of the dropouts left school to make money, and a significant number left to care for a parent or have a baby. But the boredom factor is a big one, so big that the first recommendation the Gates Foundation paper made was to improve teaching and the curriculum to make it more relevant and engaging for young people.

The boredom factor is not very surprising when you consider the gap between how Net Geners think and how most teachers teach. Net Geners are not content to sit quietly and listen to a teacher lecture. Kids who have grown up digital expect to talk back, to have a conversation. They want a choice in their education, in terms of what they learn, when they learn it, where, and how. They want their education to be relevant to the real world, the one they live in. They want it to be interesting, even fun. Educators may still think the old-fashioned lecture is important, but the kids don't, futurist Marc Prensky told me recently. He remembers one Australian principal who put it this way: "The teachers are no longer the fountain of knowledge; the Internet is."

THE GLOBAL ECONOMY AND DIGITAL AGE REQUIRE NEW ABILITIES

It's not what you know that counts anymore; it's what you can learn. This means that Net Geners need a different form of education than baby boomers had. When baby boomers went to college, they learned a competency or profession, and then moved on to their career. They were set for life. Education and work were separate. The educational model was to cram as much knowledge into your head as possible to build up your inventory of knowledge before you entered the world of work, where you could retrieve that information when needed. This worked in a relatively slow-moving world. But now we're faced with the fast-paced world of the information age, where, as jobs change, you can't take the time to send workers back to school for retraining. We have entered the era of lifelong learning. To adapt Andy Warhol's famous comment, today you're set for all of 15 minutes; if you are studying a technical topic at a university, half of what you learned in your freshman year might be obsolete by the time you graduate. On the job, employees must reinvent their knowledge base repeatedly as they move from one career to the next.

The ability to learn new things is more important than ever in a world where you have to process new information at lightning speed. Students need to be able to think creatively, critically, and collaboratively; to master the "basics" and excel in reading, math, science, and information literacy, and respond to opportunities and challenges with speed, agility, and innovation. Students need to expand their knowledge beyond the doors of their local community to become responsible and contributing global citizens in the increasingly complex world economy.

OLD PARADIGMS ARE HARD TO CHANGE

Progressive educators around the world are talking about changing the pedagogy to fit the demands of the fast-moving twenty-first century, a world in which the ability to think and learn and find out things is more important than mastering a static body of knowledge. Luis M. Proenza, president of the University of Akron, clearly gets it. "The time has come for some far reaching changes to the university, our model of pedagogy, how we operate, and our relationship to the rest of the world," he told me. "But we need to listen to these Net Generation students to see the way forward."

Yet the Industrial Age model of education will be hard to change. I received a lesson on this one day after delivering a dinner speech to a group of university presidents. At the end of my talk on what's wrong with the universities and how education needs to change, I received a polite, even encouraging, round of applause and returned to my table.

I asked the group of distinguished educators sitting with me why the shift to a new model was taking so long. One president said, "The problem is funds—we just don't have the money to reinvent the model of pedagogy." Another said, "Models of learning that go back decades are hard to change." Another got a chuckle around the table when he said, "I think the problem is the faculty—their average age is 57 and they're teaching in a 'post-Gutenberg'[15] mode."

A very thoughtful man named Jeffery Bannister, who at the time was president of Butler College, was seated next to me. "*Post*-Gutenberg?" he said. "I don't think so! At least not at Butler. Our model of learning is *pre*-Gutenberg! We've got a bunch of professors reading from handwritten notes, writing on blackboards, and the students are writing down what they say. This is a pre-Gutenberg model—the printing press is not even an important part of the learning paradigm." He added, "Wait 'til these students who are 14 and have grown up learning on the Net hit the [college] classrooms—sparks are going to fly."

Bannister, a wise man who, sadly, has since passed away, was absolutely right. Old paradigms die hard. The Industrial Age model of pedagogy is so embedded in everyday practice in America's schools that truly changing it will take time. A 2007 study on the quality of students' experiences in 2,500 of our nation's elementary school classrooms, for instance, found that students were spending the vast majority of their classroom time listening to the teacher or working alone on low-level math or reading worksheets.[16] Or consider the schedule for the majority of American high schoolers: they're running from class to class at the sound of a bell approximately every 40 minutes. For one period, they're memorizing formulas on related rates in calculus from one teacher in the math department; the next period they're regurgitating marine life taxonomy in biology from another teacher in the science department; the period after that they're taking notes about *Moby-Dick* with a teacher from the language arts department; and so on. Each time, the learning is interrupted by that bell. As Marshall McLuhan said in 1967: "Today's child is bewildered when he enters the nineteenth-century environment that still characterizes the educational establishment, where information is scarce but ordered and structured by fragmented, classified patters, subjects, and schedules."

Not much has changed in the educational system since then.

The U.S. Government's Answer: Does It Prepare Kids for the Twenty-First Century?

In the United States, the government's answer to the education crisis has not fixed the problem. While everyone wants kids to improve their math and reading skills,[17] the latest federal legislation, called No Child Left Behind, will in some ways worsen the gap between rich and poor, in terms of preparing them for the twenty-first-century digital world. The federal law that set up this system leaves it to individual states to set standards and test the kids, usually via a standardized multiple-choice test. Schools, especially those in underprivileged areas, have switched their focus to preparing kids to pass the tests, because principals of poorly performing schools could be ejected from their jobs.[18]

Now I'm not against *all* forms of testing. But is testing to assess what kids remember and what skills they have the right approach for today's digital economy? I doubt it. Take reading. The ability to read a text on paper is somewhat different from the ability to read and search online. A good conventional reader understands what she has read, and repeats it if necessary. She connects what she's reading to what she already knows and synthesizes the information.

But as Donald Leu, codirector of the New Literacies Research Lab at the University of Connecticut, has found the skills needed for effective reading of books are different from those you need to read effectively online.

The state reading tests do not measure online reading skills, he notes. They only measure the ability to read text on paper. So, Leu argues, the No Child Left Behind legislation has a perverse effect. It was designed to close the gap between rich and poor schools, to put the kids in poorer neighborhoods, which tend to produce more dropouts and poor academic results, on the same playing field as the kids in the white suburbs. But the result is that the kids in the poor neighborhoods—who have the least access to the Internet at home—are now turning away from Internet skill development to focus on the traditional reading skills. Meanwhile, kids in the affluent white neighborhoods, who have no problem passing the state math and reading tests, are devoting more time to developing the critical skills they need to master reading online. "So the rich are getting richer and the poor are getting poorer in terms on online reading skills. It's clear as light, and there's no way to measure the gap," says Leu.

That's not the only problem, either. A July 2007 report showed that nearly half of the districts surveyed had cut instruction time in social studies, science, art, music, and physical education from their curriculum in favor of those subjects that are tested, like reading and math.[19] Forty percent of school districts in America have eliminated recess.[20] That hardly helps in the battle against one of the nation's current health problems, childhood obesity.[21] What's more, exercise, as John Ratey, professor at Harvard Medical School and author of *Spark: The Revolutionary New Science of Exercise and the Brain*, suggests, may actually prime the brain for learning.[22]

WHAT WORKS? FOCUS ON THE STUDENT, NOT THE TEACHER

If schools were a business that was routinely losing one-third of its customers—and half in some places—I suspect the board of directors would insist on some fundamental changes, or simply fire the CEO. So why doesn't the school system do what some of the leading customer-faced companies are doing today? Focus on the customer, or in this case, the student. It sounds simple, but, as many companies have found, focusing on the customer requires a deep change throughout the organization. This means changing the relationship between student and teacher in the learning process. To focus on the student, educators must abandon the old system in which the teacher delivers the lecture, the same lecture to all students. First, teachers have to step off the stage and start listening and conversing instead of just lecturing. In other words, they have to abandon their broadcast style and adopt an interactive one. Second, they should encourage students to discover for themselves, and learn a process of discovery and critical thinking instead of just memorizing the teacher's information. Third, they need to encourage students to collaborate among themselves and with others outside the school. Finally, they need to tailor the style of education to their students' individual learning styles.

Some leading educators are calling for this kind of massive change; one of these is Richard Sweeney, university librarian at the New Jersey Institute of Technology. He says the education model has to change to suit this generation of students. Smart but impatient, they like to collaborate and they reject one-way lectures, he notes. While some educators view this as pandering to a generation, Sweeney is firm: "They want to learn, but they want to learn only what they have to learn, and they want to learn it in a style that is best for them."[23]

FROM BROADCAST TO INTERACTIVE LEARNING

The old system is what I call one-size-fits-all, one-way broadcast learning. It was designed for the Industrial Age, when industry needed workers who did what they were told. The teacher was the sage, and he or she was supposed to deliver knowledge to the grateful students, who were expected to write down the sage's words and deliver it back to them, often word for word, in exams if they wanted to score an A. Unusual questions were not appreciated. When I was in the second grade, for instance, I asked, "Why is there snow at the top of the mountain when it's actually closer to the sun?" The annoyed teacher told my mother that I probably wouldn't graduate from high school, and I certainly wouldn't amount to much.

In the old model, the teacher is the broadcaster. A broadcast is by definition the transmission of information from transmitter to receiver in a one-way, linear fashion. The teacher is the transmitter and student is a receptor in the learning process. The formula goes like this: I'm a teacher (or professor) and I have knowledge. You're a student and you don't. Get ready, here it comes. Your goal is to take this data into your short-term memory and through practice and repetition build deeper cognitive structures so you can recall it to me when I test you. As I often tell educational audiences, the definition of a lecture is the process in which the notes of the teacher go to the notes of the student without going through the brains of either. As someone who gives many lectures a year, I appreciate the irony of this view.[24]

So is it any surprise that teacher-broadcasters and TV broadcasters are both losing their audience? Kids who have grown up digital are abandoning one-way TV for the higher stimulus of interactive communication they find on the Internet. Sitting mutely in front of a TV set—or a teacher—doesn't appeal to this generation. But unlike the entertainment world, the educational establishment doesn't offer enough alternatives to the one-way broadcast.

There are shining examples of interactive education, though. Dr. Maria Terrell teaches calculus at Cornell University, and she definitely does not stand at the front of the class and draw on the blackboard. In the classroom with 22 students, she walks up and down the rows of desks as the class is finishing "warm-up questions" that have been assigned before class. "Talk about your answer with your neighbors," she tells the students. "Justify your answer with a theorem. No looking in your textbook."

She works the aisles like a dynamic game-show host, jumping in occasionally to help out. When one student says he has no idea how to answer the question, Dr. Terrell interjects, "Well, you do have some idea from your knowledge. Draw a picture . . ." Later, she takes the spotlight at the front of the class, jotting down the student's thoughts about how to solve the

> "Getting a chance to be able to talk to our peers and understand their way of thinking about the math and explaining how we think is cool."
> —KEENAN BORDE, 19, ITHACA, NEW YORK

problem. "Any more ideas?" No one has any. "Keenan, your stuff looks so good there," she says, eyeballing one of the students. "Do you want to put it on the board?" "No," says Keenan. "Awww, come on . . . ," Terrell says in her most persuasive game-show tone. The student, egged on by the entire class, reluctantly approaches the board, and draws the theorem and explains his answer.

At Cornell, this interactive method has been integrated into the introductory calculus courses through a National Science Foundation grant–funded program called "Good Questions."[25] One strategy being used in this program is called just-in-time teaching; it is a teaching and learning strategy that combines the benefits of Web-based assignments and an active-learner classroom where courses are customized to the particular needs of the class. Warm-up questions, written by the students, are typically due a few hours before class, giving the teacher an opportunity to adjust the lesson "just in time," so that classroom time can be focused on the parts of the assignments that students struggled with. Harvard professor Eric Mazur, who uses this approach in his physics class, puts it this way: "Education is so much more than the mere transfer of information. The information has to be assimilated. Students have to connect the information to what they already know, develop mental models, learn how to apply the new knowledge, and how to adapt this knowledge to new and unfamiliar situations."[26]

This technique produces real results. A study of 350 Cornell students evaluated the impact of a key part of the Good Questions program, called "deep questions," which elicit higher order thinking. Students who were asked "deep questions" and participated in frequent peer discussion scored noticeably higher on their math exams than students who were not asked deep questions or who had little to no chance for peer discussion. Dr. Terrell explains: "It's when the students talk about what they think is going on and why, that's where the biggest learning occurs for them. . . . You can hear people sort of saying, 'Oh I see, I get it.' . . . And then they're explaining it to somebody else . . . and there's an authentic understanding of what's going on. So much better than what would happen if I, as the teacher person, explain it. There's something that happens with this peer instruction."

FIGURE 5.3   MORE WOMEN ARE GRADUATING FROM COLLEGE

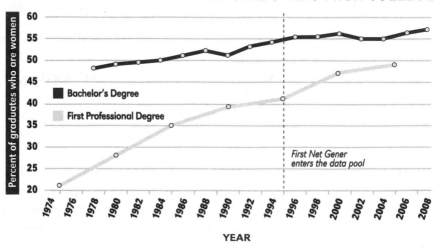

Source: National Center for Educational Statistics

*First professional degree includes the fields of dentistry (D.D.S. or D.M.D.), medicine (M.D.), optometry (O.D.), osteopathic medicine (D.O.), pharmacy (D. Phar.), podiatric medicine (D.P.M.), veterinary medicine (D.V.M.), chiropractic medicine (D.C. or D.C.M.), law (J.D.), and the theological professions (M. Div. or M.H.L.).

Interactive education enables students to learn at their own pace. I saw this myself back in the mid-1970s when I was taking a statistics course for my graduate degree in educational psychology at the University of Alberta. It was one of the first classes conducted online—an educational groundbreaker from Dr. Steve Hunka, a visionary in computer-mediated education. This was before PCs, so we sat down in front of a computer terminal that was connected to a computer-controlled slide display. I could stop at any time and review, and test myself to see how I was doing. The exam was online too. There were no lectures. Just as well: the statistics lecture is by definition a bust. Instead, we got face-to-face time with Dr. Hunka, who was freed up from lecturing to spend time with us one-on-one.

Back then, online learning was expensive, but today the tools on the Net make it a great way to teach kids and free up the teacher to design the learning experience and converse with the students on an individual and more meaningful basis. It works. The research evidence is very strong and growing. As one extensive report described over a decade ago:

"Compared with students enrolled in conventionally taught courses, students who use well-crafted computer-mediated instruction ... generally achieve higher scores on summary examinations, learn their lessons in less time, like their classes more, and develop more positive attitudes towards the subject matter they're learning. These results hold for a broad range of students stretching from elementary to college students, studying across a broad range of disciplines, from mathematics to the social sciences to the humanities."[28]

FIGURE 5.4   BROADCAST LEARNING VERSUS
             INTERACTIVE LEARNING

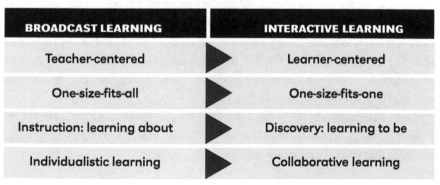

BROADCAST LEARNING	INTERACTIVE LEARNING
Teacher-centered	Learner-centered
One-size-fits-all	One-size-fits-one
Instruction: learning about	Discovery: learning to be
Individualistic learning	Collaborative learning

FROM INSTRUCTION TO DISCOVERY

Schools should be places to learn, not to teach. Net Geners need to learn how to look for information, analyze and synthesize it, and critically evaluate the information they find. This may sound obvious, but it's not what's happening in most classrooms. In the old model, students were expected to absorb vast quantities of content—some was relevant but most was not relevant to real life. A spectacular memory, and a gritty determination, helped if you wanted to score an A. Education was about absorbing content—provided only by the teacher, mind you. But now that students can obviously find the facts they're looking for in an instant, this old model doesn't make any sense. It's not what you know that really counts; it's how you navigate in the digital world, and what you do with the information you discover. This new style of learning, I believe, will suit them. Net Geners, immersed in digital technology, are keen to try new things, often at high speed. They want school to be fun and interesting.

> "I always just took information for granted before. I thought well it's in a book, it must be right. . . . But now I started to question, "What's the value of learning this right now?"[30]
>
> —CHERRIE KONG, 18, AUCKLAND, NEW ZEALAND

So they should enjoy the delight of discovering things for themselves. As Seymour Papert, one of the world's foremost experts on how technology can provide new ways to learn, put it: "The scandal of education is that every time you teach something, you deprive a child of the pleasure and benefit of discovery."[29]

John Seely Brown, a director emeritus of Xerox PARC and a visiting scholar at USC, noticed that when a child first learns how to speak, she or he is totally immersed in a social context and highly motivated to engage in learning this new, amazingly complex system of language. It got him to thinking that "once you start going to school, in some ways you start to learn much slower because you are being taught, rather than what happens if you're learning in order to do things that you yourself care about. . . . Very often just going deeply into one or two topics that you really care about lets you appreciate the awe of the world . . . once you learn to honor the mysteries of the world, you're kind of always willing to probe things . . . you can actually be joyful about discovering something you didn't know . . . and you can expect always to need to keep probing. And so that sets the stage for lifelong inquiry."

Seely Brown also hypothesizes that the most important skill to learn for the twenty-first century is to hold the weight of the world around us in awe and embrace this world of constant change.

"The fundamental mantra in the Singapore education system is 'teach less, learn more,' " Seely Brown continues. "And so the teachers in their school systems, I'd say, spend much, much less time teaching and everything kind of now turns around the notion of inquiry method ... stu-

"Most useful education for the future is not happening at school. It's happening after school, particularly in personal robotic clubs, etc., and on the entire Internet—it's happening in games. It's not on a test . . . So they go to what is really turning them on."
—*MARC PRENSKY, SOCIAL CRITIC*

dents explore in groups . . . teacher becomes a mentor . . . it's an amazing experience to go inside one of these classrooms and see that basically the classrooms are being run by the kids."

Look to the "edge" of the formal education system—the Robotics club, for instance—and you might actually be shocked at what you can learn. For instance, "tinkering" has made a comeback. The boomer generation used to play with stuff to get a sense of how things break, how they fit together, and how to fix them. "You got a real sense of how things work together to create a whole in a very wonderful, if not mysterious way that sets the foundation for a path of understanding of how complex systems work," says Seely Brown. "And that foundation turns out to be immensely useful when you move into formal learning . . . because of your tinkering, you were capable of taking the abstract notions you were being taught in school, and almost unconsciously map them back and begin to under-

"I joined the Science Olympiad and I was on the tower-building teams. It was so fun."
—*JOCELYN SVENGSOUK, 20, PRINCETON, NEW JERSEY*

stand how to explain things that you didn't quite understand when you were tinkering, but you saw kind of how things worked out anyway. Suddenly, you begin to understand why things worked out and why they didn't."

Changes in technology that happened around 1980, like computer chips in cars, prohibited a whole generation from tinkering. Then, beginning in 1995 with the Internet and today's Web 2.0 participatory tools, tinkering has come back full force, though now it's virtual and social tinkering, rather than mechanical tinkering.

The discovery mode is getting into some advanced classrooms. Harvard professor Chris Dede is the creator of "River City," a multiuser virtual environment (MUVE) in which students go back in time to solve mysteries in nineteenth-century America. Students are asked questions like "Why are poor people getting sick in much greater proportion than rich people?" They experiment in River City's virtual town by taking water samples, examining the effects of pollution on the water, tracing hospital admissions, measuring population density by socio-economic status, etc. Students' investigations are facilitated by teachers both in the virtual world and in real-life group interpretive sessions. Research on the use of River City has shown that it motivates all learners, especially lower-achievement students who were previously unengaged, to become immersed in student-directed, nonlinear learning to actively construct their own knowledge. Teachers believe the experience helps their students to become aware of inquiry methods and to develop research skills and an understanding of experimental design.[31,32]

When Barry Joseph tried to convince a New York City high school to let kids learn how to create video games after school, he met stiff resistance from educational authorities: "As our executive director likes to say, it was like trying to convince them to bring porn into the classroom."

But Joseph, the director of Global Kids Online Leadership Program, persisted. With a grant from Microsoft Corporation's U.S. Partners in Learning, plus help from staff and the gaming company Gamelab, he set up an after-school program called Playing 4 Keeps to teach kids how to create socially conscious video games. High school students worked with professional game developers to create a game. They called it Ayiti: The Cost of Life, and it challenges the player to manage the life of an impoverished family in Haiti, and attend to their health, education, and employment. Over 1.5 million people have played the game since it was launched in 2006.

Creating a game like this, Joseph says, encourages twenty-first-century learning skills, such as deep, critical thinking. "Building games and critically playing games (empowers) the youth in our programs to use games as a means to express themselves and educate others while training them to be critical consumers of the games they play," Joseph reports. "Games can teach players to develop critical thinking, comprehend sophisticated models of the world, understand complex systems theory, and more."

Students can reach this level of deep thinking because they're so engaged in the experience of creating an online, interactive game, he says: "It takes them further. You're not dragging them along; you're often running after them."

Creating a game and watching other players play it also has an important impact on the students' sense of self, Joseph says. "It means they see themselves as producers"—just like the professional game designers they're working with.

Creating games, in other words, is a powerful way to learn how to learn.

FROM INDIVIDUAL TO COLLABORATIVE LEARNING

Every boomer can remember the silence in the vast exam room at school, where the only sound was the shuffling of papers and the nervous shifting in dozens of hard seats. This was the make-or-break moment; you were on your own. Your individual mastery of the course material was to be tested, and you weren't allowed to talk or share information. Although we had study groups for some courses, the idea that you might collaborate on an essay was strictly forbidden. In fact, it was not unusual for students in law schools to hide crucial information from each other.

This do-it-on-your-own attitude still prevails in many school systems. In the spring of 2008 at Toronto's Ryerson University, not far from where I live, first-year engineering student Chris Avenir set up a Facebook group called Dungeons/Mastering Chemistry. It was pretty popular: 147 students shared tips on surviving assignments that were worth 10 percent of their grade. The teacher, who had told the students to do the work alone, was not impressed when he found out about the group. The university threatened to expel Avenir. The students were outraged; one of the Web sites supporting Avenir was even selling "Chris Didn't Cheat" T-shirts for $19.99. The university eventually backed down, but Avenir received a failing grade for his homework assignments.

This incident has shone a light on the gap between the students and the university teachers and administration. The individual learning model is foreign territory for most Net Geners, who have grown up collaborating, sharing, and creating together online. Progressive educators are recognizing this. Students start internalizing what they've learned in class only once they start talking to each other, says Xerox PARC's Seely Brown: "The whole notion of passively sitting and receiving information has almost nothing to do with how you internalize information into something that makes sense to you. Learning starts as you leave the classroom, when you start discussing with people around you what was just said. It is in conversation that you start to internalize what some piece of information meant to you."[33]

Students need to talk among themselves. In fact, research has found collaborative learning to be more effective in increasing academic performance than individual or competitive learning.[34] Dennis Harper, founder of the GenYES program, says: "If a 50-year-old teacher takes a Web development class and produces a Web site on the Civil War for their 13-year-old kids and then a 13-year-old kid makes a Web site on the Civil War, assuming they have the same content, which one do you think that the 13-year-olds are going to learn better from? We've found over and over again, the one made by the peer

"I feel the hands-on approach, with open discussion and honest critiques, is the best way of learning. It can be harsh at times, but it builds confidence and allows for collaboration with peers."

—NICK DUBOIS, 25, BUFFALO, NEW YORK

is going to be much more relevant: the music, the background, everything. Why not train the kids to do this?"

Wikis, open-source Web pages that anyone can add to or edit, are not only useful for students working on peer collaboration projects; they can also connect teachers to each other and to course management systems so that they can easily collaborate on reference lists, instructional strategies, etc.[35] There are even wikis devoted to teaching educators how to use wikis in the classroom, with pages describing how to create a wiki, wikietiquette, developing curricula, privacy and security on the wiki, and assessment of the technology (that is, wikis4education[36]).

Collaborating can help students gain empathy for people from different cultures. The Horizon Project is a joint venture among five classes ranging from grades 10 through 12 and including students from the United States, Darfur, Bangladesh, Australia, Austria, and China.[37] It's a great effort, which I have supported in various ways. The project, led by teachers Vicki Davis and Julie Lindsay, uses Skype, blogs, YouTube, Google Notebook, Flickr, Facebook, and MySpace to help students create a digital story based on the themes of Thomas Friedman's *The World Is Flat*.

"The classroom in Bangladesh had primarily students from a Muslim background while the U.S. students were primarily from a Christian background," said Davis. "At the beginning of the project there were many fears. Muslim students wondered 'What if they think we're all terrorists?,' while American students questioned portrayals of Muslims in America. But after about two weeks, students came up to me and said, 'You know what, the news media is lying to us. These kids are great and they are just like us. Attus actually listens to the same music we do (Red Hot Chili Peppers).' My students have really changed in their viewpoints. . . . When we can build bridges between individual students that our future can walk across . . . that's really the hope that we have for America . . . so that students can work together on any subject."

MIT: Opening the Door to a World of Discovery

In 2007, all of the 1,800 courses taught at the Massachusetts Institute of Technology (MIT) were posted on the Web for people all over the world to access through the Open Educational Resources (OER) movement. So anyone can now get MIT's Sustainable Energy Chemical Engineering course syllabus, lectures, notes, assignments, video, audio, etc., from the Internet for free. The university believes that by opening up their intellectual property to the world, they will help advance the frontiers of knowledge.

This decision has had a surprising effect on the kids who are actually on campus. As Xerox PARC's John Seely Brown discovered, most of them don't go to class anymore. They pick up the class material on the Internet and talk about it in study groups.

In their spare time, the MIT students said, they build things. They tinker. MIT is probably one of the greatest places in the world to build things because it offers its students extraordinary tools, equipment, and support.

Most of the students Seely Brown interviewed "were just totally immersed in a different form of learning." The new learning environment was enabled not only by the open courseware, but also by the study groups and the open attitude of MIT, which effectively says "if you want to engage in research projects, even in your freshman year, that's fine with us. Go find people to do it with and we will go along with you."

FROM ONE-SIZE-FITS-ALL TO ONE-SIZE-FITS-ONE

Mass education was a product of the industrial economy. It came along with mass production, mass marketing, and the mass media."[38] Schooling, says Howard Gardner, is a mass-production idea. "You teach the same thing to students in the same way and assess them all in the same way." Pedagogy is based on the questionable idea that optimal learning experiences can be constructed for groups of learners at the same chronological age. In this view, a curriculum is developed based on predigested information and structured for optimal transmission. If the curriculum is well structured and interesting, then large proportions of students at any given grade level will "tune in" and get engaged with the information. But too often it doesn't work out that way.

This mass-education idea, however, is being challenged. Students are individuals who have individual ways of learning and absorbing information. Some are visual learners; others learn by listening. Still others learn by physically manipulating something (these are the kids who need to get up and move around while they're in class or doing homework). "If the factory was the model of the typical twentieth-century American school, the craftsman's shop or artist's studio is the model for a twenty-first-century educational delivery system,"[39] argues a 2007 report from the 2020 Vision: Brighton Central School District, Brighton, New York. Or maybe the model for the twenty-first century is the one-room schoolhouse of yesteryear, where teachers had to customize education for each child in the room.

Advanced schools, like the 30 high schools in the Middle College National Consortium, adapt their educational style to take account of how each student prefers to learn. Middle College High School in Memphis, Tennessee, for instance, has 250 students in grades 9 through 12. It's a diverse student population, which includes kids with academic ability who have fallen through the cracks, kids with behavioral issues, and academic achievers who are too quirky to fit into a big high school. The teachers know about each kid's learning style from their entrance interviews and from the learning inventory each child has filled out to describe how she or he learns best. Teachers play off those learning styles in class by offering kids many different ways to learn—not just via a textbook, but by experiencing things outside the school.

One of the big projects in 2008 was a performance about the civil rights movement to mark the fortieth anniversary of the Reverend Martin Luther King Jr.'s death—a highly pertinent topic at a time when a black politician was making history in the Democratic primary contest. This was a classic example that highlights the new pedagogy that I'm advocating. For starters, the children had lots of different ways to investigate the topic—not just by reading books and Web sites, but by visiting the local civil rights museum, and by listening to the school secretary, Miss Kay Teel, describe what it was like to be in Memphis in the 1960s. Then the students worked together with the teacher to construct the outline of the performance. This was a collaboration. The teacher did not rule the show. Each student could contribute in different ways. "Some sang the songs, others wrote the script, created digital pieces, and contributed in many other ways. For the most part, the kids had the freedom to choose what they wanted to do," says principal Michelle Brantley-Patterson.

The big payoff came on performance day, when the kids from *other schools* came and watched and loved it. "I saw so much confidence in our kids," said Brantley-Patterson. "That's why you get up in the morning. It's contagious. You don't get that from fill-in-the-blanks tests or from lecturing."

Another way that the Memphis school customizes education is through the self-directed improvement system developed by social psychologist Dr. Jeff Howard, founder of the Efficacy Institute. In math class it gives kids the tools to check their own progress against a set criteria. It's made a big difference in class. "The kids know what they have to work on, and kids are showing kids how to master difficult skills," says Brantley-Patterson. Since Middle College implemented Howard's "Self-directed Improvement System" using their own data, the percentage of kids passing Tennessee's required math assessment for graduation has shot up from 68 percent to 86 percent.

The idea of customized education is spreading to schools across the United States. EdVisions, funded by the Gates Foundation and based on individual-centered learning, has over 40 high schools across the country. The Big Picture Company has designed nearly 50 schools on the basis of "one student at a time" and even has free online software to help students and educators monitor their progress. Student-centered programs like these have won kudos. A metastudy of 76 dissertations and other studies found that matching learning style with complementary instruction techniques improved both academic achievement and attitudes toward learning.[40]

One of the leading advocates of customized education in the United States is Carol Ann Tomlinson, author of *The Differentiated Classroom: Responding to the Needs of All Learners*, and dozens of other books and articles. In the old days, she observed, teachers thought that the best way to learn was through repetition, drills. "Now we understand more fully the role of the brain in learning—the need for students to make sense of what they learn," she told *Education World*. "Differentiation focuses also on helping students understand ideas and apply skills so that they develop frameworks of meaning that allow them to retain and transfer what they study."

Thomlinson continued, "I think kids are keenly aware of differences among themselves. "I think they fully understand they are not cookie cutter images of one another. They see that in many facets of their lives. When teachers engage kids in talking about their particular strengths, weaknesses, interests, and ways of learning—and in developing a classroom where everyone gets the help and support they need to grow as much as possible—I see kids who are very enthusiastic about that approach to teaching and learning." But this cannot happen in a classroom where teachers spend most of the time lecturing, she noted. The classroom has to focus on the student. The teacher has to be quick and flexible to adapt to the students' different learning styles.

"Become a kid watcher," Tomlinson advises teachers. "Study the kids in any way you can. Learn to see them as individuals rather than a group. Ask them how the class is working for them and how to make it work better. Then begin to respond to what you see. Each step you take will teach you, if you want to learn. If you combine that with regular pre-assessment of student competencies and begin to think about teaching with student needs in mind, you'll be off to a great start."[41]

Should We Be Training University Students Only for the Twenty-First-Century High-Tech Business World? Or Is Liberal Arts Still Important?

At the turn of the century, some of the members of the government of Ontario, Canada's most populous province, complained publicly about the value of a liberal arts education. They clearly thought a BA was a waste of time; government money should flow instead to practical courses preparing kids for a career in business.

I felt strongly that this attitude was wrong. A liberal arts education is a great way to train the mind to master precisely the kinds of skills you need to navigate in this digital world. So I hatched a counterattack with one of Canada's most famous radio hosts, the late Peter Gzowski, then the chancellor of Trent University, a liberal arts college. We asked Canada's most senior high-tech CEOs to endorse a public call for proper funding of liberal arts and science courses in Canadian universities. Of the 35 executives who received my e-mail, 31 signed the statement within 48 hours.

Many of the CEOs who supported the public statement had a liberal arts and science undergraduate education themselves. Some said their companies don't need people with just technical skills. They needed people who could think, synthesize ideas, communicate, place things in context, and understand the relationships among ideas.

For college students, some of what they learn in their freshman year may already be obsolete by the time they graduate. That's why liberal arts coupled with science training is so important: you learn how to learn, how to make sense of things that change. It certainly helped me. Whatever success I have had in the high-technology world is attributable to my liberal arts experience.

NOW THAT COMPUTERS ARE IN SOME SCHOOLS, HOW'S IT WORKING OUT?

Schools have come a long way toward integrating computers into the classroom in the last 10 years. Today, almost every American school provides Internet access and about 95 percent of schools have high-speed connections. By 2006, one in four schools were in the process of transitioning to a 1:1 environment, where every student and teacher would have his or her own wireless computing device for use at school and at home. Few of them were in this position in 2003.[42] The nation's digital schools are going wireless as students themselves increasingly access the Internet via mobile devices.[43]

What kind of impact has this had? Several studies suggest that computers in schools have not improved academic performance.[45] One of the negative studies is a 2007 U.S. Department of Education report covering over 9,000 students that assessed the effectiveness of 15 educational software products. The study concluded that after one year of testing there were no significant differences in academic achievement (as measured by scores on standardized tests) between students who used educational software and their peers who didn't.[46] However, this study examined only a limited number of educational tools, not the full range, so the study is far from definitive. What we do know is that nearly 9 in 10 school districts that had ubiquitous computing environments reported a positive impact on academics.

"There is a new fervor in American education, a new creativity—driven in part by this generation of tech-savvy students."

—ROD PAIGE, FORMER SECRETARY, U.S. DEPARTMENT OF EDUCATION (2005)[44]

There are more bright lights of hope, too: a multiyear assessment of SimCalc, interactive algebra software, showed that seventh grade kids in Texas improved their performance from the fiftieth percentile to the eightieth percentile on a proficiency test of math concepts, as a result of working with the software.[47] Other schools report better relations with teachers, better teamwork, and improved attitude and behavior.

One of the most dramatic changes occurred in Cowansville, a small city in the Eastern Townships, Quebec, a few miles north of the Vermont-Canada border. After the school board gave laptops to each kid from grade 3 to grade 6, the percentage of students reading or writing at a competent level for their age went up 12 percent! Absenteeism went down 26 percent, and behavioral incidents dropped 34 percent.[48] The impact of computers went far beyond these impressive statistics, according to Ron Canuel, director general of the Eastern Townships School Board. He tells the story of a boy with attention deficit disorder who had very serious behavioral problems. After the child was given a laptop, teachers started complaining that he was writing *too* much. "I was touring [his] school one day and he showed me a purple guitar," said Canuel. "He was trying to learn how to play 'Smoke on the Water' by Deep Purple, and I said, 'Oh, I know that song.' He looked at me with like eyes big (like I'm supposed to be somewhere between dead and gruesome) and says, 'Wow, you know that?' Well, since then, every few months he sends me poetry that he writes."

So how's it working out overall? Judging from the studies, I believe computers can't live up to their potential as an educational tool if they are deployed in the old-fashioned educational system that relied on teachers to deliver content. Jim Goodnight, CEO of SAS, a world leader in business intelligence, puts it this way: "You can't just throw computers in the schools and hope that they will be used properly. You need a Web-based curriculum for teachers." SAS is showing teachers the technology they can use to change teaching. "The teacher becomes more of a mentor than an instructor," he said. The technology will help the teacher keep track of how each student is doing.

If teachers and educators listen and change their approach to education in ways that I have described in this chapter, they'll find that computers can be an extraordinary teaching tool.[49]

THE 2.0 SCHOOL

Time and time again I've seen schools begin the process of turning into a truly student-centered place of learning and discovery only to face the hard wall of entrenched thinking about education. There are some terrific stories to be told, but students won't be prepared for the world of today unless schools use technology to implement real change to their model of education. Indeed, change in any institution is a tremendous challenge, but especially in the world of education.

Take Wellington Girls' College in Wellington, New Zealand. It was a standard teacher-gives-the-lecture kind of school until Margaret McLeod became principal in the late 1990s. She is a forward-thinking educator who knew that the old industrial model of education wouldn't prepare the girls for the digital world. So when her school brought computers into the classroom, McLeod hoped the technology would be the catalyst to change the educational model and make it a shining example of the 2.0 school—the kind of school that embraces the characteristics I have been describing.

You Can Be a New Teacher, Even after 50!

I was at a cocktail party and an older woman in her sixties came up to me and said, "I'd like to meet you; you've changed my life. I read *Growing Up Digital* and heard you give a speech and I decided I was going to do this in my classroom. I'm a math teacher in an independent school and I've been giving math lectures for more than 30 years. I got support from the administration, from local technology companies, and from parents to get laptops into the classroom. I worked with some software people to move the math curriculum to an interactive, self-paced model." She continued, "I am now a new woman. I know more about every one of those kids after a month than I did about any individual in years past. The kids love math; scores are up. I can hardly wait to get up in the morning to go to work!"

—Briony Cayley, math teacher at Bishop Straughn School in Toronto

There was just one problem: Many of the teachers didn't know how to use computers. Those who did weren't nearly as computer literate as the students, which caused understandable frustration on all sides. Then a brilliant idea emerged: Turn the students into teachers. Get the students who know how to use computers to teach the teachers who don't. So Tech Angels was born. A group of girls received sophisticated computer training, and they developed and delivered a lesson on what they learned to teachers, on a one-on-one basis. They taught the teachers everything from how to turn on a computer to how to create a Web site. Tech Angels was, the school said, a "revolutionary" approach to education because it acknowledged that the kids were authorities on how to interact with a personal computer.

The role reversal attracted plenty of interest from educators, parents, students, and the media. The students told entertaining stories about what their teachers were like as students. "All the things they tell you not to do in class, they do," said Cherrie Kong, the lead Tech Angel, in 2003. "They talk, they gossip, they interrupt. I've even been tempted to expel a few! But seriously, you see them as real people, which is part of growing up." The teachers acknowledged that students benefited too. "Part of what's really good about the Tech Angels program," teacher Ann Coster said, "is seeing students grow in confidence and maturity because they have something to give that's important to the teacher and the relationship changes."[50]

But was it a revolution? A 2006 review of the program for the New Zealand Council for Educational Research was skeptical. Many of the teachers did not share McLeod's enthusiasm for fundamentally changing the education system to prepare girls in a new way for the twenty-first century. Many didn't understand or share her vision.[51] They just thought the girls were giving them practical assistance to learn some new computer skills. They didn't see the Tech Angels as a catalyst to change the way they teach. Because McLeod, who left the school in 2007, didn't obtain buy-in from the teachers for the deeper changes she hoped to produce, the "success of the program is likely to be compromised," say the study's authors, Rachel Bolstad and Jane Gilbert. "The school's activities will continue as business as usual, and the change needed—at the level needed—will not occur."

Some 2.0 schools have emerged as start-ups, like Greenwood College School in Toronto, a few blocks from where I live. It began in 2002 with a big donation from Richard Wernham, a successful lawyer who had just cashed out on a profitable mutual fund business. From the outset, Greenwood was a 2.0

school in every sense. Students with a wide variety of learning skills are carefully evaluated before school begins, so each child gets an education that suits his learning style, and his interests. Students, for example, are given tests based on their learning style, so some get conventional tests or oral ones, while others are assigned an artistic project. Every student has a laptop, and in class the teachers work with smart boards—big screens that function like interactive Web sites. The teachers can send whatever they put up on the smart board to the students' laptops so they won't miss anything. There's no typical class—but there's always plenty of room for students to work together, experiment, and converse with the teacher. The classic one-way lecture "-doesn't happen," said David Thompson, the school's first principal. "The kids seem to enjoy school more," he said. "They have more confidence because we're playing to their strengths, not their weaknesses." Granted, the school is only six years old, but so far the dropout rate is zero.

> "The problem with the forward facing, seated lecture hall style education was the inevitable lack of context in anything I learned."
> —ERIK RUBADEAU, 26, TORONTO

There are examples of established schools that have successfully changed—like the Middle College High Schools in Memphis I mentioned earlier. This school is leading the way in the new style of education that works both for the Net Gen mind and for the digital economy they will enter. The high school hasn't totally abandoned the lecture; sometimes it's the quickest way to hand over information. "But it's only a small chunk of the learning journey," says principal Michelle Brantley-Patterson. She encourages teachers to ask questions and let kids discover the answer—even in math class. "Don't go through the formula," she tells the math teachers. "Before you start, ask the students: What do you notice? Let them show [you] what they know." Sometimes there will be a long silence, which many teachers find uncomfortable, she says. That's okay: "Let them think about it."

It's not easy. Letting kids discover for themselves involves a lot of up-front preparation on the part of the teacher. When kids work together, disputes can naturally arise—just as they do when adults work together. "We had one of those moments yesterday," she said, "but we worked it out."

Her 2.0 school produces tangible results. "I'm proud to say that in the last three years, we led the district in graduation rates," she said. In 2007, 91 percent of students graduated; the year before, all of them did. What's more, the Memphis school led the district in the percentage of kids who passed both math and English tests in their senior year. Last year, every single student passed the senior English test. "To me, it's revolutionary. It will make a difference in what we will be in the future," she said. "When kids are given the opportunity to be mature, they rise to the challenge."

Some educators and parents, she knows, are skeptical. They think the old way is the right one. They think teachers should go back to lecturing, to controlling the classroom. "I tell them, this is a school, not a plantation," says Brantley-Patterson. "I am not telling students what to do. I'm helping them to discover. I'm helping them to unearth their greatness. That is what education is all about."

> "Technology can provide us with collaborative environments where classroom discussions can be continued outside the classroom."
> —*MELISSA KENNINGER, 30, MINNEAPOLIS*

THE SCHOOL 2.0—SEVEN TIPS FOR EDUCATORS

Here are seven strategies that will help you to become a better teacher in this new digital age.

1. **Don't throw technology into the classroom and hope for good things.** Focus on the change in pedagogy, not the technology. Learning 2.0 is about dramatically changing the relationship between a teacher and students in the learning process. Get that right and use technology for a student-focused, customized, collaborative learning environment.

2. **Cut back on lecturing.** You don't have all the answers. Besides, broadcast learning doesn't work for this generation. Start asking students questions and listen to their answers. Listen to the *questions* students ask, too. Let them discover the answer. Let them cocreate a learning experience with you.

3. **Empower students to collaborate.** Encourage them to work with each other and show them how to access the world of subject-matter experts available on the Web.

4. **Focus on lifelong learning, not teaching to the test.** It's not what they know when they graduate that counts; it's their capacity and love for lifelong learning that's important. Don't worry if the kids forget the dates of key battles in history. They can look them up. Focus on teaching them how to learn—not what to know.

5. **Use technology to get to know each student** and build self-paced, customized learning programs for them.

6. **Design educational programs according to the eight norms.** There should be choice, customization, transparency, integrity, collaboration, fun, speed, and innovation in their learning experiences. Leverage the strengths of Net Gen culture and behaviors in project-based learning.

7. **Reinvent yourself as a teacher, professor, or educator.** You too can say, "Now, I can hardly wait to get up in the morning to go to work!"

THE NET GENERATION IN THE WORKFORCE

YOUNG RETAILERS MAKE THE "BEST BUY" FOR THEIR FUTURE

In the summer of 2007, Richard M. Schulze, chairman of the consumer electronics retailer Best Buy, assembled his board of directors for a very unusual presentation. The global electronics store had a pressing HR problem: employees earning less than $80,000 weren't buying into the company retirement plan. Only a measly 18 percent of them had a 401(k) plan, a number that could potentially attract unwelcome attention from the Internal Revenue Service. The solution, Schulze explained to his board, might come from the same employees who were shunning retirement saving in favor of the latest music and technology—the company's own Net Generation. These young employees had an idea, and they would present in their own way.

The lights dimmed and a synthesizer beat reverberated through the boardroom. It was time to watch a movie, a short one that had won a company contest challenging employees to use their imaginations to explain the advantages of a 401(k) plan. Enter Roy Croft, Best Buy's customer experience manager. Croft, dressed up in Ray-Ban sunglasses, a false blond mustache, and 1970s-style wig, played a character tormented by the loss of his brother in a stockroom tragedy. He looked like Hutch, the streetwise cop from the '70's TV show *Starsky and Hutch*. As the five-minute parody rolled, Croft had to work with his partner, the Starsky-esque character called "401(k) Guy," to understand and sign up for a retirement plan. The little film may not be Oscar material, but it generated lots of laughs in the boardroom, and afterward, the filmmakers made a personal appearance to talk about their film.

The film was the upshot of a serious effort by Best Buy to tap into the creativity of its Net Gen employees. The majority of Best Buy's retail employees are between 16 and 24. They are vibrant and artistic and are into the latest and greatest technology and extremely passionate about storytelling. Needless to say, anything with the word "retirement" in it was a big turnoff to a Net Gener, especially if the future savings cut into their current music-buying power. To reach this audience, Best Buy had to ditch the regular "HR-speak" and adopt the language and culture of the target audience, the Net Geners.

Hence, the contest. The call for videos was posted on the company's internal social networking site, *www.BlueShirtNation.com*, which signed up 20,000 employees within a year of the launch. Employees were asked to make a five- to seven-minute video translating the new 401(k) into something that was meaningful to them, easy to understand, and compelling to their peers—with a state-of-the-art digital recorder right off the camera department shelf! The contest produced the *Starsky and Hutch*–style video, and it worked: Best Buy employee participation in the 401(k) plan jumped from 18 percent to 47 percent as a result of the campaign.

The Best Buy story is just one example of how a major company tapped into the Net Gen's youthful energy to solve a business problem. Companies like this should be held up as an example of how to handle a new generation that comes into the workforce with very different attitudes about collaboration, about having fun at work, and about being free to work when and where they want. Yet, as we will see in this chapter, all too often the young people go to work and hit a wall of corporate procedure and a deeply entrenched hierarchy that rewards those who command large numbers of followers. The widespread banning of Facebook at work is a classic example. The Net Gen wants to take a digital break; the boomer employers shut them down. Get ready for the generational clash.

Employers, I will argue, have two options. They can refuse to adapt to the Net Gen, stick to their old hierarchies, and reinforce the generational firewall that separates the managers from the newly hired minions. But if they do, I believe, they will forfeit the chance to learn from the Net Gen—to absorb both their mindset and their tools of collaboration. In this complex business environment, that would be a bad choice. Instead, I think, the winners will be those companies in the corporate world who choose the Best Buy option—to embrace the Net Geners' collaborative ways. As we will see, some leading companies, like Deloitte and Accenture, understand this and are tapping into this generation's culture. They know that the Net Gen way of working is the twenty-first-century way—and it can help them succeed.

In this chapter, I will show what the Net Gen model of work might mean for corporate America. For starters, I think the old HR model—recruit, train, supervise, and retain—should be shelved. Instead, companies should adopt a new model—initiate, engage, collaborate, and evolve. You'll see how some organizations like the U.S. Marine Corps are finding innovative ways to wage the war for talent. We'll show you how some corporate leaders appeal to Net Geners—by customizing job descriptions, as Deloitte does; by using game-based strategies to train employees for short-term projects; by keeping in touch with alumni, the former employees, to find new people and get new ideas. Old-style job interviews are out. Two-way dialogues are the way to hire. And the first three months is a time when the employee is evaluating the company, not the other way round. You'll find plenty of examples in this chapter, along with tips for employers on how to deal with the challenges of this new generation.

I think the Net Gen can help companies win, period. Our research shows that companies that selectively and effectively embrace Net Gen norms perform better than those that don't. In fact, I'm convinced that the Net Gen culture is the new culture of work. The Net Gen norms I describe in this book may turn out to be the key indicators of high-performing organizations in the twenty-first century.

The Entitlement Generation?

You'll hear lots of older employers voice the same complaint: Young workers today are spoiled brats. They're making ridiculous demands of their employers, and they haven't even proven themselves! That feeling may be widespread. Nearly 83 percent of Americans think that America's youth feel more entitled than young people did 10 years ago, according to a national survey conducted by the Sacred Heart University Polling Institute.[1] Wayne Hochwarter, a management professor at Florida State University's College of Business, saw it in a survey of 400 business students he conducted at his university in 2008. The vast majority of the students wanted to pay their dues within five years and didn't want to start at the bottom and work their way up, Hochwarter's survey found. As one of his friends, the president of a Jacksonville food processing company, put it: "College grads today want the keys to the kingdom the first day at work."

Many employees, apparently, feel the same way. Hochwarter surveyed 500 employees in a broad range of occupations in 2006, and he found that over half believe that many employees act as if they are more deserving than others at work even though they haven't "paid their dues." Some of the quotes he collected were telling. "I don't know where these kids come off thinking they are entitled to things it took me 20 years to get," said a Chicago management consultant. "College grads aren't willing to do the grunt work necessary to learn the job, but they sure want the perks," added a vice president of human resources. Dr. Mel Levine, a pediatrics professor at the University of North Carolina Medical School and author of a book on the topic called *Ready or Not, Here Comes Life*,[2] put it this way: "We're seeing an epidemic of people who are having a hard time making the transition to work—kids who had too much success early in life and who've become accustomed to instant gratification." Here's Exhibit A, from a report about how a prominent investment bank competes in the war for talent: "A U.S. employee who was relocating to Switzerland asked his new employer to pay for a year's dog-meat because his pet would find it hard to get used to the foreign food."[3]

The Net Generation is not properly prepared for the workplace, according to a major report by a consortium led by the Conference Board. The report, based on a survey of over 400 employers, was sobering: Net Geners are "woefully ill-prepared" for the demands of the twenty-first-century workplace. And yet a closer look at this survey paints a different picture of the Net Generation. In fact, the vast majority of employers in the survey felt that college students were actually *well prepared overall* for work; it was high school students who fell short—less than half of the employers surveyed thought that high school grads were well prepared overall. The chief complaint was that high school graduates couldn't write memos and other forms of corporate communication properly. Nearly 7 in 10 thought that high school graduates' critical thinking skills were deficient too, although I wonder what they expected of a teenager starting out at an entry-level job.[4] Yet college graduates received much better marks. About three-quarters of employers thought that four-year college graduates had writing skills that were good enough for the workplace or even excellent.

It's revealing that some of the employers' sharpest criticisms were reserved for the Net Geners as people. They criticized their inability to work in teams, their motivation and their work ethic. Young employees, they complained, were neither polite nor punctual. They didn't even dress properly. Moreover, Net Geners, some complained, were not realistic about how long it would take to move up the corporate ladder.[5] The leadership skills of some of the two- and four-year-college graduates were deemed to be insufficient. It looked like employers just didn't think these Net Geners were fitting into their corporate world.

The Clash of Generations: An Irresistible Force Meets an Immovable Object

I think we're seeing the early signs of a major collision between the freewheeling Net Generation and the traditional boomer employers. It's not necessarily a clash between Net Geners and boomers as human beings. It's a clash between two ideas of how work should work. One key indicator is how long the Net Gen employees stay on the job. In one Canadian study of 18- to 34-year-olds, the average 27-year-old had already held five full-time (nonsummer) jobs.[6] But does that mean that Net Geners are not loyal or hardworking?[7] Our research shows, surprisingly perhaps, that most Net Geners say they want to work for one or two employers in their business lifetime (see Figure 6.1). They want to be loyal employees, as long as they have the chance to move and succeed within the organization, but they usually last only two years. I call this the intention-behavior paradox.

So why do they keep moving? This is a case of the irresistible force meeting the immovable object. The Net Gener arrives at work, eager to use his social networking tools to collaborate and create and contribute to the company. For starters, he's shocked to find that the company's technological tools are more

FIGURE 6.1 NET GENERS' RESPONSE TO THE QUESTION, WHICH WOULD YOU RATHER DO: WORK FOR ONE OR TWO COMPANIES OR FOR A VARIETY?

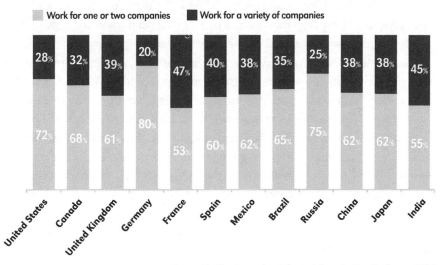

Source: The Net Generation: A Strategic Investigation, © nGenera, 2008

primitive than the ones he used in high school. The company he works for still thinks the Net is about Web sites presenting information, rather than a Web 2.0 collaboration platform. And they are surprised, perhaps naively, to learn that corporations have antiquated ways of working. Then the company bans Facebook at the office because it suspects Net Geners are wasting time chatting with friends and throwing digital snowballs when they should be working—thus depriving Net Geners of their link to friends, to fun, to coworkers. Pretty soon, the talent heads for the exit.

A lot of times, the tools kids are using in their bedroom are more sophisticated than those used by Fortune 500 companies. Here's a classic story from the New York Times: In 2003, a 22-year-old computer geek named Matthew Burton started work at the Defense Intelligence Agency. He couldn't wait to try out the systems of the sophisticated spy agency, but what he found was "a colossal letdown." The search engines were primitive compared with Google; the spies didn't even have a blog on which to share information with other spies. And this was a powerhouse spy agency that's supposed to track down the terrorists! This was one catalyst in the creation of an approach and set of tools that now enable the intelligence community to collaborate better—Intellipedia.[8]

The problem is not just technical. Too many businesses are still stuck in the old unproductive hierarchy, which divides the world into governors and the governed. "We live in a free and open society, but many of our workplace organizations use command-and-control style," said Asher Adelman, president of the Workplace Democracy Association. In late June 2008 he released a poll of 2,475 employees showing that one-quarter of working Americans view their workplace as a dictatorship, and less than one-half think it promotes creativity.[9] Said Adelman: "People go to work and they're told what to do and how to do it and they're not given any decision abilities whatsoever."

The middle managers in between act, as business thinker Peter Drucker put it, as "relays—human boosters for the faint, unfocused signals that pass for information in the traditional, pre-information organization."[10] In this hierarchy, you have two missions—to move up "the ladder," and to execute the orders that fulfill the goals determined by your boss, or by his boss, or his boss. Innovation, creativity, taking pleasure in giving customers better service, or creating new products (in other words, having fun) were typically not part of the picture. You hung in with the company until you retired or were fired. You were the "Organization Man."

This model obviously cannot work in an economy driven by innovation, knowledge, immediacy, and working via the Internet. But how much have things really changed? The most illuminating answer may come from the most widely syndicated management book of all time. The book was not written by me or Stephen Covey or even Peter Drucker. It was written by a former telephone company employee named Scott Adams. *The Dilbert Principle* (there's an excerpt below) hammered the various management buzzwords and newspeak from *empowerment* to *reengineering* as cynical decoys rather than signs of meaningful change. Adams comes through again and again with a humorous nudge on the traditional corporate hierarchies and the authority of decision makers. In the old model of economic development, worker bees are to be supervised in their honey production.

"Why does it seem as if most of the decisions in my workplace are made by drunken lemurs?"

"Decisions are made by people who have time, not people who have talent."

"Why are talented people so busy?"

"They're fixing the problems made by people who have time."

THE WAR FOR TALENT

We're on the brink of a major war for talent, as many companies that rely on knowledge workers already know. The tables have turned. Twenty years ago, when college grads poured into the workforce, companies had their pick of the best and the brightest. Employers had the power to choose; employees were grateful to get a job and did what they could to keep it, and the last thing on their mind would be to suggest radical new ways of working and managing a company. But in the next 10 years, as baby boomers retire, there won't be enough young people to fill up the management spots recently vacated.

This time it is the employees' turn, especially the best and the brightest of them. They are poised to enjoy the role of being choosy about who they work for. It sets up a classic war for talent that is already underway in some sectors. Deloitte, one of the world's largest accounting firms, hires about 10,000 people a year in the United States alone. "Many companies come to the conclusion that the only real limitation on their growth is their ability to continue to attract, develop, and retain high-quality talent," Deloitte's CEO, Jim Quigley, told me in the spring of 2008. "I don't need to look out 25 years to say, 'This is a business challenge.' I can look out next year and say, 'This is a business challenge.'"[11]

In the United States alone, there will be a shortfall of 10 million workers by the year 2010.[12] In the next 10 years, the demand for more than 30 million U.S. college-educated workers will greatly exceed the 23 million new college graduates that are expected.[13] A labor crunch at senior levels is imminent. America's 500 biggest companies will see half their senior managers retire in the next few years,[14] which leaves a lot of companies scrambling to figure out how they can accelerate the growth of Net Geners who have just entered the professional world. Ronald Logue, chief executive officer of State Street Corporation, put it this way: "A central issue for our success is how fast can we get these digitalized kids into management."

The labor shortage is particularly acute in the science and engineering sectors. One out of four of today's science and engineering workers is over 50 years old, says John Bailey, deputy director of policy for the U.S. Department of Commerce, and the rate of growth in these fields far outpaces our ability to fill these types of jobs. While the demand for knowledge workers grows, the supply is shrinking. The number of four-year engineering majors has fallen dramatically in the past decade,[15] as has nationwide course enrollment in science and engineering.[16] Universities aren't turning out a sufficient number of graduates to replace the exiting boomers, never mind hiring the new recruits necessary for corporate growth.

Given the labor shortage in some sectors on the home front, companies are looking at pools of talent abroad. In many of the rising economies, the Net Gen far outnumbers the postwar generation. China's Net Gen outnumbers its boomer-age population by 80 million. In India and Latin America, the relative sizes are much different. For example, there are almost twice as many Indian Net Geners as there are Indian boomers. India generates 2.5 million university graduates annually, mostly English-speaking. They cost 12 percent of what an American graduate would cost to hire, and work an average of 450 more hours per year.[17] This is good news for employers: The world's rising economies represent an unprecedented source of young labor, and it's often cheaper than labor in North America and Europe. There are around 390 million potential young professionals in low-wage countries versus 180 million in high-wage countries.[18]

Companies are shipping some jobs to these lower-cost pools of labor. Any job that is not confined to a particular location has the potential to be performed anywhere in the world. If the job activities do not require physical proximity, local knowledge, or complex interactions with colleagues, then location doesn't matter. Such jobs may be performed wherever a company deems most attractive. A company may choose to have a particular "location insensitive" job performed in the demand market (that is, in the market in which the resulting output is sold), in a border zone (near shore), or remotely (offshore). Not all location-insensitive jobs will move offshore, but many

will—it's estimated that today, 11 percent of the world's service jobs are performed remotely.[19]

But as the numbers suggest, that hardly solves the coming labor shortage in
the United States and Europe, especially the shortage of knowledge workers.
Companies will need a comprehensive global talent strategy to compete for the
best and brightest employees—not just Net Geners, but women, seniors, and,
as we described in *Wikinomics,* the freelance collaborators who have proved to
be an extraordinary source of innovations for major companies like Proctor &
Gamble. Says Deloitte's Quigley, "I now compete in two markets—one for customers and one for talent."

New Models of High-Performance Work

Business, in other words, needs the Net Generation—in more ways than one.
The Net Generation "is the foundation for the next three decades of employment and leadership," according to Randall Hansen, founder of Quintessential
Careers, one of the oldest and most comprehensive career development sites on
the Web. Yes, they are "the most pampered and indulged generation," he notes.
But "this generation is also the most tech-savvy and wired (or perhaps wirelessly connected) cohort. Their views of life and work are different from any
others'—and if employers want to recruit and retain these people, strategies
and policies and procedures will have to change."

I think the Net Generation will be challenging, but they'll ultimately be good
for corporate America. I believe the Net Generation will show smart companies how to collaborate in new ways. In today's working world, being able to
collaborate is hugely important—and I don't mean the kind of collaboration
that equals endless meetings. Work has become more cognitively complex,
more team-based, more dependent on social skills, and more subject to the
pressures of time. As work becomes more mobile, it depends less on geography
and more on technological competence. Thus, growing numbers of firms are
decentralizing their decision making and embracing new technologies that link
employees in teams around the world.

The new Web—which allows you not only to hunt for information, but to
contribute it—offers the technology to help us harness human skill, ingenuity,
and intelligence more efficiently and effectively than anything we have witnessed
previously.[20] By mobilizing the collective knowledge, capability, and resources
embodied within broad networks of participants, smart firms can accomplish
great things. People throughout a firm, locked into traditional organizational
structures, can be freed to share knowledge and ingenuity. Further, companies

can reach outside their boundaries to tap into vast pools of labor available in the global economy. Whether designing an airplane, assembling a motorcycle, or analyzing the human genome, the ability to integrate the talents of dispersed individuals and organizations is becoming *the* defining competency for managers and firms. This is a tremendously powerful way to do business, says Best Buy CEO Brad Anderson. It's "unleashing the power of human capital."

Net Geners know how to use the latest collaborative tools. Best Buy has figured this out. "To someone of another generation, it's a shock that kids who work in Best Buy stores can spontaneously come together to build and deploy new IT systems in a couple weeks," says Michele Azar, vice president, Emerging Customer Channels, The Internet Group.

But that's exactly what happened: The challenge was to create an employee portal that the Best Buy employees, mostly age 16 to 24, would actually want to use. Instead of using the standard approach, which would have cost millions, Scot Kersten turned to the kids in the store.

"With very limited funding (less than $500,000) we set out on a journey to find developers in our own backyard. Not just any developers—ones that actually use the Internet as a way of life." He eventually found six kids and paired them up with three developers from Best Buy's corporate office who were not in the Information Technology group.

They threw out the conventional approach, reassured skeptics within the business, and at the end of the six-week period launched five key features that increased collaboration within the business—between head office and the field, and with other business units, like call centers, that have never had a voice before. They also created an internal wiki that allows Best Buy to gather insights from all 150,000 employees on everything from the latest trends to competitive insights.

"Within weeks, the number of pages in the wiki was growing beyond what anyone had envisioned," says Kersten. "We are now in a place where the voices of each individual employee can be heard and can change the way our business is run." Kersten says the wiki has helped the company increase productivity by cutting several steps in standard processes. It has also given employees a forum in which to express themselves on topics like diversity; a move that Kersten believes will help to retain employees.

Or take Chris Rasmussen, who at 33 is a prolific blogger who teaches social networking to the United States intelligence community. His two-day course helps analysts integrate social tools into their daily work habits. It makes knowledge, and more importantly, the people that generate it, more discoverable, he said. What's more, social tools are a "powerful organizational leveler." These tools can generate and capture "emergent knowledge" as well as create "emergent leaders"—regardless of age, rank, or time spent "climbing the corporate ladder," he said. Rasmussen knows from experience; he has sat on high-level panels about the new powers of the Web. "I noticed at a recent panel that I was the only person not confirmed by the Senate or appointed by a mayor or governor," he said. "I'm just this blog guy that throws out some good ideas once in a while. It's pretty cool to gain a reputation or brand based on merit and enthusiasm, not age or rank." So look at the new employees and you will see what you need to change in order to compete in today's world. Their culture of collaboration is taking root in the workplace and already beginning to create a new corporate meritocracy that is sweeping away the hierarchical silos in its path and connecting internal teams to a wealth of external networks. This means that in the War for Talent, companies have a simple choice. Adapt to the Net Gen ways of doing things and win their loyalty—and the War for Talent. Or stick to the old ways and lose.

> Net Gener Jonathan Wolf, a 26-year-old from Worcester, Massachusetts, contributed to the Facebook group entitled, Grown Up Digital: Help Write a Book!, stating, "I'd love to work for just one or two companies for my entire life. If there were a company that offered that kind of tenure, they'd get the best work possible out of me.
>
> "What would that company look like? oh, man . . . for one thing, I like how google requires that you dedicate a portion of your work week to pet projects. That's a fantastic way to spur innovation in the workplace. That would definitely have to be a requirement: the ability to labor on something outside of my normal work, something that I've chosen and feel passionately about.
>
> "Past that . . . the ability to telecommute would be wonderful. Nobody wants to be in an off-white cubicle for their entire work day. It's both physically and emotionally stifling. Flexible hours would be nice, but if I'm working from home, that's a bit of a moot point. stock options are good. Full benefits to extend to myself and my son. travel opportunities. training so I can advance in my field. Ubiquitous data access. annual gadget expense account. masseuse.
>
> "But the number one thing my job would have to do is BE CHALLENGING. I'm not spending my time filing reports, doing menial labor, or intellectual grunt work. I need to feel valued in the workplace, and feeling valued comes directly from being challenged. It says 'we think this guy can handle something tough. he's got the skill.' Then, I'll be inclined to prove it. That means a better bottom line for my employers. Everyone wins, then."

NET GENERATION NORMS AND THE TRANSFORMATION OF WORK

When we asked Net Geners about the events that defined their worldview, they talked about the fall of the Berlin Wall in 1989, the Rio Earth Summit 1992, the attack on the World Trade Center on September 11, 2001, global warming, and their first iPod. They are different from their parents. Whereas previous generations value loyalty, seniority, security, and authority, the Net Gen's norms reflect a desire for freedom, fun, collaboration, and the other norms we've been exploring in this book. In this war for talent, employers are going to have to understand the key Net Gen norms if they want to hire them, and keep them.

Freedom

The Freedom to Work When and Where You Want

Most Net Geners reject the "nine to five" working hours that Dolly Parton described so memorably back in 1980 in a movie by that name. Some 69 percent of Net Geners we surveyed want to choose where and when they work.[21] Flexibility in hours and benefits is the most crucial way to attract and keep Net Geners.[22] Over half want to be able to work outside the office.[23] Pampered you say? Actually they may be more creative and productive this way.

The Freedom to Enjoy Work and Family Life

"Working to live" is the motto of the Net Generation, and sometimes older managers may misinterpret their need for a work-life balance as a lack of commitment. But it's not necessarily that. Net Geners crave work that is meaningful, challenging, and offers variety[24]—but they want their lives in balance. One out of every two Net Generation workers values family time more than work, compared with 41 percent of boomers.[25]

Net Geners expect to be free to mix work with their personal lives, just as they did in school. They also want to be judged on their performance, not on face time. Services that make a young parent's life easier—such as on-site day care—will attract and retain top talent. Smart companies are those that embrace nontraditional employment relationships, such as part-time work, flextime, temporary work, job sharing, seasonal employment, and on-call and shift work.

> "I would be more loyal to a company that shows respect for my efforts and time, and acknowledges any sacrifices made vis-a-vis personal life."
>
> —ADITI BAKHT, 23, DELHI, INDIA

The Freedom to Try New Jobs

Two out of three Net Geners said they would rather work for one or two companies than for a variety of companies, our research shows. But they're not loyal to an employer; they're loyal to their career path. They'll stay at a company that offers them structure and internal mobility. If a company refuses to invest in them, they'll leave.

A lot of students follow the money—no surprise given their university debt load.[26] This rings true especially in rising economies like those of India, China, and Brazil, where young workers can often double their salary after completing initial training at a multinational organization. This generation can find out quickly online who's paying what around the globe. They'll probably have multiple careers before they retire, whether through choice or of necessity.

Customization

My Job, My Life

Net Geners have grown up customizing everything—from their iPods to their ringtones—and as they start working, they want employers to manage them as individuals, not as a big group. This means individualized learning and development opportunities; adaptable, project-based role descriptions; monitoring performance with more frequent informal discussions that evaluate specific job contribution within the organization; and improvement of the manager-employee two-way working relationship through open dialogue. Net Geners will want rewards that fit their current lives—like cash to save for a house early in their careers, and more time with the kids later on. The evidence is mounting that when firms can create highly customized job descriptions, work systems, compensation plans, and the rest—it pays offs.

Scrutiny

I Know What You Did Last Night

As one CEO I know discovered, you can't keep a secret anymore. He sent a top-secret memo to 40 senior employees and two days later everybody in the company had read it. It turned out that the memo was posted on a couple of public Web sites. "I'll never do that again," he told me. "When I know something, I'm going to tell everyone."

Sixty percent of Net Geners check out a company before accepting a job offer. Count on them to check up on the company culture and any complaints that have surfaced on the "YourCompanySucks.com" Web site. They want to work for companies that are transparent. It's good for the company too. Our research shows that when companies share more information such as financial data, business plans, new-product ideas, and management compensation information with their employees, good things happen. Transparency drops collaboration costs and improves trust between employees and management. The speed of collaboration increases. There is a decline in office politics and game playing.

The scrutiny goes both ways, as we saw earlier. Companies are now checking up on potential employees in search of red flags, as they delicately put it, on Facebook or other social networking sites.

Integrity

Be a Good Company to Work For

When scrutiny increases, corporate integrity is essential. Just as trust is the sine qua non of virtual communities, integrity is the foundation of the new enterprise. In North America, Net Geners define integrity as being honest, considerate, and transparent. They expect employers to be this way, and live by their commitments.

> "The most attractive companies offer a chance to do volunteer work as part of the job."
>
> —BEN RATTRAY, 27, SAN FRANCISCO, FOUNDER AND CEO OF CHANGE.ORG

Young people respond well to management integrity and quickly become engaged. There is greater loyalty and lower turnover, and employees are more likely to do the right thing. Employees in open and trusted firms are better motivated, especially if they are working in jobs that require thinking skills. Take a look at a Net Gener's representation of her real work environment in the illustration opposite this page.

Collaboration

Teamwork Is Not Just Motherhood

Boomers grew up with hierarchies—at home, at school, at work. The goal in a hierarchy is to move up, and have more people reporting to you. But as Tamara Erickson, a widely respected expert on organizations and the changing workforce, has observed, this generation is not turned on by status or hierarchy. They want to do challenging work, but they don't necessarily want organizational responsibility. Their dream job, she says, is something like this: a job with a problem or dilemma no one knows how to solve and lots of great people to work with. How different that is from the workplace I entered after college, where the goal

A NET GENER'S IDEAL WORK SPACE

Source: Katie, 22, Vancouver, British Columbia, Canada*

*This drawing was prompted by the following instruction: "Please draw a picture or create a collage to represent your ideal work environment. Include all elements that are important to you."

was to have a corner office (which I occupied at one point, and which, I have to admit, felt good). That was having power over other people. But collaboration, as Net Geners know it, is achieving something *with* other people, experiencing power through other people, not by ordering a gaggle of followers to do your bidding. Collaboration is how Net Geners get things done. It's part of their digital upbringing. (Table 6.1, on page 164, contains some telling data about the attitude toward collaboration of the Net Geners and other generations, including the boomers.)

"There shouldn't be teamwork just for the sake of teamwork. Rather, you bring together teams when you need different types of minds to come together with certain skill sets."

—ALEX TAPSCOTT

A NET GENER'S PERFECT WORK SPACE

Source: Craig, 22, Vancouver, British Columbia, Canada*

*This drawing was prompted by the following instruction: "Please draw a picture or create a collage to represent your ideal work environment. Include all elements that are important to you."

TABLE 6.1   COLLABORATION: GENERATIONAL DIFFERENCES IN NET
GENERS' COLLABORATION IN THE WORKPLACE

	Percentage That Strongly/Somewhat Agree		
	NGeners **(16–29 years)**	**Gen Xers** **(30–41 years)**	**Boomers** **(42–61 years)**
At work, I accomplish more working in teams than I do working on my own.	26% U.S.	20% U.S.	17% U.S.

Source: The Net Generation: A Strategic Investigation, © nGenera, 2008

Entertainment

Work Should Be Fun

For my generation, there's a time for work and a time for fun. For Net Geners, work and fun are both rolled into one. One day at a panel discussion the executive VP of one of the world's largest companies asked some Net Geners what their company could do to make it more attractive to their generation.

"This place should be more fun—it's just not fun to work here," said 23-year-old Effie Seidberg. I could tell from the body language that the executives in the room didn't get it. You work and then go home to have fun. Or you work and then retire to have fun. That's the old view.

Two out of three Net Geners feel that "working and having fun can and should be the same thing."[27] That doesn't mean they want to play foosball all day long. Instead, they want the work itself to be enjoyable. Effie, for example, studied logic at Princeton, and got a job with Google on her second try. She loves the culture of work, but that's not all, "The company is insanely internally transparent, which feels like a sign of respect and trust," she said. "The hours are as flexible as

> "A lot of companies, all able to give very high salaries, are vying for a limited number of people. It's the benefits packages that catch people's attention."
>
> —ADITI BAKHT, 23, DELHI, INDIA

you'd like them to be. . . . The free food and subsidized massages are key. . . . The boundaries between work and play are fuzzy. Unlike in the corporate world, no one thinks twice if you IM with your friends in the middle of the day or go out to play some volleyball at two. The culture is designed to help employees relax into productivity, not stress into it. . . . To me this just seems, well, logical."

The debate over banning Facebook is a typical case of the boomer employers just not getting it. I remember when employers banned e-mail; they thought it was totally unproductive and that managers shouldn't be typing. I remember when companies refused to give their employees PCs. Then they banned the Internet; employers were apparently worried that employees would look at porn on the company premises or that they would be wasting

> "One day at work they took away our tools, like Facebook, Pandora, Bebo, NPR. Work is slow now, cold and boring."
>
> —STEVE RESSLER, 27, TAMPA, FLORIDA

their time. I took a different approach. When the first Web browser appeared, I was running my company, New Paradigm. I sent everybody a note: Get on the Internet, I told them. "You must go and waste your time."

To be sure, organizations need to design proper work processes. They need to compensate people so they'll be encouraged to work effectively. Then, if they do take a break on Facebook, that's fine. It's their way of cooling off, before revving up for the next round of work.

> ### The Ultimate in Entertainment: Tale of a Corporate Campus in India
>
> In India, the most successful corporate campuses are virtual theme parks that make the dot-com excesses look mild. For instance, the Infosys 54-acre campus on the outskirts of Bangalore has every possible amenity, including gyms, yoga studios, a multiplex cinema, banks, and bowling alleys. The restaurants serve 14 different cuisines. Employees are not allowed to use the amenities during work hours, but they are packed with young people mingling in the evening after work.[28]
>
> Indian Net Geners enjoy seeing their colleagues as a kind of extended family. Almost 30 percent more Indians than North Americans say their coworkers are good friends.[29] Among many families, especially in the south of India, it is common for young people to spend the vast majority of their social time with their families versus friends who are not relatives. Young Indian workers often live with their parents and even grandparents, and they can provide up to 70 percent of the family income.[30] Indian families can make the North American concept of "helicoptering" look mild by comparison; they expect to have deep understanding of and input into all of their children's decisions.
>
> So, when recruiting, successful employers reach out to parents at the same time they are doing so to Net Geners, holding information sessions that discuss "family benefit" programs (family access to gyms, theaters, etc.).[31] Such programs wed employees to the company—it can be much harder to change jobs when the whole family will lose their perks as a result! By creating comprehensive campuses with all the amenities, employers help create an atmosphere that extends the familial social circle productively into work.

Speed
Let's Make Things Happen, Now

Net Geners need speed. They're used to instant responses, so if colleague A is not available, the Net Gener will ask colleague B instead of waiting. They quickly become frustrated if they have to wait for managers or deal with a mountain of red tape. Warp speed is the preferred speed. They'll get frustrated with a lengthy, multistep recruiting process too. Smart companies are creating fast recruiting cycles—from the application process through to hiring, with lots of feedback in between.

They want to move up quickly too. When I was CEO of New Paradigm, a new and very talented employee I had hired three months earlier came into my office and shut the door to talk. Her question: "What's it going to take for me to be the CEO?" In formulating a response, one of the things that went through my mind was "I'll have to be run over by a beer truck." But I restrained myself and had a good discussion with her about her talents and opportunities to grow and develop.

Opportunities for advancement are the number one criteria used in selecting a new job, a survey of Canadian college graduates reported.[32] It means that companies will have to balance the desire of older employees to move ahead on the basis of seniority with those of younger employees expecting rapid advancement based on their achievements.

Net Geners also like continual performance feedback from management in order to gauge their progress. According to one study, 60 percent of Net Geners in the workforce want to hear from their managers on a daily basis and 35 percent want to hear multiple times a day.[33] "Superstars have an insatiable demand for honest, immediate feedback," says Graham Jones in the Harvard Business Review.[34] This can be irritating. When I started work, I got the annual performance review. Net Geners want a steady stream of it, and I find myself thinking, 'Didn't we just discuss this last week? You're doing great!'

Expect all kinds of new software programs that enable everyone in a company to give real time daily feedback on the performance of others. Net Geners will thrive on this information and improve their performance on a daily basis. Think how batch information processing of the 1970s was replaced by the real-time computer systems of today. Rather than receiving information on a monthly or yearly basis, information became real time and companies could adjust their behavior continuously. Just think what a similar shift could mean for human performance. Once again, we can learn from Net Generation culture about the requirements of the future enterprise.

Speed affects loyalty as well. Says 24-year-old Moritz Kettler, my daughter's boyfriend, who works for a large telecommunications company: "I love my job and the people I work with, but I can't see myself staying here for very long. It just takes too long for things to happen around here. It's obvious what needs to be done in so many situations, but working decisions through the bureaucracy is driving me nuts and ultimately will probably cause us to fail in the market."

Really Fast Recruiting, Chinese Style

At the Shenzhen General Talents Market[35] in China, employers interview and make an offer in one day, and expect the employee to turn up for work the next morning.

SHENZHEN GENERAL TALENTS MARKET

Source: Courtesy of China

The General Talents Market operates six days a week as a giant open market for staff. Every day, approximately 150 employers screen up to 8,000 applicants (see photo). In this vast market, employers range from small local businesses to some of Shenzhen's biggest corporate citizens, such as Foxconn.[36] With an economy running full steam, they often hire on the spot: "For my company, we offered many people interviews in the afternoon, at our company location," said Raymond Ling, age 25 and manager at Fook Wah. "They climbed on a bus and came to our offices with very little knowledge about who we were and what we did. I'm not sure I know why they were so trusting."

> "Having an opportunity to fast-track up the career ladder has to be in the foreseeable future, not 5 years down the road but 1 or 2 years."
>
> —ANITA TANG, 26, HONG KONG

Innovation: Let Me Invent

Innovation is the hallmark of Net Gen culture. If video games taught this Net Generation anything, it's that every problem has seemingly endless solutions, and digital tools like Facebook and MySpace have them "obsoleting" and creating new profiles often several times a day.

Three out of four Net Geners would like to find new ways of accomplishing their jobs.[37] This is a generation bent on being innovative in the office. Young employees want to add value, make a difference, challenge the status quo, and understand how their work contributes to organizational success.

But Can They Deliver?

The Net Generation can be challenging, but even a very large corporation can adjust and adapt to their ways in order to gain an edge in the war for talent. Take Deloitte. In 2007, *BusinessWeek* ranked the giant accounting and management consulting firm the number one company in the United States at which to launch a career. I asked Deloitte's Quigley what he thought about the Net Geners. "I think they're incredibly capable, talented people who want to be challenged and come to the workforce highly prepared," he said. "They come to the workforce with the skills that some of those with no hair or gray hair didn't come to the workforce with." Integrating them effectively into a team is "challenging a little bit," Quigley said, "because they think differently. They like to communicate. They like to collaborate in a different kind of way. But I definitely don't support the view that they have no work ethic or that they're dumb.

"They are not committed to a company and they're not committed to a manager," he continued. "They're committed to their career. Some become critical of that and say that they're selfish. I don't. I just accept that." Deloitte's response is to show the Net Geners that it is committed to them and to their career by creating a "distinct experience for them." Deloitte, he explains, customizes jobs so that for Deloitte employees, "their work can fit into their lives, and their lives fit into their work." It's helped the company retain more Net Geners, he said: "We believe that it is a new strategy for the workforce of the twenty-first century, and the workforce of the twenty-first century is different than the workforce in the last century."

The Net Generation can't deliver on their own. They need older employees to work with them. Bill McEwan, the CEO of Sobeys Inc., Canada's second largest grocery retailer, sees this every day. The most successful stores, he says, are those where the Net Geners get along with older employees. They learn from each other. McEwan's son Matthew says a lot of companies suffer from the effects of a "generational firewall" that separates the powers (older people) from the new employees (Net Geners). Permitting a generational firewall is a big mistake. That firewall will stop older people, who know the business, from absorbing the Net Gen way of collaborating, and especially their techniques of using collaborative tools, such as wikis, which allow many users to create and edit documents. It also prevents Net Geners from learning from the experience of older employees. Breaking down the firewall can separate the winners from the losers. Barack Obama broke down the firewall; Hillary Clinton didn't. Best Buy broke down the firewall; Circuit City, its troubled and far weaker competitor, didn't.

Will the Job Hoppers Set Out on Their Own?

The Net Geners are becoming seasoned job hoppers. Often Net Geners enter the work force and don't like what they see. If they don't like a job or can't change a company, they'll leave, and they have plenty of alternatives. Going from one old-style company to another is typically not an acceptable plan. But will they set up their own businesses? While it's not clear yet, there are early signs of an entrepreneurial upsurge in this generation. According to nGenera's "My Internet Life" study, approximately 1 in 4 participating Net Geners want to be entrepreneurs or own their own company. A 2007 Harris poll suggests the entrepreneurial urge might be even bigger—40 percent of young people under age 18 said they would like to start their own business some day, and another 37 percent called it a possibility.

If entrepreneurship is good for an economy, we need to ask: is this wishful thinking? The percentage of Americans age 20 to 34 that actually start new businesses each month is slightly below the average for all age groups.[38] However, another worldwide study that measures entrepreneurial activity in a different way found that young adults age 25 to 34 were the most active entrepreneurs, not only in the United States but in many other countries around the globe.[39] You might wonder what kind of employers Net Geners would be. I asked Matt Mullenweg, a Net Gen entrepreneur who cofounded a free state-of-the-art publishing platform for bloggers, called wordpress.com. As of the spring of 2008, wordpress.com had 2.8 million blogs and was growing by about 300,000 per month. There is still a heavy amount of traffic on the site, upwards of 30,000 hits per day.

The company has 24 employees. "Everyone works at home and there are no hours," Mullenweg told me. "Ninety percent of communication is on IRC (Internet Relay Chat) and the rest is on Skype. Never on the phone. Twice a year we meet at the same place. I travel around the world meeting people in their homes. People can work together virtually but it's tougher to socialize virtually. So this is tricky."

Mullenweg has some advice for Net Gen entrepreneurs, "Be open—don't worry about people stealing your idea. It's all about execution. Hiring is key. If you have bad people, you need a lot of process and structure. If you have good people, you need way less process and bureaucracy."

The Mindset to Collaborate: Trained by Games

It may sound odd, but online game playing may be a good form of business education. A recent nationwide survey of 2,500 U.S. business professionals searched for differences between those who grew up playing video games and those who did not. Professionals who grew up playing video games were more serious about achievement, more loyal to their company and their coworkers, more flexible and persistent problem-solvers, and more willing to take only the risks that make sense.[40] As I mentioned in Chapter 4 in discussing the Net Gen mind, this generation's interactive-game-playing experiences are very different from the game-playing experiences of previous generations. Today's popular video games like World of Warcraft emphasize cooperation rather than individual competition (for the highest score as in the arcade games, for example).

The new video games reward creative problem solving and trial and error, along with risk taking. There is little fear of failure, since there is always somewhere to go when you need help (a cheat code or a walk-through). However, Net Geners feel a need to discover on their own and have a willingness to keep at it. In the workplace, Net Geners have a desire to win collaboratively; they yearn to stand out as top achievers who have performed so well as a result of the speed and dexterity they developed playing video games growing up.

To be a guild master in a game like World of Warcraft, you need to be able to create a vision, find recruits and give them a platform on which to learn, and orchestrate the group's strategy. To me, it sounds a lot like the skills a corporate executive needs, doesn't it?

Yet online games obviously do not prepare you for the realities of corporate life. Take Net Gener Stephen Gillett, who, in 2004 at age 28, took a top IT job at Yahoo! after running worldwide infrastructure at CNET Networks Inc., a publicly held media company. Gillett approached Xerox PARC's John Seely Brown to ask his advice about the career change.

"Well, Stephen, I gather you accepted doing this job, right?" Seely Brown inquired.

"Yes," said Gillett.

"How many FTE, fulltime equivalents, does it take to do this job?" Seely Brown asked.

Gillett paused for a long time: "I didn't . . . I didn't ask."

"Pardon me?" Seely Brown said. "You accepted doing this job with the following goals, with the following time frames, with the following benchmarks, but at the same time you didn't guarantee being given resources?"

"No," replied Gillett. "I didn't think about that."

"Well, why?"

"Well, I thought it's just like going on a quest in World of Warcraft," said Gillett. "I just expected to be able to attract and find the most talented people around . . . I think that's what doing a job is about."

Maybe that's how it should be in the real world, but it often doesn't work out that way. The Net Generation may be in for a rude surprise once they start working in the real corporate world. Employers shouldn't just dismiss the Net Geners on account of their organizational naïveté, though. They should embrace the Net Geners' culture, or run the risk of losing both the war for talent and the opportunity to absorb new ways of working.

TALENT 2.0: RETHINKING TALENT MANAGEMENT FOR A NEW GENERATION

Instilling the Net Gen's collaborative culture into the world of work only begins with the adept use of tools like social networking. Companies have to change in a far deeper way to adapt to the Net Gen's way of working. To win the war for talent, companies will have to completely rethink the way they handle the Net Geners, from the first contact to after they leave the company. As part of our research, youth researcher and author Robert Barnard and I came to a rather significant conclusion: the old model of employee development—recruit, train, supervise, and retain—is outdated.[41] The more appropriate employer-employee paradigm for this generation, we believe, is *initiate, engage, collaborate,* and *evolve.* This model better reflects the relationship's reciprocal nature as well as the Net Gen norms. (See Figure 6.2.)

> "I think [companies] are relying on fresh approaches, young people who are trying to break paradigms, and I think they are looking for that thirst of success that young generations have."
>
> *-MONICA AGUILAR, 25, CAMARGO, MEXICO*

FIGURE 6.2 MODELS OF MANAGEMENT

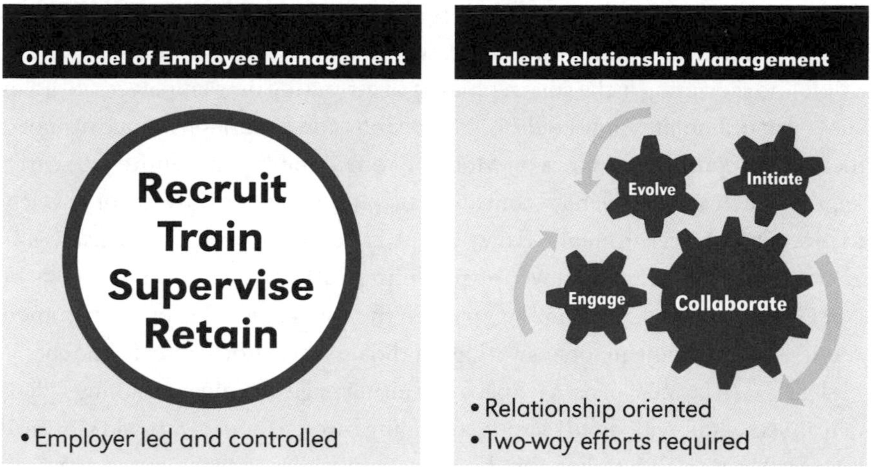

Old Model of Employee Management	Talent Relationship Management
Recruit Train Supervise Retain	Evolve / Initiate / Engage / Collaborate
• Employer led and controlled	• Relationship oriented • Two-way efforts required

The Net Generation: A Strategic Investigation, © nGenera, 2008

Telepresence: Technology Making All Work Spaces Simultaneous

Telepresence. I first heard the word in 1978, spoken by a colleague named Bill Buxton, who is now an executive at Microsoft. Medical telepresence can, for example, link an expert surgeon at Massachusetts General Hospital in Boston with an army doc in Iraq; the mobile telepresence surgical equipment can aid in the trauma care of American soldiers hurt in combat. The Mass General surgeon's actions, movements, and voice may be transmitted and duplicated in Iraq. "Because the stereographic images and the motions and forces can be readily scaled, microsurgeries of all kinds can be made easier with this technology."

DON'T RECRUIT: INITIATE RELATIONSHIPS

In the old model of human resources, potential new hires were solicited using one-way broadcast advertising methods like the placing of classified advertisements in the local newspaper or giving a talk at a school career day.

Yet traditional advertising to attract young people is a complete waste of time and money. It would be better to take all that money that is being spent in this way and use it to build a big fire to attract attention. The companies that understand the Net Generation generate online excitement by creating engaging and informative Web sites and communities using tools such as blogs and podcasts, and creating attractive multimedia material for distribution on sites such as

YouTube and/or Facebook. Smart companies are savvy at presenting job responsibilities, workload, and opportunities for professional development to potential
hires and at conveying an accurate representation of the corporate environment.

Online recruiting is the smarter means of attracting new employees. Studies
show that online sites now hold 110 million jobs and 20 million unique resumes,
including 10 million resumes on Monster.com alone.[42] Some entire job search
engines, such as hirediversity.com and naacp.monster.com, are devoted solely
to diversity job recruitment.[43] Savvy organizations will position themselves as
an attractive Net Gen employer by providing authentic, uncensored blogs by
Net Gen employees, a hiring FAQ page in the form of a wiki, and a customer-
service-like mechanism for answering candidates' questions in real-time chat.

The U.S. Marine Corps' MySpace recruiting page contains streaming videos
of drill sergeants, wide-eyed recruits struggling through boot camp, and seasoned
marines landing on beaches. On the U.S. Army's companycommand.army.mil
Web site, there are discussion threads on everything from mortar attacks to grief
counseling and dishonest sergeants. The site describes itself as "a grassroots,
voluntary forum that is by and for the profession." The military's collaborative
Web sites are a cyber-extension of the mess hall conversations that have tran-
spired for decades.

No one is suggesting that social networking sites like Facebook and
LinkedIn will replace your human resources departments, says Mike Dover,
vice president of syndicated research at nGenera Corporation in Canada. "But
any firm that does not deploy them as a recruiting tool, especially in the initial
tracking stage, will find itself at a serious disadvantage," he says.

LinkedIn, the popular social network for businesspeople, offers many
advantages, Dover explains.

LinkedIn makes it easy to find candidates who are not actively searching for
work—the most sought after candidates in the typical job competition. These
days, it's perfectly acceptable to put your CV on this popular site, and searches
can be done based on tag words, geography, number of recommendations, or
"degrees away" from the recruiter.

Unlike a paper résumé, where brevity is crucial, LinkedIn allows you to
include detailed information, such as blog sites, lists of clients and engage-
ments, and personal interests.

Candidates can list recommendations. Since these references are public,
they are more likely to be accurate. The absence of a recommendation can be
telling too.

When investigating candidates, a firm can use LinkedIn to check for references that the candidate didn't provide. For example, Candidate X worked at Unilever during 1988–93 . . . who else do we know that worked there?

What happens when you get a prospect in the door? Old-style job interviews were much like an FBI interrogation in which potential employees were grilled on their strengths and weaknesses, knowledge, and skills. Interviewees braced themselves for the barrage of questions by wearing extra deodorant that day and that was their only defense, considering that few of them were informed of the inner workings of the company or able to research the actual position they were applying for.

I think this approach should be completely revised. Employers who seek to identify, attract, and hire the best talent should see the process as a two-way dialogue. When today's young people research potential employers, they look for corporate integrity, openness, transparency, and a true picture of the employment offer.[44] They will often walk into a job interview with their own list of questions after having googled the interviewer and reviewed the company's recent press releases. The Net Geners want to make sure that a company's values and corporate culture align with their own values and working style. Some enterprises do use more informal and personal tactics in attempting to attract qualified candidates; they draw on social networks to recruit candidates (often utilizing their own Net Gen employees' contacts) and craft processes that promote two-way information exchange.

As for screening employees, try before you buy, using co-op programs or short-term training programs before you hire someone. As Mike Dover of nGenera says, "Engage the free agent nation and you can make sure that full-time hires are a good fit." He also recommends that firms "use the underground reference by communicating directly with contacts of the potential recruit. On sites like LinkedIn, all recommendations are public so referees are more likely to be truthful because they are accountable. It's so much better than the old method of single call reference check. In that system, even a serial killer could get three people to say something nice about him."

Net Geners, while still in their teens, start to think about whom they might work for, so start early in building a reputation. Most importantly, companies need to articulate a unique vision for talent—based on the eight Net Gen norms. And remember, money is typically not at the top of the list. New employees want to learn, meet interesting people, do interesting work, and yes, have fun.

Finally, don't be surprised if you see a new kind of résumé. I like to advise Net Geners to discard the old-style sections like Name, Job Objectives, Qualifications, Employment History, and References. Instead, I tell them that their resume should say: What I Know, Where I've Done It, How I Got This Knowledge, Who I Know and What They Know, Who I Want to Meet,

> "My friends are jealous; they're in typical entry level jobs, still putting off figuring out what they want to do."
>
> —ROB DEAN, 22, ARLINGTON, VIRGINIA

What I Want to Learn, What I Want to Create, What Tools Would Help Me Be Most Productive. I know this kind of résumé looks different, but I think that employers may find that it's more revealing, and therefore more useful, than the standard one. It may launch a conversation that could turn into a long term work relationship.

DON'T JUST TRAIN: ENGAGE

In physics, the smallest particle into which a substance can be divided and still have the identity of the original substance is the molecule. Molecules are held together by electrical forces. They are, in a sense, networked. The molecule is a good analogy for the optimal role of the Net Gen knowledge worker in today's digital economy. Individuals who are networked have replaced the old corporate hierarchy as the optimal structure of an organization as a vehicle of wealth creation. In other words, everything that was mass has become molecular.

In organizations this means that each employee is treated as an individual contributor. Employment is a relationship—between the employee and employer. It needs commitment from both sides, as the employer routinely taps into the needs of the individual worker: to engage and collaborate *throughout their entire careers*, at every stage of the employee life cycle.

Engagement is a two-way street—an open flow of communication relaying the specific needs of the employee and the organization. "What's in it for me?" and "What's in it for you?" are questions that must be clearly addressed with both employee and employer held accountable for delivery of their commitments. Work styles, work-flow models, workday and workplace parameters, career paths, and professional development offerings should be examined and potentially retooled by organizations to maximize fit with the generation mix of employees. Net Gen employees, in particular, will respond well if mentored and coached to contribute to corporate policies, strategy, and business performance. Says Accenture's Managing Partner of the Human Performance practice Peter Cheese, "When it comes to young knowledge workers, and we're hiring 70,000 this year, engagement is the mystery ingredient required to free the power of human capital and transform performance."

For starters, rethink the job description. Take a page from Jim Quigley, CEO of Deloitte, who has mandated that each employee have a custom description.

A traditional condition of employment in many organizations is a 90-day probationary period during which new recruits are assessed for their suitability. Nowadays, young employees regularly use this period to decide whether the employer is worth working for. Thus, employers must use creativity and flexibility when organizing the first few months of work so as to expose the new recruit to various leaders, work situations, and work content. Greater transparency, and exposure to and interactivity with the broader organization, during this initiation phase will lead to a win-win outcome. Companies that make the effort will benefit from less turnover, shorter ramp-up periods, higher levels of engagement, and earlier and greater returns on their investments in young employees.

Training has to change. For example, the National Institute for School Leadership developed an $11 million executive training course for school principals—using computer simulations to help them apply their existing knowledge to realistic new scenarios. A leadership team running a virtual school might be asked, "How will you put together a professional development system that results in raising student achievement?" Participants answer a series of forced-option questions and receive immediate feedback, thus developing good strategic skills, leadership, a team-oriented mind-set, and ethics.[45]

Other companies are using game-based training to update their employees on short-term projects. The game format is flexible and easy to distribute, just in time. DIRECTV, for example, needed to boost sales of their sports programming package, so it created a simulation game created to place the call-center agent in an interactive environment. The agent must deal with realistic characters voicing frequently asked questions about DIRECTV and their programs. By playing the game, the agent practices active-listening skills, learns telephone etiquette, and is familiarized with the benefits of DIRECTV's popular sports programming package. The scoring mode on the game gives players instant feedback on how well they're doing as sales representatives. The game-based training proved to be a huge success, making it possible for DIRECTV to reach their aggressive goal for the 2006 football season.[46]

Companies need to increase the learning component of work. Our survey tells us that Net Geners think work and learning, collaboration, and fun should be the same thing—and they've got it right. So rather than sending employees off to training programs, it makes sense to strengthen learning as part of enriching work. We try to do this at the nGenera Innovation Network. All employees are not only encouraged; they are required to blog regularly as part of their jobs. Each of them (and they're mainly Net Geners) must think about important issues facing our clients, and based on their research formulate opinions for public presentation. To do this they must read others' blogs daily, think through issues, and craft their thoughts on a regular basis. The blog delivers value to our clients and the market and, as part of their work, our employees learn from it. Work and learning—the same thing. Not to mention that they collaborate to blog and have fun, too.

DON'T JUST SUPERVISE—BUILD NEXT GENERATION COLLABORATIVE WORK SYSTEMS

For Brad Anderson, CEO of Best Buy, supervision and even management in the old sense is outdated. He notes, "The Net Geners we hire have enormous knowledge, unprecedented information, and facility with tools that in some areas is superior to their seniors." So the job of management is more to create the context whereby they can be successful, rather than to supervise them.

I recently attended a small meeting where two senior managers presented some of the company's new initiatives to Anderson. One Net Gener who had been invited, 23-year-old Adam Mulder, spoke passionately and at some length about a change he thought would improve the company's sales of media products. Brad listened attentively, taking notes, asking Adam questions, and encouraging others in the room to join the conversation.

I was struck by the exchange. Had I been a young recruit sitting with the CEO, my knees would have been shaking. But here was this young man speaking his mind to the big boss. I asked Anderson later to comment on why as a CEO he was so interested in a discussion with a relatively new employee, way down on the management structure. He told me, "Young people like him take center stage around here a lot. They've got a difference that produces unique insights. The future of this enterprise is dependent much more on him than on me." A power shift is occurring: "If I were to shut him down, he'd tell someone and soon everyone would know that I don't listen. He can shut me down as the CEO. Having power means something very different than it used to."

When I wrote *Growing Up Digital*, I described a "Generation Lap," in which "kids [are] outpacing and overtaking adults on the technology track, lapping them in many areas of daily life."[47] In 1997, young people for the first time were recognized by adults as being authorities on something truly revolutionary—digital technology, interactive media, and collaboration. As they enter the workforce, these young employees bring their experience as digital authorities with them. This challenges fundamental concepts of corporate hierarchy—where, for example, a boss in any business unit is viewed as an authority on everything that takes place in that unit. He is the superior supervisor. Instead, the boss needs to understand that he or she is a student in some areas—for example, with regards to the use of wikis, blogs, and social networks for collaboration. As John Seely Brown puts it, "What you find in leading organizations today is that each one of us is, in some way, an authority in some domains and a student in other domains. We must be prepared to learn major things from our subordinates and vice versa." Consider the issue of technology in the workplace. The nGenera survey showed that 54 percent of Net Geners rated themselves as having the top level of expertise about technology. Only 28 percent rated their bosses as having an equivalent level of expertise. (See Table 6.2.)

Lots of employers are understandably worried that employees will disclose important company information in a blog or other writing on the Internet. To guard against this risk, employers need to explain the rules to new Net Gen employees, says dana boyd, a fellow at the Annenberg Center for Communications, University of Southern California. "You have a guideline on it. You have to make it very, very clear that there is zero tolerance for [sharing company information] with the penalty of being fired for cause. No one knows discretion until you teach them. School's a public place. You are now entering the work-

TABLE 6.2   THE NET GENERATION AND THE KNOWLEDGE GAP

How would you rate your own knowledge of how to use technology?

	Total	White Collar	Gray Collar	Blue Collar
Yourself	45%	54%	38%	45%
Boss	28%	28%	27%	29%
Coworkers	26%	26%	29%	22%
AP You vs. Your Boss	17%	26%	11%	16%

Source: The Net Generation: A Strategic Investigation, © nGenera, 2008
(N - 1,750 13-29 year olds in U.S. and Canada)

*The responses in this survey of 1,750 Net Geners in the United States and Canada were prompted by the question: "How would you rate your own and your boss's and coworkers' knowledge of how to use technology?" (The top three boxes measures percentage of people who responded 8, 9, or10 on a 10-point scale.)

force for the first time. And I think that all companies have a responsibility to have a blogging policy and to make it very, very clear, from day one, how this works. The thing is that you give them an e-mail [of someone] to contact with questions. And you give them examples of things not to do. Like bitching about the really bad day at Goldman Sachs."[48]

> "I think for a lot of kids now many of your tools are the natural channels for getting things done . . . but sometimes it takes an older, wise person to light the way."
>
> —JOE O'SHEA, 22, TALLAHASSEE, FLORIDA

But many companies still treat young employees as apprentices who should do their time and keep quiet. A survey by Lee Hecht Harrison reports that more than 70 percent of older employees are dismissive of younger workers' abilities.[49] When their voice goes unheard or their contributions go unrecognized, they may feel undervalued and start looking elsewhere for more meaningful employment. In today's marketplace, young human capital is at such a premium that the need to satisfy employees is fundamental.

Companies like Best Buy know this. As Brad Anderson explains, employees are now being given far more autonomy to decide how and where they want to work. A growing number of firms are decentralizing their decision-making function, communicating in a peer-to-peer fashion, and embracing new technologies, which empower employees to communicate easily and openly with people inside and outside the firm. In doing so, they are creating a new corporate meritocracy that is eroding old hierarchies and connecting internal teams to all kinds of external networks. And who better to lead in the pilot programs to take you to the future than those who have grown up using these tools?

DON'T JUST RETAIN: EVOLVE THE RELATIONSHIP

> "And what is your reason for leaving?"
> "To be honest, I was spending way too much time thinking about creative ways to kill you."
> "Have you cleared out your desk?"
> "Why don't you go check?" (said with big smile on face)
>   —Dilbert's pointy-haired boss conducts an exit interview[50]

In the old model of employee development, ex-employees were treated as traitors. Leading companies see it differently. I personally have experience with evolving employee relationships with a Net Gener. In fact, I have hired 31-year-old Denis Hancock on six separate occasions. Denis is a talented lad, and I've been working with him for almost a decade—but not continuously. Over this time, he's left us five times—to finish his undergraduate studies in Amsterdam; to backpack through Australia and New Zealand; to gain some marketing experience at a larger company; and, most recently, to pursue a master's degree in economics. In between, his time with the company has also been a mixture of full- and part-time employment agreements, which have often involved him working from home. Sounds like a high-maintenance, unstable relationship—right?

Wrong. It's not like Denis up and vanishes in the middle of an important project—he tends to be with us for projects that he can contribute the most value to, and then is off improving himself in other ways at other times. By keeping him in our alumni network, we get the opportunity to tap into his new skills as they develop. Perhaps most interestingly, this approach has now greatly increased our chances of keeping Denis around for the long-term, in sporadic work stints. As Denis explained to me in our most recent contract "negotiations," his next big leap (into fatherhood) means that having a flexible employer will be even more important to him than before. Our track record on this front gives us a decisive competitive advantage for the next, oh, two decades or so.

Using the analogy of the university's alumni network, companies should think of employees as individuals within a web of contacts. Such alumni contain a wealth of knowledge about the company's inner workings, ever available to add great value, even after leaving the company. Social networking, communities of practice, and other Web 2.0 platforms allow employees and ex-employees alike to exchange resources and disseminate information. Net Gen employees will embrace this kind of thinking, as it comes naturally to them.

My son Alex graduated from Amherst College in May 2008. Already, he has been approached by the school to become an active alumnus—by participating in networking events and fund-raising endeavors and by soliciting donations. Colleges and universities with the strongest alumni networks have the greatest endowments, and such connections continue to strengthen the prestige of these institutions. "Businesses are not universities, but in recognizing the potential value of those employees who are leaving for the right reasons, such as professional development, businesses will see a greater return on the initial investments they make."[51]

A key to building an alumni model of retention is for companies to support employees who wish to move on to build new skills that their organization cannot offer. Having an open and honest conversation about the employee's needs and future plans increases the likelihood for her to return someday with valuable new knowledge and insights for your organization—whether that employee is working on contract or full time. Consulting and accounting firms and other professional services have utilized an alumni model for years. "It costs half as much to rehire an ex-employee as it does to hire a brand-new person; rehires are 40 percent more productive in their first quarter at work; and they tend to stay in the job longer. Research suggests that the average Fortune 500 company could save $12 million a year by actively recruiting alumni," wrote Cem Sertoglu et al., in the *Harvard Business Review*.[52] The advantages of accepting job mobility rather than regarding it as a threat are great in today's competitive marketplace; the potential to recapture the return on the initial investments you make in a company's human capital is too valuable to ignore. And, as for retention, the key is to create a culture wherein youth can contribute, grow, learn, and have fun.

CONCLUSION

The Net Generation's eight norms provide a manifesto for change that will revolutionize the workplace of tomorrow. These norms will also provide competitive advantage to companies that embrace these norms today. Managing talent today is about creating new opportunities, enhancing competitiveness, reducing costs, and increasing profits and success. The sheer numbers of the Net Generation, both from North America and nations with rising economies, offer an unprecedented bounty of talent. This wave of young workers will not only work for tomorrow's global corporations, but will increasingly shape and direct the most successful corporations, wherever their nominal headquarters might be.

This new generation of workers is forging a new way of doing business—using Web 2.0 communication tools to create a collaborative workplace that democratizes and accelerates the performance of an organization.

TALENT 2.0: SEVEN GUIDELINES FOR MANAGERS

As the Net Generation comes into the workforce, they are changing the way we think about talent and work.

(1) **Design work systems according to the eight norms.** Look to Net Generation culture and behavior as the new culture of work and the new enterprise.

(2) **Rethink authority.** Be a good leader (e.g., coach, mentor, facilitator, enabler), but understand that in some areas, you will be the student and the Net Gen employee will be the teacher. Net Geners need plenty of feedback, but recognition must be authentic. False praise doesn't work.

(3) **Rethink recruitment; initiate relationships.** Don't waste money on advertising for talent. Use social networks based on trust to influence young people about your company.

(4) **Rethink training; engage for lifelong learning.** Rather than relying on traditional training programs that are separate from work, look to strengthen the learning component of all jobs. To achieve this, encourage employees to blog.

(5) **Don't ban Facebook or other social networks.** Figure out how to harness them. New tools like wikis, blogs, social networks, jams, telepresence, tags, collaborative filtering, and RSS feeds can be the heart of the new high-performance workplace. Rethink management processes and design jobs and work for collaboration. Give the Net Geners a chance to put collaborative tools to good use—by joining one of the company's volunteering efforts.

(6) **Rethink retention; evolve lasting relationships.** Create alumni networks. Bring talent you're recruiting inside your business web, if you can't get it inside the boundaries of your organization per se. Networked business models work well.

(7) **Unleash the power of Net Gen capital in your organization.** Listen to young people. Put them in the driver's seat alongside you when designing work spaces, processes, management systems, and collaborative working models.

THE NET GENERATION AS CONSUMERS

Brian Fetherstonhaugh is the chairman and chief executive of OgilvyOne Worldwide, a global leader in managing customer relations, with more than 110 offices in 56 countries. In 2005, when he wanted to understand the Net Gen's media habits, he didn't commission the usual survey. Instead, he started right at home, by asking his 15-year-old daughter, Allison, to keep a detailed media diary for one week.

"I wanted to know how much TV she was watching, whether it was live or TiVo; how much time she was on the computer or mobile phone, what she was doing on the computer; what music was she listening to; was she reading magazines or newspapers; how many text messages she was sending and any other media activity," said Fetherstonhaugh.

Allison was happy to oblige, and when her father read her media diary, he was astonished. "What surprised me was that more than half of the television Allison was watching was not live TV. It was either TiVo, a DVD, or games," said Fetherstonhaugh.

And when watching TV this way, Net Geners are able to eliminate the ads. Fetherstonhaugh also discovered that Allison didn't read the newspapers, a scary thought for an advertising executive.

Telling results, especially for companies marketing news and entertainment to teenagers through print ads. Soon, Fetherstonhaugh's project became known as the Allison Diaries. "The information was so useful that I asked Allison to recruit friends to keep similar diaries. That worked well, so then I asked my colleagues in OgilvyOne offices around the world to ask their sons and daughters to do the same thing." Allison herself was charged with gathering the responses and creating a summary for her dad.

With the Allison Diaries, Fetherstonhaugh quickly realized that the advertising industry had underestimated the impact of the Internet. Figures showing the percentage of disposable income spent online do not tell the full story. "I knew from other sources that teenagers don't spend a lot of money online," said Fetherstonhaugh. "E-commerce hasn't really caught on, in large part because teenagers don't have credit cards. What I learned from Allison and her friends is that they spend a lot of time online, researching products they end up buying in stores. They always consult the Internet before making a purchase. This sort of behavior doesn't show up in the cold, hard e-commerce data. The Net Generation's arrival means that many of marketing's fundamental tenets must change."

In business schools they still teach the Four Ps of marketing–product, price, place, and promotion. To market a product effectively, you create products and define their features and benefits. You set the prices. You select places to sell products and services. You promote aggressively through advertising, public relations, direct mail, and other in-your-face programs. You control the message. We, the consumers, just have to listen and buy.

Yet, as we will see in this chapter, the Net Geners are changing this game. They won't accept this one-way approach, not when they've been immersed in two-way communication from childhood. They were raised in a world of marketing and advertising, so they can detect a sales pitch with heavy topspin in a second. While they are not impervious to the power of advertising, they are more adept at filtering, fast-forwarding, and/or blocking unsolicited advertising than previous generations were. They can compare the company line with other versions of the story, and they have plenty of ways to find out from a wide variety of sources—including critics of the company.

When the Net Gens go shopping, they are guided by the eight norms that I have described in this book. Among other things, they usually go online to scrutinize a product—both its features and its price—before setting foot in a store. They expect plenty of choice and high-speed service. They think fun should be embedded in the product. They're not satisfied with one-size-fits-all items that can be bought only in certain places and at certain times. They want something that fits them—where, when, and how they want it. They're no longer passive consumers of the broadcast model. That's yesterday's news. They aren't just consumers, either. Some Net Geners are eager to contribute to the brand—something that wouldn't have occurred to most boomers. Call them the new "prosumers."

In this chapter, you'll see how the Net Generation turn to their friends for shopping advice rather than trusting ads or company executives. They are developing what I call N-Fluence networks via the Internet, especially the social media. These N-Fluence networks are expanding the circle of friends you can have, and are undercutting the conventional wisdom that says we're only separated from people we don't know by six degrees of separation. N-Fluence networks have their own social structure: you have your best friends, your larger circle of acquaintances in your social network, plus the world. The rules of engagement are different for each level, which makes life tough for the marketers who are used to the old style of broadcast advertising. We'll look at how some of them are trying to penetrate the social networks. Now they find they need to be a "friend" in order to influence Net Geners, and many of them are not sure what that means. We'll offer some dos and don'ts to help. Smart companies, for instance, are making friends with their customers by posting online product reviews and by seeking out enthusiasts to spread the message for them, as well as by accepting that when they do so, they can't control the message or the brand.

The Net Geners, as we will see, are a new kind of shopper. I think they will cause marketers to rewrite the rules of marketing for this generation, and ultimately for the future. Companies will no longer have a monopoly on creating the product, setting the price, choosing the place, or doing the promotion, and controlling the message. The Net Generation is rendering these so-called "Four Ps of Marketing" obsolete. Instead, companies will play by ABCDE rules of marketing—Anyplace, Brand, Communication, Discovery, and Experience. As we'll see in this chapter, Net Geners want to buy things Anyplace, where and when they want. They'll help shape the Brand, and the product. And they won't tolerate a lecture, however amiable. The standard ad will be replaced by Communication, a two-way conversation. As in any relationship, integrity will be one of the key building blocks of this new interactive brand. Since Net Geners research the product and its price

> "I despise 'interactive' ads. If the ad has to flash and blink to get my attention, it's just going to bug me, not make me want the product. Companies that design good products seem to also make good ads—like Apple or Coke or fashion companies—or just not advertise—like Facebook or Amazon. Their product (and partially their name) is good enough that we don't need to get irritated; we just need to be convinced."
>
> —KEVIN GESSNER, ROCHESTER, NEW YORK

online, they'll negotiate the price. I call this the Discovery of Price. And finally, they expect products to be at the same time an Experience. We end the chapter with seven tips for marketing professionals.

THE NEW GENERATION OF CONSUMERS HAS MONEY, AND UNPRECEDENTED INFLUENCE

This new generation of consumers behaves differently than their parents did in the marketplace where goods and services are sold and bought. Companies are eager to understand them because they earn and spend a great deal of money. In the United States, students earn almost $200 billion a year in part- or full-time jobs,[1] and in 2006, they purchased $190 billion worth of goods.[2] But that's not the most important reason marketers need to pay attention to the Net Gen.

Net Geners have enormous influence on their baby boomer parents, and their money—some $2 trillion in spending a year.[3] Net Geners age 21 and under influence 81 percent of their families' apparel purchases and 52 percent of car choices.[4] Even younger children have powerful sway, with those between 5 and 14 influencing 78 percent of total grocery purchases.[5] And, as they age, their direct purchasing power will soar: in 2003, only 5 percent of cars were purchased by people born between 1980 and 1995; by 2020, this will climb to 40 percent.[6]

"This new generation," Fetherstonhaugh says, "is leading marketers into the digital revolution." He's right. The eight norms we have been discussing in this book inform the way they behave as consumers and foreshadow profound changes in marketing itself.

THE EIGHT NORMS: HOW THEY GUIDE NET GENERS WHEN THEY GO SHOPPING

Freedom: Give Me Choice and the More the Better

In my youth, I could choose between Levi's and Lee jeans. Net Geners, on the other hand, insist on the freedom to choose, and they generally get it. Today, there are a dozen brands of jeans on the market, and each brand has a half-dozen styles. In exchange for exclusivity of brand, Net Geners have opted for a greater range of choices—and designer jeans can cost $300 or more. Instead of being overwhelmed, the Net Geners love the variety and the challenge of finding the perfect fit.

> "I like flexibility and choice. I want to customize my products the way I want and to pay for something the way I want to and have it delivered when and where I choose. I want my purchases to be fast and easy. My motto as a consumer is 'Don't fence me in.' "
>
> —NIKI TAPSCOTT

Customization: Make It My Own

Net Geners love to customize new product offerings, even if it means hacking. Only months after Apple introduced its popular iPod player, for example, amateur iPod users had created "Podzilla," a software utility that allows users to record at a much higher quality than a separate $50 recording device. Tuner cars, favored mostly by young drivers, have become a $3 billion industry.[7] Most major auto manufacturers initially missed out on this opportunity, and only recently have begun offering more customization options.

Scrutiny: I Will Check It Out Before I Go to the Store

Consumer Reports magazine was the go-to source for product information for older generations. Today it's the Internet, with its vast library of research on products, prices, and options. Prices can be compared on Price.com, Amazon, and BizRate. Experiences with products or services can be reviewed on bulletin boards, in discussion groups, and on product- or theme-related blogs.[8]

Some 83 percent of Net Geners say that they usually know what they want before going to buy a product.[9] While online purchases account for a small but growing 16 percent of the Net Generation's annual spending,

> "When I bought my digital camera I looked at online reviews, matched prices, and did my best to learn as much about the product as I could."
> —KEVIN GESSNER, ROCHESTER, NEW YORK

most teens report reading and learning about products online before they buy them in conventional stores.[10] In a recent survey, some 80 percent of shoppers in New York said their visit to a store was not prompted by offline advertising or marketing.[11]

Integrity: Does This Company Deserve My Money?

PR and "spin" won't work for this generation. These techniques assume that you can control the media environment and send out corporate messages to consumers who will believe and internalize them. In a pervasive computing environment, these one-way conversations just aren't credible.

Net Gen consumers expect companies to do what they promise, and meet the users' expectations. The news aggregator Digg.com learned this the hard way. The company faced a user revolt after it complied with a legal order to remove from its Web site a story that included the details of a software key that could break the encryption code on high-definition DVDs.[12] In this instance, the Digg community apparently felt that integrity meant placing more of a premium on freedom of speech than on the letter of the law, and they wanted Digg to act in accordance with this expectation. Marketers who stay true to their word can reap fruitful results; for Net Geners who are looking for brands with which they can identify, integrity is a cornerstone of consumer loyalty.

Today's digital tools strip away the layers of insulation that once existed between companies and consumers.[13] It is increasingly important for companies to act with integrity—and fulfill the expectation that they will operate honestly and forthrightly, will honor their commitments, and will hold themselves accountable when they make mistakes. Many companies

> "A company which demonstrates ethics and social responsibility is more likely to attract my business (Costco versus Wal-Mart, or the RED campaign)."
>
> —ERIC POTTER, BRANDEIS UNIVERSITY

have confronted a "YourCompanySucks.com"-type Web site, on which frustrated customers and activists complain about bad products or unethical corporate behavior. So many customers ganged up online to complain about truck rental firm U-Haul's reservation system that some law firms tested the waters for a class-action suit.[14]

Collaboration: Let Me Help You Make Your Product or Service Better

Nearly 7 out of 10 youths want to work hand in hand with companies to create better goods and services. It probably didn't even occur to their parents to help a large, impersonal company do something better. They simply consumed what was in the marketplace. In any case, they didn't have the opportunity. Back then, companies conceived new products in secret. The Internet, corporate support forums, user groups, and e-mail didn't exist. Long-distance calling was expensive and 1-800 numbers weren't widespread, and companies weren't structured to receive substantial customer input.

But now many young people feel good when a company values their opinion. They believe they offer useful insights and like to feel part of a knowledgeable, exclusive group. They are willing to test product prototypes and answer survey questions. Half of Net Geners are willing to tell companies details of their lives if they believe that the result will be an improved product that better fits their needs. This number rises to 61 percent of Early Adopters (people who get new tech items before most people do) and 74 percent of the Bleeding Edgers (the first people to get new tech items). However, they hesitate to share the data if they feel a company might misuse the information, sell it to other companies, or inundate them with junk mail and spam.[15]

Leading companies are using all kinds of innovative approaches to get feed-back. Dell created IdeaStorms, an online presence that allows customers to raise all kinds of ideas about and criticisms of its products. When CEO Michael Dell was contemplating the idea, he said to me: "We've just got to open up to customers. They have great knowledge and we need to engage them better." Other companies involve their customers in actually designing products and services going as far back as a decade. Lego was an early Internet pioneer, open-ing the interfaces to its Mindstorms robotic product and engaging customers in actually building Mindstorm applications.

Entertainment: Make It Fun

Nearly three-quarters of Net Geners think that having fun with a product is just as important as simply using it, according to our survey data. For the Net Gen, entertainment and playfulness are central to socialization and education. When 92 percent of American children aged 2–17 have regular access to video games, entertainment is not just an expectation, it's a big industry—bigger than the Hollywood film industry.[16] Some leading-edge companies are revving up the fun factor. In 1998, shopping mall developer The Mills Corporation partnered with the Vans shoe company to create an indoor skate park in its "The Block" mall in Orange County, California. The project not only boosted Net Gener traffic, but also attracted their parents.[17]

Speed: Serve Me Now

Net Geners expect speed when they interact with companies. Net Geners natu-rally assume that companies can respond with the same kind of simplicity, speed, and directness that they do when they exchange instant messages with their friends. Responding to every customer query with an instant response would have been unimaginable in the past, given the amount of employee time required. But new pervasive computing could feasibly automate many processes while still answering the customers' questions. Check out what's happening around the world:

> In Japan, using a camera phone to picture, or "read," a two-dimensional bar-like code will cause users to view a URL that provides the option for more product information, one-click music downloads, and/or information exchanges with new friends.
>
> In Finland, a cell phone camera can "read" an UPCODE on the sports page, and provide a video of last night's overtime goal.

> In Korea, a cell phone can "read" a "ColorCode" during a television broadcast and download the real-time music video, or provide the detailed specifications for the car or laptop that has captured the viewer's attention.

> In Pretoria Airport, Wiremedia has posted signs encouraging travelers to turn on their mobile phones' Bluetooth connectivity.[18] If they do this, customers receive special offers on duty-free products.

Such location-based technology lets advertisements at retail locations, movie theaters, billboards, and bus stations "come alive" and deliver their message to potential customers within range. For the busy Net Gener who is hurrying past a flower shop on Mother's Day, the timely delivery of a mobile coupon may be a convenient and welcome reminder. It also might generate significant new sales for the florist. Wiremedia has opened up its software to enable Net Geners participating in social networking sites and blogging communities to communicate with each other using its technology. Colby Fede, CEO of Wiremedia, explained that this action stemmed from the desire to leverage " . . . the vast viral marketing potential that blogs and social networking sites can deliver to a burgeoning brand."

Innovation: Give Me the Latest
The Net Gen wants the latest and greatest products available—whether it's their cell phone, iPod, or game console. It makes their friends envious and contributes to their social status. And they often get what they want: new models are constantly being introduced, and in most cases offer big gains in functionality, speed, or capacity.

THE RISE OF N-FLUENCE NETWORKS
Today, social networks, driven largely by youth, are the key arena where young people talk to each other, meet new friends, and keep up with acquaintances. I'm not just referring to networks like Facebook or MySpace, but also to the myriad places on the Web where people can meet and share information. They constantly swap views on movies, music, clothes, and dozens of other topics in these networks. When they think about what to buy, Net Geners go to online social networks to see what their friends are buying—32 percent of teens say they "buy things my friends have."[19] When they lack experience with a product, 29 percent ask their friends for advice.[20]

Kids are influencing their friends as never before. When I was young, on a typical day I could influence perhaps a half-dozen people—my siblings and a couple of good friends. Not that they sought my opinion all that often, and when they did, the question was usually pretty simple: should we walk or ride our bikes to the park?

I call these communication networks and the relationships they foster "N-Fluence networks." For the Net Generation, this is where influence really lies, in these networks of friends and acquaintances. To be sure, in some senses such networks are nothing new—traveling salesmen, Tupperware parties, chain letters, and groups of friends have been around for a long time. Business executives have long understood their value: that's why they set up exclusive clubs for lunch and dinner. The problem is that these social networks didn't scale very well: they were limited by what's known as Dunbar's number.[21]

Back in 1992, Robin Dunbar, a British anthropologist, suggested that the natural size of a group—including high school friends and people you'd like to see again—is about 150. That's the number of people most humans can maintain a stable relationship with in a group or groups through personal contact. Dunbar came up with the number after observing that in nonhuman primates, the natural size of their groups depended on the relative size of their neocortex. Extrapolating from that finding, he suggested that the natural size for a human group was 147.5, which, as it happens, is roughly the same size as the number of people in a typical preindustrial village, professional army unit, Hutterite farming community, and scientific subspecialty.

The limit wasn't just a function of brain size. Nonhuman primates, he noted, keep up social ties through personal one-on-one grooming, so they don't have time to maintain a large group. Humans keep up relationships through grooming too, a form of social grooming called language, which allows them to have larger groups——but they're still limited by the number of people they can talk to at any one time. The evolution of larger groups in humans, Dunbar noted, depends on the development of a more time-efficient method for social bonding. Dunbar was developing his theory in 1992, long before social networks became a reality. But now, I would say, a social network like Facebook is the new form of social bonding that will break Dunbar's number, and allow Net Geners like Niki to maintain a stable circle of 700 friends.

Today, the Internet and social networking technologies shatter Dunbar's supposed limits. The Net Geners use communications networks that are orders of magnitude larger, far more complex, and much more efficient than those that were possible when their parents were young. When I was Niki's age, I could maintain only a handful of friends because I had to keep up with them through face-to-face contact. Phone calls were expensive; flights were out of the question. But now, many young people participate in larger and more complex social networks than we would have imagined possible 10 years ago. Geography and time zones no longer get in the way. Members of social networks can contact other people far more quickly and easily than they once could.

Say good-bye to the six degrees of separation too. The line came from the wonderful play by John Guare, but it was based on a famous study of the late 1960s by Stanley Milgram, a social psychologist from Harvard. He wanted to see how many contacts separated two random individuals, so he set up an ingenious experiment. He distributed envelopes to people living in Nebraska and Kansas and gave them the name and address of a stockbroker in Boston. Their mission was to mail the envelope to someone they knew—a friend or acquaintance—who might know the stockbroker, or someone who actually knew him. Most of the letters didn't make it, but those that reached the stock-broker via snail mail usually got there after six steps.

When that experiment was conducted, the Internet was in its early days and e-mail hadn't been invented. I'm sure that the results would be significantly different if the experiment were conducted today, now that we have e-mail, the Web, Google, and Facebook. If Niki were to ask her 700 friends if any of them knew a certain stockbroker in Boston; I doubt it would take six contacts to find him or her. So is it now two degrees of separation? Three? One of the researchers studying the small-world phenomenon is Carnegie Mellon University's Jure Leskovec. In 2007, he coauthored a study called "Planetary Scale Views on a Large Instant Messaging Network," which looked at a planetary population sample that is 4 million times larger than Milgram's U.S. study. The study, done in June 2006, covered an astounding 30 billion conversations via instant messaging networks among 240 million people around the world.

The finding: there are 6.6 degrees of separation between any two random people in this immense instant messaging universe. But Leskovec wasn't just looking at the distance between someone in Wichita and Boston. He was look-ing at two people on the entire planet: "And they're still less than seven people apart! As networks grow, they shrink," says Leskovic. "It's counterintuitive, but as people accumulate more friends, the distances shrink."

That said, I propose Tapscott's New Law of Friends. Okay, it's just a hypoth-esis: "The number of degrees of separation on the planet varies inversely to the size of your social network." A corollary to the law is: "In the new world of social networking, you can have 700 friends and find anyone else on the planet via fewer than seven contacts." This new interconnectedness means that the

N-Fluencers have unprecedented power that comes with scale. They have a larger number of friends they can influence. They can reach more people in fewer steps. And if the conditions are right, they can spread the word (be it negative or positive) about a political cause or a consumer product or service, like wildfire.

Power to the People: Friends Are More Important than Movie Reviewers

The impact of these social networks on the shopping habits of the Net Generation is immense and already visible.

The power of the Web to decentralize knowledge has prompted a profound shift in power from the producers to the consumers. Net Geners have increased access to information about products and services, and they can discern true value more easily than the generations before them. More than ever, to compete in the marketplace, firms need truly differentiated products, better service, or a lower cost, because deficiencies in value cannot be hidden as easily. True value is evidenced like never before.

Influence is also being decentralized as the Net Generation speaks out from the modern-day trenches, otherwise known as blogs. Blogs and other consumer-generated media are altering the sources of power and authority in our society. Some of these sources wield a surprising amount of influence, shifting the balance of power away from more traditional, accredited sources. Smart companies understand this power shift and embrace it.

In the film industry, for example, movie critics have historically been the gold standard for assessing movie quality. But today the blogging community is more N-Fluential than the so-called movie experts. This influence means serious money: the sequel to *Pirates of the Caribbean: Dead Man's Chest*, for example, broke all kinds of box office records because of enthusiasm from teenagers and young adults, despite an overwhelming critical disdain from conventional media sources.[22] The conversational nature of blogs allows for top content and opinions to rise, and, more important, fall, based on merit. Film producers need to find ways to influence the influencers. Russell Schwartz, marketing chief of New Line Cinema, a film studio owned by Time Warner, says: "Younger moviegoers want the immediacy of text messages or voice mail. A review from one of their peers is more important than a printed review from a third party they don't know, which is how they would describe a critic."[23]

It's not just happening with film: *New York* magazine passed over *Rolling Stone* when it created its list of key influencers in the music industry, but 26-year-old blogger Sarah Lewitinn made the list. Apparently her blog, www.ultragrrrl.blogspot.com, has "more power than any print music critic."[24] Net Generation members see little use for the traditional role of the critic. A recent poll appearing in the *Los Angeles Times*, coconducted by Bloomberg News, revealed that of Net Geners between the ages of 18 and 24, only 3 percent felt that "critics' reviews were the most important factor in their movie decision making process."[25] For firms, the power shift away from traditional influencers means that many established "go to" contacts might lack their former clout. Today, firms must identify and engage the new voices of authority, many of which will—like blogger Sarah Lewitinn—emerge from unexpected quarters. A good way to start identifying these new voices of authority is to spend time with Net Gen customers and catalog the new sources of information and "experts" that they depend upon.

Not All Influencers Are Created Equal

Influence within a network is not evenly distributed; some users have a great deal of influence while others have little or none. Early evidence suggests that the distribution of influence within an online social network may not be much different than the Pareto principle (better known as the 80–20 rule), which states that 80 percent of influence can be attributed to as few as 20 percent of the users. For example, sites like Digg.com have spawned "Digg gangs," in which the top 30 users have a disproportionate effect on top article postings.[26] Naturally, it stands to reason that identifying and reaching "key influencers" is extremely important when engaging with N-Fluence networks.

In *The Tipping Point*, Malcolm Gladwell describes three personality types— connectors, mavens, and salesmen—existing among the people who spread opinions and ideas and create new social trends. Each of them is evident in today's N-Fluence networks.

- *Connectors* are the masters of the extended social network. When looking to spread marketing messages, smart companies engage these users first. Defined as having large and distributed social circles, connectors tend to be the hubs of their social networks and are thought to be the enablers of the small-world phenomenon, whereby every individual is connected by a short chain of acquaintances. Young connectors have their fingers on the pulse of society and are able to use digital technology to manage and maintain weak ties that may have previously withered.

- *Mavens* are grassroots sages in the new world of radically decentralized authority. Mavens who build up their reputation and stature via blogs, reviews, and online game-playing environments become a trusted source of influence for friends and strangers alike. Their knowledge and expertise allows them to garner respect from and influence the decisions of strangers. Mavens like to delve into details that may escape other consumers: they notice—and comment on—overpriced products, false claims, and media errors. This is a fitting description of many bloggers.

- *Salesmen* are able to broadcast their influence to the world. Companies that attract the attention of salesmen benefit from their ability to create a lot of buzz. Salesmen are charismatic, charming, and excellent negotiators. They exert a "soft" influence rather than overpowering those with whom they interact. Social networking and multimedia sites from YouTube to MySpace provide salesmen with the venues that allow their talents to shine.

TYPES OF N-FLUENCE NETWORKS

Just as not all N-Fluencers have equal value, not all networks are equally valuable either. In working with my clients, I've developed a framework of three different categories of N-Fluence networks (see Figure 7.1 on page 198). Each one functions differently, although there's plenty of overlap. A message between best friends or acquaintances can quickly go viral, and spread over the world.

Best Friends

Best Friends is the small group of people the user knows well (on MySpace this would include your "Top 8," for instance).[27] My daughter Niki says she has 18 Best Friends. These can include siblings but not typically parents, as these are more peer-to-peer relationships. Most Net Geners are still uneasy about their parents having access to their full profile and friend communications. With Best Friends, as the name suggests, influence is directed at friends who are close to the user. This type of influence relies on personal interaction and one-to-one communications. The majority of young people (57 percent) prefer face-to-face interactions among their closest friends, though among Bleeding Edge users, only 33 percent prefer face-to-face. In general, electronic social tools are an important means of augmenting close personal relationships, but they do not replace face-to-face contact.[28]

While the basic dynamics of the Best Friends network are not new, what has changed is the degree of connectivity among Net Geners. Despite a preference for face-to-face contact, new channels such as cell phones, instant messaging, and text messaging provide more consistent access to peers and introduce stronger interpersonal dynamics into these relationships. Of course, the more things change, the more they stay the same, and one of the most important fac-

FIGURE 7.1   THREE CATEGORIES OF N-FLUENCE NETWORKS

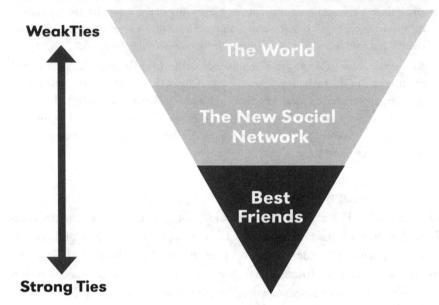

Source: The Net Generation: A Strategic Investigation, © nGenera, 2008

"Word of mouth is, has been, and always will be the most effective advertising engine. I trust my peer group more than anything when it comes to product recommendations"

—JONATHAN WOLF, WORCESTER, MASSACHUSETTS

tors in the Best Friends network continues to be who (or "what" in the case of brands, bands, or companies) you choose to "friend." In social networks, you're judged by the company you keep: friends and affinities project something about your identity and not all friends and influencers are created equal. What does this mean for companies marketing to the Net Gen?

My Social Network

A social network could be a group of 100 or so traditional acquaintances plus the much larger technology-enabled extended social network that may include hundreds, or even thousands, of "friends." Niki has over 700 of these friends—and she knows them all. Net Geners are constantly connected with their friends and members of their extended social network through social networking sites like Facebook and MySpace, personal blogs, and instant messaging. While many of these networks include people the user has never met in person, most social networks also include many of the user's "real world" social connections:

classmates, personal acquaintances, and peers. There is a wide range in the number of social connections that people establish: some users see anyone with 500-plus friends as a little "creepy" while others, like 17-year-old Brittnie Sarnes of Columbus, Ohio, won't "friend" anyone who doesn't have at least 150 friends of their own. Brittnie herself has 540 friends.[29]

One of the most intriguing aspects of N-Fluence networks is the capacity to build trusted relationships with people outside traditional social circles. As our social networks grow, so does the universe of people we rely upon to help us make decisions, and a growing number of these influencers come from nontraditional sources.

For example, one research firm says that for IT decision makers, the influence of the "expert" professional analysts is on the decline: "Analyst insight no longer has the clout it once did, and it is being displaced by emerging influencers such as blogs, systems integrators, individual consultants, academics, conferences and events and purchasing co-operatives, amongst others."[30] While 45 percent of influence on IT decisions still comes from journalists and analysts, bloggers now wield 8 percent of influence in IT decision making (up from 0 percent in 2004).[31] Those who demonstrate skill and expertise in specific areas are able to build up community credentials and exert more influence over others. Their opinions matter, and are sometimes held in higher regard than those from more traditional accredited sources. The role of social networking in the decentralization of authority, not only in IT decision making but throughout our society, cannot be overstated.

While some may question the strength of virtual social relationships with strangers, these virtual ties can be every bit as real and influential as their physical counterparts. Take the example of one avid online game player who was confined to a hospital bed for several months in 2006 following an injury. The support he received from fellow gamers included one man, whom he had never met in person, who drove with his entire family all the way from Ontario, Canada, to the hospital in Plymouth, Massachusetts, to deliver a care package. The drama and emotion invested in these communities and their relationships can be every bit as real as the cliques and pecking orders that get established in other contexts.

These social networks are dynamic and evolve rapidly; stability is the exception, not the norm. As one study concluded: "What we see . . . is a turbulent mass of individuals all making and breaking ties, and constantly shifting with respect to each other."[32] New technology, though, makes these big social networks easier to maintain. Anyone familiar with the problem of phone tag knows how much effort gets wasted in communication "overhead." New media like blogs, wikis, instant messaging, and social networking sites help eliminate that overhead with easier access to information (along with better filters). It's communication without the traditional effort required to communicate: IM "away" messages communicate your status to anyone who cares to check it; RSS provides feeds that are available on demand; MySpace bulletins update select audiences; and wikis share material among readers and authors alike. Close to a third of young people say the Internet has boosted their number of significant ties.[33] Today's typical Internet user already has 23 percent more significant social ties than a nonuser does.

The World

The "world" is the larger collective of people who the user does not know personally but with whom he or she is in contact through the network (i.e., the "weak tie" network). When today's youth broadcast their opinions to friends and family on public blogs, or on sites such as Amazon, eBay, Epinions, MySpace, or YouTube, they also influence the world around them. MySpace and YouTube rank as the third and fourth most visited sites on the Internet respectively in the United States (eleventh and fifth in Canada).[34] Today's young people are the first generation in which the audience has a voice that rivals the power of traditional broadcast networks. BoingBoing, a great blog coedited by Cory Doctorow, has a readership of 750,000, larger than many mainstream media sources. When Doctorow gets wound up about an issue—like Sony's attempt to covertly install DRM software on the PCs of unsuspecting users—people listen.[35]

This style of communication is available not only to individuals; companies are also leveraging the viral characteristics of social networks like YouTube to get their message out, just as Dove did with its popular "Campaign for Real Beauty" video (viewed more than 18.5 million times).[36] Dove's short film was featured on TV talk shows such as *Ellen*, *The View*, and *Entertainment Tonight* and generated three times the traffic that Dove's Super Bowl ads generated for the CampaignForRealBeauty.com Web site.[37] Creating material that audiences can identify with and share is a powerful way to engage them in conversation; producing something other than straight advertising makes the message more interesting.

But it isn't just young members of these sites who are influencing and being influenced. As new uses for these sites emerge, the number of adult visitors is rising. While not necessarily creating their own profiles, users between the ages of 35 and 54 are perusing others' opinions and browsing sites like MySpace to check on their children, find information on their child's future college roommate, or even to run background checks on potential employees.

How Marketers Are Trying to Penetrate N-Fluence Networks

Typical N-Fluence networks spread through instant messaging programs such as AIM, MSN, ICQ, Google Talk, and Trillian, and social networking sites such as MySpace, Facebook, Ryze, hi5, Cyworld, mixi, Friendster, orkut, and Bebo. They can also occur around multiplayer games such as World of Warcraft, Lineage, City of Heroes, EverQuest, and Second Life. Teenagers can post their product reviews or rants on sites such as YouTube. Sites such as Amazon or eBay rely on product reviews or rating systems for users, as do sites like digg.com (votes on articles) and Epinions (consumer product ratings). This connectivity creates new opportunities for firms to gain powerful advantages in the marketplace. The smart ones are applying a deft touch with technology, pinpointing the right network influencers, and abiding by principles such as authenticity and integrity. Procter & Gamble's business unit, Tremor, for example, attempts to engage the youth segment by offering influential teens an early look at product releases and free samples. Firms like Buzz Marketing pay these influencers directly in order to spread the word about products and services. Other companies use teens as a sounding board to create more suitable messages. Brain Reactions, for example, recruits college students to brainstorm new products and services or marketing campaigns.

It's no accident that some of the most successful advertising campaigns targeting young people are placing their content on popular sites like YouTube and social networks like MySpace. Instead of broadcasting to kids, they're launching on interactive media platforms where users take an active role in creating, publishing, filtering, remixing, and distributing content. There are currently 1.4 million band profiles on MySpace.[38] Apple even launched MySpace pages for the new Nano, one for each color. One of the most popular YouTube videos (22.6 million views) is the Ronaldinho Nike soccer commercial, and having the video popularized on a third-party site makes it more convenient and easier to find than if it had only been posted on Nike's own site.[39]

Treating Customers as You Would a Friend

Marketers have been quick to follow youth into these social communities, hoping to be their friend and catch their attention. When they approach Net Geners in these social networks, though, they must have something to say that is meaningful, useful, interesting, and that has personal value. Yet, traditional marketing approaches often do just the opposite, the result being that consumers don't trust them: 61 percent of consumers today say that marketers and advertisers do not treat them with respect.[40] A friend knows who you are, what you care about, and is someone you share a history with. Yet customers get the opposite impression when they're waiting for minutes on hold, when one service channel isn't aware of an interaction that occurred in another, or when a point-of-sale experience doesn't live up to expectations.

The successful companies view befriending customers in these social networks as a relationship-building exercise. The acid test for the message is simple: Does the content survive a one-on-one interaction with a person you know? Is this the way you'd treat a friend? If the answer is no, as I tell my clients, there's no point in venturing into this network of friends. As mentioned, companies have started to create MySpace profiles for their products or services. They're making thousands or even millions of new friends online. These include, the most recent *X-Men* movie (2 million friends), Adidas Soccer (81,000 friends), Toyota Yaris (58,000 friends), Cingular Sounds (27,000 friends), and a Wendy's franchise (77,000 friends).[41] In this world, the word *friend* has taken on a whole new meaning.

While Net Geners frequently discount corporate messages, they believe messages from friends because they're real. It's this authenticity that makes penetrating these social networks so difficult for marketers. Naïve attempts to turn youth into corporate mouthpieces tend to backfire or to be received with hostility, corrupting both the message and the messenger. Spreading genuine messages (for example, Dove's "Campaign for Real Beauty" video), on the other hand, can be a win-win situation, because it preserves the legitimacy of the social network while marketing a product. For Net Geners, honesty is more important than perfection. For example, while 71 percent will tolerate corporate mistakes (if corrected honestly or quickly), 77 percent say that untrue advertising would convince them to tell friends not to buy a product.[42]

The line between authenticity and manipulation is a thin one. Sony Ericsson, for instance, crossed the line into manipulative advertising with its cell phone campaigns. In one instance, the company trained 60 actors to ask unsuspecting tourists to take their picture with its new camera phone. When the charade was exposed, the public was not impressed. The company then tried a similar stunt with its new W800 Walkman phone and was hammered by bloggers when, once again, people discovered they had been deceived. With its blundering advertising, Sony inadvertently spawned a negative viral campaign. Engadget.com, the largest nonmainstream media blog, commented:

> One of the many great things about the Internet is the new transparency in which marketers are actually speaking openly and honestly with their companies' customers instead of trying to hoodwink them into buying products. We think perhaps Sony Ericsson hasn't heard about any of that, because apparently they mounted an entirely fabricated marketing campaign to get users to submit testimonials about the W800 Walkman phone.[43]

Or take Coca-Cola's launch of its new diet drink for men, Coke Zero, in 2006. It started out by creating a blog, The Zero Movement, which trumpeted sayings like "Why can't New Year's come with zero resolutions." It looked like it came from activists; the company logo was nowhere to be found. Then the bloggers pounced, setting up a new blog, The Zero Movement Sucks, which exposed the real author of the Zero Movement. The blog railed against the company's surreptitious tactics with lines like "If you buy Coke Zero, you're not just a pathetic loser, you're a pathetic loser in denial." They even sold black T-shirts, emblazoned with logos like "I joined the Zero Movement and all I got was this lousy brain tumor." The company eventually put its logo on the site and moved on. The tempest hasn't made a visible dent in sales volumes so far—the company claims that Coke Zero is the most successful launch in 20 years and is doing a fine job of driving up sales volumes. But this incident, nonetheless, points to the danger of trying to mislead the new scrutinizers in the Net Gen consumer world.

Both the Sony and Coke initiatives were, rightly so, perceived as integrity violations. Marketers need to understand the Net Gen norms so they won't blunder into such campaigns. The strongest norm is integrity. The Net Gen wants marketers to be honest, to be considerate of customer interests, to abide by their commitments, and to be open and transparent about what they're doing.

This world has its own social etiquette, and if companies want to be a friend and make more of them, they need to know the rules. One Second Life user blogged about 20 "Dos and Don'ts for Big Business." While some of the advice is specific to Second Life itself, other suggestions could apply to almost any online community. A few of the highlights (some of which are paraphrased) include the following:[44]

- Don't think a cute or dorky real-life logo or mascot will automatically fit into a virtual world.

- Offer avatars instead of fancy branding; provide something to interact with on their visit.

- Give out useful and interesting objects that users can take home. You need giveaways that are more than just "lame brand swag" with your company logo on them.

- Do not put pictures of RL [real life] people into the build. It really kills the immersion.

- Don't isolate yourself on a private island; establish a presence wherever people spend their time.

- Don't launch something big and pretentious for a one-time event and abandon it later.

- Pay attention to interface design issues (for example, avoid "laggy" objects, or podiums with seating that's outside of the 20-meter text "hearing distance").

- Watch what people actually do in the virtual world. Don't impose RL activities that will wind up looking lame . . . . Talk to people who spend time living and working as avatars in the virtual world to see what they think and what they want . . . . Do focus groups.

- If an idea doesn't work, don't be afraid of quickly deleting it and rebuilding from scratch—this is a highly changeable, malleable, fixable world where the costs of rebuilding are still low.

Giving Net Gen Consumers a Say in the Message

Companies are making friends with customers online by listening to what consumers have to say about their product or service. Product reviews from customers, for example, can help boost sales. Only one-quarter of online retailers offer space for peer ratings and reviews on their sites, but the evidence shows they are missing a big opportunity. Nearly 60 percent of Net Geners feel that customer reviews are important in influencing their purchase decisions, and savvy retailers agree: a recent Forrester Research study found that 96 percent of online retailers who offered customer ratings and reviews on their Web sites said it was effective for improving online conversion rates.[45] When CompUSA, a leading electronics retailer, decided to incorporate a customer rating system into its Web site, it immediately noticed the benefits. Shoppers who arrived at the site via review-related searches bought 50 percent more than other online shoppers.[46]

But what about negative reviews or product placement? Many say that there's no such thing as bad publicity, and a number of commercial viral videos seem to confirm the adage. From bird- and cat-killing cars (the Ford SportKa) to a clip depicting a youth crushed by his own car (Goodyear), controversy and bad taste, it seems, help spur the impulse to share (at least when presented as humor). Some companies provoke curiosity through the outrageous—videos of Qashqai car games (qashqaicargames. com) come to mind. But controversy is different than deception. Many users react against what has become known as astroturfing, that is, the posting of messages that look like they spring from grassroots sources but are in fact fake (hence the term "astroturf," as in fake grass).

For example, a blog about Wal-Mart that was allegedly authored by a couple who spent nights in their RV in Wal-Mart parking lots turned out to be staged by viral marketing firm Edelman. Public outrage was predictable. Strangely, the public seems slightly more forgiving when individuals are the ones doing the deceiving. One YouTube user known as LonelyGirl15 attracted a storm of attention with her mysterious video postings. When it turned out that she was an impostor—an actor playing the role of "Bree"—some users turned their back on the content, while others continued to follow the fictional saga. To date, LonelyGirl15 videos have been viewed 23 million times.[47] The early debate over the authenticity of LonelyGirl15 actually seemed to fuel the interest.

In contemplating word-of-mouth marketing, companies should seek to both encourage good word of mouth and minimize bad word of mouth. Dr. Paul Marsden and his colleagues at the London School of Economics found that both good and bad word of mouth could be used to predict corporate growth.[48] Marsden found that every 7-point increase in the likelihood of recommending a brand (on a scale of 0–10) correlated to a 1 percent increase in growth. However, reducing negative word of mouth by just 2 points also correlated to 1 percent growth. The study put an economic value to these word-of-mouth impacts: a single point increase in likelihood of recommending a brand was worth a $17.3 million increase in sales; while a mere 1 percent reduction in negative word of mouth would lift sales by $48.8 million. The latter result suggests that, for many firms, countering the damaging effects of negative word of mouth is an excellent place to start.

Finding People Who Really Care to Spread the Message

Information overload has made it more difficult than ever to tap into the collective consciousness of the mainstream. Still, customers like the opportunity to communicate their satisfaction with a product or service, amplifying positive momentum for the firm. In *Crossing the Chasm*, a book that quickly became a bible for high-tech marketers in the 1990s, Geoffrey Moore proposed an adaptation of Rogers's "diffusion of innovation" theory to help address the problem of reaching the mainstream. He identified the stage that is most crucial to a new product's success as the transition between early adopters and the early majority, labeling this segment of the product adoption cycle as "the chasm." Though early adopters (visionaries) are often keen to share their enthusiasm and publicize a product, their endorsement alone will not lead to adoption by the early majority (pragmatists who tend to adopt proven products). Moore's key to bridging the chasm was to target a niche market of the pragmatists by offering them a "whole product" (early adopters don't need a "whole product," just a core product that allows them to create their own solution). Proven success in meeting the needs of one niche can then be leveraged to target another niche, and another, creating a domino effect.

This strategy has useful implications for companies trying to shape opinion in N-Fluence networks. Instead of attempting to launch its message directly into the mainstream, the smart ones are targeting smaller niche communities in which the company's influence can take root. Not only will these niches be more defensible once established, but also their smaller size reduces complexity and allows their relationships to be readily understood.

O'Reilly Media, perhaps best known lately for helping to cement the term Web 2.0, is a company that uses this strategy with tremendous success. O'Reilly has a consistent track record in following the voice of the "techgeek" community, and it uses its access to this community to make forays into new subcommunities as they take shape—publishing books and hosting conferences along the way. A recent example is how the company built upon the success of *Make* magazine. O'Reilly launched a new sister publication called *Craft:* magazine, which embraces the fitting "Martha Stewart for Geeks" theme identified by *Newsweek*'s Stephen Levy.[49] O'Reilly's relationships within these specialized communities are extremely important for identifying new niche markets and carving out influential positions within them.

If these niche communities think the message is valuable, they spread it to their friends—and the message will go viral and spread like wildfire. To go viral, messages need to spark conversations—contagion can often be due to something outrageous or fantastic. Take Honda's "Cog" commercial, for example. The video depicts an amazing Rube Goldberg chain reaction occurring entirely with car parts. While the video could have easily been created using special effects, a large part of its draw was the feat of actually making the commercial; it took an impressive five months to prepare and 606 takes to film.

Paul Marsden cites a list of 10 different factors that contribute to making a message "infectious."[50]

1. Excellence: perceived as best of breed

2. Uniqueness: clear one-of-a-kind differentiation

3. Aesthetics: perceived aesthetic appeal

4. Association: generates positive associations

5. Engagement: fosters emotional involvement

6. Expressive value: visible sign of user values

7. Functional value: addresses functional needs

8. Nostalgic value: evokes sentimental linkages

9. Personification: has character, personality

10. Cost: perceived value for money

If a message is infectious enough, this positive word of mouth has a direct financial benefit. Marsden found that a measurable improvement in customers' willingness to recommend a brand correlated to millions of dollars of revenue growth.[51]

Letting Go

In the blogosphere, customer review engines, consumer advocacy sites, and other nontraditional social spheres all interact—often in unpredictable ways—to influence consumer decisions. Consider the expression "butterfly effect," coined by meteorologist and mathematician Edward Lorenz. It's the idea that a butterfly flapping its wings on one side of the world could trigger a chain reaction that produces cataclysmic weather conditions on the other.[52] In complex systems, outcomes are extremely sensitive to initial conditions; a small change can dramatically affect the end result. For marketers targeting today's networked youth, this idea has great appeal. It offers the potential to quickly pump up a product's buzz with a handful of well-placed early connections. However, this volatility cuts both ways, since a few missteps at the beginning can snowball and damage a product's reputation. As a result, companies must realize that they can no longer tightly control their marketing messages, and that they are increasingly at the mercy of their "stakeholder webs"—groups of individuals who scrutinize a firm's behavior and try to change it.[53]

Significant influence is often wielded by a small number of individuals who have a disproportionate impact on the system. Some leading-edge companies are trying to identify individual network actors, like Gladwell's mavens, connectors, and salesmen, and leverage their capabilities to help maximize their influence. Based on success with Tremor in the youth market, for example, P&G launched a new word-of-mouth initiative geared for moms called Vocalpoint. P&G screens candidates up front, and Vocalpoint moms tend to have a larger-than-average social network. Participants "generally speak to about 25 to 30 other women during the day, where an average mom speaks to just five."[54] At peer-ranked news site digg.com, a single user known as "P9" contributed a startling proportion of submissions that made it to the site's front page. Other users' complaints about "digg gangs" eventually led to a new ranking algorithm for the site, but the changes have disillusioned star contributors like P9, who has now officially "quit" digg.[55] While it's difficult to say if the community will be better off for P9's absence, there will certainly be a new crop of "superusers" anxious to fill the void. Those able to engage social network superusers—without alienating the rest of the network—will find that their influence over system outcomes rises accordingly.

TURNING CONSUMERS INTO PROSUMERS

Thanks to the Web 2.0, companies in just about every industry can turn their consumers into producers—that is "prosumers." Prosumerism is more than an extension of mass customization, customer centricity, or any of the other terms that boil down to companies making basic products and letting customers tweak the details. It's what happens when producers and consumers both actively participate in the creation of goods and services in an ongoing way.

The concept isn't new. Marshall McLuhan introduced the idea in the early 1970s,[56] Alvin Toffler introduced the term in the 1980s,[57] and I refined the idea in my 1995 book, *The Digital Economy*. It's become such a force that Anthony Williams and I devoted an entire chapter to the topic in *Wikinomics*. In each case the underlying message was the same: technological advances would, in the future, enable the producer and the consumer to merge. But again these were ideas in waiting for a new generation of consumers who would have the inclination and skills to prosume.

"So what?" you may say. Producers and consumers have always been the same group of people: collectively, we produce the value that we collectively consume. What's different about prosumerism is the blurring of the line between producers and consumers at the micro level of the economy. In the past, firms could safely ignore or even resist customer innovations that didn't fit their internal processes and business models. Today's youth, though, treat the world as a place for creation, not consumption. The Net Gen will turn its collective back on static, "read-only," noneditable products in favor of products that allow them to become directly engaged in the production of the goods and services that they consume. And, of course, they'll insist on sharing their adaptations with each other.

Prosumerism is largely the manifestation of interest-based communities working together to solve a problem or improve a product or service. Today we have the mass-collaboration and mass-communications technologies that allow those groups to function and flourish. If it's good enough, other people will want it—and the innovator becomes a prosumer overnight. With the onset of Web 2.0, blogs, wikis, and less publicized tools, such as cheap video editing software and simpler interface tools, are increasing the opportunities for prosumerism. As the tools available to consumers grow ever more similar to those the "professionals" use, anyone with the skills and interest can leverage them to create a new idea, service, or thing. Thanks to the democratization of technology availability, not only do the tools now exist, but everyone has access to them.

The nGenera research suggests that prosumerism is deeply ingrained in youth culture and that young people around the world are seeking out opportunities to engage and cocreate with companies. For example:

- Fifty-four percent of Net Geners indicate they often modify "things I own so they fit who I am." More developed nations (the United States, France, Germany and the UK) all showed less than 50 percent on this metric, while emerging nations (China, India, and Brazil) showed around 60 percent.
- Sixty percent of Net Geners agree that they "take advantage of opportunities companies give me to help them make their products and services better." (Again, those in emerging nations are the most likely to agree.)
- Given the choice between pursuing their passions and making lots of money, most Net Geners choose passion (China, Japan, and Mexico are the exceptions). The implications of this are the same as for the "fun" question—these kids think about work a little differently than their parents traditionally did (see Chapter 6).

The percentage of the Net Generation actively engaged in prosumerism is still small—many visit online product rating sites, but only a fraction add or change ratings on these sites. In the United States, for example, 30 percent of Net Geners visit the online ratings sites, but only 5 percent contribute. We're still at the thin edge of the prosumerism wedge in many major markets, but the influence of the few in this world can't be underestimated. Research shows that 5 percent of Net Geners influence about 30 percent of their peers.[58]

Prosumers Get Busy

Young people may not have money, but they have time. And they're willing to turn off the TV and spend that time forming their own prosumer communities online, where they share product-related information; collaborate on customized projects; engage in commerce; and swap tips, tools, and product hacks. NetGeners are already acting like prosumers—through mashups, sites that mix personalized content with Google's mapping service. They produce everything from UFO sighting locations (ufomaps.com) to online pedometers (gmap-pedometer.com). The popular cable comedy show *The Colbert Report* harnessed the creative energy when it issued the "green screen challenge" (a green screen video of Colbert goofing off that users could add their own backgrounds to). Dozens of user-created videos resulted in hundreds of thousands of downloads.

Sometimes saying nothing at all is the best strategy for giving users control of the message. Red Bull used this strategy quite effectively as it rode the crest of the energy drink wave. The brand's mystique is cultivated by a strangely nebulous positioning. One author describes it this way: "Usually the wizards of branding want to be extremely clear about what their product is for and who's supposed to buy it. Red Bull does just the opposite. Everything about the company and its sole product is intentionally vague, even evasive . . . the great thing about a murky brand is that you can let your customers fill in all the blanks."[59]

Consumers are starting to make physical things too. For example, student Jose Aliva used FedEx boxes to make furniture and posted photos of his creations online (www.FedexFurniture.com). While FedEx responded with a letter from its legal department, complaining that, among other things, consumers might mistakenly believe that the shipper had expanded its business, the VP of a mattress company called Dormia saw an opportunity and sent the student a free mattress. Aliva was thrilled. "This is actually the first mattress that I will have ever owned, and the first good mattress I've ever slept on," he wrote in his blog. "I had the best sleep of my life."[60] Dormia now has an ad on the FedEx Furniture site, and even FedEx had to admit that he showed "a resourceful use of objects that companies give away."

"A billion people in advanced economies may have between two billion and six billion spare hours among them, every day."

—YOCHAI BENKLER, YALE LAW PROFESSOR AND AUTHOR OF THE WEALTH OF NETWORKS[61]

Although many companies like FedEx don't like outsiders tinkering with their products, the potential value is vast when people in advanced economies have billions of spare hours a day. In order to harness that time, it would take the whole workforce of almost 340,000 workers employed by the entire motion picture and recording industries in the United States put together, assuming that each worker worked 40-hour weeks without taking a single vacation, for between 3 to 8.5 years.[62] This is an extraordinary amount of quantitative capacity that prosumer networks can tap into. Why would people want to contribute their spare time? For one thing, they're passionate about a given topic. But there's another driving force—what Columbia University law professor Eben Moglen calls the need to "conquer their uneasy sense of being too alone."[63]

This is a massive change, as *Time* signaled in 2006 when it named me, you, and everyone else as Person of the Year: "It's a story about community and collaboration on a scale never seen before. . . . It's about the many wresting power from the few and helping one another for nothing and how that will not only change the world, but also change the way the world changes."[64]

Large companies—one version of "the few"—should be a little rattled as they survey "the many" intent on wresting power from them. But it's a misplaced fear, in many cases, and those companies would be better off cultivating the prosumer opportunities that the "Person of the Year" presents.

In some ways, the *Time* article is "so 2006," as my daughter might say. Social networking is no longer about hooking up online or creating a gardening community. It is becoming a new mode of production. Social networking is becoming social production. Consumers can finally become the actual designers and even producers of goods and services.

Prosumption has already started in the music, video, and software industries, but, as start-ups such as CaféPress and Ponoko are demonstrating, it will migrate into the production of physical goods as the infrastructure for personalized manufacturing matures. For example, Mountain Dew, a soft drink subsidiary of Pepsi, got a lot of help from its Net Gen consumers in coming up with a new flavor for the soda. The soft-drink maker released a free online game featuring a live-action short film and 3-D characters. It gave users a chance to pick all the features—from logo to color to flavor—of the next version Mountain Dew would release. The winner was decided by an online vote. I think prosumption will eventually create opportunities for individuals to augment their incomes by adding small increments of value to the economy in heretofore impossible ways (think about the worldwide garage sale that is eBay). Companies that engage and cocreate with their customers will make a bigger impact with fewer resources than traditional "plan and push" businesses—as exemplified by Flickr, Lego, Second Life, and Facebook, which have all grown rapidly by ceding control to their customers.

Any company in the business of selling goods and services should start planning now to harness this force of prosumerism, or risk falling behind. Today's young customers are not waiting for an invitation to collaborate and share information—in many cases they'll hack technology to let themselves in the company's door, or invent around them and create opportunities for competitors.

THE NET GENERATION AND MARKETING 2.0:
FROM FOUR PS TO THE ABCDE OF MARKETING

The Net Gen is driving the rethinking of many of the tenets of marketing. Marketing 2.0, as I call it, can be characterized by these words: Anyplace, Brand, Communication, Discovery, and Experience—the ABCDEs of Marketing 2.0. Let's look more closely at the meaning of these words, in no particular order:

From Products to Experience

More and more goods and services are being commoditized—bought and sold almost exclusively on the basis of price. Some companies are working hard to create new genres of economic offerings by enhancing customer experience. They're creating memorable value and events that engage each customer in an inherently personal way.

The old industrial approaches to product definition and product marketing are obsolete. In a world where customers are informed, fickle, and have choice, and where margins are thin, and profitable growth can be elusive, delivering a compelling customer experience can make all the difference. Net Geners want most products and services to incorporate fun. Remember, "fun is what you're paying for." They also love to innovate and want to customize everything. They want to collaborate and be engaged. All of this suggests that products must now be mass customized, service intensive, and infused with the knowledge and the individual tastes of customers. What's more, Net Geners as prosumers want to be involved in coinnovating products, and if you let them you'll actually be setting the stage for rich, enduring experiences to occur.

This requires rethinking everything in the customer experience value chain, including value creation and coinnovation, channel management, marketing programs, customer engagement, new models of the brand, sales programs, support and service, and distribution platforms.

Price Is Negotiable: From Price to the Discovery of Price

Enabled by online marketplaces, dynamic markets and dynamic pricing are challenging vendor-fixed pricing.

In these early days of new price discovery mechanisms, marketers should question even the concept of "price" as customers gain access to mechanisms that allow them to state what they're willing to pay and for what. When you think about it, price is a crude measure of value. It reflects in a single number all the attributes that customers may value in a product—time, effort, craftsmanship, innovation, fashion, status, rarity, long-term value, and so on. As buyers and sellers exchange more information, pricing becomes fluid. As this generation becomes more influential, markets, not firms, will price products and services. Customers will offer various prices for products depending on conditions specified. *If you deliver this afternoon, I'll pay A. If I can buy this quantity, I'll pay B. I'll accept certain defects and pay C. If someone else will pay D, then I'll pay E.*

From Place to Anyplace

With the Net Gen, hearts, not eyeballs, count. Every company competes in two worlds: a physical world (marketplace) and a digital world of information (marketspace). B-webs enable firms to focus on the marketspace, by creating not a great Web site but a great b-web and relationship capital. Within a decade, the majority of products and services in many developed countries will be sold in the marketspace.

However, when you see how mobile Net Geners are, carrying their digital buddies in their pockets, you can see a new frontier of commerce emerging—the *marketface*—the interface between the marketplace and marketspace. A Net Gener may turn to her mobile, geospatial device to find the physical location of a store. Customers of the same companies can buy clothes online; if they don't fit they can return the items to the store. Or they can browse the Web at their leisure and take printouts of desired items to the store. Gap has even installed Web Lounges in some stores where customers can place orders. Net Geners love the plethora of choice and added convenience.

"There are real day-to-day behavioral changes in how people influence, shop, and buy," says Brian Fetherstonhaugh. "If you are selling fashion to the North American teenager, and you do not have a search engine marketing presence and a fantastic landing experience [when you go to that company's Web site], and you are relying on traditional media, your efforts are wasted because that's not how a customer's journey actually unfolds." Putting your "media and messaging at decisive points along that journey" from research to purchase is one of the keys to capturing the Net Gen's interest and loyalty.

Good-bye Traditional Advertising and PR: From Promotion to Communication

Traditional advertising, promotion, publicity, public relations, and most other aspects of corporate communications as we've known them until now are becoming archaic concepts. These concepts exploited unidirectional, one-to-many, and one-size-fits-all media to communicate "messages" to faceless, powerless customers. Not surprisingly, this model is completely inappropriate when marketing to the Net Gen.

This generation has huge power. They often have access to near perfect information about products. They choose the medium and the message. Customers, not external entities, can participate in a firm's business network through multidirectional, one-to-one, and highly tailored communications media. The customers, not the company, control the marketing mix. Rather than passively receiving broadcast images, they do the casting. Rather than getting messages from earnest PR professionals, they create public opinion online with one another.

Marketers are losing control. And yet it looks like many marketers still don't get it. By the end of 2007, consumers were spending over 25 percent of their time online, according to a neo@ogilvy survey.[65] Yet advertisers are spending less than 10 percent of their dollars online (see Figure 7.2).

FIGURE 7.2   ONLINE ADVERTISING DOLLARS DO NOT MATCH
THE TIME CONSUMERS SPEND ONLINE

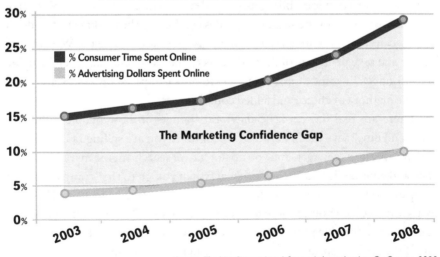

Source: The Net Generation: A Strategic Investigation, © nGenera, 2008;
Brian Fetherstonhaugh, Chairman and CEO of OgilvyOne

Of course, digital marketing does not mean banner ads on Web sites. Companies need to actually communicate—a two-way or multiway process. Consider what 26-year-old Jonathan Wolf has to say about traditional ads appearing on the Web. "I DON'T SEE THE ADS ANYMORE. obnoxious blinking flash animations, garish banners, irritating pop-ups. They've all kind of disappeared. i'm a child of the internet. i'm used to all that crap floating into my visual cortext, and I've learned to filter it out." He gives a warning to advertisers: engage with N-Fluence networks. "I'm universally filtering out a style of advertising, without any sort of bias, then the advertiser needs to figure out a better strategy. . . . I buy things if other people I know recommend them," he says. The Internet is the biggest system of word-of-mouth in existence, and advertisers are only now beginning to figure out how to effectively use it.

The New Brand

In the past, the brand was seen as a promise, an image, a badge, or, as many popular books on branding describe it, "a word in the mind."[66] A brand is something that exists in the minds of customers and in the interactions of markets. Brands are actually a by-product of the growth of mass communications. Using the one-way broadcast and print media, marketers could convince people through relentless one-way communications to "Just do it!"

The brand is becoming a more complex construct than a simple promise, word, or image. The brand has an architecture of sorts and, for a growing class of products and companies, integrity, honesty, reliability, consideration, and transparency are the foundation of brand architecture. Most brands have included some but not all of these values in the past. Coke presents itself as reliable—delivering the same taste worldwide. It communicates consideration—quality control, flavor, convenience, safety, philanthropic benevolence, even the promise of lifestyle improvements—"Things go better with Coke." If you say "Things go better with Coke" enough times, you could establish the Coca-Cola brand in the market.

But values like honesty and transparency were never really necessary for Coke's branding. In fact, the brand has always boasted of opacity, at least in the formulation of its secret ingredients (in that case appropriate). But today, things don't go better with Coke if the company is being accused of opacity and trickery in its viral marketing campaign for Coke Zero. And Coke paid the price.

Adding honesty and transparency to the formula creates a higher hurdle and more complex brand architecture. Today, Coke must endeavor to behave and present itself as a leader in corporate citizenship and a company with great integrity. It has launched programs on the environment (water and natural resources, climate change, environmental education, and waste management). It has invested considerably in fighting AIDS through employee programs and bottling partners. Over the past few years it has invested tens of millions of dollars in educational programs in the many communities in which it operates. It has, however, had little success convincing critics that it has taken adequate steps to improve labor practices in its bottling plants, or even to accept responsibility for this challenge. Coke lives in a house of glass, and consumers, especially in certain important markets (youth, developing countries), can be expected to shift loyalties as Coke's brand architecture is undermined.[67]

Given the propensity of young people to ignore advertisements in traditional media, their growing ability to scrutinize companies, and their surging power in the marketplace, they are driving a change in thinking among marketers away from focusing on brand image and brand equity to thinking about relationships with customers. A new form of marketing is emerging wherein brand managers emphasize customer engagement, brand collaboration, and, in some cases, even shared brand ownership. Smart companies are eschewing less effective, command and control marketing and communication methods. As the Net Generation comes of age, hundreds of millions of passionate users and consumers will be taking an active role in determining, shaping, and redefining brands independent of company involvement. Winning companies and brands are learning to engage and cocreate with these customers rather than shouting over or ignoring the noise of the marketplace. To bridge the marketing divide, the concept of controlling the brand is now giving way to collaborating with a stakeholder group that most companies are unfamiliar with—their customers.

CONSUMERS 2.0: SEVEN GUIDELINES FOR MARKETING PROFESSIONALS

In the culture of the first digital generation and their experiences as consumers, you will discover the new twenty-first-century values, relationships, and marketing model for your company. Here are seven rules to guide your marketing plan.

① **Don't focus on your customers—engage them**. Turn them into prosumers of your goods and services. Young people want to coinnovate with you. Let them customize your value. Open up your products and services. Remember: "If you can't open it, you don't own it."

② **Don't create products and services—create consumer experiences**. Add value to your offerings to make them richer experiences and use the Web to help deliver your new value.

③ **Radically reduce advertising in broadcast media**. Most TV and much of radio and print advertising is a waste of time, energy, ink, money, and electrons. Shift your "Marketing Communications Spending" to digital media.

④ **Develop a strategy to plug into N-Fluence networks**. The three keys to Net Gen marketing are word of mouth, word of mouth, and . . . you get the idea.

⑤ **Rethink your brand.** The brand is no longer just a promise, image, or badge—for many companies it should become a relationship.

⑥ **Bake integrity into your corporate DNA and marketing campaigns.** Honesty, consideration, accountability, and transparency are the foundation of trust for this generation. Be authentic in everything you do.

⑦ **Move the Net Generation into the center of your marketing campaigns.** They are important beyond their (huge) demographic muscle. They influence all generations like never before. The Four Ps—product, place, price, and promotion—are an inadequate framework to deal with the consumer of the future. Replace them with the ABCDE of marketing: anyplace, brand, communication, discovery, and experience.

THE NET GENERATION AND THE FAMILY

When Matthew Dreitlein graduated from college with a major in political science, he moved home to the yellow two-story suburban house with the swing set and trampoline in the backyard, where he'd grown up in Rochester, New York. At 21, he had mixed feelings about it. He was looking forward to breakfast with his brothers, but how would he handle dinner with the parents? When he was a teenager, all fired up by the information he had gathered on the Internet, they had fought at the dinner table. "I was learning and questioning everything, while they (both business professionals) were trying to make ends meet," he said.

Then, as he was unpacking his bags at home in January 2008, Dreitlein came up with an ingenious idea. He had been a night owl at the university, so in Rochester he would still stay out late with friends. Then he'd come home and stay up all night working on his novel, surfing the Web, or preparing for a political conference or one of his volunteer activities. He'd have breakfast with his brothers, and then go to sleep until mid-afternoon. After a few weeks, he realized how easy it was to live at night: "I had the house to myself during the nights," he said. For his kind of work, the Web made normal, nine to five hours completely unnecessary. "I had ample time to use the family computer, watch whatever I wanted on TV, and read in peace and quiet. It was really nice."

Matthew gets time to hang out with his friends late at night and see his girlfriend without missing out on time with his own family. It has worked out beautifully with the parents: "My mother and I have made our peace, and my dad and I talk much more, which I am really thankful for," he said. "We don't fight about what to watch or what to do, who needs the car, or doing chores. It's all based around acceptance now. We each have our space and time to do what we need to do."[1]

Matthew's parents, Janet and William, are pleased to have him back: "We remember this time in our lives and it's almost like we are getting to relive the excitement and adventure that comes with striking out on your own."

THE FREEDOM FLIP

Boomer Youth Found Freedom Outside; Net Geners Find Freedom Inside

Matthew's story is a classic for this family-oriented generation. Yet boomers are always surprised to hear that Net Geners move home after college. It's yet another sign, in the critics' view, that the Net Generation is coddled, overprotected, and unable to put a foot in front of them without praise or support from their parents.

But I see this trend in a different light. This is an example of one of the profound differences between the Net Geners and their boomer parents.

The typical boomer would never think of moving home after college, but that's because their home life was usually different. Boomers grew up in homes that were run as a hierarchical operation, like that of the family on the popular TV show *Father Knows Best* that aired when they were growing up. They went outdoors to be free; their parents didn't know what was going on there. And as soon as they were able, they moved away from home to be free and independent. Net Geners, on the other hand, grew up in homes that were democracies—they had a say in family life. It was the outdoors that was strictly controlled by fearful parents. So the first Net Geners found their freedom indoors—especially online. Then, once they could access the Net from their mobile devices, they could be free online—anywhere.

The freedom they experienced online made it easy to be close to their parents; there was no need to rebel. But it also meant that a significant part of their upbringing occurred outside of the influence of their parents, because most parents didn't know, at least not at the beginning, what their children were doing online. This poses a significant challenge for parents of Net Geners, as they begin to realize that the risks associated with the teenage quest for individuality have moved to the world the child experiences online—inside the family home, or on their mobile phones anywhere. There they can potentially face bullies, sexual predators, online porn, and any number of noxious influences.

Yet I believe there is no sense in trying to censor the Internet; smart Net Geners can always find ways to sneak around the digital fences. Rather, I think it's more important than ever for parents to talk with their kids about real human values and other important topics—at the family dinner table and elsewhere. And the good news is that this generation is well positioned to take on this topic as they begin to launch families of their own. Our research suggests that this family-oriented generation will design open families that will be well suited to handling the challenges that their kids will face when they explore the world online.

For Boomers, Indoors You Were Controlled; Outdoors You Were Free

When I was a kid growing up on the Canadian side of Niagara Falls, I used to walk a mile every day to school with my little brothers. Our route passed through a rough neighborhood. My parents weren't worried; they didn't know much about that neighborhood. After school, we used to make rockets by taking the gunpowder out of firecrackers, and one time we even blew the lid off of a garbage can. We thought that was impressive. We played ball beside a hydroelectric canal that dropped 80 feet to a rushing torrent of canal water feeding the turbines of a powerplant down river, and we often climbed the fence to chase the ball, careful to make sure not to fall over the edge into the canal and certain death. I had wonderful loving parents, but they didn't fret about the risks we were taking every single day. They didn't know what we were doing out there.

But inside the family home was a different story. Like many boomers my age, I grew up in a strict family, and we didn't dare challenge my parents' orders. When my father called, I had to answer "Yes Dad." "Children," my relatives would say, "should be seen and not heard." Those words doubtless echoed in my parents' minds when one day I mumbled the word "fart" while sitting in the car. All hell broke loose. My British-born uncle used to say, "Spare the rod, spoil the child," and no one objected. Far from it. This was perfectly normal in the small Canadian town where I grew up. Parents set the rules, and enforced them.

So when we became teenagers and started to form our identities independent of our parents, we couldn't wait to leave home, even if we loved our parents, as I most certainly did. That was the rite of passage. On the last day of high school exams, my friend and I climbed onto the top of the steep roof of our family home and sat there in the sun for hours, just talking. I felt like king of the world, knowing I was going to college and finally would be truly independent. My dad saw us up there and just chuckled—he was happy for me.

For Net Geners, Freedom Outside Was Canceled

When boomers became parents, however, they effectively canceled the freedom to play outdoors. They were afraid to let their kids do what boomers did as children—like running free in the woods, or in the park. Instead, all trips to the outdoors were scheduled, contained. In many families, lessons, drills, and plans replaced uninhibited playing. Kids were driven to school and couldn't just hang out in the park, because, after all, everyone knew that was "dangerous." Many of the fears that drove these changes were irrational: Since the early 1990s, crime—both property crimes and violent crimes including murder—has been dropping. The number of violent offences committed by juveniles ages 12 to 17 declined 61 percent from 1993 to 2005, while those committed by persons older than 17 fell 58 percent.[2] And when it comes to nightmare crimes like sexual assault, statistics show that the perpetrators are rarely strangers. Nearly all the time, they are people the victim knows, and often they are people the victim knows very well.

But the fear of the stranger persisted. In the early 1980s, when the first Net Geners were preschoolers, the fear was magnified by the profusion of new TV programming that played to their fears about child abduction, sexual predators, and tampering with Tylenol and Halloween candy. Parents' attention shifted from child rearing to child protecting. Boomers traded in their Volkswagen love vans for the first version of the five-star, crash-tested minivan fully equipped with "Baby on Board" signs suctioned to their windows—and signed their kids up for play dates, supervised sports, and lessons of all kinds.

That fear shows no sign of cooling. In 2000, four out of five parents voiced fears about their children's safety.[3] The nervousness about what happens to children outdoors has induced many parents to buy mobile phones for their children, as we saw in Chapter 2. The mobile phones came with a condition: Parents expected their children to answer their calls, according to Sherry Turkle, professor of the social studies of science and technology at MIT. "On the one hand, this arrangement gives teenagers new freedoms," she notes. "On the other, they do not have the experience of being alone and having to count on themselves; there is always a parent on speed dial. This provides comfort in a dangerous world, yet there is a price to pay in the development of autonomy."[4]

Fear was obviously not the only driving force. Boomer parents were ambitious for their kids. Taking lessons, everything from piano to math, they hoped, might keep them out of trouble and help them succeed. And for good reason—a college education is almost a prerequisite for success in a knowledge economy and entrance standards have been going up every year for a long time. Personally, with my mediocre high school grades, any decent university probably would not accept me today. Home became like work, according to Alvin Rosenfeld, author of *The Over-Scheduled Child*. This was Kid Inc., where the schedule was designed to ensure John Jr. made it to the soccer practice, the swimming lesson, the piano lesson, his psychologist, and the Kumon math tutor, who would help him pass the test he needed to pass in order to get into whatever school was on the five year plan for his brilliant future.

> "Parents need to always remember to let their kids just be kids. It's okay to spend a few hours surfing the Web, running around outside—just kid stuff."
>
> *—ALEX TAPSCOTT*

It's nuts: the image of one of my friends drilling his toddler with flash cards is still emblazoned in my mind. The culture of parenting is at one level a modified work culture,"[5] according to the Vanier Institute, a Canadian research organization. For parents, Rosenfeld says, it's "a relentless to-do list."[6]

Net Geners Found Freedom Indoors—Online

There was one place where kids could be free to play inside the home—the home computer. This was where the Net Gener was king. On the Internet, the Net Gener was the expert. He didn't have to take lessons from anyone. In fact, he could teach his parents—the Generation Lap. The kids were experts in this one area. In my home, for instance, I became the student in the computer department on many issues. It was the same story in lots of homes, where the kids were the acknowledged experts on all the gadgets flooding into the market—the MP3 players, the laptops, the mobile phone, the remote control, and all those Web 2.0 tools.

I believe the expertise of Generation Lap has helped to change the power dynamics in the family. The old-fashioned hierarchy, requiring absolute obedience and tolerating no dissent, was already being challenged by boomer parents, as we will see in this chapter. But Net Geners played a significant role too. When the Net Geners started speaking back to their parents, based on what they learned online, you knew the hierarchy was shaking. And when it turned out that they were the experts in using this new technology, the hierarchy was doomed.

With the Net Generation, this trend of freedom will continue and deepen. The reason? Mobile technologies. No longer tethered to a computer, they now have their friends in their pocket wherever they are. They can access the world of information, good or bad, with the click of a thumb.

Net Geners Shake Up the Old Hierarchy

The old family setup—with father as CEO and mother as chief operating officer—was challenged on many fronts. The empowerment of women, who flooded in the marketplace since the 1970s, has made the father-CEO look silly. New child rearing theories, publicized in parenting books and seminars, put the child at the center of the family. Demographic changes played an important role. Net Geners, for example, have grown up in smaller families—today's families have an average of 3.2 members, including the parents,[7] while at the height of the baby boom, the typical family had more than three children. That gave both parents of Net Generation children more time to spend with their kids.[8] As the org charts in Figures 8.1 and 8.2 suggest, Net Geners have also grown up in more complicated families than the straight mom-and-dad ones of the Boomer Generation. Single-parent families, run by either mother or father, have become far more common. Now a family dinner at a holiday may well include stepbrothers, the ex-husband, his spouse (of either gender), stepparents, ex-laws, and grandparents.[9]

The old hierarchy has given way to a new kind of family democracy, in which Net Geners have a voice in family affairs. It's confusing for many boomers, who are flooding into parenting classes to seek advice on how to handle the new

FIGURE 8.1   THE FAMILY ORG CHART WHEN BOOMERS WERE YOUNG

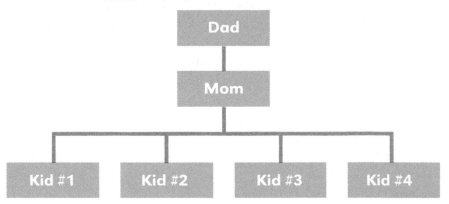

Source: The Net Generation: A Strategic Investigation, © nGenera, 2008

**FIGURE 8.2   THE FAMILY ORG CHART WITH NET
                            GENERATION KIDS**

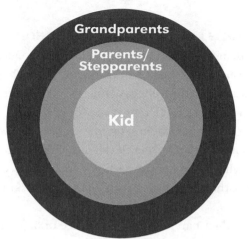

Source: The Net Generation: A Strategic Investigation, © nGenera, 2008

order. But the change to a democratic style of parenting is taking root. A recent study of over 550 mothers and fathers showed that parents felt they were less authoritarian than their parents were. They described themselves instead as the types who expected kids to follow the rules but were willing to discuss them openly.[10] Does this mean the parents have abdicated the responsibility of being parents? Absolutely not. The kids may be experts in the Internet, but that does not mean they're experts in other things. In democratic families, modern parents such as Ana and myself still had, when we were raising our children, the responsibility to draw the line between right and wrong, between safe and unsafe.

But we also talked to our kids, listened to them, and together came up with solutions to whatever problems and issues they were grappling with and found a way forward. That didn't mean that Niki and Alex were allowed to run wild. When we gave them the freedom to make choices and speak out, we also made sure they were aware of their responsibilities—to work hard in school, carry their weight at home, be socially responsible, and not harm other people. As parents, we had responsibilities too—to respect the kids, to allow them to access the Internet and form like-minded communities there, and to encourage their freedom of speech. We didn't read their diaries or other private writings online or otherwise and we didn't spy on them. As parents, we took the lead in defining rights and responsibilities, but we didn't impose them. They were discussed, often in loud and spirited discussions, before all endorsed them.

FAMILY TIES: THERE'S NO PLACE LIKE THE NEW HOME

This new style of democratic parenting has paid many wonderful dividends. In the 1960s, 40 percent of teens said they'd be better off without their parents.[11] Contrast that attitude with the feelings of today's Net Geners. Roughly 80 percent of Net Geners ages 18 to 25 report speaking to their parents in the past day, nearly three-quarters see their parents at least once a week, and half say they see their parents daily.[12] Nearly half call one of their parents a hero.[13] Even college students who no longer live at home touch base with their parents an average of more than once a day via phone, e-mail, text message, or other means.[14]

Net Geners see their parents as a vital source of happiness and security. When my son Alex wrote his thesis for his senior year in college, he included a sweet dedication page that said lovely things about me, Ana, Niki, and his girlfriend. I can't think of any college student who would have even considered such a thing in my day. Nearly three in four say their relationship with their parents makes them happy. Two out of three teens and college-aged young adults say they would first call their parents if they were in trouble. Furthermore, these young people are twice as likely to trust their parents over their friends. They are also more likely to discuss serious issues with their parents than with their friends.[15]

No wonder Net Geners are so happy to move home after college. They find both warmth and freedom there. A 2007 survey showed that 38 percent of 2006 college graduates expected to live at home, "for some time."[16] There are at least 16 million American families today with one child 18 or older living in their home . . . and thanking mom and dad for the free room and board. Of course, money is a factor: most twentysomethings are about $20,000 in the hole from college loans and credit card debt.[17] Almost three out of four Net Geners ages 18 to 25 report that their parents have helped them financially in the past year.[18]

Role Reversal: The Generation Lap

It's hard to be a Dell techie. You have to put up with people in a wild panic, people who swear at you, people who just can't understand why their computer is not working after it was drenched with cold coffee. You have to calm them down, and then patiently walk them through the repair protocol. That's when they typically become silent and obedient; they're suddenly afraid that the mysterious machine will do something terrible.

So imagine the surprise of the techie who dealt with Feroz Rauf. He had called to find out why the new hardware he had ordered online wasn't working, and was all too happy to sit and chat with the techie on the phone—for more than four hours. During that conversation, Rauf was more than just curious; he was insightful. He tried something that the rep didn't think of, and fixed part of the problem. He even showed the techie a trick or two of his own.

Then Rauf disclosed that he was putting off studying for his seventh grade language arts test to enjoy this lengthy conversation with the man from Dell. It turned out that the kid was only 13.

At age 11, Rauf began taking apart and reassembling computers with his friend Demitri. He learned the ropes by talking to engineers, friends of his parents, and visiting online forums. He swears by Wikipedia, and can defend its credibility with citations. His seventh grade French may need polishing, but when it comes to computer expertise, he's working at a college level.

Rauf is the undisputed expert in digital technology in his family. His father may have a doctorate, but even he defers to the boy when it comes to the TV set, mobile phones, entertainment devices, and of course new computer parts. It's a classic example of the Lap Generation. Rauf is lapping everyone in mastery of digital technology, and he's happy to share the information. But he sure likes to get the respect, and he did that night in his four-hour conversation with the Dell techie.

HELICOPTER PARENTS ARE HOVERING

It's made a profound difference in the family. As researchers Neil Howe and the late William Strauss wrote in their 2007 paper for nGenera, this parent-child connection is a significant feature of this Net Generation. One of the manifestations is what the media calls the "helicopter parent"—the parent who hovers over her or his kids and intervenes with teachers and employers even when the Net Geners are supposedly grown up. There are legions of stories about these parents: Dr. Robert Epstein, visiting scholar at the University of San Diego and West Coast editor of *Psychology Today*, started teaching more than 25 years ago. He says that back then he could give any assignment he wanted. But about 10 years ago, Net Gen students began to complain about assignments. Then, after the parents complained, the department chair or dean would side with the students. One time, Epstein says, he asked a student to submit a new paper after she had cut and pasted sections of her paper repeatedly to turn six pages of material into a ten-page paper: "The next thing I knew she and her mother went to the department chair, complaining."[19]

Some colleges now offer a "freshman orientation" workshop—for parents. It's no joke. An estimated 40 to 60 percent of parents, from all socioeconomic groups, can be categorized as helicopter parents, according to a study of parental involvement at 15 universities by Patricia Somers, an education professor at the University of Texas.[20] Somers says it starts long before the Net Geners reach college age; it actually begins while their kids are in secondary school. Parents, eager to ensure that their kids get into college, are using online programs to track their children's test scores, attendance, and homework production. Forget Big Brother; this is Big Mom and Big Dad. Helicopter parents don't make a landing when their children graduate either. Some employers are finding that when they interview candidates, parents come along, and stay involved, lobbying for promotions or salary increases. Nearly 10 percent of employers report that parents help their children negotiate salary and benefits, and 15 percent of employers hear complaints from parents if their kids aren't hired.[21] (See Figure 8.3.)

FIGURE 8.3   TYPE OF PARENTAL INVOLVEMENT AS REPORTED BY EMPLOYERS IN 2007

Obtaining company info	40%
Submitting résumé	31%
Promoting child	26%
Attending career fairs	17%
Complaining if not hired	15%
Arranging interviews	12%
Negotiating salary and benefits	9%
Advocating promotion, raise	6%
Attending the interview	4%

Percentages Reported by Employers

Source: Collegiate Employment Research Institute (2007)

The zeal of the helicopter parent can be truly remarkable. Howe and Strauss tell the story of the chief executive of a public relations company who got a call from the mother of one of his employees. The mother wanted to know how her daughter was doing. And could the CEO, by the way, help the mother deliver her daughter a surprise sushi lunch.

Stories like this make boomer employers shake their heads, but, as Howe and Strauss argue, the helicopter parents should not be spurned. They are a key feature in the lives of a family-oriented generation whose members are strongly connected to their parents: These Net Geners are "team-oriented, focused on achievement, trusting of adults, and eager to meet expectations—and they come with the hovering parents who made them that way." Far from being a bad thing, Howe and Strauss conclude, the resurgence of the extended family could help young people shoulder the burden of caring for elders—including aging boomers—in the future.

BULLYING, PORNOGRAPHY, AND PREDATORS

The freedom Net Geners enjoy on the Internet at home—and now in the mobile devices in their hands—has made it easy to move home comfortably, without sacrificing any of this freedom. But that freedom online has also raised some very serious parenting issues. Boomer parents, who were so careful to protect Net Gen kids outdoors and so thoughtful about nurturing a collaborative, democratic environment to replace an old hierarchical one, often have no idea what is going on online. Although the surveys produce somewhat mixed findings, a couple of findings stand out: 41 percent of U.S. teens under age 18 say their parents don't know what they're doing online, according to a 2002 survey.[22] And 38 percent of high school students sometimes hide their online activities from parents, according to a 2006 report.[23]

Bullies Find a Huge Audience Online

Some of the online hazards are the same terrors as the old ones—with a new twist. There was plenty of bullying when I grew up. At my elementary school in Niagara Falls, the thugs in my class used to line up the smaller boys against a wall and hurl snowballs at them—all the while taking a perverse pleasure at the sound of their cries of fear, as if they were characters in Lord of the Flies. But now bullying has found a way to engage the new technology in its service. Bullies, who, by definition, need an audience of bystanders to make themselves feel powerful, now are able to recruit hundreds of friends on Facebook, or millions of bystanders on YouTube. Every week there is a new story of teenagers bullying fellow students—or even teachers—in front of this new audience.

For example, eight Florida teenagers, six of them girls, lured a 16-year-old girl they knew into a house and beat her unconscious—apparently as a form of retribution in a girl-versus-girl dispute. While it was in progress, they filmed this dreadful attack, and then posted it on YouTube. The ugly case provoked howls of outrage: "We are worshipping a false god in this country and that god's name is fame and fortune," Glenn Beck, the controversial TV host, bellowed. "Teens are living in virtual reality and a voyeuristic culture of violence and humiliation, and it's all for fame and fortune."[24] The media coverage only made it worse: one of the most disgusting moments came when a heavy-set assistant working for TV psychologist Dr. Phil tried to ward off competing TV cameras that were pursuing one of the accused as she left jail. Dr. Phil, it later emerged, had paid the girl's bail and wanted an exclusive interview. (After the deal was revealed, Dr. Phil backed off.)[25]

The attack was appalling, and some of the commentators were quick to blame Internet sites such as YouTube for posting the video of the attack. Some pundits even cited the social network MySpace as the genesis of the attack because the victim was alleged to have provoked the retaliatory beating with a MySpace posting. In a poignant and heart-wrenching YouTube video, the victim's father blamed the Internet, saying, "MySpace is the Anti-Christ." To him, "these Web sites are creating a space for criminal activity, desensitizing our children."[26]

But is the Internet to blame? This terrible attack cost a 16-year-old her vision. But did it happen because of the Internet? To be sure, the democratization of content creation gives a platform to anyone to wanting their 15 minutes of fame. And there is certainly a celebrity culture pervasive in all of society, created primarily through TV reality shows, the paparazzi, *American Idol*, and countless other television contest programs. But more than anything, this is a story about bad parenting on the part of the parents of the attackers. Some of their parents seemed to endorse what the media called the "Florida beat-down." "She's a very good puncher and she's my baby girl," said one mother. "They're making a mountain out of a molehill," said the parent of one of the boys accused of being a guard.

The Florida beat-down speaks volumes—not about this generation or the technology that defines them, but about these eight teenagers and their troubled families. The girls who assaulted the 16-year-old were obviously violent bullies. They have a lot of problems but clearly they never absorbed the ancient wisdom: do unto others as you would have done unto you. I would say the same thing, by the way, about the kids at the elite prep school in New York who criticized their teachers in foul terms on Facebook—and then, once their teachers found out, got their powerful parents, school trustees, to back them up.[27] This reveals a deep lack of family values on the part of some Net Geners—of all classes, from working-class families in Florida to the highest echelons of Manhattan society.

But it does not represent all Net Geners, or even most of them—just as the millionaire crooks that ran Enron do not represent the mainstream values of the boomer generation. Why not look instead at the teenager who calls herself Lcbabieee? She posted commentary on YouTube to say how shocked she was at the assault: "It makes me question what the hell is wrong in our community," she said.[28] More than 600,000 people viewed her commentary within 24 hours of the assault being reported, and in the next months millions saw it, more than watched the original video of the assault. She calls on all youth to look hard at their values and what is happening to their generation. She was followed immediately by dozens of other Net Geners who spoke out against the horrific act. To me, the huge and clearly positive response to her challenge says more about the character of her generation than the pathological behavior of eight troubled youngsters.

Many parents, of course, are terrified that their kids could be the target of online bullying. Take the case of Megan Meier, a 13-year-old girl from Missouri. Her mother Tina took all the precautions when Megan went online. The family computer was located in a common area of the house, and she routinely checked her daughter's MySpace comments. Then Megan got a request to add her as a friend on MySpace, the social networking site. The request came from Josh Evans, who said he was a homeschooled 13-year-old boy from a neighboring town. Tina didn't see the harm. Under Tina's watchful eye, the two became fast friends and were soon exchanging flirtations online. They had never spoken in person, but for Megan, a girl who had trouble fitting in with the cool kids and had been teased about her weight, Josh was everything she could have wished for.

Then Josh changed. In October of 2006, Josh began taunting Megan, calling her a "bitch" and "slut." His MySpace friends joined in and Josh even told her the world would be a better place without her. Devastated, Megan hanged herself with a belt. Her mother found her in the closet.

This was one sad and weird story—Josh turned out to be a female neighbor in disguise—but it still shows the devastating impact of cyberbullying. Sadly, Megan is not the only one. Parry Aftab, a New York lawyer who specializes in

Internet abuse issues, says that Megan's death is one of 11 teen suicides that she knows of that were the direct result of cyberbullying.[29]

Amy Brinkman is a prevention specialist in Santa Clara County's Department of Alcohol and Drug Services who runs a program in East San Jose schools to combat bullying. She has counseled many victims of cyberbullying, including one girl who was subjected to an entire Web site that featured a figure, with a picture of the girl's face, eating and ballooning to obesity. "Cyberbullying is so powerful because it reaches into a kid's private mind space," Brinkman said. "There is almost unlimited access to your psyche and yourself."[30] Because it can take place in the home, it can reach children in the place they once felt most safe.

It's not easy to combat when 6 out of 10 teens bullied online don't tell their parents.[31] Many schools don't have programs in place to teach kids why cyber bullying is not a harmless prank and to give these kids the knowledge with which to cope. The effects of cyberbullying range from trouble at school, including low grades; to anxiety, depression and loneliness; and to health problems such as headaches, stomachaches, and lack of appetite. Meanwhile, cyberbullying is triggering widespread litigation and legislation, with everyone from teachers, parents, and school districts pursuing legal action over nasty and threatening remarks posted by students on the Web. The cyberbullies and their lawyers are fighting back by invoking free speech rights under the First Amendment. "The position that we have consistently taken is that speech that takes place at home is outside of the purview of the schools," said Kim Watterson, a First Amendment and appeals lawyer who has won four cyberbullying lawsuits in recent years on behalf of students. "They simply cannot punish for speech at home."

Dealing with either a bully or a target—in the schoolyard or online—needs careful attention from parents and educators. It requires proactive, thoughtful action, at home and at school. "Breaking the cycle of violence involves more than merely identifying and stopping the bully," Barbara Coloroso wrote in her book, *The Bully, the Bullied, and the Bystander*. "It requires that we examine why and how a child becomes a bully or a target of a bully (and sometimes both) as well as the role bystanders play in perpetuating the cycle." In her book, Coloroso describes bullying as "a conscious, willful and deliberate hostile activity intended to harm, induce fear through the threat of further aggression and increase terror." The answer, she says, is not a zero-tolerance policy or censorship, but rather a thoughtful and deliberate response. The bully needs to understand what she has done wrong, and understand that she is responsible. She needs a process to solve the problem she's created, and understand, at the same time, that she is cable of being a decent person. Parents have a profound responsibility in this healing process, but, as Coloroso suggests, there's one big problem here: Bullying runs in families. The target needs something different, Coloroso says, a strong sense of self. Once parents see the signs of bullying, they need to listen to their child, believe their child's story, and reassure the child that she is not alone and that it's not her fault. Then they have to come up with a plan to stand up to the bully and take back her power. None of this necessary healing, however, can be achieved in the courts alone, or in a legislature. The ultimate bulwark against online bullying must exist in the home—and, more precisely, in what is said in the conversations between parents and children.

I think the new democratic model of the family may help. A dozen years ago in *Growing Up Digital*, I called it the open family. The old, hierarchical system—whether it was a business one, a computer system, or a media operation—was built on a broadcast model. The CEO barked orders. The trusted TV news anchor told us what was happening in the world. Parents dished out orders and advice, without necessarily listening to the children. But in the new open model, children are active participants, experts in at least one thing—the Internet. That doesn't mean that parents can't be parents. Children are not experts in other things, like dealing with bullying. But now, if parents adopt the open family model, they can start by listening to their children, and asking them questions. This could be a far better method of helping a child discover the resources within himself to withstand the assaults of a bully, or to help the child face up to what he has done and to develop a sense of empathy.

In this model, both parents and children have to listen, and not to always be thinking about something else, or tapping out a message on the BlackBerry. Real communication about this issue doesn't necessarily happen on schedule either. But opportunities can come up when parents join their children in their world—watching a favorite TV show or checking out something online. The open family is a transparent unit, which talks openly and honestly about difficult topics and develops a mutually acceptable approach to dealing with them. I truly believe that this type of family attitude and dialogue is the best defense against the problem of bullying. There's no such thing as an invulnerable protective shield, no matter what the legislators and lawyers will tell you.

A Father and Son Talk About Pornography

When my kids went online as teenagers in the mid-1990s, I knew that sooner or later they might be tempted to check out a porn site. As Net Geners, they were in a completely different situation than I was as a teenager after we moved to

Orillia, a small city an hour north of Toronto. At that time, the only porn in town was inside a magazine, *Playboy*, which was sold at the corner store. Even if I had dared to try to buy it, the storeowner would have refused to sell it to me, and then would have called my parents. Alex and Niki, on the other hand, could potentially view any sexual image on the Internet, including pictures that might be inappropriate or degrading. What was a parent to do?

At around this time, the United States was embroiled in a huge public debate over whether to censor the Internet in order to stop children from viewing all manner of pornographic pictures online. In 1996, the U.S. Congress tried to censor the Internet with the Communications Decency Act. This Act offered a chilling preview of what censorship could look like.

The CDA decreed that a government body would decide which words and images on the Internet were "indecent" and "patently offensive" in a "contemporary community." If, in its estimation, these unpalatable words and images had no literary, artistic, or educational merit, and could be easily accessed by a person less than 18 years of age, then criminal charges would be laid. As no individual, nonprofit organization, or even large public corporation would risk prosecution for second-guessing the government, communication on the Internet would be limited and guarded. The most important tool for democratizing information since the printing press would have been suffocated at its very source.

Valuable information for young people to be able ot access, on relevant topics such as sexually transmitted diseases, rape, incest, abortion, sexual harassment—to name a few—could have been banned. Information about support groups for those who have suffered any indignity such as those just listed might also have been eliminated. Everything from contemporary films, plays, books, and online newspapers to paintings, sculpture, and photographs—especially the avant-garde ones—might be outlawed if they had been deemed to be below some unknown community's arbitrary moral standard.

The Communications Decency Act was struck down, and so was the law written to replace it. But boomer parents have not rested. By now, half of them have installed blocking devices to stop their kids from viewing pornography, or violence, crime, or other inappropriate content—customized to fit the parents' beliefs. These devices could even allow parents to track their kids' other activities—in other words to spy on them. It seems creepy to me. For the teenager the message is loud and clear: I don't trust you. What's more, online blocking devices like NetNanny and CYBERsitter, as Kathryn Montgomery notes in her new book, *Generation Digital*, are deeply flawed. CYBERsitter, for example, is supposed to protect you against porn, gratuitous violence and crime, but an online journal found that it also blocked entry to a national women's Web site. Now, even though half of American parents use them, it's unclear how effective these filters are at stopping Internet-savvy teens from going where they want online.

So when our children were entering adolescence back in the 1990s, Ana and I decided not to install these blocking devices. For one thing, we thought it might block out the local newspaper, or vital information for a school project. For another, we believed that the issue of pornography—or other inappropriate material—would provide a great opportunity to talk to our children, in order to share our values with them, and to create open relationships. If our kids came across something that was undesirable, we wanted them to talk to us about it and not feel they had done something bad that needed to be kept secret.

So we made a deal with our children. It was a social contract and they had to sign it. There were safety rules—they could never meet someone in person whom they had met on the Internet without first talking to us, and having us there at their first meeting. They could not go to inappropriate places on the Internet. And in exchange, we would not spy on them, or try to block their access to the virtual world. We had another contract for how they would behave with their friends at our cabin on the lake. It included a no-tolerance policy on drug use, no swimming after dark, and all teenage guests doing their share of chores. We trusted each other, and we both kept up our side of the bargain. Of course, as in any family there were problems and breakdowns. But we worked hard to build that trust by making sure that information flowed freely in our home.

When Alex was 12 or so, I sat down with him for a frank father-and-son chat.

"Do you know what porn is?" I asked.

"Yes," he said.

"Have you ever been to a porn site?"

"No, I haven't."

"Well, I want to talk to you about porn," I said.

"Dad, isn't that for losers who can't get a date?"

I thought that was a pretty good start. We ended up talking about porn, how it degrades women and messes up the joy of sex with someone you really like. Then we signed the social contract and shook hands.

A year later a journalist who disagreed with our approach interviewed me. She said, "But Don, blocking software has improved so much. Why not use it?" She then described a program that a parent could use to "prevent your kid from taking your credit card and buying, say, $2,000 worth of software on the Internet. I thought about it for a second and replied, "If your kid is taking your credit card to steal money, you have a big problem; and the solution is not software!" Clearly your child needs something else like some values and a relationship with his parent.

My bottom line on this issue is: if you don't like porn, talk to your kids about it.

The Big Fear: The Online Sexual Predator

It's a terrifying threat, the sexual predator trolling the Internet in disguise, like the Wolf in "Little Red Riding Hood." There are thousands of people worldwide who create and trade disgusting pictures of children being abused, as Julian Sher described in his 2007 book, *One Child at a Time.* Now the kids are making their own porn: older men disguise their true identity and age on popular social networking sites such as MySpace; they pretend to be a lonely girl's online "boyfriend" and seduce her into sending sexually graphic pictures they can use for their own pleasure, for profit, or for blackmail. As many as 10 percent of the children that the National Center for Missing and Exploited Children (NCMEC) has identified in child pornography images are older teens who take compromising pictures of themselves.[32]

What this means, Sher says, is that there's no quick legal or technological fix to protect children from Internet predators. Sites like MySpace already sift through millions of images posted every day and shut down thousands of profiles that include indecent images. It's also cracking down on registered sex offenders who are stupid enough to use their own names. But, as Sher notes, that doesn't stop predators from using fake names and e-mails. To compel sex offenders to disclose their e-mail addresses—as some U.S. legislators would like—is, Sher writes, like "telling convicted bank robbers out on parole that they cannot use unregistered guns in future hold-ups."

This is a major challenge for parents: how should they deal with their children's adventures on the Internet if the kids start veering into dangerous territory? For starters, let's put it into perspective. The biggest killer of kids is car crashes. Some 9,807 children ages 8 to 17 died in car crashes in the United States between 2000 and 2005. More than half of them were riding with a teen driver and two-thirds of the dead children were not wearing seat belts. So it would make sense for parents to get riled up about seatbelts. Yet we don't fear the common killer right in front of us. We're far more frightened of the rare and hidden threat that lurks outside of our control. That said, I've always believed in the old-fashioned way of preparing kids to venture into the world. Smart parents would not—even if they could—accompany their children every time they ventured outside the home, nor would they monitor every telephone call, scan every pamphlet or book, scrutinize every television or computer screen inside the home. Similarly, cyber-smart parents teach their children how best to protect themselves in an imperfect world where strangers may lurk in schoolyards and disturbing images may appear on the family computer. Yet, as of 2002, half of parents hadn't even talked to their kids about safe online habits.[33]

One of the ironies of the Internet is that while it makes staying in touch easier when family members are physically apart, it can also keep them apart when they're at home.[34] The family dinner table appears to be one of the casualties of this trend. In our home, we could see this coming: while Alex and Niki were growing up, it was not unusual to find each family member clicking away at our keyboards in separate rooms. As a result, we insisted that the kids join us every night at the table for a family supper. No one left until the conversation was over. We all worked hard to make it a pleasant and interesting experience. Some days were *a lot* harder than others. But at the end of the day, Ana and I usually slept tight knowing we were doing the right thing. Dinner table discussions are an incredibly valuable medium for collaboration in problem-solving and future planning. Family members don't just tell stories to one another for entertainment's sake; rather, they relate these stories to each other to make sense of events in their lives.[35] "Family narratives may be a particularly important thing for children's emerging sense of self, both as an individual and as a member of a unified family."[36] And generally speaking, positive family interactions have a significant impact on child well-being: nearly four out of every five Net Geners said that talking with family members made them feel happier.[37]

> "It was my parents in my family, who set the stage for more open dialogue; the technology just pushed their cause, maybe further than they had originally wanted."
>
> —NIKI TAPSCOTT

WHAT WILL NET GENERS DO AS PARENTS?

How will Net Geners handle this challenge? Unlike boomer parents, they start out knowing full well what's happening online. And they'll be deeply knowledgeable about what they got away with as teens. How will they deal with the online freedom *their* children will grow up with? From my limited and unscientific experience, the family dinner is making a comeback now that Net Geners are becoming parents. This may be the manifestation of the open family in action. This is where they'll talk about what their children find on the Internet. They'll discuss it openly rather than installing blocking devices that they—as Net Geners—know are bogus and easy to avoid. They won't try to spy on their kids; they value freedom too highly. So instead they'll collaborate over dinner, and the father (or the mother) will not necessarily be at the head of the table. The family dinner will be the signature of the Net Generation—just as the helicopter parent was of mine.

They Will Value Family Time

This generation is committed to nurturing connections within the family. A 2007 poll revealed that Net Geners feel a strong sense of commitment toward family and show renewed interest in traditional family structures.[38] Of the Net Geners surveyed, 85 percent think that getting married will make them happy, and 90 percent think it is likely that they will be married to the same person their whole life. And 56 percent say that having a family of their own is very important.[39] A study among women aged 18 to 24 revealed that over 90 percent planned to be mothers (or already were). Nearly half of those women anticipated having given birth by the time this book was published in 2008.[40]

Net Geners developed their expectations about being a parent by watching their own boomer parents. As children, they were the center of attention. Their parents made time to watch the soccer practices and ferry them between activities. But Net Geners could also see the reality behind the Supermom façade. Nearly two-thirds of mothers worked outside the home,[41] and started the second shift as a homemaker the minute they walked in the door. They were doing the double shift, which left little or no time for themselves.

These big social changes, woven into the fabric of home life, are making Net Geners place a high value on family. For 63 percent of Net Gen women, getting married, having children, or owning a home is more important than becoming a manager, earning a certain salary, or starting a business (23 percent).[42]

The vast majority of Net Gen women want to work after having children. They're highly ambitious, but it looks like they don't want to sacrifice time with their children to achieve their career goals. Ninety percent of women aged 17 to 28 say they would take a pay cut to be able to spend more time with their children, according to one study.[43] That goes for men and women. "We see the apparent downtrend in career ambition as the real revolution, where very sizeable numbers of women and men are working hard, but not wanting the tradeoffs they would have to make by advancing into jobs with more responsibility," said scholars at the Family and Work Institute.

They'll Connect, Search for Information Online

As parents, this generation will be immersed in the digital world—to check parenting advice, talk to other parents, and play with their kids. Profiles on social networking sites will turn into showcases of baby photo albums. Busy Net Gen parents will make time to use the Internet not only for socializing, but for social support—gaining advice and knowledge about child development, and finding products and services that will make their offline lives with their children richer and better.

When they travel, it will be easier to stay in touch. Andy Shimberg travels all the time for his work for nGenera. His 12-year-old daughter Madison really missed him; she couldn't really connect with her dad on the phone. Then Andy bought her an Apple MacBook with a built-in camera, and the 12-year-old figured out that she and her dad could use iChat to talk and see each other after work and school. Now when Andy's on the road, he and Madison fire up their respective Macs to talk to each other, with the live pictures. "There is something about that face-to-face picture that completely changed the conversation. She is engaged in the conversation, can show me things from school or maybe a new outfit. I can pick up my computer and show her my surroundings, and what some of these cities and locations look like that I travel to," he says. "After a long day on the road, there's nothing quite like firing up my computer and entering an iChat with my daughter and wife."

Screen Time for Babies?

For some families, the screen has become the babysitter. Recently, a Kaiser Family Foundation survey revealed that 61 percent of babies one year or younger were spending an average of one hour and 20 minutes per day with screen media (TV, computers, and video games). Forty-three percent of babies this age watch TV every day and 18 percent watch videos or DVDs every day. Nearly one in five babies one year or younger had a TV in their bedroom, as did 29 percent of children aged two to three, showing that some families have created an environment where TV is ever present.[44]

That is unhealthy for babies; they obviously need close contact with parents to develop properly. Parents obviously need to read to their children and spend time with them. A 2007 study among parents of preschoolers found that increased exposure to electronic media leads to a decrease in parental reading and teaching activities in the home.[45]

But I'm not knocking all screen time in childhood. Obviously, it depends on whether the child is immersed in passive TV watching, or interactive media that stimulate their minds and their imaginations. It also depends on whether the TV or Internet experience is educational or not. If it's enriching, even experts at the Society for Research on Child Development acknowledge that screen time can help develop children's minds: "If educational television has been success-ful in fostering children's cognitive and social development, one might expect that interactive media would have similar, if not greater, potential."[46]

Net Geners, like their parents, are already struggling with the issues of screen time for the kids. One 29-year-old mother says she tries to limit her 9-year-old daughter's time with the plethora of electronic devices and movies in the house. But now the girl is "slightly disconnected from other children her age," the mother says. "Her computer skills are starting to meet those of other children her age, but she still lags in that department. It is a very tough balanc-ing act when we live in a day full of modern technology . . . some days I am grate-ful that she doesn't know everything about pop culture and technology and other days I feel like I have done her a disservice."

The Open Family

The Net Gen's affinity for both the family and technology will, I believe, finally bring to life the open family that I saw budding a decade ago. Net Gen parents will collaborate with their children in creating an interactive, open family that lives according to a different model of authority—one that disregards conven-tional family hierarchies and roles—one that is topical, situational, and fluid. Net Geners are quick to recognize that the best way to achieve power and con-trol is *through* people, not *over* people.

The new Net Gen family is free to explore online, and open to discuss what they find and what it means with their parents. The setting is the old-fashioned, traditional, family dinner table. Parents don't just talk; they listen. They're open and curious about new ideas, including things that they or their children have discovered on the Internet. Instead of censoring or spying or ordering, parents negotiate, explain, and build a common view—like the model CEO that garners praise these days in business journals. Open families are learning, adjusting, and evolving. In my family, we've created an open platform, so I will hand over the conclusion of this chapter to my daughter Niki, a consultant who still loves to do her work on her laptop on the kitchen table, with all the family buzzing around.

"When my parents became adults, they discovered their chutzpah in their independent passions, causes and interests, including socialism, freedom, peace and feminism," she said. "They demanded their voices be heard and they respected those who gave them the opportunity to speak. In my family, this respect of the individual's voice translated to my dinner table and discussion with the family.

"I will allow my kids authority in areas they know more than I do, but I will quickly try and catch up. I will listen more to their 'crazy ideas' about new things in the world that I may not know about. I will not be scared by things I do not understand. I will have a much larger 'support' network of information and backup online to help me along the way."

SEVEN PARENTING GUIDELINES FROM THE KIDS WHO HAVE GROWN UP DIGITAL

(1) **Have a family vision.** Create an open family based on multidirectional communication, mutual trust, and respect for a fluid notion of authority.

(2) **Interact.** Get involved beyond the daily lives of your family; prioritize spending quality time with one another.

(3) **Customize your parenting.** Differentiate the environment and the opportunities available to address individual children's needs.

(4) **Consciously design your family to balance work and personal lives.** Recognize the trade-offs you are willing to make and attack them one by one.

(5) **Collaborate in parenting.** Value diversity and build community in the raising of your children, their lives will be so much richer for it.

(6) **Let kids be kids.** Take cues from the children themselves, capitalize on their spontaneous interests, and foster the motivation to learn for the pure joy of discovery.

(7) **Play.** Get down on the floor with your children and let out a hearty, full-bellied laugh at their silliness!!!

⑨

OBAMA, SOCIAL NETWORKS, AND CITIZEN ENGAGEMENT

THE NET GENERATION AND DEMOCRACY

When 23-year-old Chris Hughes signed on to work for Barack Obama in the winter of 2007, he knew the young senator from Illinois would have to do things differently to win. Obama was the underdog. He had little political experience at the national level and no executive experience. He was the only African American in the race. He was trailing the established front-runner, Senator Hillary Clinton, by a hefty margin. All the pundits said she had it locked up. Clinton was raising immense sums of money and lining up powerful supporters. She had a seasoned team of old-style consultants skilled at manipulating the old media. She was presenting a strong case to explain why she would be the best leader. "It became clear that if he was going to be running, he would need to have a people-powered campaign," said Hughes. "And there was no way to do that without the Internet."

Hughes knew how to help, and it wasn't by knocking doors like he did for Al Gore's presidential run in 2000. At Harvard, Hughes had roomed with Mark Zuckerberg, the cofounder of Facebook, and had helped to develop lots of features—like the "poke," a digital version of the tap on the shoulder—for the social networking site. He knew how social networks like Facebook had transformed life on college campuses, and now he wanted to deploy the power of sharing for Obama. So Hughes moved to Chicago, took a substantial pay cut, and started work as director of online organizing for the Obama campaign.

The online efforts that Hughes organized—which revolved around my.
barackobama.com—or My Bo, as its called inside the campaign—changed the
way politics is played on the Internet, and on the ground. The digital tools that
Hughes put on Obama's social networking site helped to create an online community with over one million people. But instead of trying to control the message from campaign headquarters, as traditional campaign organizers often do,
he gave the individuals in the community the digital tools to organize themselves, share information, and create rallies and fund-raisers for the candidate.
Suddenly, you could share for a cause—propelling Barack Obama, the Net
Geners' favorite candidate, toward the presidency. The results were astonishing: by June 2008, Clinton's powerful campaign had been beaten by a new
model—the Net Generation's version of digital, friend-to-friend networking.

The Obama story, which unfolded during the writing of this book, is a spectacular illustration of the power of the Net Geners, equipped with their digital
tools, to disrupt convention, topple authority, and potentially change the world.
As of this writing, no one knows how the remarkable Obama story will end, but
one thing's for sure: politics will never be the same. And it's just the beginning.
The Net Generation is turning into a political juggernaut that will dominate
twenty-first-century politics in America. Indeed, they have the numbers to do
it. Already they are one-fifth of overall voters, and by 2015, once they all are old
enough to vote, they will be one-third of the voting public. And, as you'll see in
this chapter, they're shaking off years of skepticism and even cynicism about
the political process to vote in greater numbers—usually for a Democrat and
for socially progressive people and causes.

As they get more and more political, they will no doubt sweep away the conventional broadcast model of politics with its "you vote, we rule" style of operating. In this old system, citizens listen to speeches, debates, and television ads,
give money, and vote—but when it comes to having input into policy and real
decisions, they are relegated to the sidelines. They are supposed to sit passively
watching while the real powers—the politicians, their financial supporters, and
the lobbyists—make all the decisions, often according to their own interests.
But this generation won't settle for that model. Having grown up digital, they
expect to collaborate with politicians—not just to listen to their grandstanding
speeches. They want to be involved directly: to interact with them, contribute
ideas, scrutinize their actions, work to catalyze initiatives not just during elections but as they govern. And they will insist on integrity from politicians—
they will know very quickly if a politician says one thing and does another. They
are going to shake up both politics and government.

I believe that this generation will be an unstoppable force for change in the country's political processes. Their digital tools, such as the social networking sites, have already changed the way elections are run, and in this chapter, I'll show you some innovative ways that digital tools are already being used to change the way government decisions are made, and the way services are delivered. It could change the nature of democracy itself. The coming era of political life in America will be Democracy 2.0, driven by the Net Generation. The first wave of democracy in America established elected and accountable institutions of governance, but with little real involvement in decision making on the part of voters. The second wave, the one driven today by the Net Generation, will create a true marketplace of ideas, characterized by a new culture of public deliberation and active citizenship. The United States will never be the same, and as these changes ripple throughout the world, citizen engagement could drive some very positive and long-overdue changes.

THEY'RE NOT THE ME GENERATION: THEY CARE

Net Geners are often called the Me Generation. According to the common stereotype, they care only about themselves and popular culture. They don't read newspapers and feel little attachment to their community or their country. Conventional wisdom holds that young voters can't be bothered with voting. According to Mark Bauerlein, author of *The Dumbest Generation*, Net Geners have "embarrassing voter rates" and "they don't follow politics."[1]

But conventional wisdom is wrong, and grows more wrong with each election. They do care about their communities. As you'll see in Chapter 10, they are volunteering in record numbers to tackle some of the world's most difficult problems, like poverty and global warming. Their civic engagement shot up after the horrific attack on the World Trade Center in 2001, and it has stayed up in the years afterward, unlike that of other age groups.[2] Yet, while they volunteered in huge numbers after 9/11, they have steered clear of formal politics. Fewer than half of 18- to 24-year-olds voted in the 2004 presidential election— a figure far below the 64 percent of voting-age citizens who went to the polls.[3]

Their apparent lack of interest did not stem from a cynicism about the role of government in society, though. They don't support the libertarian view that governments should just get out of the way and let markets rule.[4] Nearly two-thirds of youth age 15–25 strongly believe that government should do more to solve problems, according to a 2006 "Civic and Political Health of the Nation" survey conducted by CIRCLE (Center for Information and Research on Civic Learning and Engagement).[5] They don't feel powerless either. Several polls show that a huge majority of Net Geners feel they have the power to change their country.[6] Nor can the reticence of young people to go to the polls be interpreted as a sign that they don't care. On the contrary, 84 percent of 18–26-year-olds said that it seemed the gap between rich and poor had grown in the last 20 years, and a remarkable 94 percent thought this growing gap was a bad thing.[7] These figures are higher than those for older generations. In a Magid Associates 2006 survey for the New Politics Institute, young adults were more likely than any other age group to favor governmental action to reduce economic differences among Americans.[8]

TRADITIONAL POLITICS ARE A TURNOFF

So why have they stayed away from the polls? The answer, in a few words, is aversion to traditional politics. A big majority of Net Geners see elected officials as selfish, too partisan, and too negative."[9] They don't trust the institutions of government either. Only 30 percent trusted the president (any president) to "do the right thing" all or most of the time. Far more trusted the military (53 percent) and the Supreme Court (52 percent).[10]

> "I'm proud to be an American. We have great minds and good intentions. But I'm not proud of the government we've had."
> —BEN ELROM, 17, CHARLOTTESVILLE, VIRGINIA

Many Net Geners believe that the mechanics of power and policy-making are controlled by self-interested politicians and organized lobby groups.[11] "A lot of us have lost faith in politicians. We don't believe that anything will be done by electoral politics. It's too frustrating and takes too long," says Danny Herbst, 23, of Portland, Oregon. Typical of his generation, he believes, "If you want to get something done, you need to do it yourself."

The Net Generation does not put much trust in politicians and political institutions—not because they're uninterested, but rather because political systems have failed to engage them in a manner that fits their digital and ethical upbringing. As a result, their interest in political life has been tepid, at best. In 2006, when asked if they would like to support a candidate beyond just voting, only 35 percent said they would volunteer for the campaign. Only 11 percent said they would donate $10 or more, while fewer than half said they would attend a rally or event. Only half would bother to put a bumper sticker on their car or a sign in front of their home. What nearly 6 out of 10 would do is join an online group.[12]

> "Politics should be about policies— what you stand for, not about your personal life. Who cares if someone smoked or has marital problems. That's their business."
> —KATIE TINKHAM, 16, RIVER FOREST, ILLINOIS

Clearly, by their own admission, their participation in the political process has been anemic. While half of the respondents had signed an online petition, only 14 percent had volunteered for work on behalf of a candidate or issue, 21 percent had attended a rally or demonstration, 15 percent had donated money to a campaign, and 33 percent had written an e-mail or letter. But, as we have noted, their lack of participation has been due, not to apathy or cynicism, but to the legitimate reservations they have had about endorsing a person or program they could not really believe in, and a process they strongly believed to be antiquated.

A GENERATION MOVES FROM CIVIC ACTION TO POLITICAL ACTION

But now things are changing. Few people realize it, but in 2004, more people under the age of 30 cast votes than did people over 65, according to John Della Volpe, cofounder of SocialSphere Strategies and director of polling for the Harvard Institute of Politics. That may be surprising because a far smaller percentage of people under 30 voted in 2004 than did senior citizens. But there are so many more young people than seniors, they still outnumbered their elders at the ballot box.[13] What's more, while the 2004 election attracted a larger percentage of voting-age citizens of all ages, the biggest increase was in the 18–24 age group. In that group, voter turnout climbed 11 percentage points.[14]

In the 2008 primaries, young people flocked to the polls. Although they hadn't caught up to older Americans in terms of the percentage of eligible voters who turned out, they substantially increased their presence in the game. The youth turnout in Georgia and Montana was three times higher than it was in 2004, and in Tennessee and Oklahoma it was four times higher. Every state that voted on Super Tuesday saw at least a five-point increase in youth voting, except for New York, which saw no increase.[15]

Net Geners now realize that who's in power matters. "In the late '90s, the Net Generation chose community volunteerism over political action because feeding the hungry or mentoring a child was immediate, tangible, and felt good—making the same impact through politics could take years because of the slow bureaucratic process and the seemingly selfish and too-partisan ways of elected officials," said Harvard pollster Della Volpe. "Politics did not become relevant for many members of the Net Gen until after September 11. It was this renewed belief in the relevance of politics—married with mobilization efforts of nonprofit groups and social networking tools—that were the groundwork for the rapid rise in participation we are seeing today."

Many Net Geners are getting involved in politics because they oppose the Iraq war and President Bush. Fully 72 percent disapprove of the job George W.

Bush is doing, and only 10 percent think the country is headed in the right direction.[16] They have seen the consequences of Bush's two terms in office, and they understand that the values and competency of a president can have a profound impact on the quality of American citizens' lives. UCLA's annual freshman survey indicates that the interest in politics increased sharply in 2001 and has been rising ever since. The studies reveal that "discussing politics" is more prevalent for today's freshman than at any other time in the survey's history. And, in Harvard University's Institute of Politics Fall 2007 survey of young people, 63 percent of respondents said they believe political engagement is a viable and important method of addressing national issues. University students are hungry for political conversation, according to a 2007 report by CIRCLE and the Charles F. Kettering Foundation, but it's got to be "free of spin." That's a big change from 1993, when many youth said politics was "irrelevant to their lives" and they had no interest in being politically active.[17]

Net Geners like the choice they're being given in the 2008 presidential campaign. At the beginning of the primary season, 84 percent of Americans, young voters included, felt there was a candidate running who would make a good president. The view was bipartisan, held by 85 percent of Republicans and 89 percent of Democrats.

"Our entire generation supports Obama because we desperately need change and he has a vision."
—BEN ELROM, 17, CHARLOTTESVILLE, VIRGINIA

By comparison, at the same time in 1992, when the elder President Bush was running for reelection against a wide Democratic field, just 40 percent felt that way.[18] (See Figure 9.1)

FIGURE 9.1   THE NET GEN STARTS VOTING

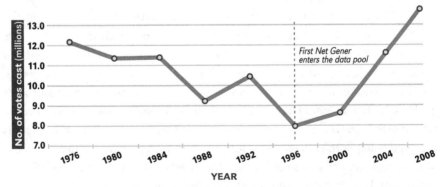

Source:Center for Information and Research on Civic Learning and Engagement* (CIRCLE)[19]
*2008 data extrapolated by John Della Volpe and Jonathan Chave, Cofounders of SocialSphere Strategies.

The Politicization of Mollie Merry

In the summer of 2007, 23-year-old Mollie Merry flew from Little Rock, Arkansas, to the Republic of Malawi in Africa. It is one of the five poorest countries in the world. The overseas project was part of her curriculum as a graduate student at the Clinton School of Public Service. Mollie's job was to help in the areas of health, agriculture, food security, clean water and sanitation, and education.

Partisan politics was not on Mollie's agenda, but in preparing for work, she learned a lot about President Clinton's postpresidential work. "It was incredible to realize how many countries he had been to and how many local organizations he had been able to help link to and help. It kind of hit me that wow, this post-president has a real power. It's almost limitless. There he was changing lives in Malawi, Africa."

Mollie then decided to become active in the 2008 election, working for four months on the Hillary Clinton campaign as a women's outreach coordinator. She told me this involved "very grassroots organizing, bringing people together around shared concerns and shared issues and then helping them organize themselves into action. If I have the power to bring people together around things that I care about, my personal conviction is that I have the responsibility to do that.

"With Facebook we were able to organize and push women like no other campaign before. There were a lot of older political people in that campaign that have been in politics a long time, but they were really smart and hired lots of young people to come in who were really knowledgeable about this technology. They really relied on us to organize groups such as 'Wellesley Women for Hillary.'

"It was really the young people that were spearheading the organization of the supporters. And once you find that you are in a group of 500 other people that are driven to do the same thing you are, you find yourself empowered and energized. Most had never actively participated in the democratic process. Tools such as Facebook make it so easy to be involved, there's no excuse not to be."

NET GENERS ARE MORE LIKELY TO BE DEMOCRATS

More of the Net Generation will vote, but what kind of voters will they be? They're likely to lean harder to the Democratic side than the Gen X that proceeded them. According to a 2008 poll, 57 percent of Net Geners were leaning Democrat, compared with 51 percent of Gen Xers and late boomers (born between 1956 and 1976).[20]

When they think of social issues and economic inequalities, Net Geners are less conservative than Generation Xers were. According to the Pew Gen Next study, in 2003, 89 percent of white 18–25-year-olds said they agreed that "it's all right for blacks and whites to date each other," including 64 percent who "completely" agreed. When the same question was posed in 1987–88, only 56 percent agreed with this statement.[21]

As well, they are more willing to accept gay marriage than older Americans are. In a 2007 Pew survey, 56 percent of 18–29-year-olds supported allowing gays and lesbians to marry, while only 37 percent of the general public do.[22]

"In the circles I travel everyone is a liberal."
—MIKE LAZEAR, 28, PORTLAND, OREGON

In a 2006 Pew survey, 61 percent of 18–25-year-olds thought gays should be allowed to adopt, while only 44 percent of other adults do.

UNLEASHING THE GENIE: HOW BARACK OBAMA USED SOCIAL NETWORKING TO ENGAGE A GENERATION

Like many Net Geners, Chris Hughes was inspired by Obama. "Barack Obama is a new kind of politician who wants to usher in a new kind of politics in our country—one based on reason and consensus rather than sound bites and partisanship. Not only is he remarkably intelligent, but also he's able to genuinely listen and understand other people's perspective. He's not a product of the Washington insider culture where lobbyists and special interests dominate the legislative process."

When he took the job of director of online organizing, Hughes's mission was not only to build energy online but to transfer it to the ground, to the hard business of getting out the vote and raising money. "The overarching goals of the campaign have been about getting supporters to reach out to other supporters by giving them the right information," said Hughes. "We make sure all of the tools we build are geared toward electoral success. For example, we let supporters make their own fund-raising page, import their address book, and share the reasons they think it's important to donate with their network. We also let them track their progress on a thermometer."

The campaign's social networking site, my.barackobama.com, is designed to give supporters the power to build support, hold rallies, and raise money. Users are invited to post blogs, get into groups, meet people in their neighborhood, and track the money they're raising. A strong sense of community is always emphasized. When making a donation to the campaign, users are asked to write a short note expressing their feelings about Obama, the campaign, or anything that crosses their mind. Once a person donates, a confirmation is sent along with a thank-you, and includes a randomly selected message written by another donor. The exchange boosts the connection that donors feel toward the campaign.

It's had a remarkable impact. As of May 1, 2008, Obama had raised an amazing $265 million, half of which came from donors who pledged less than $200. Well over $28 million in contributions has been reported online. In February 2008, for example, 256,000 people logged onto Obama's donations page,[23] and 43 percent of Obama's donors gave less than $200.[24] In contrast, Clinton had fewer donors who gave more money (171,000 donors, and only 27 percent gave less than $200).[25]

This is people power in action—very different from the classic top-down political system of campaigning. Unlike the Howard Dean campaign of 2004, which used Meetup.com to organize events and generate interest, the Obama campaign empowered each individual user by giving them the tools they need to act. "We make it much easier for people on a local level to find other supporters," said Hughes. As a result, "we have local grassroots Obama groups in the vast majority of high schools, colleges, and general regional networks."

Obama also has a big presence on other social networking sites like MySpace, Facebook, and Bebo. Not surprisingly, the online campaign made sure that all information and events were easy to transfer to their supporters' Facebook profiles, where they could be shared with friends, and friends of friends. Giving the power to the supporters wasn't always trouble-free, though. When one volunteer put up a MySpace page with the senator's name on it, the volunteer recruited 160,000 friends. But, in the view of the Obama campaign, there was a snag: it might look like the messages were coming from the candidate himself. So the Obama campaign took over the site—which angered the volunteer so much that he refused to hand over the 160,000 contacts.

E-mails are a key feature of the online campaign. Supporters who turn up at events give their e-mail addresses, which are then added to region-specific lists. They are also encouraged to sign up for issue-specific lists that matter to them. With that information the Obama campaign can send them e-mails with relevant updates about their region and about the issues that are most important to them.

"The Obama effort is the first real trans-media political campaign of the twenty-first century, where the role of engaging, two-way technologies—including mobile devices, laptops, and social networking sites—became as important as traditional media," branding consultant Brian Collins told me during the primaries. A prime example came from a Toronto blogger (and U.S.

politics junkie) who compared the way Obama and Clinton used Twitter, a Web site that lets people send text messages from their mobile phones to friends. You could sign up to follow messages from both candidates, but only Obama repaid the favor by signing up to follow your messages. It's a small thing, blogger Jason Oke notes, "but it's an important gesture that shows [Obama] understands the grammar of social media. Clinton is basically using Twitter as another broadcast medium; Obama is using it as a tool for connecting with people on an individual level."

The strategy has made Obama a lot of friends—over one million of them. Obama had by far the largest Internet presence of any of the three candidates still vying for the presidency in the spring of 2008. Hillary Clinton came in second at 330,000 friends, and Republican nominee John McCain trailed with 140,000 friends. While Obama and Clinton had the same number of Facebook friends in the spring, most of Clinton's "friends" were actually against her candidacy. Obama had his own detractors, with the largest group having 30,000 members, but those paled in comparison with his strongest group of supporters, which had over 500,000 members.

Giving volunteers the power to organize had an amazing impact, as Obama described in a talk captured on YouTube: People were asking him how he won the Idaho primary by a huge margin, he said: "It was because volunteers got together. They really built the campaign. We weren't even there in Idaho and suddenly we got a call from somebody—'I'm here in Idaho and I'm organizing. Can the senator stop by sometime?' We didn't have big plans for Idaho, but people made the structure."

People like Meredith Segal, a junior at Bowdoin College. She was so inspired by Obama's 2004 Democratic National Convention speech that she went to work setting up a pro-Obama group. Today, it has over 60,000 members and chapters at 80 colleges. The group got the chance to meet the senator at a rally they organized themselves at George Mason University that drew a crowd of 3,000 students.

In the 2008 Democratic primaries, Obama was favored by the Net Gen by an over two-to-one margin. This represents a major generational shift. Morley Winograd and Michael D. Hais, coauthors of a new book, *Millennial Makeover: MySpace, YouTube, and the Future of American Politics*, point out:

> that the rise of new, large and dynamic generations, which vote against the established patterns of older generations, is one of the primary causes of the political realignments that have transformed American politics every four decades throughout our country's history.

The impact of these realignments on the political system and the country depends on the kind of generation that produces the realignment. The last previous generation gap in 1968 featured the ideological, moralistic, and highly divided Baby Boomer generation vs. the gung ho, institution building beliefs of their parents—members of the GI generation, the nation's previous "civic" generation. It split the Democratic Party apart in that year's presidential election and created the cultural wars that the country has endured for 40 years since. This year's generation gap (and resulting political realignment) is caused by the rise of a civic, unified Millennial Generation with its penchant for win-win, group-oriented solutions to the country's challenges.[26]

Obama could see this demographic wave coming, and with Chris Hughes's help, he tapped into it brilliantly. As *New York Times* columnist Frank Rich put it: "The millennials' bottom-up digital superstructure was there to be mined, for an amalgam of political organizing, fund-raising and fun, and Mr. Obama's camp knew how to work it. The part of the press that can't tell the difference between Facebook and, say, AOL, was too busy salivating over the Clintons' vintage 1990s roster of fat-cat donors to hear the major earthquake rumbling underground."[27]

A Candidate—and a Campaign—That Echoed the Net Gen Norms

It's not surprising that the Obama campaign captured the imagination of so many Net Geners. His campaign embodied some of the key Net Gen norms we have been discussing throughout this book.

His campaign was customized to each Net Gener with my.barackobama.com. His Facebook presence was innovative. The campaign was deeply collaborative. Online supporters were encouraged to take action, tell their friends, raise money, and hold rallies. They were not directed from above, as they would have been in a typical campaign. The collaborative ethos paid handsome dividends. In February 2008, a video was uploaded onto YouTube called "Yes We Can." It was an inspiring four-minute musical version of Obama's New Hampshire concession speech that was released by will.i.am of the Black Eyed Peas musical group, with a little help from celebrities like actress Scarlett Johansson. The song, which echoed Obama's direct quotes as his voice echoed in the background, was any campaign operative's dream. But will.i.am had nothing to do with the Obama campaign; he was just an enthusiastic supporter. And what an impact he had! In less than two months the video was viewed by over 17 million people and would be described as one of the defining moments of any Democratic primary presidential campaign.

After Obama won the Democratic primary race, his campaign found another innovative way to tap into Net Gen supporters' desire to collaborate. FighttheSmears.com gave supporters a chance to deal with accusations appearing in any media against Obama and his wife Michelle. The site confronted the accusations head-on: to counter the claim that Obama was not born in the United States, his birth certificate was posted online. To disprove claims that Obama refused to say the Pledge of Allegiance with his hand over his heart, a YouTube video was posted that clearly showed Obama doing just that.

The site dealt with claims about Obama's wife Michelle as well. "On May 30, Rush Limbaugh said he heard a rumor that a tape exists of Michelle Obama using the word 'whitey' from the pulpit of Trinity United Chruch of Christ," the site said. "Truth: No such tape exists. Michelle Obama has not spoken from the pulpit at Trinity and has not used the word." Of course, the site also gives Obama supporters plenty of help and encouragement to spread the truth to friends and acquaintances.

As we've seen, Net Geners value integrity and expect politicians to show it too. Obama's moment to show this side of his character came when he delivered a remarkable speech in March 2008 on race.

Race issues are a challenge for any politician. The Reverend Jeremiah Wright, Obama's pastor and the man who had married him and baptized his children, had made a number of incendiary comments on video, such as the suggestion that America deserved what it got on 9/11. "America's chickens are coming home to roost," he said in one speech. Yet Obama did not immediately cut his pastor loose, as the conventional politician might have done. Instead he confronted the race issue head-on in a thoughtful speech about race relations that was viewed millions of times on YouTube. At the time, it looked like a great example of integrity in politics. Obama made it clear that while he didn't agree with the pastor, he nonetheless would continue to sit in his congregation because the pastor had many other laudable facets to his personality and his public service. But then, Wright supplied Obama with another challenge. More videos emerged showing Wright in full flight, claiming that the U.S. government had somehow infected African Americans with the HIV virus. Finally, Obama pulled the plug. "I gave him the benefit of the doubt," he said in late April, but the latest round of comments "offended me." Obama denounced the pastor for dividing the races. "He contradicts everything I'm about," he said. "Reverend Wright does not speak for me."

Obama supported Wright after the first round of outrageous comments emerged; then he renounced him. Was this the kind of flip-flop that erodes trust? I don't think so. This was a tough moment in his campaign, but Obama didn't lose the trust of his Net Gen supporters because he was up-front about changing his mind. He didn't try to rewrite history, or weasel his way out of it. He was honest and transparent. It was a good example of how to keep your integrity in the challenging environment of YouTube politics.

The digital campaign has also played on the Net Gener need for speed and entertainment. Obama, for example, gives his 20,000 followers on Twitter instant updates on his campaign, his location, and even his mood. On April 3, for instance, Obama was "troubled by today's unemployment figures, the latest indicator of how badly America needs fundamental change from Bush-McCain policies." On March 12, he was "grateful to be with distinguished generals & admirals. Between them, they've served 9 Commanders-in-Chief. Honored to draw on their counsel." It makes supporters feel they've got an immediate connection with the leader.

NOW THEY WANT A SAY IN GOVERNMENT—OR THEY COULD TAKE IT TO THE STREETS

The Obama campaign helped to engage a significant number of Net Geners in the political process, not just as donors and voters but as active collaborators in the campaign. But I believe that's only the first stage of the politicization of this Net Generation. During the campaign, Obama promised that he would make decision making at the federal government more visible so that the ordinary person knows what's going on inside the government machine and can contribute his or her views. I believe the Net Generation will expect this, no matter who is president. If they face the usual wall of silence or cloud of obfuscation when they try to communicate with the federal government, watch out: we could see a new wave of youth radicalism on the streets. They've shown they have the tools to organize themselves, and they've shown that they care. If they become agitated about an issue, they can whip up a powerful protest movement.

Just look at the huge protests in South Korea in the summer of 2008. When President Lee Myung-Bak agreed in April 2008 to lift a five-year-old import ban on U.S. beef, despite fears that the meat might be tainted with mad cow disease, teenage girls started talking about it on fan Web sites for television personalities, according to the *International Herald Tribune*. Then the teen concerns about American beef moved to Agora, a popular online discussion forum at the Web portal Daum.

"When a high school student began a petition on Agora calling for Lee's impeachment, it gathered 1.3 million signatures within a week," according to the *Herald Tribune*. "The police were caught off guard on May 2 when thousands of teenagers networking through Agora and coordinating via text messages poured into central Seoul, holding candles and chanting 'No to mad cow!'"

At first, mainstream media and the government paid no attention. American beef imports were suspended in 2003 following a mad cow case in the United States, and five years later the U.S. government insisted that its beef was safe. However, the U.S. government tests less than 20,000 of the country's 100 million cows, unlike in Europe, where every animal above a given age gets tested.[28]

Ignored by the mainstream, the young South Koreans decided to make their own news. "Protesters stepped forward as "citizen reporters," conducting interviews, taking photographs and, thanks to the country's high-speed wireless Internet, uploading videos to their blogs and Internet forums. One video showing the police beating a female protester caused outrage on the Internet and prompted even more people to join the demonstrations," according to the *Herald Tribune.*

The protests gathered power as anti-government supporters such as labor unions joined in. Dozens of Web sites broadcast the demonstrations live, with the help of BJs—"broadcast jockeys"—to enliven the action, the newspaper reported. This was a classic "Web 2.0 protest."

"Mad cow" became the emblem for widespread complaints against Lee's government: "mad cow education," "mad cow labor policy," and "mad cow health care." It shook Lee and his government. In an attempt to placate the growing protest, Lee fired three of his cabinet ministers in July.

"The thirtysomethings were completely disinterested in taking it to the streets," said John Della Volpe, who was present in Korea for the protests. "It was the Net Geners who led the protest. This huge upheaval in Korean society was driven by teenagers!"

Leaders in the United States and elsewhere should take heed. Consider these polls. In its fall 2007 survey of young people, Harvard's Institute of Politics found that a plurality of 37 percent thought that the two parties did such a poor job of representing the American people that a new third party was needed. Only 31 percent of youth felt the two main political parties did an adequate job, while 33 percent were undecided.

True, that dissatisfaction may have diminished for the legions of Net Geners who worked for Obama, or McCain, but after the election these youngsters will be energized and have unprecedented tools at their disposal to continue championing for change. They will want to see their issues stay at the top of the list for proposed presidential and congressional action.

If that doesn't happen, you might see them out on the streets or organizing a highly effective protest online. As Newfoundland high school student Charlotte-

Anne Malischewski recently pointed out in *The Globe and Mail*, "young people are more vocal during this first decade of the twenty-first century than they were in the 1960s. Canadian protests against the war in Iraq thus far have drawn 10 times more people than all the Canadian protests against the war in Vietnam combined. The largest protest in the United Kingdom, that attracted nearly two million people, was not in 1968. Rather, it was in 2003 and it, too, was against the war in Iraq. In the United States, the largest protest was not against the war in Vietnam, nor the war in Iraq. The largest wave of demonstrations in United States history took place in April 2006 when more than two million people took to the streets in favor of immigrant rights."

Government leaders need to understand that youth activism is healthy and should be embraced. They're not just another constituency who needs to be mollified. This generation wants change, and will demand its rightful role at the decision-making table.

Reinventing Government Service Delivery

Net Geners, like the public in general, are not content to stand in line for routine transactions, or passively receive media-fed campaign bulletins. They'll demand better service, more convenient access to information, and an ongoing opportunity to personalize or customize the services they receive from government. They want the public sector organized in ways that maximize convenience to the citizen as opposed to the bureaucracy.

As you've seen, Net Geners have become accustomed to unfettered choice in virtually all aspects of their lives. In most public sector 'marketplaces,' governments maintain a monopoly on service provision and most services are delivered on a one-size-fits-all basis. Even in the shift to e-government, many agencies have simply replicated physical-world distribution systems on the Web.

I see tremendous potential for government to create new forms of value by focusing on what it does best while creating partnerships for other activities. By assembling networks of citizens, private firms, nonprofit organizations, and other agencies on a Web-based platform, for instance, governments can offer greater innovation, choice, and variety to their service customers. In some areas, it could even be advantageous to go one step further by offering citizens a basket of services and providers to 'purchase' with their tax dollars or to offer many other possible business models that emphasize choice in service venues, providers, and options.

Most governments are offered and delivered on a one-size-fits-all basis. Web services, widgets, RSS, and other Web 2.0 technologies could enable service providers to satisfy expectations for customizable or personalized interactions with government. Imagine, for example, that all citizens were granted their own MyGovernment page from birth—an interactive space through which they channeled all of their interactions with government, whether renewing a driver's license, filing taxes, finding a new doctor, or registering a business. The service would actively anticipate their needs and deliver information to their platform of choice, including their desktops, mobiles, or perhaps their favorite social-media sites.

Given the significant growth in the mobile Web around the world, many governments are already migrating their services to mobile devices. Canada's Wireless Portal provides access to real-time government information, such as border-crossing wait times, real-time currency exchange rate information, and location-specific information such as phone numbers and hours of operation for various offices. Providing such instantaneous and mobile "on-demand" services meets the Net Generation's expectation for speed and immediacy.

Throughout Asia, mobile government services have become an integral aspect of political and social developmental strategies. In the Philippines, for instance, the municipal government of Manila has teamed with citizens and environmental nongovernmental organizations to help steward the local environment. The Bantay Usok project allows citizens to act as environmental stewards by texting the location of vehicles that are belching smoke from their exhaust pipes. The project, which began in 2002, drew over 50,000 text messages in its first two months of activity.

DEMOCRACY 2.0: FROM BROADCAST TO INTERACTIVE

There is a new age of participation emerging in the economy—and Obama has unleashed the desire to participate deeply in political activity. The Net Generation, as I explained earlier, is driving the democratization of information content: a blog makes you a publisher and YouTube makes you a broadcaster. Young people innovate and participate in economic activity in ways that were previously unimaginable. If you're a high school student in Dallas or Zurich, you can join the Innocentive network to help P&G find a new molecule. Rather than reading the encyclopedia, you can write one together with thousands of others to help create Wikipedia. Rather than watching the evening news, you can make a news clip for yourself, and if it's good it'll be broadcast on Al Gore's Emmy-winning cable television network Current TV. If you're a poor student in India you can "attend" MIT on the Web and if you become a kick-ass programmer, you can join the TopCoder network and be gainfully employed from your village. Every company needs to find ways to become tied into this explosion of peer production. The economy and the ways firms orchestrate capability to innovate and create goods and services is changing—what Anthony Williams and I call *Wikinomics*—innovation is being democratized.

But when it comes to political democracy, we're all pretty passive. Almost all democratic systems around the world are best described as "broadcast democracies." Politicians in capital cities use the media to broadcast their opinions to citizens, and in the run-up to an election, they buttress these messages with paid advertising. Then the citizens get their one shot at participating in the governing process, i.e., they vote. After the ballots are cast, voters go back to their passive role as recipients of political messages. Between elections there is no real engagement by the citizens in the important decisions that affect their lives.

This "we vote, they rule" system of representative democracy made sense when it was devised centuries ago. Our ancestors didn't have the education, time, resources, or communication tools to participate in the governing process. They chose their representatives in the expectation that they would learn about issues and make reasoned decisions on the voters' behalf. The system worked because public policy issues were simple and evolved at a horse-and-buggy pace. Government could credibly assert that they had a mandate from the electorate and the legitimate authority to implement its views.

Back then, there was a much richer and greater amount of public discussion and debate than exists today. No one explains it more eloquently than Al Gore, the former vice president who won an Oscar and shared a Nobel Peace Prize. Back in the early days of America, printing presses were almost everywhere and accessible to most people who wanted to print an essay, pamphlets, a book, or flyers, Gore explains. It was easy, in other words, for the public to participate in the political discussion. But now, "some extremely important elements of American Democracy have been pushed to the sidelines. And the most prominent casualty has been the 'marketplace of ideas' that was so beloved and so carefully protected by our Founders. It effectively no longer exists." Gore is speaking about the rise of a one-way, centrally controlled communications medium—television. "Consider the rules by which our present 'public forum' now operates, and how different they are from the forum our Founders knew. Instead of the easy and free access individuals had to participate in the national conversation by means of the printed word, the world of television makes it virtually impossible for individuals to take part in what passes for a national conversation today," he said.

It's easy to watch TV; television is more accessible than any source of information has ever been in all of history, he noted. "But here is the crucial distinction: it is accessible in only one direction; there is no true interactivity, and certainly no conversation." This has created a broadcast model of democracy. "To the extent that there is a 'marketplace' of any kind for ideas on television," Gore said, "it is a rigged market, an oligopoly, with imposing barriers to entry that exclude the average citizen."[29]

> "Politics today is entertainment. But you don't really find out what's going on by watching TV."
> —TINA STURGEON, 30, PORTLAND, OREGON

To be sure, government leaders have attempted to test public opinion through instant polling, by many accounts creating a hyperdemocracy where elected leaders are buffeted daily by the capricious winds of pollsters and the public mood. Notwithstanding laudable efforts of some government leaders, they have failed to create flexible, responsive, or efficient government. And they have failed to engage citizens in a real marketplace of ideas. No wonder our democratic institutions are in a deep crisis of credibility and functionality. In a world where TV dominates the democratic life, Gore is deeply worried. "I truly believe that America's democracy is at grave risk," he warns.

Let's face it—governments everywhere seem ineffective and out of touch; political corruption in high places is unabated; interest groups and lobbyists seem to dominate everything; and real change seems glacial, from improving healthcare, the environment, and education to finding peace and security in the world.

We must change, and the Net Gen model of interactivity, collaboration, and enablement points to the right way. What the current system lacks are mechanisms enabling government to benefit on an ongoing basis from the wisdom and insight that a nation can collectively offer. Citizens can and should become involved, learn from each other, take responsibility for their communities and country, learn from and influence elected officials, and vice versa. We could revitalize the marketplace of ideas.

I'm not proposing some kind of *direct* democracy—where citizens can vote every night on the evening news or Web sites. That would be tantamount to a digital mob. Democracy is much more than majority rule on a nightly basis. Many people don't have the time, inclination, or expertise to become well informed on all issues. Governments want reasoned opinion, not just any opinion.

What I am proposing is a way to allow citizens to contribute ideas to the decision-making process, to get engaged, to learn, and to innovate new solutions to society's problems. This is long overdue. These days, the policy specialists and advisers on the public-sector payroll can barely keep pace with defining the problems, let alone craft the solutions. Government can't begin to amass the in-house expertise to deal with the myriad challenges that arise. Governments need to create opportunities for sustained dialogue between voters and the elected. Courtesy of the Internet, public officials can now solicit citizen input at almost no cost, by providing Web-based background information, online discussion, and feedback mechanisms. Government can now involve citizens in setting the policy agenda, which can then be refined on an ongoing basis. Such activity engages and mobilizes citizens, catalyzing real-life initiatives in communities and society as a whole.

Real, deliberative democracy requires an enhanced notion of citizenship. Even the language we use in discussing matters of government betrays an outdated view. When it comes to providing services like utilities, we speak of citizens as "rate payers" rather than customers. When it comes to democracy we describe citizens as "the electorate," "voters," and "electors." In

> "In theory we have input into policy now. But not in reality. There should be a World Economic Forum for youth."
> —BEN ELROM, 17, CHARLOTTESVILLE, VIRGINIA

doing so we reduce citizens to people who execute transactions in a voting booth every two or four years. Surely citizens could be involved more deeply in the political life of their country, to the benefit of all.

How can governments solicit opinions of citizens in a more effective way? They can start by looking at the private sector. New digital tools have paved the way for profound transformations in how companies function. Businesses are using these digital tools to deepen their existing relationships with customers or developing new relationships. It's a rare (and foolish) business today that doesn't operate at least an online forum of some sort that allows customers to pose questions and share insights they have into the company's products. As I explained in Chapter 6, the Net Generation are moving beyond e-mail; they use wikis, blogs, social networks, and digital brainstorms to engage and enable their employees, customers, and other stakeholders. The typical results are better collaboration, innovation, and customer engagement.

As the Obama 2008 juggernaut demonstrated, political figures can seize on these creative techniques to reconfigure and revitalize outdated democratic processes. Governments can use digital tools to involve citizens on an ongoing basis. As they contribute to the decision-making process, citizens can learn from one another, take responsibility for their communities and country, and influence elected officials. I think the nation would be stronger for it.

The Digital Brainstorm

I worked with the Clinton White House in 2000 on exactly this issue—exploring techniques for conducting a discussion among all Americans. The topic President Clinton chose for this exercise was "the Digital Divide"—how to close the gap between digital haves and have-nots in the country and the world. Because our efforts came at the end of his term, we ran out of time and were unable to execute the plan. But the idea was a good one. Flash forward almost a decade. To quote the French writer Victor Hugo: "There is nothing so powerful as an idea whose time has come" . . . again.

Here's how it would work. The president would say, "We're going to have a national discussion on revitalizing our cities. It starts on Monday at noon and ends the same week on Friday at noon. Anyone can participate through the Web 2.0 discussion community we've set up. If you don't have Internet access, I've partnered with corporations, schools, libraries, community computing centers, and shopping malls to give you access. We'll post background papers. We'll organize the discussion by region and also by interest groups. There'll be a business discussion, a discussion among public transit users, and so on. As you participate in the discussion rate the ideas that you come across and the best ideas will rise to the top. I'll participate daily and give my views. At the end of the process we'll explore our options for further action."

The goal is not for citizens to instruct politicians. It's to have a conversation in which people become engaged in political life; think about issues; get active in improving their communities; and mobilize society for positive change. Politicians and citizens alike would become more informed and learn from each other. And collectively we would take a step away from broadcast and toward participatory democracy.

Habitat Jam—the New Marketplace of Ideas

Some countries are already experimenting with digital brainstorms. In December 2005, the government of Canada teamed up with IBM to implement Habitat Jam, an online forum that brought together over 39,000 people from 158 countries in a three-day online discussion about urban sustainability. A "jam" is a "massive online discussion that develops actions out of a multiplicity of perspectives and expertise."[30] (IBM began online "jamming" in 2001 as a means of engaging its 300,000-plus employees in every facet of the company's operations—from corporate values to concrete solutions for growth, productivity, and innovation.) With Habitat Jam, more than 600 actionable items were brought forth by participants, with more than 4,000 pages of rich dialogue on the problems, challenges, and opportunities of urban development. Ninety-one percent of Habitat Jam participants noted that the process brought together people who otherwise might never share ideas and information. Kevina Power Njoroge, a Canadian who lives in Kenya and helped with the Jam, says that when problems are complex, it helps to engage youth because they can suggest solutions that haven't been explored. "As well," she said, "because many of the poorest communities of the world are in the majority youth, the best way to engage the greatest number, in the most meaningful way, is through a youth peer-to-peer model—youth engaging other youth. Massive digital brainstorms could be applied to virtually any issue and can provide an essential tool for reengaging young citizens—via the classroom, home computer, or mobile phone— in a democratic process of idea-sharing and priority-setting."

A Wealth of New Approaches

The Office of the Prime Minister in the United Kingdom launched E-Petitions in November 2006 to provide a platform for constituents to influence policy direction. UK CIO John Suffolk notes that E-Petitions have had a tangible impact on the consultative process, particularly in cases where the number of signatories exceeds 1 million. It successfully stimulated a lengthy debate that garnered over 1.8 million signatories and a lengthy response from the prime minister regarding proposed changes to a national vehicle-tracking and road-pricing proposal.

On the local level, virtual town hall meetings—such as those developed by the Utah State Legislature in the United States—provide effective models for discussion and debate among community members, especially in remote, rural areas, where geographic distances inhibit citizens from gathering in one physical location. In Utah, this meant equipping state legislators with BlackBerrys so they could participate in a 48-hour online discussion with community residents across the state. State legislator for Utah, Steve Urquhart, is a pioneer in new democratic models. Through his site Politicopia.com, people can post and edit information about legislation under consideration in the senate. When colleagues complain about not liking what people have said about their bills, his response is simple: "That's not my problem." As he says on the site, this is an experiment in open democracy, and one that's been a long time coming.

> "What we lose in face-to-face contact will be mitigated by what we gain in inclusiveness and accessibility."
> —GREG CURTIS, SPEAKER OF THE UTAH HOUSE OF REPRESENTATIVES

Other digital democracy initiatives could include:

- **Online citizen panels.** Randomly chosen citizens serve as policy advisors on an issue. They use the Web to hear evidence, ask questions, and deliberate in order to arrive at policy recommendations. Permanent advisory bodies could consist of a cross section of citizens who use the Web to debate ideas and share information.
- **Deliberative polling.** This gives citizens the resources to learn about and reflect upon the issues in a collaborative and deliberative fashion. This would combine small-group discussions on the Internet with scientific random sampling to provide more informed public input in policy-making than instant polling can furnish.
- **Virtual question periods.** This activity would make political representatives available online for regular question-and-answer sessions with their constituents.
- **Scenario planning.** Public planners would create alternate scenarios using simulation and modeling software in order to project possible future policy and to understand the long-term consequences of various decisions. Politicians, bureaucrats, and citizens could assess the potential impacts of these decisions on a range of issues, from health care to the environment to the economy.

Web 2.0 technologies make the process of engaging citizens in policy making easier and less costly than ever before by providing tools to support knowledge-creation and community-building—two core aspects of digital-era policy making. Rather than ask how elected representatives can be protected from a deluge of e-mail or endless online discussion, politicians, agencies, and political parties need to adapt institutional engagement strategies to the needs and expectations of digital citizens. Just as political journalists and spin doctors are expert in disseminating information and publicizing their agendas, the new model of political communication and engagement calls for equivalent skills in the art of listening, learning, responding, and absorbing public knowledge and experience into the policy cycle.

The changing nature of democracy in the twenty-first century raises many questions. Three of the most important are:

- What are the obligations and what are the prospects of ordinary individuals fulfilling these obligations given that most people think their personal schedules are already overloaded?

- When should citizens be engaged in decision making and how can policy makers ensure that public consultations are not mere window dressings on preconceived policy strategies?
- What are the most promising models of Web-enabled citizen engagement and what are the keys to successful consultations?

The ultimate goal is not simply to provide citizens with more information, but to integrate their insights and perspectives into a more authentic and engaged model of representative democracy.

> "The new participatory culture offers many opportunities for youth to engage in civic debates, to participate in community life, to become political leaders."
>
> —HENRY JENKINS, DIRECTOR, MIT COMPARATIVE MEDIA STUDIES PROGRAM

BUILDING TRUST WITH A NEW GENERATION

The Net Gen norms discussed throughout this book have enormous implications for government leaders. Youth want governments that are customizable, fast, and innovative. They want choice and the opportunity to collaborate. They will scrutinize candidates and elected officials like never before. Above all, to win their trust, politicians must behave with integrity.

In the 1960s and 1970s, many Americans looked no further than Walter Cronkite, "the most trusted man in America," for all world news. While Cronkite was a journalist of the highest integrity, his show, the *CBS Evening News*, offered only one perspective and one access point for information. At that time, there were few other ways of getting the news. Today, older people often lament that newspaper readership and the popularity of evening news shows have waned, as if this reflects apathy about politics and current events. What they fail to recognize is that more people, especially Net Geners, are using the Internet to read blogs and online newspapers, to watch the news that they care about most, to create and share user-generated multimedia, and to participate in political forums. As our Net Gen sample told us, why wait until 7 p.m. for one network to deliver 23 minutes of news and 7 minutes of advertising when information, commentary, debate, and entertainment are being updated and generated around the clock online?

Governments today must recognize that they face a trust vacuum. To win the trust of Net Geners, governments have to be transparent. At a minimum, policy makers should publicize their overall goals and objectives and, for specific issues and decisions, the documents they relied on, the names of the partic-

ipants in the decision making process, and their underlying rationales and criteria, and they should provide reasons why alternative policy options have not
been pursued. True transparency, however, will extend beyond posting policy
documents on Web sites. It must make the processes, underlying assumptions,
and political presuppositions (including supporting research) of policy explicit
and subject to criticism. Freedom of information should be extended to
include not just data, but also the tools of policy making: the models, simulations, problem-structuring tools, and geographical information systems that
policy makers use themselves.

There's a new communication standard for government and politicians
today courtesy of YouTube and social networking sites. For all politicians today
there is a permanent searchable record of what they say and stand for. Go
online and watch "John McCain versus John McCain," in which he contradicts
himself endlessly. Is this fair to Senator McCain? Perhaps not—but viewers are
watching. One 2002 video showing McCain flip-flopping on the Iraq war
has been viewed 600,000 times on YouTube. The online accuracy patrols hit
Democrats, too—as Hillary Clinton found out when she claimed she had
landed in Bosnia "under sniper fire." As a video on YouTube so graphically displayed, she never had to run for cover. Instead she was all smiles as a little girl on
the Tarmac welcomed her.

Accountability is one of the cornerstones of trust, and is integral to engaging the Net Generation. Accountability isn't new in politics. In 1988, George
H.W. Bush told the American people, "Read my lips, no new taxes." After
assuming the presidency, he was pressured to raise taxes to reduce the
national budget deficit. With a Democratic-controlled Congress leaning on
him, Bush in fact raised a number of taxes as part of a 1990 budget agreement. By not abiding by his commitments, he lost the respect of many American voters, and ended up losing the presidency to Bill Clinton in 1992.[31]
Voters were angry with Bush not because he raised taxes, but because he had
betrayed their trust.

The rise of the Internet has provided young voters with a huge new memory
archive of political backflips. Bush's mistake was massive and glaring. Today,
any violation of trust or faith by a politician goes on record. Every sound bite
and every video is put online. Many young people today, particularly college
students, watch *The Daily Show*, which lampoons politicians and gives poignant and amusing commentary on current affairs. A favorite tactic of the show
is to compare a politician's recent statements with those he or she made in
the past. The flagrant contradictions—sometimes jaw-dropping—always get

laughs, but they reinforce the Net Generation's propensity to scrutinize and attack those who lack integrity.

Trust depends on transparency. If a government or politician withholds information, Net Geners will only assume it is for nefarious reasons. While C-SPAN has a Web site that allows users to track important stories in Congress, in the White House, and in the courts, it doesn't go far enough. Compare it something like OpenCongress.org, a nonpartisan nonprofit Web site that allows users to track all of their representatives, and see what they said or if they showed up for session every day.[32] Convincing Net Geners that transparency is a core value of government and politicians will be of critical importance to those who wish to establish trusting, long-term relationships with the Net Generation.

Most recent innovations in transparency and political communications have been driven not by government, but by third parties—usually citizens, foundations, or nonprofits—seeking to encourage greater involvement of young people in politics. Sites such as PoliticalBase.com and OpenCongress .org aggregate news and information on U.S. presidential candidates, and provide a platform for citizens wanting to track their representatives. "We want to make it much easier for people to understand the web of political connections—not only who did John Kerry vote for, but who contributed to his campaign, and what were his stances on various issues," says PoliticalBase cofounder Mike Tatum. Meanwhile, groups like Sunlight Labs and IBM's alphaWorks are taking advantage of new visualization technologies to help nonexperts access and understand publicly available data that highlights government spending, political contributions, and the possible connections between the two.

People in positions of power are reluctant to give up the control they have over processes and are afraid of being held accountable for something they can't control. This has been true throughout history: leaders of the old paradigm are reluctant to embrace the new. The rise of a generation that scrutinizes, demands integrity, and wants to see changes in the political system is a terrifying thought for those who don't understand that change can be good.

Governments can sit back and wait for Net Geners to force them to become more transparent, or they can be active participants in shaping the flow of communications to citizens. Adopting transparency as a core value and actively encouraging and fostering its application by making information readily available, will be critical in establishing trusting, long-term relationships with the generation that will dominate politics in the twenty-first century.

DEMOCRACY 2.0: SEVEN GUIDELINES FOR GOVERNMENT LEADERS

1. **Hire more young people.** Demographically speaking, most governments are like the population pyramid of Italy—i.e., no young people. You can't change your agency, organization, or your party unless it is populated by Net Geners. Listen to them. In their culture of enablement is the new culture of government. Empower them to bring about real change inside your organization.

2. **Embrace Democracy 2.0.** Don't broadcast to Net Geners. Think interaction, not unidirectional communications. Think enablement, not control. Reach out to engage them in different ways. You should have a blog. Set up a wiki or digital brainstorm on some topic of importance. Let Net Geners lead the process.

3. **Rethink your e-government and Internet strategy.** Forget about putting "government online." That's old-school. Government is more than paving the cow path. Don't have "Web sites"; create communities for new models of service delivery. Use the Web 2.0 to rethink how governments orchestrate capability to create services.

4. **To create trust, act with integrity—honesty, consideration of the interest of youth, accountability, and transparency.** Dig deep and ask yourself if you measure up to Net Gen expectations for integrity. Change your behavior if it doesn't measure up. You'll find yourself a better person for it. You're going to be naked, politically speaking, so get buff. And if you're not buff, open the kimono a bit to get yourself motivated.

5. **If you're a politician, stop using attack ads.** They are toxic to the body politic. Your advisors tell you they are necessary to win, but they are wrong. Be straight with journalists and tell them to stop grilling you about your personal life. If you're a TV journalist, stop the dumbing down of political life. Net Geners are sick of vacuous politics. They want to know what politicians stand for and what they will do to bring about change and what they are in fact doing. They want to revitalize the Founding Fathers' marketplace of ideas.

6. **If you're a government manager or executive, get together with Net Geners and develop a strategy for the wiki workplace.** Rather than banning social networks as many governments have done, embrace them—with an effective strategy. Let Net Geners lead the process. Stop spying on individual Net Geners on Facebook, MySpace, or other social networks.

7. **If you're a senator or congressman,** "Please heed the call / Don't stand in the doorway / Don't block up the hall. / For he that gets hurt/ Will be he who has stalled / There's a battle outside/ And it is ragin' / It'll soon shake your windows / And rattle your walls / For the times they are a-changin'." (A little advice from Bob Dylan.)

MAKING THE WORLD A BETTER PLACE—AT GROUND LEVEL

Last winter, my wife Ana and I flew to Davos, the Swiss ski resort that every year hosts the World Economic Forum. It's a gathering where you can literally bump into Bill Gates, Bono, Google CEO Eric Schmidt, and Pakistan's President Pervez Musharraf all in one day. At the parties, along the corridors, and in the panel discussions, people were talking about some of the world's biggest problems. Ana and I, however, went looking for some good news, and ended up attending a panel discussion with six teenagers.

The "Davos Six," as they're called, were a global group, all activists in their communities. They had been chosen out of 300 contenders by the British Council, a nonprofit that seeks to build ties between the United Kingdom and the rest of the world. The kids, ages 16 to 19, were by far the youngest people in a convention center room, packed mostly by men with thinning hair.[1] "Get ready to be inspired," British actress and screenwriter Emma Thompson told me as we entered the room. At the start of the session, the moderator asked Emma what she was thinking about when she was a teenager like the Davos Six. Thompson, who has tackled some pretty serious gender issues in her work, had a one-word description for what was on her mind at age 16: "Boys."

When the laughter subsided, we heard from the Davos Six teenagers. They were thinking of far weightier issues. "I'm Rhadeena De Alwis," said a confident 18-year-old teenager from Sri Lanka. "I work with street and slum children who are marginalized and ostracized in their own country," she said, looking straight at us in the graying audience. "I truly believe you have to be the difference you want to see in the world and that's why I do what I do."

Next up was Whitney Burton, a first-year university student from the United States. "In North America, every year we spend $20 billion on ice cream. It would only cost $10 billion to build enough schools to put all the world's children into primary school. To me, this shows it's not a problem of resources but of allocation." Whitney didn't just talk about it. She had already raised $16,000 to build a school in Sierra Leone and staff it with teachers.

We heard from a 19-year-old from Cape Town who was fighting racism by helping children to have confidence in their own identities, and from a teenager who had emerged from a spell of drugs and prostitution to help gay kids on the streets in Scotland.

Then there was an amazing 17-year-old boy in a shiny red jacket, Yunan Jin. "I want you guys to imagine what your childhood was like," he said. He paused for a moment as we all tried to remember. When he was a kid growing up in Beijing, Yunan dreaded spring. Sandstorms blew in and choked his lungs, which was particularly difficult for someone with a delicate respiratory system. "It was a veritable hell on earth." So in 2005, at age 14, Yunan had an idea: recruit people to travel to Mongolia, where the sands take flight, and plant 365 trees, one for each day in the year. It was hugely inspiring. But some of the adults in the audience told me afterward that they didn't buy it—these were just a few extraordinary kids; they didn't represent their whole generation.

I disagree. While clearly a very special group, they are more representative of the values and effectiveness of their generation than not. I'm optimistic that this generation will make this world a better place. The reason is simple: not only is this a generation that cares about social problems, they are the first to grow up with a powerful tool that can be used to make a far more substantial difference than my generation ever could. It's a tool of unprecedented power to inform, engage, and mobilize their generation.

In this chapter, you'll see how Net Gen activists are using this tool to make the world a better place. I'll tell you about young people who are simply good citizens, doing what they can in a low-key way. I'll also introduce you to some of the Net Generation's most innovative activists—like the tens of thousands of college students in the United States who have deployed the Internet to mount a targeted attack on the companies that are indirectly financing the horror in Darfur. Some aim to do good by deploying the power of the Internet on a global scale, like Michael Furdyk, an entrepreneur who made his first million in high school and then helped to launch TakingItGlobal, a Facebook-style social network for global do-gooders. You'll meet young people who are using popular music and "widgets" to enter the social networking worlds and to engage fellow Net Geners in a debate about one of the most profound issues of our time— global warming. As Net Geners, these activists know how to appeal to youth— by tapping into the norms that we have discussed throughout this book, such as integrity, collaboration, and speed.

And we know that the majority of Net Geners will be a receptive audience. The media says they are a generation of shoppers who don't give a damn, but this just doesn't match the data. We know from our global surveys that they have sound values, and care about their fellow human beings. In this chapter you'll see that masses of young people are volunteering as never before to make their communities and the world a better place. While they are not protesting in the streets, our research shows they are active in other ways— raising funds for everything from hospitals and animal shelters to civil rights organizations.

What's more, a majority of young people in the United States are changing their own behavior and becoming green consumers. They want kids around the world to have a chance for a better life than their parents had, in a cleaner and healthier world. Of course, these values may differ, depending on where you go. In India, for example, the Net Geners entering the workforce want to make money, but look a little closer and you'll find out why: they need to support their extended families. Elsewhere, making money is not as important; when those Net Geners enter the workforce, they want to learn and meet interesting people.[2] But overall, our research shows, they care about their fellow citizens. So I see hope.

I see it in the handsome 16-year-old boy from the suburbs of Buenos Aires who flew to Davos to become part of the Davos Six. "Think of the amount of money a cup of coffee costs—$5 or so—that's the money a family of six in Argentina has to survive for the whole week," Juan Niscimbene told the assembly of powerful people in that conference room. Juan comes from an activist background: his grandfather, a lawyer, was imprisoned by the military dictatorship.

Now he's looking for a way to pull kids out of a life of poverty by offering them a ladder, a decent education. He's extraordinarily well informed; he used the Internet to see how farm subsidies in North America and Europe deepen the poverty in rural Argentina. Juan is trying to set up a library and a community forum for youth in a shelter not far from his home, and now he's using the connections he made at Davos, and through the Internet, to raise money for it.

As I listened to Juan and the Davos Six, I thought about the values of this generation and the potential of the digital tools they possess to help them organize themselves. I felt that these kids were indeed great examples of their generation, no matter what the skeptics said. That was when I typed a new entry into the blog I had been running at the conference, one that surprised many of my readers: "As far as I'm concerned, these are the six most important people at Davos."

THE NET GENERATION IS INHERITING A MESS

The world they are inheriting is a challenging and difficult one, to say the least. True, there is lots of good news. Innovation is at an all-time high. Trade is flowing more freely. A billion people have entered the global economy in the last two decades.[3] Thanks to the Web and Wikinomics, people can participate in the economy in ways previously unimagined. There is newfound interest in political involvement all around the world.

But let's face it; overall my generation is handing over a global mess. Poverty is everywhere and over a billion people still live on less than a dollar a day. Countless people have no safe water or are without electricity, let alone broadband. Most people have no access to decent healthcare, and even in the richest country in the world there are tens of millions of people with no health insurance.[4] Everyone now agrees that global warming is a huge problem, and that it won't be solved only by conservation. We need new forms of energy and we need to reindustrialize the planet, and in a hurry. Around the world there is strife: new forms of military conflict and violence. There are tectonic shifts in the global economy, and, as the engines of growth shift to Asia, no one knows what kind of displacement and fallout will occur. The nuclear threat of my generation has reemerged, but in a different form: nuclear weapons seem to be all over the place and there is the potential danger of their falling into the hands of rogue powers or individual terrorists.

Comedian Jon Stewart put it well in his frank commencement address to the 2004 graduating class of the College of William and Mary: "Let's talk about the real world for a moment. I guess this is as good a time as any. I don't really know how to put this, so I'll be blunt. We broke it. Please don't be mad. I know we were supposed to bequeath to the next generation a world better than the one we were handed. So, sorry. I don't know if you've been following the news lately, but it just kinda got away from us. Somewhere between the gold rush of easy Internet profits and an arrogant sense of endless empire, we heard kind of a pinging noise, and uh, then the damn thing just died on us. So I apologize."

Then he calls out to the graduates, "But here's the good news. You fix this thing; you're the next greatest generation, people."

THE LIFE OF AN ACTIVIST BEFORE THE INTERNET

I remember what it was like to be a student radical without the help of the Internet, or even a fax machine, to try to drum up some support for a cause. As a teenager in the 1960s, I protested against the war in Vietnam. I defended a doctor who championed women's right to choose whether to have a child when they became pregnant. I criticized the Canadian government, then under Prime Minister Pierre Elliot Trudeau, when it sent troops into Quebec to round up hundreds of innocent people after terrorists kidnapped a British diplomat and a Quebec cabinet minister. I was an activist, '60s style.

It started in high school, in small-town Ontario, when I wrote a protest song about the bombing by the Ku Klux Klan of a Sunday school basement in Birmingham, Alabama. Then I organized a demonstration in Orillia, a small lakeside town an hour or so north of Toronto, where my family moved when I was 11 years old. We were protesting the fact that the town council had banned the Mariposa Folk Festival. Apparently, the folks there didn't like the long-haired weirdos camping on their lawns. The protest was big news; I ended up on the front page of the sober *Toronto Globe and Mail*, Canada's national newspaper. The publicity was awkward, though. For one thing, my name is the same as my dad's, and people in town couldn't understand why a high school French teacher was organizing a protest that ended up on the front page of the national newspaper. What's more, the somewhat unsophisticated sign I held, which read "Burn the Stump," contained an unfortunate reference to our mayor. Nonetheless, when we went to the town hall, the mayor graciously gave me a chance to give a speech, and I jumped at the opportunity to say how the folk festival would put the town on the map and be good for its economic development. I didn't convince the town council that day, although a few years later the town saw the light and hosted the festival.

I was an activist on several issues, but I didn't have the tools. We were working in the dark. Up in Orillia, we had no way to find out what was going on in the United States, where students were protesting the Vietnam War. We couldn't find anything in the local paper, or on TV. The closest I could get to the news was by listening to a Bob Dylan album or to someone who had been to a peace rally when they came through town. I had no other way of finding out.

At college, I managed to help organize some big protest marches, and thousands of kids came out to protest the war or the testing of nuclear weapons. To spread the news of the demonstrations, we used the technology that was available. We had no fax machine, of course, so we bought an offset printing press in order to create our own flyers. We also published our own newspaper, printed posters and pinned them to telephone polls or billboards. But if you really wanted to get the message out, you had to meet groups—day care activists or civil rights people or a labor group—and convince them to take on your cause. It was all about getting groups of people who really cared to tell other groups of people about your issue. It was all about word of mouth—but the word traveled at the speed of atoms, not bits.

STAYING IN TOUCH WITH YOUR FRIENDS TAKES ON A NEW MEANING

Nowadays, every young activist or volunteer has a printing press at his or her fingertips. It's a digital one that can instantly shoot out information around the world. Social networks like Facebook can spread the news in a spectacular way. If one friend sends a message to an acquaintance in another group, that friend can instantly alert everyone in her group—say 500 people—and each one of them can potentially spread the news to another round of friends. Within days, news can spread to hundreds of thousands, or even millions, of people, without any huge up-front investment. It means that ordinary citizens can make change without convincing the power structures to move. This is one of the big reasons why I think the Davos Six, and activists like them, will be able to make a far greater impact than my generation ever did.

The Net Gener who wants to change the world now has not only a digital printing press, but the digital equivalent of a million volunteers to pass the flyers from friend to friend. Thanks to entrepreneurs like Mark Zuckerberg, this capability now exists, but how will the Net Generation use it? Will they use it to procrastinate, as critics in my generation will tell you? Will they just stick to trading pictures and jokes and gossip about the celebs? The record suggests the opposite.

Even before Zuckerberg worked to create Facebook, college students in the United States were volunteering in record numbers and using the Internet to mobilize their generation.[5] Take, for example, the campaign by U.S. college students to end the killing in Darfur, the region in the western part of Sudan where the ethnic and tribal conflict that broke out in 2003 has cost hundreds of thousands of lives and displaced millions of people. It's a human catastrophe, as militias supported and financed by the Sudanese government have been destroying entire villages, murdering and raping all those in their way.

In the United States, it is not any of the mainstream networks that has given the most complete coverage to the Darfur crisis. Instead, it has been MTV, the network known mostly for its music videos. In 2004, MTV bought a college TV network, which broadcast to five million students in cafeterias, fitness centers, and lounges at colleges and universities across the United States. In MTV's hands, the college network, called mtvU, turned into a full-blown TV-, Internet-, and wireless-based venue for college kids, operating 24/7.

Stephen Friedman, who took over as mtvU's general manager, was a long-time activist in his own right. He had already won three Emmys and a Peabody Award for the Fight for Your Rights campaign he created for MTV. Now Friedman wanted to see activism on mtvU, along with new music and the ever-popular chance to rate the professors. He listened to his audience for inspiration. "We handed over the channel as a megaphone," said Friedman.

The Darfur campaign began when Friedman heard about a Georgetown University senior, Nate Wright, who had a modest but effective idea: ask students to give up a cup of coffee or a video rental for one day and donate the money to the people suffering in Darfur. Friedman loved the idea—it was "a little incremental action" that could raise awareness—and tracked Wright down in his dorm to propose that he take the campaign across the United States with MTV's help. Over the next few months, Wright's action group, STAND, contacted organizations on college campuses throughout the country, with the result that on April 7, 2005, tens of thousands of students at over 200 campuses gave up a luxury, like a $5 cup of coffee, in order to contribute to the Darfur campaign.

The campaign had been a successful one, based on a clever idea; beyond this it had used fairly standard tactics to accomplish its goal. But then Friedman began to realize how students could use the Internet—with brand-new social networking sites like Facebook—to ramp up interest in a cause like never before. It was a classic case of student-to-student activism, spreading like wildfire among groups of friends on the Internet. The power of social networking revealed itself only one year after the one-day luxury fast (Participants gave up a purchase of a frivolous item—ice cream, chips, cappuccino—and donated what they would have spent to humanitarian relief efforts.) that Nate Wright had organized in April of 2005; it happened in the spring of 2006, when students convinced the University of California to divest from companies that were indirectly financing the crackdown in Darfur. The Darfur activists were far smarter and more sophisticated than had been the anti-apartheid movement in the early 1990s, said Friedman. "This is a new breed of activism. They're reinventing what it means right in front of us."

A few months later, Friedman noticed that a whole spate of vile video games were being used by neo-Nazis to try to recruit kids into their ranks. The games gave kids the chance to kill a Jew, a black, or a gay person. Friedman, revolted at what he saw, decided to create something entirely new for mtvU—a game that would reach out to kids who didn't know where Darfur was. "We had no clue how to create a viral video game, but we had confidence in our audience," he said.

So, with $50,000 sponsorship money from Reebok, he announced a contest to create the game. It was controversial: was it appropriate? How would it do justice to the terror in Darfur and not trivialize it? Friedman knew that it had to be addictive. If it sounded like a PBS educational game, it would fail. The winner, an activist at the University of Southern California in Los Angeles, created a game that asks you to put yourself in the shoes of a person in Darfur (Do I go get water before the Janjaweed comes?). It's been played over three million times and still gets passed on through circles of friends in the social networking sites. A lot of people who have played the game probably didn't know that the Darfur killings were real, Friedman said, but once they get into the game, "it gets under their skin." It has helped people who know nothing about Darfur to walk in the shoes, digitally speaking, of someone in Darfur. While it's hard to say exactly what impact it's had, Friedman thinks the game, called Darfur Is Dying, "is another tool that moves youth toward activism."

The campaign for Darfur shows that kids these days are willing to embrace big causes, Friedman says, "They're yearning to be part of something really big. This is an incredibly optimistic generation that has the belief they can do something that's bigger than just themselves. People ask me: why Darfur? A genocide is a hard issue if you're looking for pragmatic solutions, and yet they're embracing those big ones because they feel empowered to do something about it."

Friedman says his audience, college students, wants tangible ways to get involved. "They want specific tools to get involved—that's a really hopeful sign—and people who ignore that miss out on the potential to partner with them." The MTV campaign, for instance, gives the kids lots of options through which to get involved—by donating money, joining a divestment campaign, passing on a message, or starting or joining an association. It's all helping to create a deeper connection between MTV and its on-campus audience, and it's paying off. In only four years, the network's college audience has shot up 30 percent.

"For many young people, volunteering is an ideal way to combine travel, cultural education, valuable work experience and active participation."

—KAREN SHIM, CANADA[6]

THE GOOD CITIZENS

Surveys confirm what Friedman is seeing on campus: Kids are engaged in their communities in a way their parents never were. The idea that the Net Gen are spoiled, lazy, self-centered kids who expect parents and employers to wait on them hand and foot, is dead wrong. It's true that young people still don't vote as much as their parents and grandparents, although that is changing, thanks to Barack Obama, the 9/11 disaster, and George Bush. Yet this doesn't mean that young people have no sense of community. On the contrary, the exhaustive research done by Harvard's Institute of Politics cited in Chapter 9 shows that the youth are volunteering, raising money, and working with other people to fight poverty, pollution, disease, and the big issues confronting the world today.

Volunteering, on the part of teenagers and college freshmen, has hit an all-time high. In 2005, some 83.2 percent of incoming college freshmen classes throughout the United States had volunteered in the previous year—and 70.6 percent did it on a weekly basis, according to the Higher Education Research Institute, which conducts the huge annual survey, "The American Freshman."[7] The same survey found that two-thirds of the college freshmen thought it was very important to help other people; about the same percentage said it was very likely that they would do community service in college. All indications are that youth volunteering is continuing to rise (see Figure 10.1).

Kids are nearly as likely to do community service as are their boomer parents. This was confirmed by a telephone survey of 1,700 young people aged 15–25

FIGURE 10.1   MORE YOUTH VOLUNTEERING IN THE UNITED STATES IN THE PAST 12 YEARS

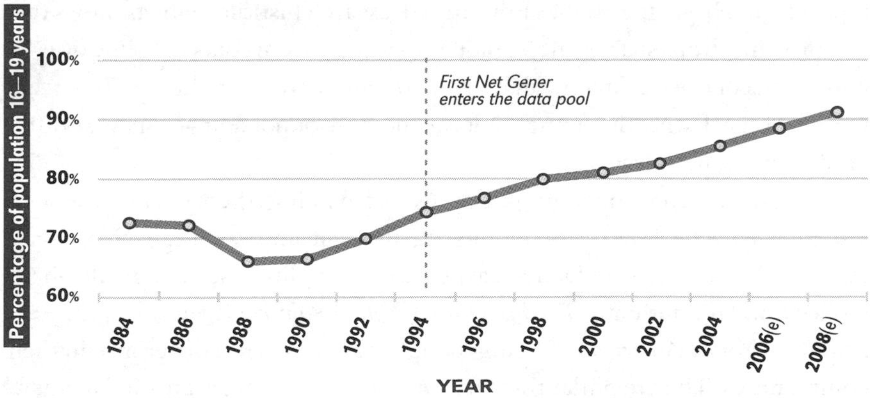

Source: Higher Education Research Institute (HERI)

that was published in 2006 by CIRCLE. It found that 36 percent had volunteered in the previous year. They were more likely to volunteer than adults age 25 and older, although they were less likely to do it on a regular basis.[9] CIRCLE also reported that 38 percent had boycotted a product because of the conditions under which it was produced, or because of the values of the company that produced it.[10]

The Net Geners are a lot more engaged than Generation X was, according to focus groups organized by CIRCLE at a dozen U.S. colleges and universities in 2006. "Our focus groups revealed a generation of college students who have a great deal of experience with volunteering (mostly face-to-face and local) and who believe in their obligation to work together with others on social issues. They are neither cynical nor highly individualistic."[11]

> "[Millennials] do not want to write off politics, despite their many criticisms; instead, they seek ways to engage politically."
> —CIRCLE, NOVEMBER 2007

The numbers show that young people are, contrary to their parents' suspicions, good citizens who volunteer for community causes. In fact, teens 16 to 19 years of age spend twice as much time volunteering as they did in 1989, according to a 2006 report for the Corporation for National and Community Service.[12] It's easy to be cynical and say that they are doing so just because they have to. In many high schools, students are obliged to do community service, for laudable reasons—research shows that educational success is linked to community service. The cynics say that lots of students do it just to pad their résumés for college applications. Bolstering the résumé-padding theory is a report from HERI, the Higher Education Research Institute, which shows that volunteering drops sharply after students graduate from college. While over 80 percent of college freshmen volunteer, that number drops to under 70 percent when you check what the young adults are doing—or not doing—six years after graduating from college.[13]

Yet you have to wonder about the résumé-padding theory when research also shows that the level of community engagement among college *seniors* is rising steadily. According to Dan Shea, professor of political science at Allegheny College, and the author of *The Fountain of Youth: Political Parties and the Mobilization of Young Americans*, "Young people want to make a difference in their communities. They're philanthropic. They've become more attuned to social and economic issues in their communities." Shea thinks this is because the Internet is encouraging kids to help out by giving them a way to learn about the problem with a few clicks. "It's one of the big myths of our day that young people are absent, disengaged, amoral."

Of course, you don't need to be a social activist to make a contribution to society. Most youngsters I've worked with and studied are becoming solid contributors as they enter the workforce in trades or professions. Some will do great things in science. Others are already becoming entrepreneurs. In most countries those with education or even skills training will be swept into the workforce by the global crisis of talent and make an important contribution.

You don't have to look far to be impressed. Last Christmas, I had a glass of wine with my daughter and her best friends from high school. They had gathered at our home for their annual "lipstick" party, and, as we sipped wine, they shared their news. Ashley Gillman entered her third year of practicing medicine. Emilee Irwin works for Journalists for Human Rights and just returned from a three-month stint in Africa. Joanna Griffiths is a publicist for Universal Studios and hopes to bring about big changes in the music industry. Eva Szymanski has set up an event planning company and has her first couple of clients. She's using her skills and Facebook to organize pro bono events for the Multiple Sclerosis Society. Victoria Clarke is doing marketing for the huge London department store Selfridges, where among other things she promotes green products. Nadine Straka is now a scientist looking for the causes of cancer. Caitlin Peddie studies at the London School of Economics working on a master's degree in international relations. She taught English as a second language to underprivileged kids to help pay her way through school.

None of them is organizing demonstrations, but they all contribute. It sounds hokey, but they're good citizens. They don't drink and drive. They are all good daughters who spend infinitely more time with their parents than I did. They fulfill their civic duty by voting, and every one of them has a cause that they're passionate about. My daughter Niki, for example, raises money for a Toronto mental health organization that seeks to end the stigma of mental illness. For Niki and her friends, the Web is key to the personal and philanthropic success of all these young women.

The civic engagement that I see in Niki and her generation may have deep roots. Historian and nGenera collaborator Neil Howe, who coauthored *Millennials Rising*, argues that individual people are shaped by their generation. The Millennials, as he calls them, do things in teams, in groups, because they wanted to fill the void left by their individualistic and self-centered baby boomer parents. According to Howe, they didn't try to compete with their parents in the area of music; they listen to some of the same tunes on their iPod. Instead, they became community-minded, something their parents didn't bother with. In Howe's view, this team spirit and community-mindedness explains why kids are volunteering so much these days. It also explains why, once the Net Geners sat in front of a computer, they immediately used it to chat with their friends and create social networks like Facebook.

Does the generation influence the technology, or is it the other way around? I think it's a two-way street. Technology is influencing the way kids think, and the way kids think is influencing how they use and shape the Internet and every institution in society. In the twenty-first century, knowledge is flowing more freely than ever thanks to the Internet, but its true potential was not realized until the Net Generation started using computers and the Web. Back in the 1990s, when I was writing *Growing Up Digital*, the Internet was a place for outsiders, geeks, radicals, or visionaries to engage in marginalized debates. As one of those people, I thought at the time that someday this milieu might become a force for change. It wasn't at that time—mainly because the type of people using the technology weren't interested in deploying it for social change. Now they are, and they have new tools with which to realize their goals. So the Net Gen is finally making my hope of those years a reality. Through them, the Net is becoming a medium for good citizenship and social awakening.

TAKING IT GLOBAL

I first met Michael Furdyk back in 1997 when he and Jennifer Corriero were working on the Web site for my book *Growing Up Digital*. Jennifer was a project manager and graphic designer; Michael was the lead Web site developer. Michael would quickly become a star in his own right. When he was in ninth grade, he and a couple of friends launched an online magazine about computers called MyDesktop.com. In May 1999, when Michael was in eleventh grade, they sold it for over $1 million. Michael told me that he was very happy. He bought an Infiniti QX4 sports utility vehicle—but his parents had to drive around with him because he only had his learner's permit. He invested the rest in a business that was shooting out ideas for the Internet so quickly that Michael could barely sit down long enough to hold a meeting. It sounded like the classic story about the overnight kid millionaires, the kind that make baby boomers grind their teeth at night, and seek dental help in the morning. Michael even got to meet Bill Gates. But then Michael turned into an emblem of his generation, a classic case of what happens when the values of the Net Gen meet up with the potential of the Internet.

In October of 1999, during a reunion of the *Growing Up Digital* contributors, Michael and Jennifer envisioned an online space where kids could work together with other kids around the world to do something good. Nothing like this existed at the time. It would be "the next hangout for young people," says Michael. "We really saw the Internet as a place for that to happen." They called it TakingItGlobal. Young people could take whatever "It" is to a global audience. The idea was for peers—young people—to exchange ideas among themselves, instead of always calling (or e-mailing) experts like Michael. "It would be a global support network to encourage young people to get involved and support those who want to do something."

After visiting Ghana and South Africa in 2002, Michael says, "I didn't really think that putting all of my efforts into making millions was as important as what we could do with technology to empower people to have sustainable lives."

"Thousands all over the world are devoting their talent and resources to bringing hope and putting smiles on the faces of marginalized communities."

—RASHID, 22, GHANA

This was before Facebook, before MySpace. As it evolved, TakingItGlobal became an online meeting place where people, social activists from around the globe, could exchange ideas about how to make the world better. It's like Facebook—each member has her own page and can communicate with friends in the same way that Facebook communities exchange news. But instead of circulating gossip and pictures of last night's party, they talk about doing good. (The mission is to "inspire, inform, and involve.") "That meant it grew a little slower than Facebook and MySpace," says Michael with a laugh. "It grew a little bit more slowly because it was about things that mattered."

As an advisor to the organization, I've watched TakingItGlobal blossom. It's truly international; only 30 percent of members are from North America, and the conversation takes place in 248 languages, many of which are translated by volunteers or by online translators. "We see it as a pathway to action," says Michael. It also strengthens and amplifies efforts to combat scourges like HIV-AIDS and climate change. As Jennifer and Michael explain it, they're creating a bridge to connect people who care—the majority—with people doing something.

"There are so many small ways to get involved, to have their voice heard," says Michael. "I think if you look at a cross section of their involvement, which is much broader than voting, it's actually much, much higher. The average baby boomer, they might vote, but do they know anything about the conflict in Darfur? Are they using paper plates? Or are they just voting and saying that's fine. This is civic participation."

TakingItGlobal is "the deluxe version of international youth dialogue," according to a 2004 report, "Youth as E-Citizens," by academics at American University's Center for Social Media.[14] It was one of the 300 youth-oriented civic sites that study coauthor Kathryn Montgomery and her colleagues reviewed in 2004 to assess the landscape of online youth civic activism. Their conclusion: youth civic culture is thriving on the Internet, in a multitude of creative and engaging forms. Even in 2004, it was already roaring, as kids who came of age in the shadow of 9/11 sought to do something their way, via the Internet. But since the "E-Citizen" report was published, the youth civic culture has expanded like a helium balloon, as activists use the friends-telling-friends power of the social networks. Now it's far easier than ever for young people to connect with each other and with the rest of the world, and this could encourage even more youth activism and straight-out volunteering, says Montgomery.

Saving Planet Earth—Literally

It's fair to say that this generation is using the Internet in a multitude of creative ways that rewrites the playbook on how to reach out to fellow youth.

Take the issue of the environment. Mark Twain famously said about the weather that "Everyone's talking about it but no one's doing anything about it." Well, the joke's over: humankind needs to change the weather. To do this, we will need to reindustrialize the planet. Thomas Friedman, in *The World Is Flat*, explains well the enormity of this challenge, pointing out that the people most aggrieved by climate change are not yet born. So boomers, who currently run the world, are not motivated to change things because global warming doesn't affect them directly. "We're being called upon to do the greatest act of steward-ship ever," Friedman says.[15]

Net Geners, on the other hand, can see that in their lifetime and that of their children, things on earth will get very ugly if our course is not reversed. And they're beginning to get involved, by the millions, in many ways—from chang-ing their own behavior as consumers to using everything from their burgeoning purchasing power, voting muscle, and good old-fashioned activism—to bring about real change.

I'm convinced we're in the early days of something unprecedented. Young people, and with them the entire world, are beginning to collaborate—for the first time ever—around a single idea: changing the weather. For the first time in history young people have affordable, global, multimedia, many-to-many communications systems enabling them to research, collaborate, and organize in order to bring about this needed change. Of course, resolving the crisis will require leadership from every demographic, country, and sector in society. But the energy is coming from the Net Generation. Their hopes, determination, knowledge, and facility with the Net are being applied to one of the greatest challenges ever—saving planet earth, literally.

Consider the Natural Resources Defense Council, a New York City–based organization that uses highly effective political and legal tactics to pursue its mission: "to safeguard the Earth, its people, its plants and animals and all the natural systems on which all life depends." Founded in 1970, it has 1.2 million members and online activists and a staff of hundreds of lawyers, scientists, and activists.

But for Kelly Cox, a twentysomething environmentalist from New York City, the NRDC was missing a key target—young people 18 to 34 years of age. So she convinced the NRDC to let her use the Internet to reach out. She could see how corporations were engaging kids on the Internet, and she thought the NRDC had to play the same game. "We had to think like marketers, not like grassroots activists," she said. "You don't want to lose that integrity but you have to be out there thinking from a business perspective because my generation grew up on advertising and marketing; you just have to utilize those tools to your advantage, or else you'll get lost in the shuffle." She looked around her, at what her own friends were doing. They were on social networking sites, of course. That's where she would find her new audience. "You go where they are. You don't make them come to you," she said.

This was in 2006 just before Al Gore's movie, *An Inconvenient Truth*, won an Oscar and helped to popularize the worldwide concern about climate change. She started by traveling to music festivals and interviewing artists about the environmental challenges they saw, and what they hoped for. The videos were initially posted on YouTube. Green Day, the hugely successful California rock band, teamed up with NRDC to speak out against the overdependence on oil and George Bush's oil-drilling plans in the Arctic. "We grew up in a huge refinery town," the lead singer Billie Joe Armstrong says on one of the videos as one of their hit songs from the *American Idiot* album plays in the background. "I learned from an early age, just from the mere smell of it, what the oil industry does and what it does to the air I was breathing in as a kid." This is not Hollywood. The lighting is bad. They're not made up. The video was posted in December 2006, and, in the next year, well over 300,000 kids watched it just on

YouTube, not counting how many watched it as kids zapped it across their Internet networks.

But that was just the start. In March 2007, Cox launched a new micro site, itsyournature.org, a catchy site where you can talk to people, check out the latest on *GOOD Magazine*, watch videos of the top snowboarders physically flipping and worrying about the effects of global warming on the snow, and check out tips on how to green your office or ditch the plastic bag.

Then in October 2007, Cox took another innovative step. As a Net Gener environmentalist from New York City, she knew she had to get NRDC into the social networking sites. So she created the itsyournature widget, a digital button for the social networking world. It's designed to be passed from friends to friends in the social networking sites. Click on the button and you'll find music videos, tips, news, events, petitions, and green guides. One of the most popular features was a goofy little video, "The Office of the Living Dead," a spoof on a zombie who does all the wrong things at the office (like wasting paper). "You can easily grab it and put it on your page, your Web site, your blog, or whatever," says Cox. It's updated automatically. "So people can get all of my content without leaving their profile page on MySpace." This little widget allows Cox to track how many people are watching a video or clicking onto a blog. "I'm getting 200 new grabbers each week"—people who put the little digital button onto their own sites or pages or blogs. And 30,000 young people are checking out the itsyournature content on social networking sites each week. "I'm seeing thousands of new activists join my community each week."

Activists like Cox at itsyournature.com and Friedman at MTV know that they can reach young people today if they talk to them in their language. The days when you broadcast a campaign on TV to shame people into donating, without inviting their feedback, are over—at least for this generation.

HOW ACTIVISTS ARE TAPPING INTO NET GEN NORMS

These activists are tapping into the same characteristics that describe the Net Gen, the norms we have described at length in this book, especially entertainment, speed, integrity, collaboration, scrutiny, freedom, customization, and innovation.

Freedom. The Internet obviously opens up a world of possibilities both for young activists looking for a bigger audience, and for young people considering which cause or causes to back. On TakingItGlobal, for example, activists can choose from 75 causes or issues being discussed, and over 10,000 nonprofit organizations. They can think about attending any one of the 10,000 events worldwide, or read one of over 250,000 blog posts, which are translated by a computer translator.

Customization. Maybe they want to be digital activists, helping out by hunting for information or spreading the word through social networks. Or maybe they want to give something up—like plastic bags. Or maybe they want to organize something or volunteer in a part of the offline world that they care deeply about. Today's top activists give Net Gen volunteers a choice.

Scrutiny. Young people are watching companies' behavior. Over half of young people say they rewarded or punished companies based on their perceived social performance, according to a 2002 survey of over 2,000 people whose ages ranged from 15 to 30 for the World Bank Institute. Over 80 percent of young people said they paid attention to the social behavior of companies in their countries. Our nGenera study of the Net Generation—conducted in Canada and the United States—found that 40 percent of the Net Geners would abandon a product they love if they discovered that a company has suspect social practices. If they do as they say, Net Geners could exert substantial pressure on companies. They'd better be ready.

Integrity. Honesty, transparency, and authenticity are crucial if you want to get through to the Net Gener. Says itsyournature founder Cox: "We are people who do not like to watch the news. We know how full of crap it is. Having grown up on marketing and advertising, we've been trained to smell the rat." Her friends, new to the business of environmentalism, set the tone: "It's digestible content for the audience. It's not formalized or laden with facts and statistics and overemphasized drama. It's just oh, cool. That's great, you know? It's peer-to-peer content. That's what's happening online."

Collaboration. MTV's campaign for Darfur wouldn't have happened without the help of college students. The spark came from a senior at Georgetown with a modest proposal to give up a luxury for a day and give the money to an organization working in Darfur. The fire spread when digital activists targeted the companies that are allegedly indirectly financing the massacre. And it turned into a wildfire when an innovative Californian activist created an addictive game that made regular kids walk in the shoes of a teenager in Darfur. TakingItGlobal is all about collaboration—between activists around the globe who have never met each other in person.

Entertainment. "It all comes down to entertainment, irreverent humor," says Cox. "There's sort of a shock value to it. It's really hard as an environmental group to find a comfortable line. You have to integrate entertainment

into it or no one will pay attention, especially the younger demographic."
You've got to be fun to engage kids these days, says Cox. Young people are
skeptical about the effectiveness of actual tree hugging. "You have to engage
them on a softer level. Radical protest didn't kick Bush out of office. It didn't
get us out of the war in Iraq. You have to put them back on the path, and walk
them slowly."

Speed. Activists are operating at speeds we've never seen before. They can
reach millions of people in minutes. They are aware that their audience wants to
know what they can do, specifically, right now. That is why mtvU gives its viewers lots of options for different ways to do something to help, from just passing
on a message to donating money, or joining a divestment campaign. These Net-
Geners like to do something tangible, like choosing a homegrown apple over an
imported one, says Cox. It gives you "an immediate sense of gratification."
That's why the green tips on how you can make a difference by giving up those
plastic bags work so well. "It makes them feel empowered by bringing their own
bag for a day"—instead of using a new plastic one.

Innovation. Instead of knocking on doors to ask people to sign a petition,
activists reach millions of people online in an instant. Instead of holding fancy
fund-raisers, or scheduling a march, they're inventing widgets to gain access to the places where kids are gathering and talking—the social networking sites. "It's all online," says Cox. "It's the new form of tree hugging. It's the digital mix that we have access to and can connect us to people in a second all over the world. The
opportunities were not this clear even two years ago. It's a cost-effective way to
engage, interact, and understand. We didn't have that back then. It was knocking door to door, mailing, which is so costly, so wasteful, and the return is not
always the best."

> "Spend an hour a week at a school
> helping a child to read, or visiting
> people in a care home, or put a Web
> page together for a local charity . . .
> there's so much you can do."
> —HELGA, 29, UNITED KINGDOM

I listen to these Net Geners, and I think back to the 1970s and the lengthy,
ideology-laden conversations we had in smoky, dimly lit rooms deep into the
night. Radicals in my day usually subscribed to one of the big ideologies—like
one of the many bitter flavors of socialism perhaps, or Che Guevera's third-
world ideology, or radical feminism, or anarchy. We broke away from the values
and ideology of our parents, government, business, and other major social institutions. But when we saw a horrific image of Vietnam on TV, we wanted to
know how we could learn more and meet like-minded people. Unless you lived

in a city like Boston or New York, your options were limited. You might see a poster, or pick up an article. You might join a march or a demonstration if one was happening in your town. Despite the limitations, my generation did help stop the Vietnam War. We helped to drive the massive change in society that made it possible for the two leading contenders for the Democratic nomination in the 2008 U.S. presidential race to be a woman and a black man. We found a way around the limitations of the distribution system.

Now young activists have a tool we couldn't even have dreamed about. The instant access to global information has made kids not only more knowledgeable about the big issues, but more sophisticated in their attack, as the student divestment campaign has shown. They know they have this power, and they're using it. As Martha McCaughey and Michael Ayers noted in their anthology, *Cyberactivism*: "Activists have not only incorporated the Internet into their repertoire but also . . . have changed substantially what counts as activism, what counts as community, collective identity, democratic space, political strategy. And online activists challenge us to think about how cyberspace is meant to be used."[16]

We're in the early stages of this trend—activists have only been using social networking sites for a year or so. The extent and degree of the Net Generation's commitment to volunteering to address social issues is still unknown. Is this a trend that will last, or just a fad? How effective are they in making people's lives better? You have to wonder what will happen when this generation moves inside existing organizations, instead of focusing their energy outside the boundaries of formal political and economic organizations. How will these activists handle the complex issues involved in changing an institution from the inside? It's too early to answer any of these questions. Will they inspire their generation and change the world? There is hope.

SEVEN WAYS TO GET NET GENERS TO VOLUNTEER AND WORK EFFECTIVELY FOR YOUR CIVIL SOCIETY ORGANIZATION

(1) **Don't just use them as foot soldiers.** Treat them as peers. Listen to their suggestions. Let them collaborate with you. Don't run your group like a Dilbertian hierarchy. Give them real power and they'll surprise you positively.

(2) **Let them develop your Web strategy.** Look for ways that the Net Geners can help online. Maybe they can help you get into the social networks where kids hang out. Don't tell them what to do—brainstorm around objectives.

(3) **Forget the guilt trip.** It won't work.

(4) **Don't be afraid to get them involved in a hard issue that's hitting people far away.** They love to travel. Can you provide opportunities?

(5) **If you've got a smart group, give them a big, tough problem to solve.** Something that is unstructured and that no one knows how to even begin to tackle.

(6) **Show integrity yourself.** Be honest, considerate, accountable, and transparent. No BS to the generation with finely tuned BS detectors.

(7) **Design your organization around the eight Net Generation norms.** For example, give them lots of options for ways in which they can help. Look for ways to inject fun or even entertainment into your cause. Check out the Games for Change—a Web site dedicated to the creation of "real world games" to make a "real world impact"—for inspiration. Give Net Geners something to do, right now, which has an immediate, tangible impact.

⨀

IN DEFENSE OF THE FUTURE

This definitive research project on this generation has produced some profound and inspiring conclusions. The most important of these is: not only are the kids alright, but as a generation they are poised to transform every institution of society—for the better. Yet, as I've explained throughout the book, this generation is being criticized on many fronts. They're "the dumbest generation," says Professor Mark Bauerlein. They're narcissistic, says psychology professor Jean Twenge. The Internet has eaten their neocortex, says Robert Bly. As high school students, they're "woefully ill-prepared for work," claims a U.S. employers report.

To read the criticisms you might conclude the Net Generation are a bunch of dull, celebrity-obsessed, net-addicted, shopaholic exhibitionists with a taste for violence, online and offline. You might even want to follow the advice offered by Professor Bauerlein on the front cover of his book *The Dumbest Generation*: "Don't trust anyone under 30."

Net Geners themselves either laugh at the line (see some of their comments below), or respond in such a thoughtful way that the dumbness theory is invalidated. But when you add up all the charges and criticisms, they represent a serious critique of youth today. Throughout this book I have attempted to sort out what is true, what is false, and what is unknown. But when you scrutinize the situation—as the young people I've worked with would have us do—a shocking conclusion emerges. But it is not what most would think. Let us begin to do this now by addressing the top 10 Dark Side issues.

THE DARK SIDE REVISITED

1. The Dumbest Generation?

This line of thought suggests that because they spend so much time staring at the screen, the young people forfeit the ability to think deeply or creatively. Augmenting this sense of alarm is a survey suggesting that young people spend a lot less time reading literature than young people once did. If they only ingest bits and bites of online information, English neurobiologist Baroness Greenfield says, they will fail to develop intellectual skills needed for higher-order thinking. Some of them may even develop a digital version of attention deficit disorder—zigging and zagging from one idea to the next without really thinking about or finishing anything.

There's a lot we don't know about the brain, but it has become evident that this most complex of human organs can change its physical structure and its functioning throughout a person's life, far more than scientists thought it could when I was a teenager. The brain is especially malleable during adolescence, which is just when teens are immersed in digital technology and spend hours playing games.

The typical boomer grew up watching more than 22 hours of TV a week. They just watched, zoned out. As I've explained, Net Geners watch less TV and when they do, they treat it as background Muzak while they hunt for information, play games, and chat with friends online. They spend a lot less time zoning out in front of the TV than their boomer parents did at the same age.

While the full impact of this digital immersion is still unknown, there is emerging evidence that the Net Gen brain is adapting to this wired world. Some of the early research is about the video games played by 8 out of 10 teenagers. Net Geners who play action video games can process information more quickly than non-game-players. They can track more objects than can nonplayers too. Research on games suggests that video games might help players practice decision making. To become an expert player, you have to master many of the same skills that are essential for success in the educational system and later in life, such as understanding design principles, practicing, developing strategies, organizing information, and discovering. And when your success depends on collaborating with dozens of other people worldwide, you have to develop management skills that are not so different from the ones that the best corporate executives develop.

General online activity—hunting for information, reading, and responding—is far from mindless. Kids are, in fact, reading, but they're reading fewer books of literature and more nonfiction online. Online reading requires many of the same mental skills that are required to read a book—and then some. You are not led along every step of the way by the hand; you have to construct your own narrative and scenarios, and you must critique whatever it is you are reading along the way. You have to be able to detect a fraud—like the Pacific Northwest tree octopus that fooled most of the seventh grade students who participated in one of literacy expert Dr. Donald Leu's studies. You have to be able to keep the question in mind and not get distracted by all the interesting factoids out there. What's more, you're reading and writing as you go. That's why some people call Web 2.0 the "read-write Web." It's challenging. This is why experts are talking about a new literacy that may be even more intellectually demanding than the old one.

Because the Internet gives young people a world of information at their fingertips, they have to struggle to understand and synthesize. It can be a great intellectual exercise. And yes, they do multitask, and switch from one stream of information to the next, with an ease that surprises their parents. Of course, they need to focus deeply to accomplish a complex task, but the rest of the time, they're developing multitasking skills that are very useful, even essential, in the modern digital world.

So is there any evidence that the Internet is making kids "the dumbest generation"? If anything, test scores suggest the opposite.

Although IQ scores are controversial and measure only one facet of intelligence, raw IQ scores have been going up three points a decade since World War II. Some researchers believe that the recent increase in IQ scores has been influenced by the complex media and technology environment.[1]

In the United States, average test scores have been improving in most subjects—especially in math. Yet this is no time to celebrate, not when so many young people are dropping out of school and college. That's why I say this is the story of two generations: the top students are doing fabulously and using the Internet to boost their academic accomplishments, but at the same time, the United States is facing a massive dropout problem, especially among city kids who are black or Hispanic. It's a scandal. Yet we shouldn't blame the Internet for this problem. Instead, let's fix class sizes, alleviate poverty, motivate teachers with better pay, improve childcare, and deal with the factors that directly cause kids to drop out and lose hope. In particular, let's get laptops and the Web into classrooms so that teachers can be freed to customize a learning experience rather than being forced to remain broadcasters of information. Don't make the Internet, a global system for communication and the sharing of knowledge, the scapegoat. That is like blaming the library for ignorance.

No one, by the way, has shown a shred of evidence that Net Geners are more ignorant than we were at their age. And when it comes to ignorance, remember the words of Samuel Johnson: "Knowledge is of two kinds. We know a subject ourselves, or we know where we can find information upon it."[2] Or, as Rob Cross and the authors of *The Hidden Power of Social Networks*, put it:" [Who] you know has a significant impact on what you come to know, because relationships are critical for obtaining information, solving problems, and learning how to do your work."[3] If Cross and colleagues are correct, and I believe they are, Net Geners' ability to network and access the world of information and appropriate people should put this generation in the driver's seat to be the smartest.

One of the executives who surely has one of the world's most insightful views of the Net Gen is Eric Schmidt, CEO of Google, the omnipresent search engine. He counts millions of Net Geners as customers, and has nearly 20,000 of them on the company payroll. In the spring of 2008, just after *The Dumbest Generation* was published, I asked him about the Net Geners he hires at Google. "Are they the dumbest generation? Do you have any other thoughts on how this generation is different?" Schmidt e-mailed me within an hour: "This generation is the smartest, not the dumbest," he wrote. "They are quicker, more global, more savvy, and better educated. The clear fact that they have been connected to each other since near birth through mobile phones, chat, and now social networks means they are the most connected generation; they care deeper about each other than we ever did. And you can quote me!"

I Don't Read Books . . .

In the spring of 2008, I was invited to lunch with the leaders of Florida State University to discuss the twenty-first-century university. Amid the deans and department heads who expressed profound thoughts about the future of the institution, was a 22-year-old student, Joe O'Shea. He was a handsome young man, dressed in a crisp white shirt and tie, as if he were headed for a high-priced job on Wall Street. It was his turn to speak:

"I don't read books per se," he told the erudite and now somewhat stunned crowd. "I go to Google and I can absorb relevant information quickly. Some of this comes from books. But sitting down and going through a book from cover to cover doesn't make sense. It's not a good use of my time as I can get all the information I need faster through the web. You need to know how to do it—to be a skilled hunter."

His perspective initiated, as you can imagine, a lively debate. "I don't know whether this portends the end of civilization," said Frank Patterson, the dean of the university's prestigious film school, "or a profoundly exciting and different future."

O'Shea is no slouch. It turns out that he was president of the student government, with a $10.1 million budget. He sat on dozens of university committees representing the students. With a couple of other friends he started Global Peace Exchange, which coordinates student collaboration in sustainable development projects. After Hurricane Katrina, he founded a free health clinic in the lower Ninth Ward of New Orleans that sees 10,000 people per year. He said he was impressed by how much other people were willing to give: "Human beings have innate compassion," he said. "A lot of times this is masked by society, but it can come forward with the right conditions. We're social beings; we live in communities. We care about others—that's our nature."

I was so impressed by O'Shea that I offered him a ride on a plane I had chartered for the day. It had been a very sad year for him: Both his parents had passed away. But now he gets together with his brothers online by playing video games, like World of Warcraft. "It's such a fun way to work together, to feel like a team together," he said. "Games provide great opportunities for people to work together and learn together. The three of us are a little team."

He was continuing his education, he told me, at Oxford: "I'm really looking forward to it; I'll have health care for the first time," he said. "We never did growing up. We just never went to the doctor."

I was impressed: Oxford sets an extraordinarily high bar for acceptance. I wondered, of course, whether he had funding. Yes, he had a scholarship, he said.

I pressed him for details.

"It's called a Rhodes Scholarship," he said.

2. Screen Addicted? Losing Social Skills?

I often hear pundits and even some parents express concerns that their kids are spending so much time online that they might not develop proper social skills. It's an understandable concern; we all want our kids to grow up with friends and a healthy ability to relate to other people. And young people should have balance in their lives. Addiction to anything—drugs, alcohol, sex, or video games—is a cause for serious concern.

But there is more to this issue than meets the eye. If in the past a young person spent a lot of time reading novels, no one would call her or him "reading addicted." So, assuming a young person has some kind of balance in his or her life, but still seems to spend a lot of time online, the underlying concern is over what exactly that young person is doing.

The fact is that young people are spending a lot of their time with *social media*—talking with friends and participating on social networks. The Net Geners are a community-minded generation, historian Neil Howe has observed; they are quite different from their individualistic baby boomer parents. They like to do things together. Some 81 percent of tweens (ages 8–12) and 53 percent of teens (13–18) say that the number one way they like spending time with their friends is in person. They're so social that they make sure all of their friends on Facebook know what's up with them day and night. Just watch them as they're walking down the street. Chances are they're talking to a friend on their cells or BlackBerrys.

True, interviews with Net Geners conducted by nGenera suggest that many of them prefer to communicate via instant messaging rather than in person for certain kinds of interactions. "It allows you to think about your responses, motives, and overall reduces the awkwardness of conversations," one of the young people told us. But this doesn't mean they are losing their social skills; after all, expressing one's feelings in writing was standard practice in the nineteenth century. In the end, look at what they do: instead of zoning out alone in front of the TV or bickering with siblings about what TV show to watch, they're interacting with friends, plenty of them, online or in person. The facts show that this is the most social generation ever, and from what I can see, they have all the social capabilities they'll need to be successful adults.

3. Are They Giving Up Their Privacy?

This is a very real problem. Net Geners *are* giving up their privacy without realizing it—or understanding the consequences. When I see what they're posting on Facebook or other social networking sites, I get really worried for them. Young people like to share pictures and stories about themselves, and they don't see any reason why they shouldn't. But they don't realize that this openness may come back to bite them when they're competing for the big job or a political post later in life. Everywhere I travel I meet recruiters who are already checking out the sites. "The term they've used over and over is 'red flags,' " says Trudy Steinfeld, executive director of the Center for Career Development at New York University. "Is there something about (a candidate's) lifestyle that we might find questionable or that we might find goes against the core values of our corporation?"[4]

Net Geners must wake up, now. For starters, they must use the privacy features on social networking sites like Facebook. They've got to be very careful about the pictures they post. If you tell something to 500 friends, you'd better assume you're telling everyone. This is not just about social networking sites either. Privacy is a huge and unresolved issue on the Internet.

4. Are They Coddled? Do They Lack Independence?

Friends of mine often raise their eyebrows when they hear that their kids or those of others are moving home—at age 24. It confirms their suspicions: these kids have been coddled all their lives. So who's surprised when they move home instead of striking out on their own, as baby boomers did? I think we have to look at this trend with a new viewfinder. Baby boomers couldn't wait to move out of the model of the family home because that was the only way they could seek freedom—away from the family hierarchy with the father in the ruling position. These Net Geners, on the other hand, were more likely to grow up in a family democracy, where they had their say. They don't have to move away to have freedom. They have it in their home, not only with the new, more open family structure, but with their computer and their handheld device, which give them access to the Internet anywhere.

They're happy to move home because they have much closer relationships with their parents. It also makes sense because they're confronted with a massive student debt, which is eight times higher than it was for boomers (adjusted for inflation). No wonder 40 percent of Americans between the ages of 18 and 25 still live with their parents and 46 percent depend on family for financial help.[5]

So moving home might make a lot of sense for an energetic Net Gener who wants to save money while he or she is launching a career. It's not necessarily a sign of apathy or emotional weakness.

The real concern is whether Net Geners can think for themselves. They've been raised to be dependent on their parents, some experts say. Young people are subject to more than 10 times as many restrictions as mainstream adults, twice as many as active duty U.S. marines, and almost twice as many as incarcerated felons, according to Dr. Robert Epstein, West Coast editor of *Psychology Today*. The Net Generation were the most overscheduled generation in history.

So if now they're calling on the helicopter parents for help when they run into trouble, who should we blame: young people or their helicopter parents? There is an upside for employers, though. Yes, helicopter parents can be annoying, and they need to be confronted or ignored if they're insisting that a low performer get undue credit. But think of the other side of this coin: parents can be recruited to help nurture a better employee or student. Is that so bad?

And don't think it will last. Most Net Geners simply ask their hovering parents to back off.

5. Does the Internet Encourage Youth to Steal? Are They Cheaters?

Our research shows that the Net Generation are big believers in integrity—honesty, consideration, accountability, and transparency. Yet, according to nGenera research, 77 percent of Net Geners have downloaded music, software, games, or movies without paying for it. It sounds like a contradiction until you start talking to them. They don't see it as stealing and their assessment of the situation is pretty sophisticated. They think this is a case of a business model that needs to be changed. Net Geners, they say, pay more for music than ever—but not the old-fashioned way. They buy some music online and they spend a big chunk of their disposable income on concerts, ringtones, and artists' products.

This old model of owning and selling music makes no sense for this entire generation, or for anyone else for that matter. I don't think it is stealing. It's a classic example of a disruptive technology. For a decade I've described a model that would work. Music should be a service, not a product. Instead of purchasing tunes, you should pay a small monthly fee for access to all the songs in the world. They could be streamed to you when you want and where you want via the Internet. I call my vision of music bliss Everywhere Internet Audio. I'd listen to my own Don Channel. I could slice and dice the massive musical database anyway I liked—by artist, by genre, by year, by songwriter, by popularity, and so on. The Don Channel would know what I like, based on what I've chosen in the past. I could even ask my Everywhere Internet Audio service to suggest new artists that resemble my known favorites.

If Everywhere Internet Audio existed, no one would ever "steal." Why would they take possession of a song? Once again young people are showing how we need to change our business models—if we would only listen to them. Rather than build bold new approaches for digital entertainment, the industry has built a business model around suing its customers. And the industry that brought us the Beatles is now hated by its customers and collapsing. Sadly, obsession with control, piracy, and proprietary standards on the part of large industry players has only served to further alienate and anger music listeners.

What about intellectual property in the corporate world? Should employers be worried that the Net Geners will blog it to the world? This is not a complicated problem. Simply tell Net Geners what's confidential, and set rules about security. As for revealing corporate secrets, experience shows that they have good judgment. When Jonathan Schwartz became CEO of Sun Microsystems, he gave every employee the right to blog publically. They have never had a problem releasing inappropriate information.

It's a big issue in the university too. The Internet makes it easy to plagiarize, and, according to one 2003 survey, 38 percent of college and university students cut and paste information they find on the Internet.[6] Plagiarism appears to have gone up by eight percentage points since the early 1960s. But Don McCabe, a Rutgers Business School professor and expert on plagiarism, sees no widespread increase in plagiarism on campus. Rather, the students who are plagiarizing are using the Internet to do it more. It's not clear whether cheating overall has increased, either. Sixty percent of high school students admitted to cheating on an exam "at least once" on a 2006 survey conducted by the Josephson Institute—virtually the same number who admitted to cheating in 1992.[7]

Whether or not it's gone up, cheating is clearly a problem. The Internet cuts the cost of stealing or buying someone else's work, and young people are under enormous pressure to score good grades so that they'll get into universities of their choice. So what's the answer? UCLA and other U.S. universities, as well as several others in Canada and elsewhere, are using an online program called Turnitin.com to detect plagiarism. The company claims it can cut "measurable rates" of plagiarism to "almost zero." My own kids say that online programs like this are an effective deterrent—because then most students wouldn't even think about trying to plagiarize when the penalty could be a failure or even a suspension. Yet the Center for Academic Integrity, a coalition of hundreds of educational institutions, does not think that technology can solve the problem completely. "Instead, we should be encouraging respect and fairness among the students," says the center's director, Dr. Stephen Satris.

6. Does It Encourage Bullying?

Every month we read appalling stories of online bullying, which can range from comments that aim to humiliate the target to outright physical violence. You can see the ugly evidence on YouTube or on the social networking sites. About 6 percent of respondents in one survey reported harassment incidents (threats, rumors, or other offensive behavior) during the past year. Another 2 percent of the surveyed youth reported episodes of distressing harassment (i.e., the incident made them feel very or extremely upset or afraid).[8]

But should we blame the Internet? Hardly. Bullying was a real problem when I was at school, but parents didn't know about it, and schools did nothing about it even if they did know. Now there's evidence—right there on YouTube—and parents, schools, and authorities can do something about it.

Bullies, experts tell us, need an audience, and the Internet provides an audience of millions, which amplifies the problem. It also allows people to bully targets while they're in the apparent comfort of their own homes.

But the bullies leave a permanent, searchable record; they can be detected, and confronted. It's going to be a lot harder to be a cyberbully, and get away with it. The response to bullying, experts tell us, needs to address the root of the problem. The bully needs to develop empathy. The target needs to develop a powerful sense of self to enable him or her to fend off attacks, in the playground or online. Only by addressing the human issues in a thoughtful way can we tackle this problem.

7. Does It Incite Youth Violence?

Sometimes the picture doesn't tell the story. In the spring of 2008, as we saw in Chapter 8, a group of teens posted an appalling video of several of them beating up a 16-year-old girl. It was all too easy for some commentators to jump to the conclusion that the desire to achieve notoriety on the Internet is driving some teens to violence. Fueling that concern is a 2007 book in which the authors argue that playing violent video games creates a significant risk factor for later aggressive and violent behavior.[9]

The research cited by this book is disturbing. One study randomly assigned elementary and college students to video games that were violent, or not. When they were later tested by a standard laboratory measure of aggressive behavior, the young people who had been playing violent video games displayed more aggression. That finding was bolstered by a survey and a longitudinal study.

This is cause for concern, especially when the video game Grand Theft Auto IV was such a mammoth hit when it launched in the spring of 2008. It's a violent action-adventure game: the protagonist has to commit multiple acts of mayhem while searching for the person who betrayed his army unit. In the first week it was released, it sold $500 million worth of games—more than 11 of the top movies in the past 13 years made in the entire year of their release. Grand Theft Auto IV is on track to becoming one of the biggest products in entertainment history. If Iowa State psychology professor Craig Anderson and his coauthors are correct, we could be in for trouble.

But there are many unknowns. It's very hard to prove that violent video games, and not early childhood violence by parents, poverty, neglect, genes, or other well-researched factors cause young people to be violent. It's not showing up yet in the number of actual violent acts. In fact, violence overall—including violent acts by youths—has been going down. Both violent crime and property

FIGURE 11.1   YOUTH CRIME IN THE UNITED STATES IN PAST 30 YEARS

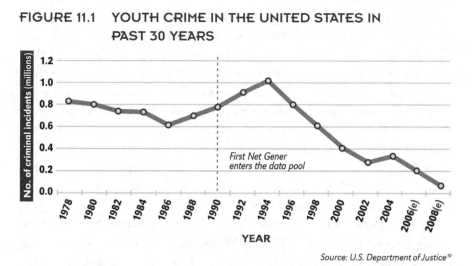

First Net Gener
enters the data pool

YEAR

Source: U.S. Department of Justice[10]

crime have been dropping since the early 1990s,[11] and victim reports show that the number of serious violent offenses committed by persons ages 12 to 17 declined 61 percent from 1993 to 2005 (see Figure 11.1), while those committed by persons older than 17 fell 58 percent.[12]

More study is clearly needed. In the meantime, parents should be sensible. Impressionable youngsters should not be allowed to play games such as Grand Theft Auto IV that are clearly aimed at adult audiences—just as they're not allowed to view acclaimed but violent movies such as *Pulp Fiction* or *Silence of the Lambs*. It only makes sense.

8. Does the Net Gen Have a Misguided Sense of Entitlement and a Bad Work Ethic?

"Woefully ill-prepared" for work is how the Conference Board and its partners described the Net Gen in their results of a survey of 400 employers. Many boomers say even worse things, less publicly perhaps, about this generation. They think the Net Geners are entering the workforce with unrealistic expectations. They want to be rich and/or powerful—without putting in the work. They're hooked up with their friends on Facebook, and cannot tolerate the slightest bit of criticism from their employer—or they'll call their helicopter parent for help. "We are developing a generation that is going to be codependent on the parent," says Stephen Seaward, director of career development for Saint Joseph College. "Let's say they're at work, and they're working with a key account or a critical client: if they're on the spot, are they going to be able to make the kind of decision that you want them to make or are they going to get on the mobile phone and talk to mom or dad and see what they think?"

Yet I believe their concerns reflect something different. They don't like how this generation wants to work. Net Geners have seen the movie *Office Space* and a hundred YouTube videos that parody Dilbert Inc. They don't see why they should be stuck in a cubicle with the nine to five routine when they have technology that lets them work anywhere, anytime. This generation wants to be judged on its merits, not on its face time. They typically want to collaborate at work, not blindly follow the rules of an unproductive hierarchy. They want to use their tools of collaboration—like Facebook—while they're at work. They think that customized jobs and more regular feedback on performance makes sense, not just for them, but for their employers. They have ideas about how work could be more collaborative and innovative.

To some, this work ethos represents a threat to the old order. Yet other companies are finding ways to work with Net Geners. The smart companies are embracing not only this generation but their collaborative ways and are getting big results. Let me quote the head of the company rated as the best place to launch a career, Jim Quigley, CEO of Deloitte: "I have a simple measure for how capable this generation is—billings. Our new recruits deliver far greater value for clients than any previous generation—and this is reflected as a significant increase in the average revenue generated per employee. They do more good work and our clients are happier."

Case closed.

9. Are They Narcissistic?

Psychology professor Jean Twenge says this generation is more narcissistic than the previous one. They're Generation Me, a "little army of narcissists" that has been nurtured by the self-esteem movement. Twenge's study has been sharply criticized on many fronts—including by one group of researchers who found no evidence of narcissism rising at either colleges or universities.

But the bottom line is what they do. As you can see from the charts in this chapter (Figures 11.1 and 11.2), Net Geners are not self-centered risk takers. They drink and smoke less than their parents did. They commit fewer crimes. They volunteer more than previous generations have. Their actions contradict Twenge's claim that they are the most narcissistic generation in history.

10. What About Their Values? Do They Just Want to Be Rich and Famous?

Yes, the Net Generation loves celebrities, and they love the idea that anyone can be a celebrity. There are lots more ways to be a celebrity now, compared to the days when boomer girls swooned over the Beatles and Elvis. It's no surprise

FIGURE 11.2   RISING PERCENTAGE OF "CLEAN" TEENS*

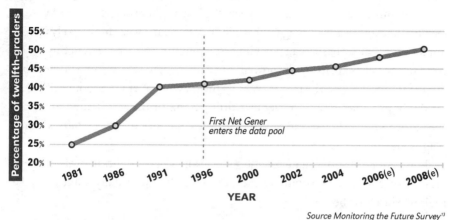

Source *Monitoring the Future Survey*[13]

*The term "clean" indicates that the person has not used illicit drugs, smoked cigarettes, or consumed alcohol in the past 30 days.

that the most popular career choice for 13-year-old girls is to be an actress, while the boys want to be a pro athlete.

They do appear to be more interested in making money than boomers were at their age. According to U.S. Census data, 79 percent of freshmen in 1970 said an important personal objective was "developing a meaningful philosophy of life." In 2005, three-quarters of freshmen said their number one objective was to be "very well off financially."[14]

But who can blame them? Their college debt load and housing costs are much higher than it was for boomers. So, as the late William Strauss, founding partner of the LifeCourse Associates consulting firm, noted: it only makes sense to make money to pay off debt and pay the rent or the mortgage.

And yes, they shop. That's no surprise. The Net Generation has been exposed to more media and marketing than any other generation; this is the first generation to be targeted by marketers as a "tween" segment when they were between the ages of 8 and 13.

But what's wrong with loving choice, innovation, new products, and even fashions and brands? What's wrong with communicating with our friends on social networks, or for have fun playing games? You can easily see it as a positive thing.

That is the glitter side of this generation. But they have another side that is quite different.

Volunteering, on the part of teenagers and college freshmen, has hit an all-time high. In high school, many of them are obliged to volunteer, but in college and in their early careers, they don't stop. About 36 percent of Net Geners ages 15–25 volunteered in the previous year, slightly higher than the rate of volunteering for Americans over age 25.[15] (Older Americans were more likely to volunteer on a regular basis than Net Geners, though.) As we've seen in this book, Net Gen activists are using the power of the Internet to tackle some of the most dreadful problems on the planet. What's more, when Net Gens got political in 2008, they displayed their power by helping Senator Barack Obama to topple the Clinton powerhouse and rewrite the rules of contemporary political campaigns in America.

This is not a shallow, materialistic generation. On the contrary, this is a generation of community volunteers and activists. They actually want to make their world a little better.

Are You "The Dumbest Generation"? Does the Digital Age "Stupefy Young Americans and Jeopardize Our Future" As the Book with This Title Says?

"I'd like to better understand exactly how having a vast repository of knowledge and information at my fingertips somehow makes me dumber, or how being able to communicate with anybody else on the planet instantaneously somehow leaves me more ignorant of the world's workings."
—Jonathan Wolf, 24, Worcester, Massachusetts

"A modern Reefer Madness: embarrassing for its creator, and unintentionally funny to its readers." —Alex Salzillo, 22, Atlanta, Georgia

"Our generation is awash in the present but we may be underinformed about the past. We are perpetually connected to events across the planet as they occur in realtime, making us self-important and complacent. Rather than get up and do something, we convince ourselves that by blogging about events we somehow affect their outcome." —Mike Kanert, 29, Saitama, Japan

"I'm going to start handing this book out. It's great. A perfect way to manage expectations about what a loser I must surely be."
—Daniel Williamson, 27, Toronto

"Fiddlesticks! . . . or some other expression from the 'smartest' generation."
—Eva Szymanski, 24, London, Ontario

"I went online today, googled this book, found a short preview, read some reviews, read multiple bios of the author. Followed a link to the WSJ online, and read another one of his pieces. Then I stopped and laughed. The Internet is the driving force behind ignorance and apathy?"
—Brooke Rosenkrantz, 21, Boca Raton, Florida

"People believe what they read on the Internet without question when not all of it is true. Alot of it, namely blogging and other sources of personal posting, are opinions and ideas, not fact. One can be conditioned to believe anything, especially younger minds that soak up everything like a sponge."
—*Nick Dubois, 25, Brooklyn, New York*

"This diatribe is full of sound and fury, signifying nothing."
—*Del McLean, 22, San Diego, California*

"Sure I'm dumb. My role model on this is Socrates, who said: 'I know nothing save for the fact of my own ignorance.' Oh, that quote came from a book . . ."
—*Graham Smith, 24, currently working in Rwanda*

"My physics teacher came to class one day and told us that she had just looked at the physics tests from 30 years ago and that we had no chance of even imagining being able to complete the test correctly. She never directly explains why, but other times in class she talks about the negative effects on children today from technology." —*Alex Zajack, 15, Las Vegas, Nevada*

"This is sensationalist nonsense—for one group or generation to categorize another as stupid or ignorant based on arbitrarily valued differences is baseless unproductive rhetoric." —*Eric Potter, 22, Waltham, Massachusetts*

"I don't think we're the 'dumbest' generation, but in all that we have gained in this 'digital age' we may have lost something of ourselves. People are inherently different, always were, and always will be, so each will make use of the abundance of knowledge differently. As Sandara Carey said: 'Never mistake knowledge for wisdom. One helps you make a living; the other helps you make a life.' " —*Aditi Bakht, 23, New Delhi, India*

"Bauerlein needs to be careful not to mix up stupidity with efficiency. Why would I waste my time memorizing hundreds of statistics and facts, when with the click of a mouse I can pull up just about anything I need to know?"
—*Vanessa Kenalty, 25, Toronto*

"We're destroying the English language? NFW [No F**king Way]!"
—*Bobbi Munroe, San Francisco, California*

"There is plenty of cause for alarm and/or optimism when it comes to my generation; even I can see that. Still I think the negative views of us come from a fear of the unknown, a fear of change. Our world is evolving at a rapid rate, and that can be scary for older generations."
—*Savannah Jones, 17, Portland, Oregon*

"Take a close look at what the baby-boom generation has left us: a bloated, unsustainable and selfish infrastructure of cars, homes, cities, and commerce. My Net Generation is critical of such development, largely thanks to the education and knowledge available at our 'lazy' fingertips (they didn't teach sustainability in high school)." —*Aaron Hay, 24, Toronto*

"Ask a teenager what is the capital of Belgium, and he might not know the correct answer. But put that teenager in front of a computer, and he'll find Brussels, its population, geographic location, GDP, and all about its role as the administrative center of the European Union."
—*Ben Elrom, 17, Charlottesville, Virginia*

"I didn't walk 50 miles in the snow to school, but I've dealt with pop-up ads all my life. Just because information is at my fingertips and that's made me lazy, doesn't mean the wealth of accessible knowledge has made me dumb."
—*Matt Ceniceros, 29, Memphis, Tennessee*

"This generation is becoming more and more dependant on technology, but the effect is questionable. We cannot allow our basic skills to suffer at the cost of convienience. (I would also like to point out my dependance on wrod proccessors as I have had many gramatical and spelling errors above, and without the red underlines, I am none the wiser.)"
—*Nate Lewin, 16, Scarsdale, New York*

"Lazy is the mask for the entitlement we feel; the right to have access to end-less information on the Internet, the drive to find our own innovative path, and the desire to see and understand the world. Sometimes the world gets so loud we need to cocoon ourselves in self-composed entertainment bubbles, but really we want to go places, enact change, and have our voices meaning-fully heard above the cacophony." —*Jen Shaw, 25, Hoboken, New Jersey*

"Ignorant and fearful—nothing less than a modern-day McCarthy in his cam-paign against youth." —*Alex Tapscott, 22, Amherst, Massachusetts*

FEAR OF THE UNKNOWN

The shocking conclusion from my research is not that the generation is some-how fatally flawed. Rather, it is that the mean-spirited, gleefully contemptuous characterization of youth today is pretty much without foundation. The cynics appear to be making up most of this stuff. Their scorn is without basis.

To be sure, there are real concerns. For some of these, for example, the issue of privacy, the problem is crystal clear, as is the solution. For other issues, the research is not yet completely clear, and for some of these I have done my best to make informed hypotheses—for example, regarding the effects of digital immersion on the brain. Yet many of the concerns are simply unfounded and based on ignorance, fear, or overt hostility toward youth.

We fear what we don't understand. To a certain degree, adults have always mistrusted youth. A Sumerian cuneiform tablet from circa 2000 BC says: "Our civilization is doomed if the unheard actions of our younger generations is allowed to continue."

A Greek philosopher is said to have complained: "The children now love luxury; they have bad manners, contempt for authority; they show disrespect for elders and love chatter in place of exercise. Children are now tyrants, not the servants of their households. They no longer rise when elders enter the room. They contradict their parents, chatter before company, gobble up dainties at the table, cross their legs, and tyrannize their teachers."[16] Sound familiar?

If the good philosopher were alive today, the quote would be altered by a few words: "The children now love *Gucci*; they have bad *corporate communications protocols*, contempt for authority; they show disrespect for elder *Gen Xers* and love *chatting* in place of exercise. Children are now *friends* not the servants of their *parents*. They no *longer look up from their mobile phones* when elders enter the room. They contradict their parents *with Wikipedia references on their mobile devices*, they *text message* before company, gobble up *crudités* at the table, *stretch* their legs, and *ignore* their teachers."

When I was growing up, children were to be seen and not heard. Then when we were teenagers, we shook things up, and often shocked our parents and grandparents. This time, the traditional generation gap is exacerbated by a new communications medium that boomers don't fully understand. It is the kids who get it. They are, for the first time, an authority on something really important in the world. That technology has helped to shape their new youth culture that challenges and could positively transform every institution of society. Some digital immigrants just don't get the digital natives. Some threatened boomers don't understand them—or the technology that they have mastered. So you've got a potent cocktail for fear.

We fear what we don't understand. I saw this fear a dozen years ago when I wrote *Growing Up Digital*. Fear leads to irrational behavior. We can become hostile and strike out at the cause of our fear.

Some people, such as some of the academics quoted in this book, use what looks like sophisticated arguments to criticize this generation. As a student of research methodology, I find the pundits' methods, which appear designed to confirm preconceived notions, irritating enough. But it's worse when, based on nothing but bias, these pundits go on a rant—dismissing an entire generation as dumb, narcissistic, distracted, violent, whatever. Youth and the Internet: it's the perfect combination for unfounded hostility.

It's as if the baby boomer pundits have become their own parents and have discovered the new sex, drugs, and rock and roll.

Summing up all these criticisms, there is a collective point of view that is fraught with contradictions. The boomers' children are supposed to be over-programmed, superstressed overachievers—but in the same breath they are described as slackers and moochers. Which is it? They have ADD and can't focus; yet at the same time they sit for hours in front of the screen, their eyes focused like a laser on a game or their social networking activities. They don't give a damn, but at the same time they want to change everything—from how their company is run to who's the president of the country. They are selfish, egomaniac control freaks but at the same time they but slavishly dependent on their parents. They are lost and confused, but their self-esteem and confidence has reached pathological levels of narcissism.

Give us a break!

Clearly something other than true research and rational thought is under-way.

No doubt Professor Bauerlein, as a lover of the English language, would know the meaning of the word *neologism*—a new word. Let me provide one: NGenophobia—the irrational and morbid fear of youth, especially with regards to their use of the Internet.

> (n) NGenophobia: eNet Gen-o-pho-bi-a (en-jen-uh-foh-bee-uh) (from Greek: ∫φόβος, *phobos,* "fear") Noun—the irrational and morbid fear of youth, espe-cially with regards to their use of the Internet. Origin, D. Tapscott, 2008: Fear (phobia) of the Net Generation (NGen). New in a family of anxiety disorders. As in "He's not really familiar with the Internet, which helps explain his NGenophobia." See NGenophobe (n). "She's a real NGenephobe who has never trusted kids." Or NGenophobic (adj). "Sometimes old-school managers become NGenophobic when the new young employees want to keep up with friends on Facebook at the office."

The real pathology emerging is not youth narcissism, stupidity, attention deficit disorder, or generational violence. It is NGenophobia.

A FORCE FOR CHANGE IN EVERY INSTITUTION

NGenophobia is a symptom of a looming generation gap, but one that is very different from the mile-wide fissure that cracked open between boomers and our parents on every front—from clothes and music to politics and values. As we've seen in this book, the Net Geners and their boomer parents seem to be coming together inside many families. Net Geners generally feel close to their parents as people; they even like their music. That's no surprise: it was the boomers who took the lead in democratizing the family to give their kids a say.

The Net Geners may not be challenging their parents as people, but they certainly are challenging the institutions the boomers are running. We saw them do it in the 2008 Democratic primary when they helped Obama grab victory from the established leader. This was the political version of the disruption that Net Geners have been causing in every world they enter, starting with the music business. Now that they're launching their careers, they're confronting the corporate hierarchy, an institution that's far more resistant to change than family structures were. No wonder this is where were seeing the most striking signs of a new generation clash.

I believe you'll see a generation clash in other worlds too, if the established authorities refuse to adapt to this new generation. After all, the Net Geners possess a tool of unprecedented power and are driving changes that could topple many established orders. As we have seen in this book, the new Web is distributing power and democratizing the economy. People no longer have to follow the leaders and do what they're told. Now they can organize themselves, publish themselves, inform themselves, and share with their friends—without waiting for an authority to instruct them. This has already had profound implications for the music business, and it will rock every other world that this generation enters.

Net Geners are already overturning the traditions of marketing. They are aggressive, demanding consumers who trust each other more than any expert, and certainly more than any ad. This is a profound challenge for old-media newspapers, broadcasters, and the companies that relied on those ads. It also presents a challenge for marketers who try to befriend kids on their social networking sites, often with disappointing results. It's already clear: the old rules of marketing don't work anymore for this generation.

In the corporate world, this generation is starting to shake up the world of management as well. The oldest Net Geners are turning 30 this year, and they're starting careers with expectations that many employers don't appreciate—especially when those expectations are driven home by hyperactive helicopter parents. But rather than shake their heads, employers should embrace the positive attributes of this generation as an opportunity to change in order to position themselves to compete and win in the twenty-first-century digital economy. The winners in this new world will be those who understand what collaboration means, and if they listen to the new generation of talent, they might find the way.

We have seen how the current Industrial Revolution model of education—where children are expected to sit still and listen to the teacher—is not appropriate for kids who have grown up digital and are used to interacting with people, not just listening. The old educational model might have been suitable for the Industrial Age, but it makes no sense for the new digital economy, or for the new generation of learners. The kids are right. We should change the education system to make it relevant to them. Teachers should stop lecturing. They should instead be mentors to young people who are using this marvelous tool to explore the world. Education should be customized to the individual student. And let them collaborate. That's how the world will be.

As they become politicized, the Net Generation will not settle for the traditional role of the voter, which involves putting in an appearance at the local voting booth and perhaps contributing some money, and then sitting quietly doing nothing until the next campaign two or four years away. Net Geners will want to be active in the work of government—not by making the decisions, but by contributing information that could help leaders make better decisions. Their digital tools will bring to the surface key information that will help that decision making—for example, information that connects a politician with financial sources and enables her or him to access them. If this generation succeeds, this will be a historic new wave of democracy.

None of this means that hierarchies will vanish completely. Society still needs authority and control in areas ranging from child rearing and executive decisions to law and order. But as the Net Generation grows in influence, the trend will be toward networks, not hierarchies, toward open collaboration rather than command, toward consensus rather than arbitrary rule, and toward enablement rather than control. As students, children and consumers, they are pressuring schools, families, and markets to change. As knowledge workers, educators, government leaders, entrepreneurs, and customers, they will be an unstoppable force for transformation.

In the past, many of these so-called postmodern concepts were ideas whose time had not come. They were ideas in waiting—for a new generation that could embrace and implement them.

NGenophobes: Fighting the Future

By gleefully attacking youth, the critics are fighting against the future. They say it's wrong to tell kids they can become anything they want or to follow their dreams. It might, Twenge suggests, "give kids the idea that the world is an ever-expanding, scarily large universe of possibilities."[17] If true, I plead guilty. I've said this a dozen times to my own kids and any other young person who will listen. Is it wrong to tell kids they should have a passion and follow their aspirations? I'm guessing trailer park boy Bill Clinton would say no. As would the countless other young people who set out to become president and, midcourse, adjusted to pursue another passion.

Sure, such advice should be coupled with counseling to be sensible and alternatives should be weighed in order that wise life choices are made. But why deny kids hope and the chance to dream? Can you see the conversation with your own 10-year-old daughter or niece? "Listen up. I know you want to be president of the United States, but that isn't going to happen because you don't have the IQ, money, or connections. Besides you're a girl and the odds are stacked against you."

The NGenophobes are fighting the future. When young people show confidence and want to be leaders, they are labeled as the entitlement generation. When students press for a new model of pedagogy, the old-line professors say their lectures are fascinating, and kids should just pay attention. The NGenophobes don't want a new generation to think that they can have power, innovate, and change the course of things. They want children to stay in their place.

Perhaps they will be successful in demoralizing and crushing the spirit of a generation. But I think not.

WILL WE LET THIS GENERATION RESHAPE THE WORLD?

Will the Net Generation be good for us? There are risks in letting go. The tool at their fingertips can be anything they want it to be. Unlike the old broadcast media or newspapers, which reflected the values of their powerful owners, this new media displays awesome neutrality. It will do what we command. Some young people will demand peace and social justice; others will use it to commit acts of unspeakable evil. Obviously there are all kinds of people in this generation. Online games, for instance, are used for recruiting neo-Nazis. White supremacists are besmirching the reputation of genuine heroes like Dr. Martin Luther King Jr. Al Qaeda is using the Internet to induce teenagers to blow themselves up, and kill many others in the process.

But we need to remember that in this world, there appears to be more good than bad.

As we enter the new age, the future won't just happen. It will be created—and primarily by them. Whether they become an entrepreneur like Mark Zuckerberg, raise money for mental health research like Niki and her friend Joanna, change their communities like the Davos Six, organize youth around the world like Michael Furdyk and Jennifer Correiro, build networks to stop global warming like Kelly Cox, fight genocide in Darfur like U.S. college students, or join a political campaign like millions of American Net Geners did in 2008, they are becoming an unprecedented force for change.

Through their massive demographic muscle and unconstrained minds, they are creating a new world. Unlike the tepid, sterilized one-way conduit of the mass media, the place they are constructing gives any idea, no matter how threatening to the contemporary order, a voice. They are using the Web and their social networks to discover and collaborate. For better or for worse, the biggest generation in American history is beginning to use its medium to discover, debate, and take action.

The second half of the twentieth century was dominated by a generation—the baby boomers. During that period, strong models of mass media, the enterprise, work, commerce, family, play, and social life were established. The new Web and the new generation are beginning to shatter these old ways—and our evidence points to a better world, if we permit them to succeed. This massive wave of youth has rights, growing aspirations, truly awesome capabilities, and nascent demands that are far-reaching.

If *Growing Up Digital* got anything right, it was the assertion that this generation will change the world. They are already bringing and implementing radical views regarding the way business should be conducted and about the process of democratic governance. They are a generation that can learn together, as a unified generation, unlike any other. They are seeking to protect the planet and they find racism, sexism, and other vile remnants of bygone days to be both weird and unacceptable. They will seek to share in the wealth they create. They will want power in every domain of economic and political life.

The big remaining question for older generations is whether that power will be shared with gratitude—or whether we will stall until a new generation grabs it from us. Will we have the wisdom and courage to accept them, their culture, and their media? Will we be effective in offering our experience to help them manage the dark side? Will we grant them the opportunity to fulfill their destiny? I think this will be a better world if we do.

LEADERSHIP 2.0: SEVEN GUIDELINES FOR A NEW GENERATION

I have a few final words of advice for Net Geners:

1. **Go to college.** It's way more interesting than high school, and you'll need more than a high school diploma to succeed in a knowledge economy. Besides, you'll need to continue to learn throughout the course of your life anyway. Read books of fiction and you will be enriched. Hone your writing skills, and your grammar. And don't use netspeak or slang at school or at work. It doesn't belong there.

2. **Be patient at work**—especially when you see old, outdated technology and bureaucratic ways of doing things. Instead of bolting right away, hang around for a while and fight for change. You're worth it: your knowledge about collaboration will drive innovation and success this century. Boomers might be your best allies. They have kids like you and are more likely to understand you and your use of technology. And you're right about the idea of the work–life dichotomy. It shouldn't be an oxymoron.

3. **Don't buy bad products.** Make companies act with integrity. You have the power to scrutinize companies and organize collective responses. You can strip them naked, and this is good for them, and for everyone. You'll force corporations to get buff.

4. **Bring back the family dinner.** This is a great place to talk to your kids about values. You might even make a social contract with your kids in order to protect their online safety and privacy, and to ensure that they have balance. They'll stay away from unsafe or inappropriate activities, and you will promise not to spy on them, or hover over them. Helicopters should be a mode of transportation, not a modus operandi for parenting.

5. **Don't discount experience.** You are an authority on something important—but you're not an authority on everything. As you enter adult institutions, you have much to teach, but much to learn. If it doesn't work out, your experience will make you a better entrepreneur, activist, teacher, or whatever you chose.

6. **Aspire to live "a principled life of consequence."**[18] You have one life—make it count. You're right to say that money isn't everything. By all means aspire to be prosperous. But the future needs more from you. Think about the world your kids will inherit and do what you can to make it a better one. Work in your community. Get engaged politically. Do the right thing.

7. **Don't give up.** When adults criticize your generation, don't take it personally. You are the smartest generation—really. You are the first global generation. You have a better world within your grasp. Reach out; hold on; make it happen.

APPENDIX

FIGURE A.1   NET GENERS' RESPONSE TO THE QUESTION:
COMPARED TO ALL HOUSEHOLDS IN YOUR
COUNTRY IN 2006, WHAT DO YOU THINK YOUR
FAMILY'S INCOME WAS?

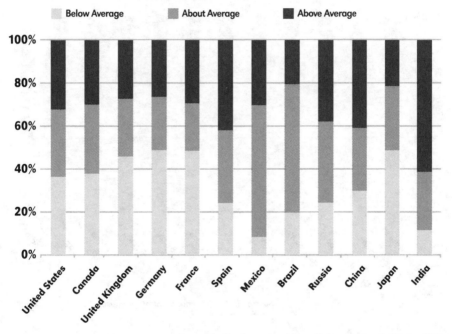

Source: The Net Generation: A Strategic Investigation, © nGenera, 2008

FIGURE A.2   NET GENERS' RESPONSE TO THE QUESTION: WHICH WOULD YOU RATHER DO: SPEND TIME WITH FAMILY OR SPEND TIME WITH YOUR FRIENDS?

Spending time with family takes precedence for most Net Geners, except in Central Europe and Japan, where they prefer to spend time with family and time with friends almost equally.

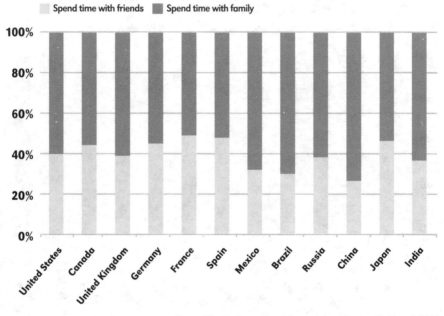

Source: The Net Generation: A Strategic Investigation, © nGenera, 2008

**FIGURE A.3   PERCENTAGE OF NET GENERS WHO VISITED
MULTIPLAYER GAMING OR ONLINE VIRTUAL
WORLD SITES IN THE PAST MONTH**

More Indian and Chinese Net Geners visit MMOG* and virtual world
sites than other Net Geners.

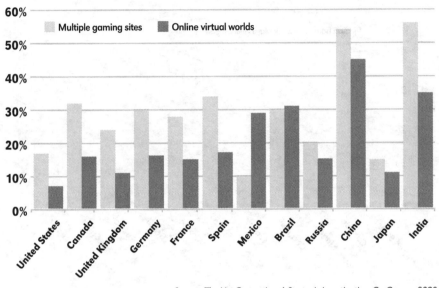

Source: The Net Generation: A Strategic Investigation, © nGenera, 2008

*Massively multiplayer online games.

FIGURE A.4   NET GENERS' RESPONSE TO THE QUESTION:
             HOW MANY HOURS DO YOU SPEND PLAYING
             VIDEO GAMES PER WEEK?

Chinese and Indian Net Geners report playing video games about
two hours a week more than other Net Geners.

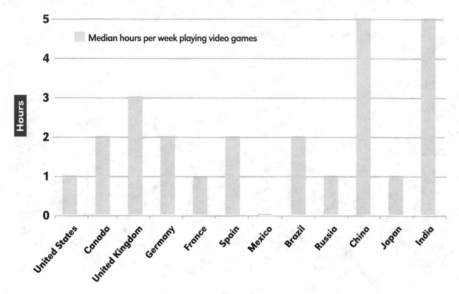

Source: The Net Generation: A Strategic Investigation, © nGenera, 2008

**FIGURE A.5   PERCENTAGE OF NET GENERS PER COUNTRY
                        WHO LISTENED TO MUSIC ON MOBILE PHONES IN
                        THE PAST MONTH**

Net Geners from the East are far more likely to listen to music on a
mobile/cell phone compared to North American Net Geners.

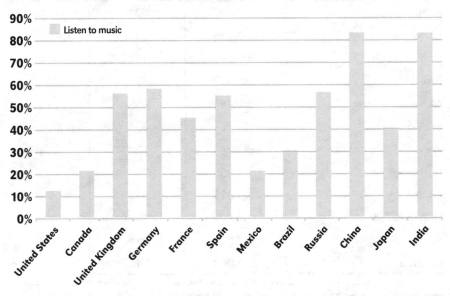

Source: The Net Generation: A Strategic Investigation, © nGenera, 2008

TABLE A.1   THE NET GENERATION IS A GLOBAL FORCE[1]

Country	Population under 25 in 2005 (thousands)	Percentage of total population under 25	Growth in under-25 population since 1980
India	593,293	52%	46%
China	501,558	38%	−9%
United States	105,246	35%	11%
Brazil	87,437	47%	22%
Mexico	50,986	49%	14%
Russia	46,209	32%	−15%
Japan	31,846	25%	−27%
Germany	21,655	26%	−20%
France	19,029	31%	−7%
United Kingdom	18,676	31%	−10%
Spain	11,500	27%	−27%
Canada	10,004	31%	−4%

Source: U.N. Department of Economic and Social Affairs, Population Division

[1]Population Division of the Department of Economic and Social Affairs of the United Nations Secretariat.
World Population Prospects: The 2006 Revision and World Urbanization Prospects: The 2005 Revision;
http://esa.un.org/unpp.

NOTES

INTRODUCTION

1. Mark Bauerlein, *The Dumbest Generation: How The Digital Age Stupefies Young Americans and Jeopardizes Our Future*, New York: Penguin/Tarcher, 2001, 26.
2. Robert Bly, *The Sibling Society*, New York: Vintage, 1997, 60.
3. Megan K. Scott, "Parents Turn the Miley Moment into a Teachable One," Associated Press, April 29, 2008.
4. William Damon, *The Path to Purpose: Helping Our Children Find Their Calling in Life*, New York: Free Press, 2008.
5. Ibid., Damon, *The Path to Purpose*, 3.
6. Charles McGrath, "Growing Up for Dummies," *New York Times*, April 20, 2008.
7. Bauerlein, *The Dumbest Generation*, 201.

CHAPTER 1

1. Inspired by John Geraci et al., "Meet the Net Generation," nGen Big Idea, December 2006, nGenera, www.ngenera.com.
2. David Foot, *Boom, Bust, Echo: How to Profit from the Coming Demographic Shift*, 1st ed., Toronto: Macfarlane Walter Ross, 1996, 19.
3. "The Statistical Abstract of the United States," Bureau of the Census, U.S. Department of Commerce (various years).
4. Ibid., inspired by Geraci et al., "Meet the Net Generation."
5. "Families by Presence of Own Children Under 18: 1950 to Present," Demographic characteristics of Households and Families, U.S. Census Bureau, www.census.gov.
6. Peter Stoler, *The Computer Generation*, 1st ed., New York: Facts on File, 1984, 8.
7. "Internet Access in U.S. Public Schools and Classrooms: 1994–2005," U.S. Department of Education, National Center for Education Statistics (NCES 2007–020), 2007.
8. Alex Williams, " 'But I Neeeeeed It!' She Suggested," *New York Times*, May 29, 2005, www.nytimes.com.
9. "Reports: Family, Friends and Community. Teenage Life Online: The Rise of the Instant-Message Generation and the Internet's Impact on Friendships and Family Relationships," Pew Report, June 21, 2001.
10. Taylor Humphrey, "More than One-Third of Internet Users Now Have Broadband," *Harris Poll* #3, January 14, 2004.
11. Don Tapscott, *Growing Up Digital*, 1st ed., New York: McGraw-Hill, 1997, 39.
12. Ibid. *Growing Up Digital*, p. 255.

13. "BBM Neilson Meters," Neilson Net Ratings, www.bbm.ca.

14. Tapscott, *Growing Up Digital*, 255.

15. "World Internet Statistics," Miniwatts MarketingGroup, www.internetworldstats.com.

16. Jennifer Topiel, "College Board Announced Advanced Placement Result: A Greater Percentage of the Nation's Students Succeed on AP Exams, Predictors of Success in College Report Points to the Need for Better Preparation in Earlier Grades," Press Release, The College Board, February 13, 2008.

17. Debra Viadero, "Nature x Nurture = Startling Jump in IQs," *Education Week*, vol. 21, no. 19, January 23, 2002.

18. Ibid., 12.

19. Anne Tergesen, "What Price College Admission?" *BusinessWeek*, June 19, 2006, 82.

20. "'Helicopter Parents' Land in the Workplace," *Trends*, May 2006.

21. Mike Myer, "COOL Solutions: Say Hi to Y," Filene Research Institute, 2005.

22. Jacqueline L. Salmon, "Firm Support for Stricter Upbringing: Disciplinarians' Advice Finds Parental Favor," *Washington Post*, Metro, November 24, 1996, B01.

23. Jane Kwiatkowski, "Armed Teens Hold Death in Their Sights," *Buffalo News*, June 4, 1996, nl.newsbank.com.

24. Judy Sheindlin, a judge on the juvenile bench in New York City for 24 years said: "You're dealing with a population of kids who have been deprived of their childhood. They don't think of themselves as growing old. They are out for immediate gratification."

25. Tapscott, *Growing Up Digital*, ch. 13.

26. Neil Howe and William Strauss, Millennials Go to College: Strategies for a New Generation on Campus, Washington, D.C.: American Association of Collegiate Registrars, 2003, 23.

27. Ibid., 15–17.

28. Ibid.

29. "The Monitoring the Future Study," Press Release, University of Michigan, December 11, 2007, www.monitoringthefuture.org.

30. John Geraci, Presentation at Boston Net Gen Meeting, YouthPulse, 2007.

31. Roberto R. Ramirez, "Analysis of Multiple Origin Reporting to the Hispanic Origin Question in Census 2000," U.S. Census Bureau: Population Division, working paper no. 77, November 21, 2005, www.census.gov.

32. "Guess Who's Coming to Dinner," Pew Research Center, March 14, 2006.

33. Jon Stewart's address is at www.wm.edu.

34. Don Tapscott and David Ticoll, *The Naked Corporation: How the Age of Transparency Will Revolutionize Business*, New York: Free Press, 2003, 22.

35. Lora Kolodny, "Global Video Game Market Set to Explode," *BusinessWeek*, June 23, 2006.

36. Marshall McLuhan and Quentin Fiore, *The Medium Is the Massage: An Inventory of Effects*, Corte Madera, Calif.: Gingko Press, 1996, 76, 78.

CHAPTER 2

1. "BBM Neilson Meters," Neilson Net Ratings, www.bbm.ca.

2. In Canada, teens 12–17 watched 22.4 hours of TV a week in 1967–68, but only 17.4 hours a week in 2007–08, according to BBM Diaries and 2008 BBM Nielsen Meters. However, in the United States a different picture emerges from a Mindshare analysis of Nielsen data. It shows that teens' TV viewing has increased—from just under 19 hours in 1966–67 to nearly 23 hours a week in 2007–08. It's not clear why the Canadian and American TV viewing statistics differ so markedly. But one way or another, TV has become a background activity while Net Geners talk on the phone or go online. It is clear that youth today are doing a lot less passive watching and a lot more interacting.

3. "NACTAS 2006 Benchmark Survey," North American Consumer Technographics, Forrester, February 2006, www.forrester.com (accessed May 20, 2008). (N—66,707) This survey found that Net Geners aged 18–26 spent 12.2 hours a week online, but 10.6 hours watching TV. Boomers aged 41–50 spent 7.7 hours online and 12.1 hours watching TV.

4. Stephen Abram and Chris Pulleyn, "Just Hitting the Surf: Millennials in the Information Age," SirsiDynix and Buck & Pulleyn, April 19, 2006.

5. Sam Diaz, "Teen Cell Phone Usage Soars in Summer," *Washington Post*, July 2, 2007, blog.washingtonpost.com.

6. Toni Fitzgerald, "For Teens, Grammys Are about Dipping," *Media Life*, Februay 15, 2008, www.medialifemagazine.com.

7. John Geraci and Lisa Chen, "Meet the Global Net Generation," Syndicated Research Project, nGenera, July 2007.

8. Vivian Vahlber et al., "If It Catches My Eye: An Exploration of Online New Experiences of Teenagers," Media Management Center, Kellogg School of Management, January 2008, www.mediamanagementcenter.org.

9. Amanda Lenhart et al., "Teens and Social Media: The use of social media gains a greater foothold in teen life as they embrace the conversational nature of interactive online media," Family, Friends and Community Report, Pew Internet & American Life Project, December 19, 2007, www.pewinternet.org.

10. Amanda Lenhart, et al., "Teens and Social Media," Special Report, Pew Internet and American Life Project, December 19,2007, www.pewinternet.org.

11. Don Tapscott and Anthony D. Williams, *Wikinomics: Harnessing the Power of Mass Collaboration*, New York: Portfolio, 2006.

12. "Aricent Survey: Safety Trumps Fun When Kids Receive Mobile Phones as Holidays Gifts," Business Wire, December 20, 2007.

13. Mike Dover, Nikki Papadopoulos, and Karoline Kibis, "The Net Generation: Key Findings from the Qualitative Study 'My Internet Life,'" Syndicated Research Project, nGenera, July 2007.

14. While I don't doubt Context's findings, I do doubt that they are exclusive to teens and young adults. Once in late 2007, and again in early 2008, the BlackBerry North American network shut down for a few hours, and I saw business people of all age groups act as if their link to the world had been severed. I saw these results mirrored in my own research.

15. Don Tapscott and Anthony D. Williams, *Wikinomics: Harnessing the Power of Mass Collaboration*, New York: Portfolio, 2006.

16. "ICTs in Africa: Digital Divide to Digital Opportunity," International Telecommunications Union, March 18, 2008, www.itu.int.

17. Olga Kharif, "Asia's U.S. Wireless Foray: Asia's Wireless Operators Are Looking to the U.S. Market. Their experience in mobile data services could pay off stateside," BusinessWeek.com, December 11, 2007.

18. Onishi Norimitsu, "Thumbs Race as Japan's Best Sellers Go Cellular," *New York Times*, January 20, 2008.

19. Dimitrios Matsoulis, "Japanese Cellphone Novels Become Best Sellers!" WordPress.com, *wordpress.com/tag/cellphone-novel/* (accessed April 24, 2008).

20. Ibid., 18.

21. "DFC Intelligence Forcasts Video Game Market to Reach $44 Billion by 2011," *Business Wire*, Sept 26, 2006, www.businesswire.com.

22. "Casio Introduces Two Stylish New Exilim Digital Cameras with YouTube Capture Mode," Press Release, Casio, July 10, 2007, www.casio.com.

23. The winner of the nGenera Photo contest, www.takingitglobal.org (accessed April 25, 2008).

24. "Learn to Dance like the Stars!" Kreeda.com, *dancemela.kreeda.com* (accessed April 24, 2008).

25. "OurStage Announces Strategic Partnership with AOL Music," Business Wire, March 5, 2008, www.businesswire.com.

26. "Our Vision," OurStage.com, www.ourstage.com.

27. "Without Tomorrow," MySpace.com, May 30th, 2008.

28. "Colombians in huge FARC protest," BBC, February 4, 2008, news.bbc.co.uk.

29. Ralph Gross and Alessando Acquisti, "Information Revelation and Privacy in Online Social Networks," Conference Presentation, Carnegie Mellon University, November 7, 2005, www.heinz.cmu.edu.

30. Ida Berstrom, "Facebook Can Ruin Your Life: And So Can MySpace, Bebo . . ." *The Independent*, February 10, 2008, www.independent.co.uk.

31. Facebook, as of May 2008, www.facebook.com.

32. Adrienne Felt and David Evans, "Privacy Protection for Social Networking APIs," University of Virginia, April 24, 2008, www.cs.virginia.edu.

33. "Road Map for Memories for Life Research," Memories for Life, April 24, 2008, www.memoriesforlife.org.

CHAPTER 3

1. "Talent 2.0—Big Idea Paper," Syndicated Research Project, nGenera, 2008.

2. "The Net Generation: A Strategic Investigation," Syndicated Research Project, nGenera, 2008 (survey of 1,750 respondents aged 13–29, September–October 2006).

3. Tamina Vahidy, "Best Commuter Workplaces," *Line 56*, October 20, 2006.

4. Frank Giancola, "Flexible Schedules: A Win-Win Reward," *Workspan*, July 10, 2005, www.worldatwork.org.

5. Michelle Conlin, "Smashing the Clock," *BusinessWeek*, December 11, 2006.

6. Bill Ward, "Power to the People," *Minneapolis Star Tribune*, June 2, 2008.

7. "The Net Generation: A Strategic Investigation," Syndicated Research Project, nGenera, 2008 (survey of 1,750 respondents aged 13–29, September-October 2006).

8. Ibid.

9. Lillie Guyer, "Scion Connects in Out of Way Places: Toyota reaches out to Gen Y drivers without screaming, 'Buy this car!'" *Advertising Age*, February 21, 2005, adage.com.

10. "The Net Generation: A Strategic Investigation," Syndicated Research Project, nGenera, 2008 (survey of 1,750 respondents aged 13–29, September-October 2006).

11. Almost two-thirds of Net Geners tell us they search for information about products that interest them before purchase. They compare and contrast product information online; they read blogs, forums, and reviews; and they consult friends. In the digital world, it's easy to be a smart shopper. Those at the top of the technology-adoption curve were the most demanding: our survey found that 69 percent of the Bleeding Edge or first adopters said they "wouldn't buy a product unless it has the exact features I want." This number slowly dropped as one went down the technology scale, reaching a level of 46 percent for Luddites.

    Almost two-thirds of Net Geners say they take the time to find the lowest price, which isn't surprising, since many work for minimum wage or a limited salary. They want value without jeopardizing quality. Interestingly, most Net Geners are dubious about online reviews, thinking many are the product of disgruntled buyers. "People who write reviews are those who are really bitter about stupid little things," a 22-year-old woman told our researchers. Only 15 percent of Net Geners as a whole agreed with the statement; however, when we study the statement, "I frequently write online reviews for products I have bought," the number jumps to 42 percent of those atop the technology-adoption pyramid.

12. "Campaign for Real Beauty," Internally computed numbers, Dove, www.youtube.com, April 30, 2008. Number of views tabulated on April 30, 2008, includes multiple copies of identical videos posted to YouTube; includes only videos with more than 100,000 views.

13. "The Net Generation: A Strategic Investigation," Syndicated Research Project, nGenera, 2008 (survey of 1,750 respondents aged 13–29, September–October 2006).

14. Ibid.

15. U.S. Patent No. 6820062 (issued Nov. 16, 2004).

16. Don Tapscott and David Ticoll, *The Naked Corporation: How the Age of Transparency Will Revolutionize Business*, New York: Free Press, 2003.

17. Jean Twenge, *Generation Me: Why Young Americans Are More Confident, Assertive, Entitled- and More Miserable Than Ever Before*, New York: Free Press, 2006, 136.

18. Ibid., 223.

19. Jean Twenge, "Egos Inflating over Time: A Cross-Temporal Meta-Analysis of the Narcissistic Personality Inventory," *Journal of Personality*, no. 94, 2008.

20. Kali H. Trzesniewski et al., "Do Today's Young People Really Think They are So Extraordinary? An Examination of Secular Trends in Narcissism and Self-Enhancement," Psycholooical Science, vol. 2, no. 19, Feb 2008, 181–188, http://lib.bioinfo.pl/pmid:18271867. (University of Western Ontario psychologist Kali H. Trzesniewski led a study of 26,000 students at the University of California from the early 1980s to today. She found no evidence of an increase in narcissism. What's more, when she looked at a far bigger group—over 400,000 high school students—she found no evidence over the past 30 years that they are more narcissistic either.)

21. Brent Donnellan and Kali H. Trzesniewski, "How Should We Study Generational 'Changes'—or Should We? A Critical Examination of the Evidence for 'Generation Me,'" unpublished.

22. "Fewer High School Students Engage in Health Risk Behaviors; Racial and Ethnic Differences Persist," Press Release, Center for Disease Control and Prevention, June 2005, www.cdc.gov.

23. "The Net Generation: A Strategic Investigation," Syndicated Research Project, nGenera, 2008 (survey of 1,750 respondents aged 13–29, September–October 2006).

24. Ibid.

25. Ibid.

26. David Richards, "Free Illegal Music Beats iTunes," SmartHouse, November 30, 2005, www.smarthouse.com.au.

27. "The Net Generation: A Strategic Investigation," Syndicated Research Project, nGenera, 2008 (survey of 1,750 respondents aged 13–29, September-October 2006).

28. Mary Madden and Amanda Lenhart, "Pew Internet Project Data Memo," Report, Pew Internet and American Life Project, July 31, 2003.

29. Frank Rose, "And Now, a Word from Our Customers," *Wired,* vol. 14, no. 12, December 2006, www.wired.com.

30. "The Net Generation: A Strategic Investigation," Syndicated Research Project, nGenera, 2008 (survey of 1,750 respondents aged 13–29, September–October 2006).

31. Alvin Toffler, *Future Shock*, New York: Bantam Books, 1971.

32. Don Tapscott, *The Digital Economy: Promise and Peril in the Age of Networked Intelligence*, New York: McGraw-Hill, 1995.

33. Lee Rainie, "Digital 'Natives' Invade the Workplace: Young people may be newcomers to the world of work, but it's their bosses who are immigrants into the digital world," Internet Survey, Pew Internet and American Life Project, September 27, 2006, www.pewinternet.org.

34. "The Net Generation: A Strategic Investigation," Syndicated Research Project, nGenera, 2008 (survey of 1,750 respondents aged 13–29, September–October 2006).

35. Ibid.

36. Steve Hamm and Ian Rowley, "Speed Demons," *BusinessWeek*, March 27, 2006.

37. Jena McGregor, "The World's Most Innovative Companies," *BusinessWeek*, April 24, 2006.

CHAPTER 4

1. C. Shawn Green and Daphne Bavelier, "Action Video Games Modify Visual Attention," *Nature*, vol. 423, 2003, 534–37.

2. Norman Doidge, M.D., *The Brain That Changes Itself*, New York: Viking Adult, 2007, xiii.

3. Ibid., xiv.

4. Thomas Elbert et al., "Increased Cortical Representation of the Fingers of the Left Hand in String Players," *Science*, New Series, vol. 270, no. 5234, October. 13, 1995, 305–7.

5. Stan and Matthew Kutcher, "Understanding Differences of a Cognitive and Neurological Kind: Digital Technology and Human Brain Development," Syndicated Research Project, nGenera, June 2007.

6. Sharon Begley, "Survival of the Busiest: Parts of the Brain That Get Most Use Literally Expand and Rewire on Demand," *Wall Street Journal*, October 11, 2002, B1.

7. Kutcher and Kutcher, "Understanding Differences of a Cognitive and Neurological Kind," 4.

8. Marc Prensky, *Digital Game-Based Learning*, 1st ed., New York: McGraw-Hill, 2000.

9. Jay N. Giedd et al., "Brain Development during Childhood and Adolescence: A Longitudinal MRI Study," *Nature Neuroscience*, vol. 2, 1999, 861–63, www.nature.com.

10. Miranda Hitti and Louise Chang, M.D., "Teen Brain: It's All About Me," WebMD Medical News, May 5, 2008, www.ivorweiner.com.

11. J. C. Rosser et al., "The Impact of Video Games on Training Surgeons in the 21st Century," *Archives of Surgery*, vol. 142, 2007, 181–86, digiplay.info.

12. Patricia Marks Greenfield et al., "Action Video Games and Informal Education: Effects on Strategies for Dividing Visual Attention," *Journal of Applied Developmental Psychology*, vol. 15, 1994, 105–23, h.

13. Prensky, *Digital Game Based Learning*.

14. Steven Johnson, *Everything Bad Is Good for You*, New York: Riverhead, 2005.

15. James Paul Gee, *What Video Games Have to Teach Us about Learning and Literacy*, 1st ed., New York: Palgrave Macmillan, 2003.

16. Hesham M. Mesbah, "The Impact of Linear vs. Non-linear Listening to Radio News on Recall and Comprehension," *Journal of Radio and Audio Media*, vol. 13, no. 2, December 2006, 187–200, www.leaonline.com.

17. Wendy Sutherland-Smith, "Weaving the Literacy Web: Changes in Reading from Page to Screen," *The Reading Teacher*, vol. 55, no. 7, April 2002, 662. ("The Internet provides opportunities to extend thinking skills beyond the hierarchical,

linear sequential model that serves so well in the world of the print text.")
tapor.ualberta.ca.

18. Prensky, *Digital Game Based Learning*.

19. See note 8, on page 325.

20. Wim Veen and Ben Vrakking, *Homo Zappiens: GrowingUp in a Digital Age*,
    London: Network Continuum Education, 2007.

21. Robert J. Sternberg and David Preiss, eds., *Intelligence and Technology*, Florence,
    Ky.: Routledge, 2005, 41.

22. Dave Roos, "How Net Generation Students Learn and Work," Howstuffworks,
    May 5, 2008, communication.howstuffworks.com .

23. Ibid.

24. Donald F. Roberts et al., "Generation M: Media in the Lives of 8–18 Year-Olds,"
    Kaiser Family Foundation Study, March 2005, www.kff.org.

25. "Screenagers," Netlingo, www.netlingo.com.

26. Tom Alderman, "Welcome to the ADD Generation," The Huffington Post, May 5,
    2008, www.huffingtonpost.com.

27. Sarah Scott, "The Myth of Multitasking," *Chatelaine*, 2006, scottreports.com.

28. "Too Many Interruptions is Like a Kick in the Head," Oxford Research &
    IIIP Research Roadmap, 2007, http://www.iii-p.org.

29. Prensky, *Digital Game Based Learning*

30. "Lord Hansard's Text for 20 April 2006," Lords Publications, June 25, 2008,
    www.parliment.uk.

31. While a 2007 survey in the United States (To Read or Not to Read, NEA Research
    Report no. 47) points to a steep decline in the percentage of teens who read literature,
    Net Geners who do read tend to read novels, like J. K. Rowling's Harry Potter series,
    which, as of April 2007, had sold an astounding 400 million copies around the world.

32. Steven Johnson, "Dome Improvement," *Wired*, vol. 5, no. 13, May 2005,
    www.wired.com/wired/archive/13.05/flynn.html. Clancy Blair et al., "Rising Mean
    IQ: Cognitive Demand of Mathematics Education for Young Children, Population
    Exposure to Formal Schooling and the Neurobiology of the Prefrontal Cortex,"
    Intelligence, vol. 33, no. 1, January–February 2005, 93–106, www.sciencedirect.com.
    (This graph is created using the rates of increase of raw scores discovered by Flynn
    and later confirmed by the scientific community. It uses a slightly different rate for the
    1990s based on recent data revealing the rates' increase during that decade. It is set at
    100 for 1970 to emphasize the difference between the raw scores of those in 1970
    and 2000. It should also be noted that these scores are estimated raw scores, as the IQ
    test is normalized every year and the actual statistical average has been, and will
    always be, 100.).

33. Roberts, "Generation M," (Young people read 48 minutes online, use a computer
    online, and spend 43 minutes offline (books, magazines, newspapers) every day.).

34. Elizabeth Schmar-Dobler, "Reading on the Internet: The Link between Literacy
    and Technology," *Journal of Adolescent and Adult Literacy*, September 2003,
    www.readingonline.org.

35. Catherine E. Snow and RAND Reading Study Group, *Reading for
    Understanding: Toward an R&D Program in Reading Comprehension*,
    RAND Corporation, 2002.

36. Donald J. Leu et al., "Evaluating the Development of Scientific Knowledge and New Forms of Reading.Comprehension during Online Learning," Exploratory Research, New Literacies Research Team, June 28, 2005.

37. "Total Group Profile Report: Total Group," Report of All College-Bound Seniors, The College Board, 2007. This chart was created from The College Board data on combined scores to show the trends for the past 30 years.

38. Kutcher and Kutcher, 5.

39. Henry Jenkins, "Confronting the Challenges of Participatory Culture: Media Education for the 21st century," Internal White Paper, The John D. and Catherine T. MacArthur Foundation, www.projectnml.org.

40. Patricia Cohen, *Dumb and Dumber: Are Americans Hostile to Knowledge?" New York Times*, February 14, 2008.

41. Steven Johnson, *Everything Bad Is Good for You*, New York: Riverhead, 2005. "Think of the cognitive labor—and play—that your average 10-year-old would have experienced outside school 100 years ago: reading books when they were available, playing with simple toys, improvising neighborhood games like stickball an kick the can, and most of all doing household chores—or even working as a child laborer. Compare that with the cultural and technological mastery of a 10-year-old today: following dozens of professional sports teams; shifting effortlessly from phone to IM to e-mail in communicating with friends; probing and telescoping through immense virtual worlds; adopting and troubleshooting new media technologies without flinching."

42. NCES, "NAEP 2004 Trends in Academic Progress: Three Decades of Student Performance in Reading and Mathematics," Statistical Analysis Report no. 2005463, National Center for Educational Statistics, December 21, 2005, nces.ed.gov/nationsreportcard/ltt/results2004/. (The National Assessment of Educational Progress (NAEP) reports that children in grades four and eight have improved significantly in math and posted slight gains in reading since the early 1970s. Seniors' performance didn't change much overall. In reading, Bauerlein reports that a larger percentage of seniors scored "below basic" [27 percent in 2005 compared with 20 percent in 1992], but he also says seniors' reading comprehension scores haven't budged.)

43. Bauerlein, *The Dumbest Generation*, 36.

CHAPTER 5

1. "Educational Attainment in the United States: Table 8," U.S. Bureau of the Census Tabulation, 2005, www.census.gov. The earning power of high school dropouts has declined over the past three decades. Male dropouts earned an average of $35,087 in 1971 (adjusted for 2005 dollars), but their earnings declined by 39 percent to $21,393 by 2005.

2. "Percentage of Persons Age 25 and Over and 25 to 29, by Race/Ethnicity, Years of School Completed, and Sex: Selected Years, 1910 through 2005: Table 8," Digest of Education Statistics 2005, National Center for Educational Statistics, nces.ed.gov. The percentage of 25- to 29-year-olds who had completed college rose from 16.4 percent in 1970 to 28.6 percent in 2005. "Enrollment Rates of 18- to 24-Year-Olds in Degree-Granting Institutions, by Sex and

Race/Ethnicity: 1967 through 2006: Table 195," Digest of Educational Statistics 2007, National Center for Educational Statistics, nces.ed.gov. College enrolment rates for 18- to 24-year-olds rose from 25.7 percent in 1980 to 37.3 percent in 2006.

"Number and Percent Change of Students Taking Advanced Placement (AP) Examinations, by Race/Ethnicity: 1999–2005, Table 13a."

Status and Trends in the Education of Racial and Ethnic Minorities, National Center for Educational Statistics, NCES 2007 039, September 2007, nces.ed.gov. The number of students taking AP exams increased by 75 percent between 1999 and 2005.

3. "Measuring Up 2006: National Report Card on Higher Education," National Center for Public Policy and Higher Education, www.measuringup.highereducation.org.

4. Neil Howe and William Strauss, *Millennials Go to College: Strategies for a New Generation on Campus*, Washington, D.C.: American Association of Collegiate Registrars, 2003.

5. Ibid. (Chartwell's 2006 College Student Survey released by LifeCourse Associates and Crux Research).

6. "NCHEMS Information Center," HigherEdInfo.org Graduation Rates, www.higheredinfo.org.

Given the state of education in many colleges and universities, students question whether it's worth it:

Affordability: In 2004, the average cost of tuition at public universities increased four times the rate of inflation, rising 11 percent over a one year period. This information is often not clear to students when they enroll in college.

Quality of education: Undergraduate education often is at the bottom of the priority totem pole at top research schools; professors are focusing on their own research. Plagiarism and grade inflation are common; students are not truly held accountable for learning.

Innovation: There are plenty of opportunities to embrace new teaching methods that are good for lifelong learning, but not enough universities and colleges have embraced them.

The result: Although two out of three new jobs in the U.S. require a college degree, employers don't think today's graduates are properly prepared. Over the past decade, literacy among college graduates has actually declined.

7. Paul Barton, "One Third of a Nation: Rising Dropout Rates and Declining Opportunities," Policy Information Report, Educational Testing Service, February 2005, www.ets.org, The graduation rate is also described in Christopher B. Swanson, *Who Graduates? Who Doesn't? A Statistical Portrait of Public High School Graduation, Class of 2001*, Washington, D.C., 2004. These graduation rates are widely referenced by experts, such as John Bridgeland, John DiIulio, and Karen Burke Morison, authors of the 2006 report, The Silent Epidemic: Perspectives of High School Dropouts. They note that there are many ways to calculate graduation and dropout rates, so there are many different statistics. They also note that official graduation rates reported by the states and the federal government are believed to be too optimistic.

8. This topic is intensely controversial. Policy makers and number crunchers are debating how many Americans graduate from high school, and whether that

number is going up, or down. One issue is how to count the dropouts who are given makeup GED diplomas, which according to some experts do not show they have the academic skills of a high school grad. According to James Heckman and Paul LaFontaine, authors of a report for the National Bureau of Economic Research, the GEDs have inflated graduation rates by over 8 percentage points. The real story, they say, is that high school graduation is declining.

9. Numbers taken from the National Center for Educational Statistics and extrapolated for the years 2006 and 2008 based on rate of increase from 1978 to 2004.

10. Only 9 percent of American 15-year-olds joined the top students in science achievement, while 24 percent were at the bottom. Countries like high-performing Finland had little variance in the distribution of their student's scores, while the U.S. was in the top three countries showing the greatest variation of scores based on student background factors like socioeconomic status.

11. Basmat Parsad and Laurie Lewis, "Remedial Education At Degree-Granting Postsecondary Institutions in Fall 2000: Table 4," Statistical Analysis Report, National Center for Education Statistics, NCES 2004010, November 28, 2003, nces.ed.gov.

12. "Consider the perspective offered by American political philosopher John Rawls, in his renowned book, *A Theory of Justice*," Marx said. "Rawls proposes that we support only that society we would want if you and I were to enter it behind a "veil of ignorance"-unaware of our own gender, race, heritage, economic status, or even of whether we bear any disability. Rawls envisions a society wherein the accident of birth does not limit that society's capacity to benefit from what each of us has to offer. We must be satisfied only with a society in which any one of us might begin with that advantage."

13. Christopher B. Swanson, Ph.D., "Cities in Crisis: A Special Analytical Report on High School Education," Education Research Center, April 1, 2008.

14. Ibid., Swanson, "Cities in Crisis."

15. The first Gutenberg printing press was assembled in 1439.

16. Robert C. Pianta et al., "Opportunities to Learn in America's Elementary Classrooms," *Science*, vol. 315, no. 5820, 2007, 1795–96.

17. "Percentage of eighth-graders at or above *Basic* was higher in 2007 than in 1992 and 2005," National Assessment of Educational Progress (NAEP), 2007 Reading Assessments, nationsreportcard.gov About 74 percent of eighth graders are not proficient in reading and may never catch up.

18. Sadly, this means that many schools are focused on improving test scores, not instilling a love of reading literature. We all know from the immense success of the Harry Potter books that children love to read if the subject matter interests them; they just need some encouragement to read more at home.

19. Jennifer McMurrer, "Instructional Time in Elementary Schools: A Closer Look at Changes for Specific Subjects," Report in the Series From the Capitol to the Classroom, Center on Education Policy, February 20, 2008, www.cep-dc.org.

20. Kathy Hirsh-Pasek et al., *Einstein Never Used Flashcards: How Our Children REALLY Learn—And Why They Need to Play More and Memorize Less*, New York: Rodale, 2003.

21. Helyn Trickey, "No Child Left out of the Dodge Ball Game?" CNN.com, August 24, 2006.

22. Debra Viadero, "Exercise Seen as Priming Pump for Students' Academic Strides: Case grows stronger for physical activity's link to improved brain function," *Education Week*, February 12, 2008, vol. 27, no. 23, 14–15.

23. Scott Carlson, "The Net Generation Goes to College," *Chronicle of Higher Education*, October 7, 2005, chronicle.com.

24. But I speak mainly to groups who are older and for whom the broadcast model is not completely ineffective. And when I give a lecture, my goal is actually not to educate. I hope to open up someone's mind, or get an audience member to investigate something for themselves, or to do something differently. I doubt if anyone actually remembers the four principles of *Wikinomics* or the seven new business models or for that matter the four themes of the new model of pedagogy. A great lecture inspires and motivates; that's about it. But real learning, especially for this generation, occurs through collaboration and discovery.

25. "Good Questions Project," Good Questions at Cornell, May 6, 2008, www.math.cornell.edu.

26. Eric Mazur, "Reflections on a Harvard Education." *Harvard Crimson*, June 6, 2007.

27. Numbers taken from National Center for Educational Statistics. Variables plotted on a normalized 2 year x-axis for ease of reading. However, First Professional Degrees were taken from a different study than the one detailing undergraduate degrees. This is why there is only data available for first professional degrees every 5 years.

28. Warren Baker et al., "Technology in the Classroom: from Theory to Practice," *Educom Review*, vol. 32, no. 5, September–October 1997, 42, 44, 46–50.

29. Papert, Seymour, *The Connected Family*, Atlanta: Longstreet Press, 1996, 68.

30. Rachel Bolstad and Jane Gilbert, "The Tech Angels Project: Inviting Teachers into the World of Digital Learning," New Zealand Council for Educational Research, September 2007, www.techangels.org.nz.

31. Stefanie Olsen, "Digital Kids: Are Virtual Worlds the Future of the Classroom?" CNET News.com, June 12, 2006.

32. Chris Dede, "Planning for Neo Millennial Learning Styles: Shifts in students' learning style will prompt a shift to active construction of knowledge through mediated immersion." *Educause Quarterly,* vol. 28, November 1, 2005, www.educause.edu.

33. Steve Hargadon, "John Seely Brown on Web 2.0 and the Culture of Learning (School 2.0, Part 6)," www.stevehargadon.com.

34. David H. Jonassen, *Handbook of Research for Educational Communication and Technology*, Mawah, N.J.: Lawrence Erlbaum Associates, 2004, 785–812.

35. Brian Lamb, "Wide Open Spaces: Wikis Ready or Not," *Educause Review*, September–October 2004, www.educause.edu.

36. wikis4education, wikis4education.wikispaces.com, May 6, 2008.

37. HorizonProject, "About Us," May 6, 2008, horizonproject.wikispaces.com.

38. "2020 Vision: Brighton Central School District," Report, 2007, bcsd.org/files ("If the factory was the model of the typical 20th century American school, the

craftsman's shop or artist's studio is the model for a 21st century educational delivery system.").

39. Ibid., 42.

40. Maryann Kiely Lovelace, "Meta-Analysis of Experimental Research Based on the Dunn and Dunn Model," *Journal of Educational Research*, vol. 98, no. 3, January–February 2005, 176–83.

41. Cara Bafile, "Different Strokes For Little Folks: Carol Ann Tomlinson on Differentiated Instruction," Wire Side Chat, Education World, www.education-world.com.

42. "America's Digital Schools 2006," An Education Survey of National Significance, www.ads2006.org.

43. Some of the brightest ideas are not even in the physical school. As part of the Aspirnaut Initiative to encourage rural children to enter math and science fields, schoolchildren in Grapevine, Arkansas, are given video iPods and laptops to use on their long commute via an Internet-enabled school bus. The iPods and laptops are filled with educational materials and National Geographic videos, making the 15-hour weekly commute into a "one-house school bus" of discovery.

44. "Toward a New Golden Age in American Education: How the Internet, the Law and Today's Students Are Revolutionizing Expectations," National Education Plan 2004, U.S. Department of Education, October 2004, www.ed.gov.

45. Mark Bauerlein, *The Dumbest Generation*.

46. "Effectiveness of Reading and Mathematics Software Products: Findings from the First Student Cohort," Report to Congress, Mathematica Policy Research, Inc. and SRI International, March 2007, ies.ed.gov.

47. Jeremy Roschelle et al., "Scaling Up SimCalc Project: Can a Technology Enhanced Curriculum Improve Student Learning of Important Mathematics?" Technical Report, SRI International, May 2007, math.sri.com.

48. "Eastern Townships School Board announces exciting positive results from Laptop Initiative," Press Release, December 14, 2005, www.etsb.qu.ca, June 16, 2008.

49. David Williamson Shaffer, *How Computer Games Help Children Learn*, first ed., New York: Palgrave Macmillan, 2006. (Consider, for example, the research on computer games as a learning tool. According to University of Wisconsin professor David Williamson Shaffer, "Computer and video games can help kids develop the creative skills that are so crucial today. They allow learners to adopt roles, try out things with a low cost for failure, and learn from experience. They're governed by rules; you need a 'practical and intellectual discipline' to play.")

50. Bolstad and Gilbert, "The Tech Angels Project."

51. Bolstad and Gilbert, "The Tech Angels Project."

CHAPTER 6

1. "Majority of Americans Cite Sense of Entitlement Among Youth, Says National Poll," Press Release, Sacred Heart University News, www.sacredheart.edu.

2. Martha Levine, "The Young Labeled Entitlement Generation," Associated Press, June 2005.

3. David Pollitt, "How Credit Suisse Competes in the Global War for Talent," *Human Resource Management International Digest*, vol. 13, no. 6, 2005, 3, 15.

4. Jill Casner-Lotto and Linda Barrington, "Are They Really Ready to Work? Employers' Perspectives on the Basic Knowledge and Applied Skills of New Entrants to the 21st Century U.S. Workforce," Report, Conference Board, Corporate Voices for Working Families, Partnership for 21st Century Skills, and the Society for Human Resource Management, 2006, www.conference-board.org. When asked about the overall preparation for entry-level jobs, 80 percent of employers said that two-year-college graduates were adequately or well prepared, and 88 percent of employers felt that way about four-year-college graduates. But only about 46 percent of employers thought that high school graduates were adequately prepared. Employers were more critical about writing skills. Over 70 percent of employers thought that high school graduates' writing skills were deficient. Over half of employers shared that view about two-year-college grads, while 25 percent of employers thought four-year-college grads couldn't write.

5. Pollitt, "How Credit Suisse Competes in the Global War for Talent," 15.

6. John Gerasi et al, "Meet the Global Net Generation," Big Idea Paper, nGenera, July 2007, www.ngenera.com.

7. Lynne C. Lancaster and David Stillman, *When Generations Collide: Who They Are. Why They Clash. How to Solve the Generational Puzzle at Work*, New York: HarperCollins, 2003, 240, "When everyone's hiring pounding the pavement doesn't seem half as hard."

8. Clive Thompson, "Open-Source Spying," *New York Times*, December 3, 2006, www.nytimes.com.

9. Lara Hertel, "Workers Blast Workplace Dictatorships," Thomson Reuters, June 25, 2008, uk.reuters.com.

10. Peter Drucker, *The New Realities In Government and Politics/In Economics and Business/In Society and World View*, New York: Harper and Rowe, 1989, 209.

11. Or as Peter Cheese, the leader of Accenture's talent management practice says: "Talent has become a strategic issue and a human capital strategy is an essential part of any business strategy." He describes the high-performance company as "The Talent Powered Organization."

12. Nancy R. Lockwood, "The Aging Workforce: The Reality of the Impact of Older Workers and Eldercare in the Workplace," *HR Magazine*, December 2003.

13. "The American Workplace 2003: Realities, Challenges, and Opportunities," Employment Policy Foundation, August 2003.

14. "The Battle for Brainpower," *The Economist*, October 5, 2006.

15. Geoffrey H. Fletcher, "How to Get Our Groove Back: As China and India threaten the supremacy of the U.S. economy, our best hope for keeping pace is putting ed tech funding to use to galvanize education (Using Technology to Maintain Competitiveness)," *THE Journal (Technological Horizons in Education)*, vol. 33, no. 12, July 2006, 18–21, 4p, 1c, goliath.ecnext.com.

16. "Evolution of Student Interest in Science and Technology Studies Policy Report," Policy Report, Organization for Economic Co-operation and Development Global Science Forum, May 2006, www.oecd.org.

17. "The World Is Your Oyster," *The Economist*, October 2006.

18. Diana Farrell et al., "The Emerging Global Labor Market," Special Report, McKinsey Global Institute, June 2005, yalegroup.yale.edu. Young Professionals refers to engineers, finance and accounting, analysts, life science researchers, and professional generalists, doctors, nurses, and support staff.

19. Ibid.

20. Don Tapscott and Anthony D. Williams, *Wikinomics: Harnessing the Power of Mass Collaboration*, Toronto: Canada, Portfolio, 2006.

21. "The Net Generation: A Strategic Investigation," Syndicated Research Project, nGenera, 2007. n=1,750, 13–20-year-olds in the United States and Canada.

22. "Canadian Employers Struggle to Attract and Retain Employees," *Canadian Manager*; vol. 31, no. 2, Fall 2006; 12 ABI/INFORM Global, findarticles.com.

23. "The Net Generation: A Strategic Investigation," Syndicated Research Project, nGenera, 2007. n=5,935, 16–29- year- olds in 12 countries United States, Canada, UK, Germany, France, Spain, Mexico, Brazil, Russia, China, Japan, and India.

24. Karen A. Foelich, Attracting Today's Educated Workforce: Opportunities and Challenges for Small Business Firms," *Journal of Small Business Strategy*, vol. 15, no. 2, Winter 2005, 1, 17, findarticles.com.

25. "Study Examines Differences among Generations in the Workforce over the Past 25 Years," National Study, Families and Work Institute, October 2004, familiesandwork.org.

26. Neil Howe and William Strauss, *Millennials Go to College: Strategies for a New Generation on Campus*, Washington, D.C.: American Association of Collegiate Registrars, 2003.

27. Ibid.

28. "The World Is Your Oyster," *The Economist*, October 2006.

29. "The Net Generation: A Strategic Investigation," Syndicated Research Project, nGenera, 2007 n=1,750, 13–20-year-olds in the United States and Canada.

30. Jennifer Alsever, "Parental Consent," *Fast Company*, no. 111, December 2006, www.fastcompany.com.

31. Raja Simhan, "Refer Candidates and Get Rewarded at IT Companies," Hindu Business Line, September 24, 2003, www.blonnet.com. Mary Hayes Weier. "Tata and Infosys Set the Bar: 15 percent Raises This Year in India," *InformationWeek*, April 21, 2007, www.informationweek.com.

32. "From Learning to Work 2004," Campus Recruiting in Canada, D-Code/Brainstorm Communications, 2004, j.b5z.net.

33. Katherine Spencer Lee, "Some Tips for Gen Y Workers," *Computerworld*, May 12, 2008, computerworld.com.

34. Graham Jones, "How the Best of the Best Get Better and Better," *Harvard Business Review*, June 2008, 124.

35. Various Authors, "Forums," www.szhr.com (translated from Chinese by nGenera staff).

36. David Ticoll and Darren Meister, "Hon Hai: Winning by Design," Syndicated Research Project, nGenera, June 2005.

37. Ibid.

38. Robert W. Fairlie, "Kauffman Entrepreneurial Activity, National Index 1996–2005," National Report, 2005, Ewing Marion Kauffman Foundation, 2006, www.kauffman.org .

39. Ulrich Schoof, "Stimulating Youth Entrepreneurship: Barriers and Incentives to Enterprise Start-ups by Young People," SEED Working Paper No. 76, Small Enterprise Development Programme, 2006, www.ilo.org.

40. John C. Beck and Mitchell Wade, "The Generation Lap: Video Games Put the Young Way Ahead," *Boston Globe*, January 2, 2005.

41. Don Tapscott and Robert Barnard, "Talent 2.0: The Net Generation and the World of Work," Syndicated Research Project, nGenera, October 2006.

42. Steven D. Maurer and Yuping Liu, "Developing Effective E-Recruiting Web Sites: Insights for Managers from Marketers." Science Direct, May 2007, www.sciencedirect.com.

43. Ines Bebea, "Diversity Recruiting; Where the Action Is," *Network Journal: Black Professionals and Small Business Magazine*. New York: September 2005, vol. 12, no. 9, 16, www.tnj.com.

44. Don Tapscott and David Ticoll, *The Naked Corporation: How the Age of Transparency Will Revolutionize Business*, Penguin, Toronto: Canada, 2003, 22.

45. Lynn Olson, "Computer Simulations Hone Leadership Skills," *Education Week*, October 30, 2007.

46. "Sports Package Sales Knowledge Training," Visual Purple Understand Everything, www.visualpurple.com.

47. Tapscott, *Growing Up Digital*, 31.

48. Mike Dover and Anastasia Goodstein, "The Net Generation 'Dark Side': Myths and Realities of the Cohort in the Workplace and Marketplace," Syndicated Research Project, nGenera.

49. Stephanie Armour, "Generation Y: They've Arrived at Work with a New Attitude," *USA Today*, November 6, 2005.

50. "Dilbert Quotes," Eircom.net, http://homepage.eircom.net/%257Eodyssey/ Quotes/Popular/Comics/Dilbert.html (accessed May 7, 2008).

51. Robert Barnard et al., "The Net Generation and the World of Work," Syndicated Research Project, nGenera, 2005, 25.

52. Cem Sertoglu et al., "Cultivating Ex-Employees," *Harvard Business Review*, vol. 80, no. 6, June 2002, 20–21, 2p, 1c.

CHAPTER 7

1. Committee on Food Marketing and the Diets of Children and Youth et al., "Food Marketing to Children and Youth: Threat or Opportunity?," Congressional Directed Research Project, Institute of Medicine, www.nap.edu.

2. Don Tapscott and Robert Barnard, "Grown Up Digital: The Net Generation as a Consumer," Syndicated Research Project, nGenera, August 2005, www.ngenera.com.

3. "Baby Boomers Have 2 Trillion to Spend," SeniorJournal.com.

4. Jayne O'Donnell, "Gen Y Sits on Top of Consumer Food Chain," *USA Today*, October 2006.

5. Goliath: Business Knowledge on Demand, goliath.ecnext.com.

6. Michael Joseph Goss, "A Box of Dreams," *New York Times Magazine*, September 28, 2003, 72.

7. James Guyette, "Tuners Take Over," *Motor Age*, vol. 123, no. 6, June 2004, 146–53.

8. "Gizmodo, the Gadget Guide," April 29, 2008, www.gizmodo.com.

9. Bill Gillies and Don Tapscott, "The 8 Net Gen Norms: Characteristics of a Generation," Syndicated Research Project, nGenera, February 6, 2007, www.ngenera.com.

10. Tapscott, "Grown Up Digital: The Net Generation as a Consumer." Harris Interactive found that youth aged 8–21 spend an average of $385 a year online. In total, they spend about $2,454 a year. Between 72 percent of youth aged 13–15 and 81 percent of youth aged 18–21 reported first researching products online before buying them at a regular store.

11. Sandra O'Loughlin, "What's That Smell? Maybe, the Future of Marketing," *Brandweek*, vol. 48, no. 1, January 1, 2007.

12. Kevin Rose, "Digg This: 09-f9–11–02–9d-74-e3–5b-d8–41–56-c5–63–56–88-c0," May 1, 2007, Digg.com.

13. Don Tapscott, David Ticoll, *The Naked Corporation: How the Age of Transparency Will Revolutionize Business*, New York: Free Press, 2003.

14. "Hall of Shame," www.u-haulsucks.com, April 30, 2008.

15. "The Net Generation: A Strategic Investigation," Syndicated Research Project, nGenera, 2008, Survey of 1,750 respondents aged 13–29, September–October 2006, www.ngenera.com.

16. John C. Beck, and Mitchell Wade, *Got Game: How the Gamer Generation Is Reshaping Business Forever*, Boston: Harvard Business School Press, 2004, 3.

17. Lauren Keating, "The In Crowd Rushes to Keep Pace with Generation Y," *Shopping Center World*, vol. 29, no. 5, 2000, 160–210, retailtrafficmag.com.

18. Jan Chipchase, "You Like This. Or Not," Personal Blog, Future Perfect, www.janchipchase.com.

19. Suzanne Martin et al. "Trends and 'Tudes," Newsletter, Harris Interactive, vol. 5, no. 7, August 2006.

20. Ibid.

21. R. I. M. Dunbar, "Co-evolution of Neocortex Size, Group Size and Language in Humans," *Behavioral and Brain Science*, vol. 14, no. 4, 1993, 681–735, www.bbsonline.org/Preprints/OldArchive/bbs.dunbar.html.

22. Patrick Goldstein, "More Movies Are Giving Critics the Finger: Bloggers Often Have More Influence Now," *Toronto Star*, August 19, 2006, H15.

23. Ibid.

24. Patrick Goldstein, "Critics' voices become a whisper," *Los Angeles Times*, August 15, 2006.

25. Ibid.

26. Barry Schwartz, "Digg to Change System to Stem Gamin; Top Digger Quits," SearchEngineWatch.com, September 7, 2006.

27. Each MySpace page has a spot reserved for an individual's list of top eight "friends" on the site. While individuals may have hundreds and even thousands of friends,

the "Top 8" is a much more exclusive group that has become a social lightning rod. The small number of top positions necessitates a ranking of one's closest peers, so choosing who to place on one's Top 8 can be a politically charged decision for anyone's social network.

28. "Meet the Net Generation," nGenera.

29. Janet Kornblum, "Meet My 5,000 New Best Pals," *USA Today*, September 20, 2006.

30. "Analyst Influence Is Diminishing (but Who Is Displacing Them?)," Influencer50.com, July 2006.

31. Duncan Brown, "The Influence of Blogs," September 26, 2006, www.influencer50.com.

32. "Analysis of a Network of 14.5 Million E-Mail Messages," Press Release, Institute for Social and Economic Research and Policy (ISERP), Columbia University, January 2, 2006, www.iserp.columbia.edu.

33. Jeffrey Boase et al., "The Strength of Internet Ties," Report on Family, Friends and Community, Pew Internet & American Life Project, January 25, 2006. www.pewinternet.org.

34. "Top 10 Websites According to Country," Alexa.com, April 30, 2008, www.alexa.com.

35. Don Tapscott and Anthony D. Williams, *Wikinomics: How Mass Collaboration Changes Everything*, New York: Portfolio, 2007, 34–35.

36. "Campaign for Real Beauty," Internally computed numbers, Dove, www.youtube.com, April 30, 2008. The number of views tabulated on April 30, 2008, includes multiple copies of identical videos posted to YouTube; it includes only videos with more than 100,000 views.

37. Jack Neff, "A Real Beauty: Dove's Viral Makes Big Splash for No Cash," *Advertising Age*, vol. 7, no. 44, October 30, 2006, goliath.ecnext.com.

38. Kim Haines, "MySpace for Your Kind of Music," *The Times-Standard Tech-Beat*, August 15, 2006, nl.newsbank.com.

39. "Ronaldinho: Touch of Gold," YouTube video, youtube.com, April 30, 2008.

40. "Comments of the Electronic Privacy Information Center," Federal Communications Commission Testimony, Electronic Privacy Information Center, April 30, 2004, epic.org.

41. "Various Profile Pages," Friend totals, MySpace.com, January 15, 2008.

42. "The Net Generation: A Strategic Investigation," Syndicated Research Project, nGenera, 2008. Survey of 1,750 respondents aged 13–29, September–October 2006.

43. Barb Dybwad, "Sony Ericsson Falls Off Clue Train in Marketing the W800," Engadget.com, September 7, 2005.

44. User Prokofy Neva, "Dos and Don'ts for Big Business," Blog, Second Thoughts, October 26, 2006, secondthoughts.typepad.com.

45. Brant Barton, "Ratings, Reviews and ROI: How Leading Retailers Use Customer Word of Mouth in Marketing and Merchandising," *Journal of Interactive Advertising*, vol. 7, no. 1, Fall 2006, 1–7, jiad.org.

46. Ibid.

47. LG15, "LonelyGirl15," YouTube, April 30, 2008, www.youtube.com. Tabulated in April 2008. The figure was derived by taking sum totals for all individual video "episodes."

48. Dr. Paul Marsden et al., "Advocacy Drives Growth: Customer Advocacy Drives UK Business Growth," Telephone Study, London School of Economics and The Listening Company, September 5, 2005, www.lse.ac.uk. Study was conducted on 1,200 randomly selected individuals and their opinions were compared to the sales records of the companies asked about in the past year.

49. "About Craft," *Craft:* craftzine.com, April 30, 2008.

50. Paul Marsden, "Tipping Point Marketing: A Primer," Tipping Point Research, April 30, 2008, www.viralculture.com.

51. Ibid., Marsden, "Advocacy Drives Growth."

52. "Butterfly Effect," Wikipedia, en.wikipedia.org, April 30, 2008.

53. Sandra O'Loughlin, "What's That Smell? Maybe, the Future of Marketing," *Brandweek*, vol. 48, no. 1, January 1, 2007.

54. Robert Berner, "I Sold It through the Grapevine," *BusinessWeek*, May 29, 2006, www.businessweek.com.

55. "Kevin Rose Promises Digg 'Algorithm Change': Top Digg User Quits," *Jonty*, September 7, 2006, www.internet20.org.

56. Marshall McLuhan and Barrington Nevitt, *Take Today*, New York: Harcourt Brace Jovanovich, 1972,

57. Alvin Toffler, *The Third Wave*, New York: Bantam Books, 1984.

58. Ibid., "Meet the Net Generation," nGenera.

59. Rob Walker, "Bull Market," *Outside*, April 2002, outside.away.com.

60. "FedexFurniture.Com," FedexFurniture, www.fedexfurniture.com, April 30, 2008.

61. Yochai Benkler, *The Wealth of Networks: How Social Production Transforms Markets and Freedom*, New Haven, Conn.: Yale University Press, 2006.

62. Ibid., 55.

63. Eben Moglen, "Anarchism Triumphant: Free Software and the Death of Copyright," *First Monday*, 1999, http://emoglen.law.columbia.edu .

64. Lev Grossman, "Time's Person of the Year: You," *Time*, December 13, 2006, www.time.com.

65. Cathy Taylor, "The Future of Advertising," Special Report, The Project for Excellence in Journalism, www.stateofthenewsmedia.org.

66. Al and Laura Ries, *The 22 Immutable Laws of Branding: How to Build a Product or Service into a World-Class Brand*, New York: HarperCollins, 1998.

67. Ibid.

CHAPTER 8

1. Dreitlein worked as a researcher for me on this book, which is how I discovered this amazing story. Every morning when I started work, I'd have a ton of new information to work with that he had found overnight.

2. "Victim's Perception of the Age of the Offender in Serious Violent Crime, 1973–2005," Bureau of Justice Statistics, www.ojp.usdoj.gov.

3. Liana C. Sayer et al., "Are Parents Investing Less in Children? Trends in Mothers' and Fathers' Time with Children," *American Journal of Sociology*, vol. 110, no. 1, July 2004, 1–23, www.soc.upenn.edu.

4. Sherry Turkle, "Can You Hear Me Now?" *Forbes*, May 7, 2007, www.forbes.com.

5. Kerry Daly, Ph.D., "The Changing Culture of Parenting," Vanier Institute of the Family, 2004. www.vifamily.ca.

6. Alvin A. Rosenfeld, Ph.D., and Nicole Wise, *The Over-Scheduled Child: Avoiding the Hyper-Parenting Trap*, New York: St. Martin's Press, 2000.

7. "2006 American Community Survey," U.S. Census Bureau, Selected Social Characteristics, factfinder.census.gov/servlet.

8. Although about two-thirds of mothers are in the workforce, they sacrificed personal time to spend it with the kids. It increased from 10 hours per week in 1975 to 14 hours in 2003. Fathers spent more time changing diapers and watching soccer games—7 hours a week in 2003, up from 2.5 hours in 1975. Each Net Gen child got more extra time with his or her parents, of course, because families were smaller than they were in the baby boom.

9. In 1950, one-parent families made up 11 percent of all homes with children under 18 years old. Today this number has almost tripled due to the increasing divorce rate and greater numbers of those who choose to never marry. Single-parent households run by fathers are on the rise, with males now accounting for one in four of every single-parent household. With 5 million households run by a man flying solo, this blurring of gender borders is the reality that Net Geners are shaping.

10. Jennifer Campbell and Linda Gilmore, "Intergenerational Continuities and Discontinuities in Parenting Styles," *Australian Journal of Psychology*, vol. 59, no. 3, 2007, 140–50, www.informaworld.com.

11. Don Tapscott, "Talent 2.0," Conference Presentation, May 14, 2008.

12. "A Portrait of 'Generation Next,'" The Pew Center for People & the Associated Press, January 9, 2007, people-press.org (accessed April 21, 2008).

13. "MTV and the Associated Press Release Landmark Study of Young People and Happiness," Press Release, Associated Press and MTV, New York, New York, August 20, 2007.

14. Neil Howe and William Strauss, *Millennials Go to College*, 2nd ed., Great Falls, Va.: Lifecourse Associates, 2007.

15. "YouthPulse," Research Publication, Harris Interactive, 2006.

16. Neil Howe and William Strauss, "Helicopter Parents in the Workplace," Syndicated Research Report, nGenera, November, 2007, www.ngenera.com.

17. Anya Kamenetz, *Generation Debt*, New York: Penguin, 2006; reprint of Riverhead edition.

18. Ibid., "A Portrait of 'Generation Next.'"

19. Mike Dover and Anastasia Goodstein, "The Net Generation "Dark Side": Myths and Realities of the Cohort in the Workplace and Marketplace," Syndicated Research Project, nGenera.

20. "Youthpulse."

21. Ibid.

22. "Connected to the Future: A Report on Children's Internet Use from the Corporation for Public Broadcasting," Report, Corporation of Public Broadcasting, 2002, www.cpb.org.

23. "50 Percent of Students Talk with Internet Strangers; 20 Percent Admit Face-to-Face Meetings," Press Release, i-SAFE, November 6, 2006, www.isafe.org.

24. Glenn Beck, "Teens Arrested for Beating Girl Unconscious; Iran still a Concern in the Iraq War; First Grader Cited for Sexual Harassment," CNN Broadcast, April 8, 2008, transcripts.cnn.com.

25. Dave Goldiner, " 'Dr. Phil's Staff Bails Out Florida Girl," Daily News, April 14, 2008, www.nydailynews.com.

26. "Eight Teenagers Invite Girl Over and Beat Her," YouTube, April 9, 2008, www.youtube.com.

27. Gabriel Sherman, "Testing Horace Mann," New York, May 30, 2008, www.nymag.com.

28. "Eight Teenagers Invite Girl Over and Beat Her."

29. Sue Hutchinson, "On the Net, Bullying Takes an Insidious Turn," San Jose Mercury News, January 22, 2008.

30. Ibid.

31. "Cyberbullying in Schools to Be Fought Thanks to $20,000 Qwest Foundation Grant to Seattle Public Schools: Funds to Help Develop Educational Programs for Parents, Students and Teachers," Business Wire, February 13, 2008.

32. Julian Sher, "The Not-So-Long Arm of the Law," USA Today, May 1, 2007, blogs.usatoday.com.

33. "YouthPulse."

34. Carol Mithers, "The Fractured Family," UCLA Magazine, July 1, 2006, www.magazine.ucla.edu.

35. Stuart Wolpert, "OCHS Wins MacArthur 'Genius' Grant," UCLA Today, 1998, www.today.ucla.edu.

36. Jennifer G. Bohanek et al., "Family Narrative Interaction and Children's Self-Understanding," Working Paper no. 34, The Emory Center for Myth and Ritual in American Life, 2004, www.marial.emory.edu.

37. "A Portrait of 'Generation Next.' "

38. "Youthpulse."

39. "MTV and the Associated Press Release Landmark Study of Young People and Happiness."

40. "The U.S. Mom Market," Telephone Survey, Packaged Facts and Silver Stork Research, October 16, 2003, www.marketresearch.com.

41. "American Community Survey," U.S. Census Bureau, Table B23007, 2006.

42. "Lifetime Television Women's Pulse Poll of Gen Y Women," National Telephone Survey, Lifetime Networks, WomanTrend and Lake Research Partners, December 13, 2006, www.pollingcompany.com.

43. Jim Carroll, "Integrating Gen-Y into the Workplace," The Boardroom, www.jimcarroll.com/articles/assoc-12.htm.

44. Victoria Rideout and Elizabeth Hamel, "The Media Family: Electronic Media in
     the Lives of Infants, Toddlers, Preschoolers and Their Parents," Report, Kaiser
     Family Foundation, May 24, 2006, www.kff.org.

45. Suzy Tomopoulos et al., "Is Exposure to Media Intended for Preschool Children
     Associated with Less Parent-Child Shared Reading Aloud and Teaching
     Activities?," *Ambulatory Pediatrics*, vol. 7, no. 1, January–February 2007, 18–24,
     www.sciencedirect.com.

46. Ellen Wartella et al., "From Baby Einstein to Leapfrog, From Doom to The Sims,
     From Instant Messaging to Internet Chat Rooms: Public Interest in the Role of
     Interactive Media in Children's Lives," SRCD Social Policy Report, vol.18, no. 4,
     2004, www.srcd.org.

CHAPTER 9

 1. Mark Bauerlein, *The Dumbest Generation*, 184.

 2. "Cone 2006 Millennial Cause Study," Press Release, Cone Inc.,
     www.causemarketingforum.com. This first in-depth study of its kind found that 63
     percent of the Net Generation felt personally responsible for making a difference in
     the world.

 3. "Voting and Registration in the Election of November 2004: Population
     Characteristics," Population Characteristics Report P20–556, U.S. Census
     Bureau, March 2006, www.census.gov.

 4. "How Young People View Their Lives, Futures and Politics: A Portrait of
     'Generation Next,'" National Study, Pew Research Center, January 9, 2007,
     people-press.org. Sixty-four percent of 18–25-year-olds disagreed with the notion
     that projects run by the federal government are inefficient and wasteful—the
     stereotype of many older and more traditional commentators.

 5. Mark Hugo Lopez et al., "The 2006 Civic and Political Health of the Nation: A
     Detailed Look at How Youth Participate in Politics and Communities," Center for
     Information and Research on Civic Learning and Engagement, October 2006,
     www.civicyouth.org.

 6. "Rock the Vote: Post Super Tuesday 2008," Lake Research Partners and the
     Tarrance Group, February 2008, www.rockthevote.com. Of the Net Geners
     surveyed, 88 percent agreed with the statement that young people today have the
     power to change their country. Additionally, 75 percent of respondents felt that
     they personally have the power to affect this type of change.

 7. Peter Leyden et al., "The Progressive Politics of the Millennial Generation,"
     Generational Study, New Politics Institute, June 20, 2007, www.newpolitics.net.

 8. Ibid.

 9. Ibid., Leyden. Of those polled, 78 percent agreed that "elected officials seem to be
     motivated by selfish reasons"; 74 percent agreed that "politics has become too
     partisan"; 69 percent agreed that "the political tone in Washington is too negative";
     and 75 percent agreed that "elected officials don't seem to have the same priorities
     that I have."

10. "The 13th Biannual Youth Survey on Politics and Public Service," National Survey,
     Harvard Institute of Politics, November 2007, www.iop.harvard.edu.

11. Ibid. Of those surveyed, 30 percent of Americans aged 18–24 trust the president "all or most of the time," while 75 percent of them said that elected officials do not have the same priorities that they do.

12. "America's Young Adults Make Their Mark," Biannual Youth Survey, Harvard University Institute of Politics, November 2006, goliath.ecnext.com.

13. In 2004, voter turnout was the third highest since 1972, said Karlo Marcelo, a research associate for the nonpartisan Center for Information and Research on Civic Learning and Engagement (CIRCLE).

14. Voting and Registration in the Election of November 2004: Population Characteristics.

15. "Over Three Million Citizens under the Age of Thirty Participate in Super Tuesday Primaries," Press Release, Center for Information and Research on Civic Learning and Engagement (CIRCLE), February 6, 2008, www.civicyouth.org.

16. "The 14th Biannual Youth Survey on Politics and Public Service," National Survey, Harvard Institute of Politics, April 2008, www.iop.harvard.edu.

17. "Dissonant Discourse Turning Off College Students to Formal Politics," Research Project, Center for Information and Research on Civic Learning and Engagement, November 2007.

18. Susan Page and William Risser, "Americans Revved Up—and Ready to Vote: Iraq, Economy, 'Fresh Faces' Boost Interest," *USA Today*, January 16, 2008, www.usatoday.com.

19. In an effort to show the powerful impact the Net Geners have had on the voting in the past few elections, the various styles of computing percentage of the youth population (18–24) are not represented here; instead only the raw data is shown. I believe that showing the increase of nearly 4 million voters in just two elections paints the accurate picture in terms of both magnitude and significance.

20. Scott Keeter et al., "Gen Dems: The Party's Advantage Among Young Voters Widens," Pew Research Center for the People & the Press, April 28, 2008, pewresearch.org.

21. Leyden, "The Progressive Politics of the Millennial Generation."

22. "How Young People View their Lives, Futures and Politics: A Portrait of 'Generation Next.'"

23. "SnapShot of Barackobama.com (rank #752), hillaryclinton.com (#1585)—Compete," Compete.com, siteanalytics.compete.com.

24. "2008 Donor Demographics," 2008 Presidential Elections, OpenSecrets.org.

25. Ibid.

26. Morley Winograd and Michael D. Hais, "Millennial Makeover," Blogspot.com, March 23, 2008, millennialmakeover.blogspot.com/.

27. Frank Rich, "Party Like Its 2008," *New York Times*, March 11, 2008, www.nytimes.com/2008/05/11/opinion/11rich.html.

28. "Consumers Union Michael Hansen's Statement on Mad Cow Disease Found in Canada," Consumers Union, Press Release, May 20, 2003.

29. "Text of Gore Speech at Media Conference," Associated Press, www.breitbart.com (accessed May 6, 2008).

30. "Habitat Jam Participation Backgrounder," IBM, 2006.

31. Jack W. Germond and Jules Witcover, *Mad as Hell: Revolt at the Ballot Box*, New York: Warner Books, 1993.

32. "Open Congress," OpenCongress.org, www.opencongress.org/ (accessed May 6, 2008).

CHAPTER 10

1. "Davos Annual Meeting 2008: The Voice of the Next Generation," YouTube: Broadcast Yourself, www.youtube.com.

2. "The Net Generation: A Strategic Investigation," Syndicated Research Project, nGenera, 2008, www.ngenera.com.

3. Peter Mandelson, "Europe and the US: Confronting Global Challenges," Speech, November 8, 2007, europa.edu.

4. Carmen DeNavas-Walt et al., "Income, Poverty, and Health Insurance Coverage in the United States: 2006." Special Report, U.S. Census Bureau, August 2007. www.census.gov. Nearly 47 million Americans, or 16 percent of the population, were without health insurance in 2005, the latest government data available.

5. "The 14th Biannual Youth Survey on Politics and Public Service," National Survey, Harvard Institute of Politics, April 2008, www.iop.harvard.edu.

6. Karen Shim, "Travel with a Purpose: Overseas Volunteering," *Panorama*, September 28, 2004, www.takingitglobal.org.

7. Sylvia Hurtado and John H. Pryor, "The American Freshman: National Norms for Fall 2005," National Survey, Cooperative Institutional Research Program (CIRP) Higher Education Research Institute (HERI), January 26, 2006, www.gseis.ucla.edu.

8. Alexander W. Astin and Lori J Vogelgesang, "Conceptualizing, Measuring and Understanding Students' Post-College Civic Engagement: What we know about the impaction of service-learning. Presentation at the Continuums of Service Conference, Portland, April 2005," Understanding the Effects of Service Learning: A Study of Students and Faculty, Higher Education Research Institute (HERI), 2005, www.gseis.ucla.edu. The chart was created using data obtained in this report; the points for 2006 and 2008 were extrapolated using the average increase measured from 1990 to 2004.

9. Mark Hugo Lopez et al., "The 2006 Civic and Political Health of the Nation: A Detailed Look at How Youth Participate in Politics and Communities," Research Study, Center for Information and Research on Civic Learning and Engagement, October 2006.

10. Scott Keeter et al., "The Civic and Political Health of the Nation: A Generational Portrait," Center for Information and Research on Civic Learning and Engagement, September 19, 2002, www.civicyouth.org.

11. Abby Kiesa et al., "Millennials Talk Politics: A Study of College Student Political Engagement," Research Study, Center for Information and Research on Civic Learning and Engagement, November 7, 2007.

12. Robert Grimm et al., "Volunteer Growth in America: A Review of Trends Since 1974," Research Report, Corporation for National and Community Service, December 2006.

13. "Thousands of College Students Using Their Spring Breaks to Help Gulf Region Rebuild from Hurricanes," Press Release, Campus Compact, March 3, 2006.

14. Kathryn Montgomery, Ph.D. et al., "Youth as E-Citizens: Engaging the Digital Generation," Report, Center for Social Media School of Communication, March 2004.

15. "Green Is the New Red, White, and Blue (2007)," YouTube, www.youtube.com.

16. Martha McCaughey and Michael D. Ayers, eds., *Cyberactivism: Online Activism in Theory and Practice*, Florence, Ky.: Routledge, 2003.

CHAPTER 11

1. Steven Johnson, *Everything Bad Is Good for You: How Today's Popular Culture Is Actually Making Us Smarter*, New York: Riverhead, 2005. Steven Johnson, "Dome Improvement," *Wired*, vol. 5, no. 13, May 2005. Clancy Blair et al., "Rising Mean IQ: Cognitive Demand of Mathematics Education for Young Children, Population Exposure to Formal Schooling and the Neurobiology of the Prefrontal Cortex," *Intelligence*, vol. 33, no. 1, January–February 2005, 93–106.

2. "Samuel Johnson," Wikiquote, en.wikiquote.org.

3. Robert L. Cross et al., *The Hidden Power of Social Networks*, Cambridge, Mass.: Harvard Business School Press, 2004, 11.

4. Alan Finder, "For Some, Online Persona Undermines a Resume," *New York Times*, June 11, 2006.

5. Anastasia Goodstein and Mike Dover, "The Net Generation 'Dark Side': Myths and Realities of the Cohort in the Workplace and Marketplace," Syndicated Research Report, nGenera, July 2007, www.ngenera.com.

6. "New Study Confirms Internet Plagiarism Is Prevalent," Press Release, Rutgers University, August 2003, ur.rutgers.edu. The survey of 18,000 students was conducted in 2003 by Professor Donald McCabe, a management professor at Rutgers University.

7. "2006 Josephson Institute Report Card on the Ethics of American Youth: Part One—Integrity," Press Release, Josephson Institute, October 15, 2006, johnsoninstitute.org.

8. "Juvenile Offenders and Victims: 2006 National Report," U.S. Department of Justice, ch. 2, 38, 2006, ojjdp.ncjrs.gov.

9. Craig Anderson et al., *Violent Video Game Effects on Children and Adolescents: Theory, Research and Public Policy*, Cambridge, UK: Oxford University Press, 2007.

10. "The Proportion of Serious Violent Crimes Committed by Juveniles Has Generally Declined since 1993," U.S. Department of Justice, Office of Justice Programs, Bureau of Justice Statistics, www.ojp.usdoj.gov (accessed May 22, 2008). Data taken from the United States Department of Justice and extrapolated into 2006 and 2008 was not available at that time. The extrapolated points are estimated using the rate of decline starting at 1994, they are signified with an (e).

11. "The Decline in Crime: Why and What Next?" Urban Institute, October 2000, www.urban.org (accessed May 22, 2008).

12. "The Proportion of Serious Violent Crimes Committed by Juveniles Has Generally Declined since 1993."

13. "Child Trends Databank," Table 3, www.childtrendsdatabank.org/tables/
    80_Table_3.htm (accessed May 26, 2008). Data taken from the Monitoring the
    Future Study was extrapolated out to 2008 using trends from 1991 to 2006.

14. "Nearly Half of Our Lives Spent with TV, Radio, Internet, Newspapers, According
    to Census Bureau Publication," Press Release, U.S. Census Bureau, December 15,
    2006, www.census.gov.

15. Mark Hugo Lopez et al., "The 2006 Civic and Political Health of the Nation: A
    Detailed Look at How Youth Participate in Politics and Communities," Center for
    Information and Research on Civic Learning and Engagement (CIRCLE),
    October 2006, www.civicyouth.org.

16. There is much discussion about who actually said this. Socrates is said to have been
    the most likely candidate.

17. Jean Twenge, *Generation Me: Why Today's Young Americans Are More Confident,
    Assertive, Entitled—and More Miserable Than Ever Before*, New York: Free Press,
    2006, 226.

18. Adapted from the Amherst College charter: "Amherst College educates men and
    women of exceptional potential from all backgrounds so that they may seek, value,
    and advance knowledge, engage the world around them, and lead principled lives of
    consequence."

BIBLIOGRAPHY

Abram, Stephen, and Chris Pulleyn, "Just Hitting the Surf: Millennials in the Information Age," National Research Project, SirsiDynix and Buck & Pulleyn, April 19, 2006, www.sirsidynix.com.

Alderman, Tom, "Welcome to the ADD Generation," *The Huffington Post*, www.huffingtonpost.com.

Alsever, Jennifer, "Parental Consent," *Fast Company*, no. 111, December 2006, www.fastcompany.com.

Alsop, Ron, *The Trophy Kids Grow Up: How the Millennial Generation is Shaking Up the Workplace*, San Francisco: Jossey-Bass, 2008.

"AmCham Members to Get Inside Scoop on Coke Zero, Coca-Cola's Most Successful Project in 20 Years," Press Release, AmCham Marketing and Communications Committee (MCC), newsweaver.co.uk.

"The American Freshman: National Norms for Fall 2005," National Report, Higher Education Research Institute.

"America's Digital Schools 2006," An Education Survey of National Significance, www.ads2006.org.

"Analysis of a Network of 14.5 Million E-mail Messages," Press Release, Institute for Social and Economic Research and Policy (ISERP), January 2, 2006.

Anderson, Craig A., Douglas A. Gentile, and Katherine E. Buckley, *Violent Video Game Effects on Children and Adolescents: Theory, Research, and Public Policy*, New York: Oxford University Press, 2007, www.psychology.iastate.edu.

Armour, Stephanie, "Generation Y: They've Arrived at Work with a New Attitude," *USA Today*, November 6, 2005.

Arrington, Michael, "Obama Sets Record with January Donations; Online Donations 88% of Total," TechCrunch, February 4, 2008, www.techcrunch.com.

Astin, Alexander W., and Lori J. Vogelgesang, "Conceptualizing, Measuring and Understanding Students' Post-College Civic Engagement: What We Know about the Impaction of Service-Learning. Presentation at the Continuums of Service Conference, Portland, April 2005," Research Project, Understanding the Effects of Service Learning: A Study of Students and Faculty, Higher Education Research Institute (HERI), 2005, www.gseis.ucla.edu.

Bafile, Cara, "Different Strokes for Little Folks: Carol Ann Tomlinson on Differentiated Instruction," Wire Side Chats, EducationWorld.com, June 5, 2008, www.education-world.com.

Baker, Warren et al., "Technology in the Classroom: from Theory to Practice," *Educom Review*, vol. 32, no. 5, September–October 1997.

Barnard, Robert et al., "The Net Generation and the World of Work," Syndicated Research Project, nGcncra, 2005.

Barton, Brant, "Ratings, Reviews & ROI: How Leading Retailers Use Customer Word of Mouth in Marketing and Merchandising," *Journal of Interactive Advertising*, vol. 7, no. 1, Fall 2006, jiad.org.

Barton, Paul, "One Third of a Nation: Rising Dropout Rates and Declining Opportunities," Policy Information Report, Educational Testing Service, February 2005, www.ets.org.

"The Battle for Brainpower," *The Economist*, October 5, 2006, www.economist.com.

Bauerlein, Mark, *The Dumbest Generation: How the Digital Age Stupefies Young Americans and Jeopardizes Our Future*, New York: Penguin Tarcher, 2008.

Bebea, Ines, "Diversity Recruiting—Where the Action Is," *The Network Journal: Black Professionals and Small Business Magazine*, vol. 12, no. 9, September 2005, www.tnj.com.

Beck, John C., and Mitchell Wade, "The Generation Lap: Video Games Put the Young Way Ahead," *Boston Globe*, January 2, 2005, www.boston.com.

Beck, John C., and Mitchell Wade, *Got Game: How the Gamer Generation Is Reshaping Business Forever*, Boston: Harvard Business Press, 2004.

Beck, John C., and Mitchell Wade, *The Kids are Alright: How the Gamer Generation Is Changing the Workplace*, Boston: Harvard Business School Press, 2006.

Beckel, Michael, "Taking Action Now: An Interview with Nate Wright," *Mother Jones*, September 1, 2005, www.motherjones.com.

Begly, Sharon, "Survival of the Busiest—Parts of the Brain That Get Most Use Literally Expand and Rewire on Demand," *Wall Street Journal*, October 11, 2002.

Benkler, Yochai, *The Wealth of Networks: How Social Production Transforms Markets and Freedom,* New Haven, Conn.: Yale University Press, 2006.

Bennett, W. Lance, "Civic Life Online: Learning How Digital Media Can Engage Youth," book 1, The John D. and Catherine T. MacArthur Foundation Series on Digital Media and Learning, December 2007, mitpress.mit.edu.

Bergman, Mike, "Nearly Half of Our Lives Spent with TV, Radio, Internet, Newspapers, according to Census Bureau Publication," Press Release, U.S. Census Bureau, December 15, 2006.

Berner, Robert, "I Sold It through the Grapevine," *BusinessWeek*, May 29, 2006, www.businessweek.com.

Bergstrom, Ida, "Facebook Can Ruin Your Life: And So Can MySpace, Bebo . . ." *The Independent*, February 10, 2008, www.independent.co.uk.

Blair, Clancy et al., "Rising Mean IQ: Cognitive Demand of Mathematics Education for Young Children, Population Exposure to Formal Schooling and the Neurobiology of the Prefrontal Cortex," *Intelligence*, vol. 33, no. 1, January–February 2005, www.sciencedirect.com.

Bly, Robert, *The Sibling Society*, New York: Vintage, 1997.

Boase, Jeffrey et al., "The Strength of Internet Ties," Report on Family, Friends and Community, Pew Internet & American Life Project, January 25, 2006, www.pewinternet.org.

Bohanek, Jennifer G. et al., "Family Narrative Interaction and Children's Self-Understanding." Working Paper No. 34, the Emory Center for Myth and Ritual in American Life, 2004, www.marial.emory.edu.

Bolstad, Rachel, and Jane Gilbert, "The Tech Angels Project; Inviting Teachers into the World of Digital Learning," Special Report, New Zealand Council for Educational Research, September 2007, www.techangels.org.

Bridgeland, John M. et al., "The Silent Epidemic: Perspectives of High School Dropouts," Report for the Gates Foundation, Civic Enterprises, and Peter D. Hart Research Associates, March 2006, www.gatesfoundation.org.

Brown, Duncan, "The Influence of Blogs," September 26, 2006, www.influencer50.com.

Buckingham, David, "Youth, Identity, and Digital Media," book 6, The John D. and Catherine T. MacArthur Foundation Series on Digital Media and Learning, December 2007, mitpress.mit.edu.

Burton, Whitney, "I'm a Fan of This Blogger (Get Email Alerts)," *The Huffington Post*, March 28, 2008, www.huffingtonpost.com.

Campbell, Jennifer, and Linda Gilmore, "Intergenerational Continuities and Discontinuities in Parenting Styles," *Australian Journal of Psychology*, vol. 59. no. 3, 2007, www.informaworld.com.

"Canadian Employers Struggle to Attract and Retain Employees," *The Canadian Manager*, vol. 31, no. 2, Fall 2006, findarticles.com.

Carlson, Scott, "The Net Generation Goes to College," *Chronicle of Higher Education*, October 7, 2005, chronicle.com.

Carr, Nicholas, *The Big Switch: Rewiring the World, from Edison to Google*, New York: W.W. Norton & Company, Inc., 2008.

Carroll, Jim, "Integrating Gen-Y into the Workplace," *The Boardroom*, www.jimcarroll.com.

Casner-Lotto, Jill, and Linda Barrington, "Are They Really Ready to Work? Employers' Perspectives on the Basic Knowledge and Applied Skills of New Entrants to the 21st Century U.S. Workforce," Report, The Conference Board, Corporate Voices for Working Families, the Partnership for 21st Century Skills, and the Society for Human Resource Management, 2006, www.conference-board.org.

Cheese, Peter, Robert J. Thomas, and Elizabeth Craig, *The Talent Powered Organization: Strategies for Globalization, Talent Management and High Performance*, London: Kogan Page Ltd., 2008.

"Child Trends Databank," Table 3, www.childtrendsdatabank.org, accessed May 26, 2008.

"Children between Five and Fourteen Influence 78% of Total Grocery Purchases," Goliath: Business Knowledge on Demand, goliath.ecnext.com/coms2/gi_0199–2822838/Children-between-five-and-fourteen.html#abstract (accessed April 1, 2008).

Chipchase, Jan, "You Like This. Or Not," Future Perfect, www.janchipchase.com.

"Coca-Cola Teaches African Teens about AIDS," Press Release, Coca-Cola, November 20, 2007, www.scoop.co.nz.

Cohen, Patricia, "Dumb and Dumber: Are Americans Hostile to Knowledge?" *New York Times*, February 14, 2008.

"Colombians in Huge Farc Protest," BBC, February 4, 2008, news.bbc.co.uk.

Coloroso, Barbara, "The Bully, the Bullied, and the Bystander," New York: Harper Resource, 2003

"Cone 2006 Millennial Cause Study," Press Release, Cone Inc., www.coneinc.com.

Conlin, Michelle, "Smashing the Clock," *BusinessWeek*, December 11, 2006, www.businessweek.com.

Conway, Susan D., *The Think Factory: Managing Today's Most Precious Resource, People!* New Jersey: John Wiley & Sons, Inc., 2007.

Coombes, Andrea, "Companies Need New Tools To Recruit Today's Grads," Dow Jones News Service, May 23, 2008.

Correa, Javier, "Murder . . . It's the Real Thing," Killer Coke Target: Colombian Labor, www.corporatecampaign.org.

Cross, Robert L., Andrew Parker, and Rob Cross, *The Hidden Power of Social Networks: Understanding How Work Really Gets Done in Organizations*, Boston: Harvard Business Press, 2004.

"Cyberbullying in Schools to Be Fought Thanks to $20,000 Qwest Foundation Grant to Seattle Public Schools: Funds to Help Develop Educational Programs for Parents, Students and Teachers," Business Wire, February 13, 2008.

Daly, Kerry, Ph.D., "The Changing Culture of Parenting," Vanier Institute of the Family, 2004, www.vifamily.ca.

Damon, William, *The Path to Purpose: Helping Our Children Find Their Calling in Life*, New York: Free Press, 2008.

Deal, Jennifer J., "Retiring the Generation Gap," 1st ed., San Francisco: Wiley : Center for Creative Leadership, 2007.

"The Decline in Crime: Why and What Next?" The Urban Institute, October 2000, www.urban.org.

Dede, Chris, "Planning for Neo Millennial Learning Styles: Shifts in Students' Learning Style Will Prompt a Shift to Active Construction of Knowledge through Mediated Immersion," *Educause Quarterly*, vol. 28, November 1, 2005, www.educause.edu.

Diaz, Sam, "Teen Mobile Phone Usage Soars in Summer," *Washington Post,* July 2, 2007, blog.washingtonpost.com.

DiFonzo, Nicholas, *The Watercooler Effect: A Psychologist Explores the Extraordinary Power of Rumors*, New York: Avery, 2008.

"Dissonant Discourse Turning Off College Students to Formal Politics," Report, Center for Information and Research on Civic Learning and Engagement, November 2007.

Doidge, Norman, M.D., *The Brain That Changes Itself: Stories of Personal Triumph from the Frontiers of Brain Science*, New York: Viking Adult, 2007.

Dover, Mike, and Anastasia Goodstein, "The Net Generation 'Dark Side': Myths and Realities of the Cohort in the Workplace and Marketplace," Syndicated Research Project, nGenera, www.ngenera.com.

"Dropout Rate in the United States: 2004," National Longitudinal Report, National Center for Educational Statistics, NCES 2007–024, November 2006, nces.ed.gov.

Drucker, Peter, *The New Realities in Government and Politics | In Economics and Business | In Society and World View*, New York: Harper and Row, 1989.

Dunbar, R. I. M., "Co-Evolution of Neocortex Size, Group Size and Language in Humans," *Behavioural and Brain Sciences*, vol. 14, no. 4, 1993, www.bbsonline.org.

Dybwad, Barb, "Sony Ericsson Falls Off Clue Train in Marketing the W800," Engadget.com, September 7, 2005, www.engadget.com.

Dychtwald, Ken, Tamara J. Erickson, and Robert Morison, *Workforce Crisis: How to Beat the Coming Shortage of Skills and Talent*, Boston: Harvard Business School Press, 2006.

"Eastern Townships School Board Announces Exciting Positive Results from Laptop Initiative," Press Release, December 14, 2005, www.etsb.qc.ca.

"Educational Attainment in the United States, Table 8," U.S. Bureau of the Census Tabulation, 2005, www.census.gov.

"Effectiveness of Reading and Mathematics Software Products: Findings from the First Student Cohort," Report to Congress, Mathematica Policy Research, Inc. and SRI International, March 2007, ies.ed.gov.

Elbert, Thomas et al., "Increased Cortical Representation of the Fingers of the Left Hand in String Players," *Science*, vol. 270, no. 5234, October 13, 1995.

"The Emerging Global Labor Market," Syndicated Report, McKinsey Global Institute, June 2005, yaleglobal.yale.edu.

"Enrollment Rates of 18- to 24-year-olds in Degree-Granting Institutions, by Sex and Race/Ethnicity: 1967 through 2006, Table 195," *Digest of Educational Statistics*, 2007, National Center for Educational Statistics, nces.ed.gov.

Everett, Anna, "Learning Race and Ethnicity: Youth and Digital Media," book 5, The John D. and Catherine T. MacArthur Foundation Series on Digital Media and Learning, December 2007, mitpress.mit.edu.

"Ernst & Young Personalizes the Job Search for Gen Y with New Interactive Careers Web Site; Redesigned Careers Web Site Features In-Depth Videos, Photos, and Personal Journals as Part of Firm's Effort to Recruit Close to 10,000 Employees in 2008," PR Newswire, March 19, 2008.

"Evolution of Student Interest in Science and Technology Studies Policy Report," Policy Report, Organization for Economic Cooperation and Development Global Science Forum, May 2006, www.oecd.org.

"Facts on Health Insurance Coverage," National Coalition on Health Care, www.nchc.org.

Fairlie, Robert W., "Kauffman Entrepreneurial Activity, National Index 1996–2005," national report, 2005, Ewing Marion Kauffman Foundation, 2006, www.kauffman.org.

Felt, Adrienne and David Evans, "Privacy Protection for Social Networking APIs," University of Virginia, www.cs.virginia.edu.

Ferriss, Tim, "No Schedules, No Meetings—Enter Best Buy's ROWE—Part 1," The Blog of Tim Ferriss, www.fourhourworkweek.com.

"Fewer High School Students Engage in Health Risk Behaviors; Racial and Ethnic Differences Persist," Press Release, Center for Disease Control and Prevention, June 2005, www.cdc.gov.

Finder, Alan, "For Some, Online Persona Undermines a Resume," *New York Times*, June 11, 2006.

Fitzgerald, Toni, "For Teens, Grammys Are about Dipping," *MediaLife*, February 15, 2008, www.medialifemagazine.com.

Fletcher, Geoffrey, "How to Get Our Groove Back: As China and India Threaten the Supremacy of the US Economy, Our Best Hope for Keeping Pace Is Putting Ed

Tech Funding to Use to Galvanize Education (Using Technology to Maintain Competitiveness)," *T H E Journal* (Technological Horizons in Education), vol. 33, no. 12, July 2006, goliath.ecnext.com.

Foot, David, *Boom, Bust, Echo. How to Profit from the Coming Demographic Shift*, Toronto: Macfarlane Walter Ross, 1996.

"The 14th Biannual Youth Survey on Politics and Public Service," National Survey, Harvard Institute of Politics, April 2008.

Froelich, Karen A., "Attracting Today's Educated Workforce: Opportunities and Challenges for Small Business Firms," *Journal of Small Business Strategy*, vol. 15, no. 2, Winter 2005, findarticles.com.

"G8 Truant on Education Aid," Press Release, Global Campaign for Education, April 21, 2006, www.campaignforedcuation.org.

Gee, James Paul, *What Video Games Have to Teach Us about Learning and Literacy*, New York: Palgrave Macmillan, 2003.

"Generation Digital, Politics, Commerce and Childhood in the Age of the Internet," The MIT Press, Cambridge, Mass., 2007.

Geraci, John, "YouthPulse," Presentation at Boston Net Gen Meeting, 2007.

——, and Lisa Chen, "Meet the Global Net Generation," Syndicated Research Project, nGenera, July 2007, www.ngenera.com.

Gerdes, Lindsay, "The Best Places to Launch a Career: The Top 50 Employers for New College Grads," *BusinessWeek*, September 18, 2006.

Germond, Jack W., and Jules Witcover, *Mad as Hell: Revolt at the Ballot Box*, New York: Warner Books, 1993.

Giancola, Frank, "Flexible Schedules: A Win-Win Reward," *Workspan*, July 10, 2005, www.worldatwork.org.

Giedd, Jay N. et al., "Brain Development during Childhood and Adolescence: A Longitudinal MRI Study," *Nature Neuroscience*, no. 2, 1999, www.nature.com.

Gillies, Bill, and Don Tapscott, "The Eight Net Gen Norms—Characteristics of a Generation," Syndicated Research Project, nGenera, February 6, 2007, www.ngenera.com.

Goldstein, Patrick, "More Movies Are Giving Critics the Finger: Bloggers Often Have More Influence Now," *Toronto Star*, August 19, 2006.

Goss, Michael Joseph, "A Box of Dreams," *New York Times Magazine*, September 28, 2003.

Green, C. Shawn, and Daphne Bavelier, "Action Video Games Modify Visual Attention," *Nature*, no. 423, 2003.

Greenfield, Patricia Marks et al., "Action Video Games and Informal Education: Effects on Strategies for Dividing Visual Attention," *Journal of Applied Developmental Psychology*, no. 15, 1994, cat.inist.fr.

Grimm, Robert et al., "Volunteer Growth in America: A Review of Trends since 1974," Research Report, Corporation for National and Community Service, December 2006.

Gross, Ralph, and Alessando Acquisti, "Information Revelation and Privacy in Online Social Networks," Conference Presentation, Carnegie Mellon University, November 7, 2005, www.heinz.cmu.edu.

Grossman, Lev, "Time's Person of the Year: You," *Time*, December 13, 2006.

"Guess Who's Coming to Dinner," National Report, Pew Research Center, March 14, 2006.

Guyer, Lillie, "Scion Connects in Out of the Way Places: Toyota Reaches Out to Gen Y Drivers without Screaming, 'Buy This Car!'" *Advertising Age*, February 21, 2005, www.adage.com.

Guyette, James, "Tuners Take Over," *Motor Age,* vol. 123, no. 6, June 2004.

Haines, Kim, "MySpace for Your Kind of Music," *Times-Standard Tech Beat*, August 15, 2006, newsbank.com.

Hamm, Steve, and Jan Rowley, "Speed Demons," *BusinessWeek*, March 27, 2006, www.businessweek.com.

Hargadon, Steve, "John Seely Brown on Web 2.0 and the Culture of Learning," www.stevehargadon.com.

Hastings, Rebecca, "Millennials Expect a lot from Leaders," *HR Magazine*, January 1, 2008.

Heckman, James J., and Paul A. LaFontaine, "The Declining American High School Graduation Rate: Evidence, Sources, and Consequences," Report, Voxeu.org, February 13, 2008, www.voxeu.org.

Hirsh-Pasek, Kathy et al., *Einstein Never Used Flashcards: How Our Children REALLY Learn—And Why They Need to Play More and Memorize Less*, New York: Rodale, 2003.

Hitti, Miranda, and Louise Chang, "Teen Brain: It's All About Me," *WebMD Medical News*, www.ivorweiner.com.

"How Young People View Their Lives, Futures and Politics: A Portrait of 'Generation Next,'" National Study, The Pew Research Center, January 9, 2007, people-press.org.

Howe, Neil, and William Strauss, "Helicopter Parents in the Workplace," Syndicated Research Project, nGenera, November 2007, www.ngenera.com.

——, *Millennials Go to College: Strategies for a New Generation on Campus*, Washington, D.C.: American Association of Collegiate Registrars, 2003.

Howe, Neil, and William Strauss, *Millennials Rising: The Next Great Generation*, New York: Vintage Books, 2000.

Humphrey, Taylor, "More than One-Third of Internet Users Now Have Broadband," Harris Poll No. 3, January 14, 2004.

Hurtado, Sylvia, and John H. Pryor, "The American Freshman. National Norms for Fall 2005," National Survey, Cooperative Institutional Research Program (CIRP) Higher Education Research Institute (HERI), January 26, 2006, www.gseis.ucla.edu.

Hutchinson, Sue, "On the Net, Bullying Takes an Insidious Turn," *San Jose Mercury News*, January 22, 2008.

"ICTs in Africa: Digital Divide to Digital Opportunity," International Telecommunications Union, March 18, 2008, www.itu.int.

"IDC Finds Online Consumers Spend Almost Twice as Much Time Using the Internet as Watching TV," Press Release, IDC, February 2008, www.idc.com.

"Industry Statistics," Bazaarvoice, www.bazaarvoice.com.

"Internet Access in U.S. Public Schools and Classrooms: 1994–2005," Research
    Project, U.S. Department of Education, National Center for Education Statistics
    (NCES 2007–020), 2007.

Jacoby, Susan, *The Age of American Unreason*, New York: Pantheon Books, 2008.

Jenkins, Henry, "Confronting the Challenges of Participatory Culture: Media
    Education for the Twenty-first Century," research project, The John D. and
    Catherine T. MacArthur Foundation, www.projectnml.org.

Johnson, Steven, "Dome Improvement," *Wired*, vol. 5, no. 13, May 2005,
    www.wired.com.

——, *Everything Bad Is Good for You: How Today's Popular Culture Is Actually Making Us
    Smarter*, New York: Riverhead, 2005.

Jonassen, David H., *Handbook of Research for Educational Communication and
    Technology*, Mahwah, N.J.: Lawrence Erlbaum Associates, 2004.

"Juvenile Offenders and Victims: 2006 National Report," U.S. Department of Justice,
    chap. 2, 38, ojjdp.ncjrs.gov.

Kamenetz, Anya, *Generation Debt*, New York: Riverhead, 2006.

Kanges, Sonja, "Techsoup," TechSoup, October 2006, souplala.blogspot.com.

Keating, Lauren, "The In Crowd Rushes to Keep Pace with Generation Y," *Shopping
    Center World*, vol. 29, no. 5, 2000, retailtrafficmag.com.

Keen, Andrew, *The Cult of the Amateur: How Today's Internet is Killing Our Culture*,
    New York: Currency, 2007.

"Kevin Rose Promises Digg 'Algorithm Change,' Top Digg User Quits," *Jonty*,
    September 7, 2006.

Kharif, Olga, "Asia's U.S. Wireless Foray: Asia's Wireless Operators Are Looking to the
    U.S. Market," *BusinessWeek Online*, December 11, 2007.

Kiesa, Abby et al., "Millennials Talk Politics: A Study of College Student Political
    Engagement," Research Study, The Center for Information and Research on Civic
    Learning and Engagement, November 7, 2007.

Kolodny, Lora, "Global Video Game Market Set to Explode," *BusinessWeek*, June 23,
    2006, www.businessweek.com.

Kornblum, Janet, "Meet My 5,000 New Best Pals," *USA Today*, September 20, 2006.

Kutcher, Stan, and Matthew Kutcher, "Understanding Differences of a Cognitive and
    Neurological Kind: Digital Technology and Human Brain Development,"
    Syndicated Research Project, nGenera, June 2007, www.ngenera.com.

Lamb, Brian, "Wide Open Spaces: Wikis Ready or Not," *Educause Review*,
    September–October 2004, www.educause.edu.

Lancaster, Lynne C., and David Stillman, *When Generations Collide: Who They Are. Why
    They Clash. How to Solve the Generational Puzzle at Work*, New York: Collins, 2003.

Lenhart, Amanda et al., "Teens and Social Media: The use of social media gains a greater
    foothold in teen life as they embrace the conversational nature of interactive online
    media," Family, Friends and Community Report, Pew Internet & American Life
    Project, December 19, 2007, www.pewinternet.org.

Leu, Donald J. et al., "Evaluating the Development of Scientific Knowledge and New
    Forms of Reading Comprehension during Online Learning," Exploratory
    Research, New Literacies Research Team, June 28, 2005.

Levine, Martha, "The Young Labeled Entitlement Generation," Associated Press, June 2005.

Leyden, Peter, Ruy Teixerira, and Eric Greenberg, "The Progressive Politics of the Millennial Generation," National Report, New Politics Institute, June 20, 2007, www.newpolitics.net.

"Lifetime Television Women's Pulse Poll of Gen Y Women," National Telephone Survey, Lifetime Networks, WomanTrend and Lake Research Partners, December 13, 2006, www.pollingcompany.com.

Lockwood, Nancy R., "The Aging Workforce: The Reality of the Impact of Older Workers and Eldercare in the Workplace," *HR Magazine*, December 2003.

Lopez, Mark Hugo et al., "The 2006 Civic and Political Health of the Nation: A Detailed Look at How Youth Participate in Politics and Communities," Research Study, The Center for Information and Research on Civic Learning and Engagement, October 2006.

Lovelace, Maryann Kiely, "Meta-Analysis of Experimental Research Based on the Dunn and Dunn Model," vol. 98, no. 3, January–February 2005, www.findarticles.com.

Madden, Mary, and Lenhart, Amanda, "Pew Internet Project Data Memo," Report, Pew Internet and American Life Project, July 31, 2003.

Mandelson, Peter, "Europe and the US: Confronting Global Challenges," Speech for Carnegie Endowment, November 8, 2007.

Marsden, Paul, "Tipping Point Marketing: A Primer," Tipping Point Research, www.viralculture.com, accessed April 30, 2008.

Marsden, Paul et al., "Advocacy Drives Growth: Customer Advocacy Drives UK Business Growth," Telephone Survey, London School of Economics and the Listening Company, September 5, 2005, www.lse.ac.uk.

Marston, Cam, *Motivating the 'What's in it for Me' Workforce*, Hoboken, N.J.: Wiley, 2007.

Martin, Carolyn A. and Tulgan Bruce, "Managing the Generation Mix: From Collision to Collaboration," Amherst, Mass: HRD Press, 2002.

Martin, Suzanne et al., "Trends and 'Tudes," *Harris Interactive*, vol. 5, no. 7, August 2006.

Maurer, Steven D., and Lui, Yuping, "Developing Effective e-Recruiting Websites: Insights for Managers from Marketers," ScienceDirect, May 2007, www.sciencedirect.com.

Mazur, Eric, "Reflections on a Harvard Education," *Harvard Crimson*, June 6, 2007.

McCaughey, Martha, and Michael D. Ayers, eds., *Cyberactivism: Online Activism in Theory and Practice*, Florence, Ky.: Routledge, 2003.

McGrath, Charles, "Growing Up for Dummies," *New York Times*, April 20, 2008.

McGregor, Jena, "The World's Most Innovative Companies," *BusinessWeek*, April 24, 2006, www.businessweek.com.

McLuhan, Marshall, and Barrington Nevitt, *Take Today: The Executive as Dropout*, New York: Harcourt Brace Jovanovich, 1972.

McLuhan, Marshall, and Quentin Fiore, *The Medium Is the Massage: An Inventory of Effects*, new ed., Corte Madera, Calif.: Gingko Press, 1996.

McPherson, Tara, "Digital Youth, Innovation and the Unexpected," book 3, The John D. and Catherine T. MacArthur Foundation Series on Digital Media and Learning, December 2007. mitpress.mit.edu.

McMurrer, Jennifer, "Instructional Time in Elementary Schools: A Closer Look at Changes for Specific Subjects," Report in the Series From the Capitol to the Classroom, Center on Education Policy, February 20, 2008, www.cep-dc.org.

Mesbah, Hesham M., "The Impact of Linear vs. Non-linear Listening to Radio News on Recall and Comprehension," *Journal of Radio and Audio Media*, vol. 13, no. 2, December 2006.

Metzer, Miriam J., Andrew J. Flanagin, "Digital Media, Youth, and Credibility," book 2, The John D. and Catherine T. MacArthur Foundation Series on Digital Media and Learning, December 2007, mitpress.mit.edu.

Miller, Mary Helen, "Segal '08 Rallies Students for Obama," *Bowdoin Orient*, September 14, 2007, orient.bowdoin.edu.

Mithers, Carol, "The Fractured Family," *UCLA Magazine*, July 1, 2006, www.magazine.ucla.edu.

Moglen, Eben, "Anarchism Triumphant: Free Software and the Death of Copyright," *First Monday*, August 1999, emoglen.law.columbia.edu.

"Monitoring the Future Study," Press Release, University of Michigan, December 11, 2007, www.monitoringthefuture.org.

Montgomery, Kathryn C., *Generation Digital: Politics, Commerce, and Childhood in the Age of the Internet*, Cambridge: MIT Press, 2007.

Montgomery, Kathryn, Ph.D., et al., "Youth as E-Citizens: Engaging the Digital Generation," report, Center for Social Media School of Communication, March 2004.

Myer, Mike, "COOL Solutions: Say Hi to Y," unpublished, Filene Research Institute, 2005.

"NACTAS 2006 Benchmark Survey," National Survey, North American Consumer Technographics, Forrester, February 2006, www.forrester.com.

"NAEP 2004 Trends in Academic Progress: Three Decades of Student Performance in Reading and Mathematics," Statistical Analysis Report, National Center for Educational Statistics (NCES 2005–463), December 21, 2005, nces.ed.gov.

Neff, Jack, "A Real Beauty: Dove's Viral Makes Big Splash for No Cash," *Advertising Age*, vol. 77, no. 44, October 30, 2006, goliath.ecnext.com.

"New Study Confirms Internet Plagiarism Is Prevalent," Press Release, Rutgers University, August 2003, ur.rutgers.edu.

Norimitsu, Onishi, "Thumbs Race As Japan's Best Sellers Go Cellular," *New York Times*, January 20, 2008.

"Number and Percent Change of Students Taking Advanced Placement (AP) Examinations, by Race/Ethnicity: 1999–2005, Table 13a," Status and Trends in the Education of Racial and Ethnic Minorities, National Center for Educational Statistics, (NCES–2007–039), September 2007, nces.ed.gov.

O'Donnell, Jayne, "Gen Y Sits on Top of Consumer Food Chain," *USA Today*, October 2006.

O'Loughlin, Sandra, "What's That Smell? Maybe, the Future of Marketing," *Brandweek*, vol. 48, no. 1, January 1, 2007.

Olsen, Stefanie, "Digital Kids: Are Virtual Worlds the Future of the Classroom?" CNETNews.com, June 12, 2006.

Olson, Lynn, "Computer Simulations Hone Leadership Skills," *Education Week*, October 30, 2007, www.edweek.org.

"Over Three Million Citizens under the Age of Thirty Participate in Super Tuesday Primaries," Press Release, The Center for Information and Research on Civic Learning and Engagement (CIRCLE), February 6, 2008, www.civicyouth.org.

Page, Susan, and William Risser, "Americans Revved Up—and Ready to Vote: Iraq, Economy, 'Fresh Faces' Boost Interest," *USA Today*, January 2008.

Papert, Seymour, *The Connected Family: Bridging the Digital Generation Gap*, Atlanta: Longstreet Press, 1996.

Parsad, Basmat, and Laurie Lewis, "Remedial Education at Degree-Granting Postsecondary Institutions in Fall 2000: Table 4," statistical analysis report, National Center for Education Statistics (NCES 2004–010), November 28, 2003, nces.ed.gov.

"Percentage of Persons Age 25 and Over and 25 to 29, by Race/Ethnicity, Years of School Completed, and Sex: Selected Years, 1910 through 2005, Table 8," *Digest of Education Statistics 2005*, National Center for Educational Statistics, nces.ed.gov.

Pianta, Robert. C. et al., "Opportunities to Learn in America's Elementary Classrooms," *Science*, vol. 315, no. 5820, 2007.

"Politicians and Estate Agents 'Least Trusted' Professions," *MailOnline,* December 4, 2006, www.dailymail.co.uk.

Pollitt, David, "How Credit Suisse Competes in the Global War for Talent," *Human Resource Management International Digest*, vol. 13, no. 6, November 2005.

"A Portrait of 'Generation Next,'" National Report, The Pew Center for People and The Associated Press, January 9, 2007.

Prensky, Marc, *Digital Game-Based Learning*, 1st ed., New York: McGraw-Hill, 2000.

"The Proportion of Serious Violent Crimes Committed by Juveniles Has Generally Declined since 1993," U.S. Department of Justice, Office of Justice Programs Bureau of Justice Statistics, www.ojp.usdoj.gov.

Prokofy, Neva "Do's and Don'ts for Big Business," Second Thoughts, October 26, 2006, secondthoughts.typepad.com.

Rainie, Lee, "Digital 'Natives' Invade the Workplace: Young People May Be Newcomers to the World of Work, but It's Their Bosses Who Are Immigrants into the Digital World," Internet Survey, Pew Internet & American Life Project, September 27, 2006, www.pewinternet.org.

Ramirez, Roberto R., "Analysis of Multiple Origin Reporting to the Hispanic Origin Question in Census 2000," U.S. Census Bureau, Population Division, Working Paper No. 77, November 21, 2005, www.census.gov.

Regine, "Forget QR Code: Here Comes ColorCode," June 17, 2008, www.we-make-money-not-art.com.

"Reports: Family, Friends and Community: Teenage Life Online: The Rise of the Instant-Message Generation and the Internet's Impact on Friendships and Family Relationships," Pew Report, Pew Research Center, June 21, 2001.

Resto, Chris, Ian Ybarra, and Ramit Sethi, *Recruit or Die: How Any Business Can Beat the Big Guys in the War for Young Talent*, New York: Portfolio, 2007.

Richards, David, "Free Illegal Music Beats iTunes," SmartHouse.com, November 30, 2005.

Rideout, Victoria, and Elizabeth Hamel, "The Media Family: Electronic Media in the Lives of Infants, Toddlers, Preschoolers and Their Parents," Report, Kaiser Family Foundation, May 24, 2006, www.kff.org.

Ries, Al, and Laura Ries, *The 22 Immutable Laws of Branding: How to Build a Product or Service into a World-Class Brand*, New York: HarperCollins, 1998.

Roberts, Donald F. et al., "Generation M: Media in the Lives of 8–18-Year-olds," Kaiser Family Foundation Study, March 2005, www.kff.org.

"Rock the Vote: Post Super Tuesday 2008," Lake Research Partners and the Tarrance Group, February 2008, www.rockthevote.com.

Roos, Dave, "How Net Generation Students Learn and Work," Howstuffworks.com, May 5, 2008.

Roschelle, Jeremy et al., "Scaling Up SimCalc Project: Can a Technology Enhanced Curriculum Improve Student Learning of Important Mathematics?" Technical Report, SRI International, May 2007, math.sri.com.

Rose, Frank, "In a Risky Experiment, Chevrolet Asked Web Users to Make Their Own Video Spots for the Tahoe: A Case Study in Customer Generated Advertising," *Wired*, December 12, 2006, www.wired.com.

Rose, Kevin, "Digg This: 09-f9–11–02–9d-74-e3–5b-d8–41–56-c5–63–56–88-c0," Digg.com, May 1, 2007.

Rosenfeld, Alvin A., and Nicole Wise, *The Over-Scheduled Child: Avoiding the Hyper-Parenting Trap*, New York: St. Martin's Press, 2000.

Rosser, J. C. et al., "The Impact of Video Games on Training Surgeons in the 21st Century," *Archives of Surgery*, no, 142, 2007, digiplay.info.

Sacher, Emily, "60% of U.S. High School Students Cheat, 28% Steal, Study Finds," Bloomberg.com, October 14, 2006.

Salan, Katie, "The Ecology of Games: Connecting Youth, Games and Learning," book 4, The John D. and Catherine T. MacArthur Foundation Series on Digital Media and Learning, December 2007, mitpress.mit.edu.

Salmon, Jacqueline L., "Firm Support for Stricter Upbringing: Disciplinarians' Advice Finds Parental Favor," *Washington Post*, Metro, November 24, 1996.

Sayer, Liana C. et al., "Are Parents Investing Less in Children? Trends in Mothers' and Fathers' Time with Children," *American Journal of Sociology*, no.110, 2004, www.soc.upenn.edu.

Schmar-Dobler, Elizabeth, "Reading on the Internet: The Link between Literacy and Technology," *Journal of Adolescent & Adult Literacy*, vol. 47, September 2003, www.readingonline.org.

Schoof, Ulrich, "Stimulating Youth Entrepreneurship: Barriers and Incentives to Enterprise Start-ups by Young People," SEED Working Paper No. 76, International Labour Organization, Development Department, 2006, www.ilo.org.

Schwartz, Barry, "Digg to Change System to Stem Gamin: Top Digger Quits," SearchEngineWatch.com, September 7, 2006.

"Science Competencies for Tomorrow's World Executive Summary," International Report, The Program for International Student Assessment, Organization for Economic Cooperation and Development (OECD).

Scott, Megan K., "Parents Turn the Miley Moment into a Teachable One," Associated Press, April 29, 2008.

Scott, Sarah, "The Myth of Multitasking," *Chatelaine Magazine*, 2006, scottreports.com.

Sertoglu, Cem et al., "Cultivating Ex-Employees," *Harvard Business Review*, vol. 80, no. 6, June 2002.

Shaffer, David Williamson, *How Computer Games Help Children to Learn*, New York: Palgrave Macmillan, 2006.

Sher, Julian, "The Not-So-Long Arm of the Law," *USA Today*, May 1, 2007.

Sherman, Gabriel, "Testing Horace Mann," *New York*, March 30, 2008.

Shirky, Clay, *Here Comes Everybody: The Power of Organizing Without Organizations*, New York: The Penguin Press, 2008.

Simhan, Raja, "Refer Candidates and Get Rewarded at IT Companies," *The Hindu Business Line*, September 24, 2003, www.blonnet.com.

Snow, Catherine E., and RAND Reading Study Group, "Reading for Understanding: Toward an R&D Program in Reading Comprehension," RAND Corporation, 2002.

"Speed Matters: A Report on Internet Speeds in All 50 States," CWA Policy Paper, Communications Workers of America, www.speedmatters.org.

Sternberg, Robert J., and David Preiss, eds., *Intelligence and Technology: The Impact of Tools on the Nature and Development of Human Abilities*, Florence, Ky.: Routledge, 2005.

Stoler, Peter, *The Computer Generation*, first ed., New York: Facts on File, 1984.

"Study Examines Differences among Generations in the Workforce over the Past 25 Years," National Study, Families and Work Institute, October 2004, familiesandwork.org.

Sutherland-Smith, Wendy, "Weaving the Literacy Web: Changes in Reading from Page to Screen," *The Reading Teacher*, vol. 55, no. 7, April 2002, tapor.ualberta.ca.

Swanson, Christopher, "Cities in Crisis: A Special Analytical Report on High School Education," National Report, Editorial Products in Education Research Center, April 2008, www.americaspromise.org.

Tapscott, Don, *The Digital Economy: Promise and Peril in the Age of Networked Intelligence*, New York: McGraw-Hill, 1995.

———, *Growing Up Digital*, New York: McGraw-Hill, 1997.

———, "Talent 2.0," Conference Presentation, May 14, 2008.

Tapscott, Don, and Robert Barnard, "The Net Generation as a Consumer," Syndicated Research Project, nGenera, August 2005, www.ngenera.com.

———, "Talent 2.0—The Net Generation and the World of Work," Syndicated Research Project, nGenera, October 2006, www.ngenera.com.

Tapscott, Don, and David Ticoll, *The Naked Corporation: How the Age of Transparency Will Revolutionize Business*, New York: Free Press, 2003.

Tapscott, Don, and Anthony D. Williams, *Wikinomics: Harnessing the Power of Mass Collaboration*, New York: Penguin Portfolio, 2006.

Taylor, Cathy, "The Future of Advertising," Special Report, State of the News Media 2008, www.stateofthenewsmedia.org.

Tergesen, Anne, "What Price College Admission?" *BusinessWeek*, June 19, 2006, www.businessweek.com.

"Thousands of College Students Using Their Spring Breaks to Help Gulf Region Rebuild from Hurricanes," Press Release, Campus Compact, March 3, 2006.

Ticoll, David, and Darren Meister, "Hon Hai: Winning by Design," Syndicated Research Report, nGenera, June 2005, www.ngenera.com.

Toffler, Alvin, *Future Shock*, New York, Bantam Books, 1984.

——, Alvin, *The Third Wave*, New York, Bantam Books, 1984.

Tomopoulos, Suzy et al., "Is Exposure to Media Intended for Preschool Children Associated with Less Parent-Child Shared Reading Aloud and Teaching Activities?" *Ambulatory Pediatrics*, vol. 7, no. 1, January–February 2007, www.sciencedirect.com.

Topiel, Jennifer, "College Board Announced Advanced Placement Result: A Greater Percentage of the Nation's Students Succeed on AP Exams, Predictors of Success in College; Report Points to the Need for Better Preparation in Earlier Grades," Press Release, The College Board, February 13, 2008.

"Toward a New Golden Age in American Education: How the Internet, the Law and Today's Students Are Revolutionizing Expectations," National Education Plan 2004, U.S. Department of Education, October 2004, www.ed.gov/.

Trickery, Helyn, "No Child Left Out of the Dodge Ball Game?" CNN.com, August 24, 2006.

Trunk, Penelope, "What Gen Y Really Wants," *Time*, July 16, 2008.

Trzesniewski, Kali H. et al., "Do Today's Young People Really Think They Are So Extraordinary? An Examination of Secular Trends in Narcissism and Self-Enhancement," *Psychological Science*, vol. 2, no. 19, February 2008, lib.bioinfo.pl/pmid:18271867.

Turkle, Sherry, "Can You Hear Me Now?" *Forbes*, May 7, 2007.

Twenge, Jean, "Egos Inflating over Time: A Cross-Temporal Meta-Analysis of the Narcissistic Personality Inventory," *Journal of Personality*, no. 94, 2008.

——, *Generation Me: Why Today's Young Americans Are More Confident, Assertive, Entitled—and More Miserable Than Ever Before*, New York: Free Press, 2006.

Tyler, Kathryn, "The Tethered Generation", *HR Magazine*, May 1 2007.

"2006 American Community Survey," U.S. Census Bureau, Selected Social Characteristics.

"The U.S. Mom Market," Telephone Survey, Packaged Facts and Silver Stork Research, October 16, 2003, www.marketresearch.com.

"U.S. Teenage Pregnancy Statistics: National and State Trends and Trends by Race and Ethnicity," National Report, The Guttmacher Institute, 2006, www.thenationalcampaign.org.

Vahidy, Tamina, "Best Commuter Workplaces," *Line 56*, October 20, 2006.

Vahlber, Vivian et al., "If It Catches My Eye: An Exploration of Online New Experiences of Teenagers," Media Management Center, Kellogg School of Management, January 2008, www.mediamanagementcenter.org.

Veen, Wim, and Ben Vrakking, *Homo Zappiens: Growing Up in a Digital Age*, London, Eng.: Network Continuum Education, 2007.

Viadero, Debra, "Exercise Seen as Priming Pump for Students' Academic Strides: Case Grows Stronger for Physical Activity's Link to Improved Brain Function," *Education Week*, vol. 27, no. 23, February 12, 2008.

——, "Nature + Nurture = Startling Jump in IQs," *Education Week*, vol. 21, no. 19, January 23, 2002.

——, "Poor Rural Children Attract Close Study," *Education Week*, vol. 27, no. 22, February 5, 2008.

"Voting and Registration in the Election of November 2004: Population Characteristics," Population Characteristics Report (P20–556), U.S. Census Bureau, March 2006, www.census.gov.

Walker, Rob, "Bull Market," *Outside*, April 2002, outside.away.com.

Ward, Bill, "Power to the People," *Minneapolis-St. Paul Star Tribune*, June 2, 2008, www.startribune.com.

Wartella, Ellen et al., "From Baby Einstein to Leapfrog, from Doom to the Sims, from Instant Messaging to Internet Chat Rooms: Public Interest in the Role of Interactive Media in Children's Lives," SRCD Social Policy Report, vol. 18, no. 4, 2004, www.srcd.org.

Weier, Mary Hayes, "Tata and Infosys Set the Bar: 15 percent Raises This Year in India," *InformationWeek*, April 21, 2007, www.informationweek.com.

Weinberger, David, *Everything is Miscellaneous: The Power of the New Digital Disorder*, New York: Henry Holt and Company, LLC, 2007.

Williams, Alex, "'But I Neeeeeed It!' She Suggested," *New York Times*, May 29, 2005.

Wolpert, Stuart, "OCHS Wins MacArthur 'GENIUS' Grant," *UCLA Magazine*, 1998, www.today.ucla.edu.

"The World Is Your Oyster," *The Economist,* October 2006, www.economist.com.

"World Internet Statistics," Miniwatts, MarketingGroup, www.internetworldstats.com.

"Workforce Wake-Up Call: Your Workforce is Changing, Are You?" Hoboken, N.J. : Wiley, 2006.

"YouTube Beating Bruises Dr. Phil," *Newser*, April 14, 2008, www.newser.com.

Yeaton, Kathryn, "Recruiting and Managing the 'Why?' Generation: Gen Y," The CPA Journal, April 1 2008.

INDEX

ABCDEs of Marketing, 212–216
Absorption of information, 104–106
Accountability, 266
Activism, 257, 269–288
    capabilities available for, 274–276
    before the Internet, 273–274
    by Net Gen, 277–280
    and norms of Net Gen, 284–287
    protests, 62, 255–257, 283–284
    and world inherited by Net Gen,
        272–273
    (*See also* Civic action; Political activity)
Adams, Scott, 155
Adelman, Asher, 154
Aftab, Parry, 231–232
Aguilar, Monica, 172
Aliva, Jose, 210
alphaWorks, 267
Anderson, Brad, 158, 178, 180
Anderson, Craig, 298
Anime music videos, 45
Apple, 48, 95, 201
Armstrong, Billie Joe, 283
A Swarm of Angels, 61
Avenir, 137
Ayers, Michael, 287
Azar, Michele, 158

Baby boomers, 7, 11–16
    children's influence on spending of, 188
    family life of Net Gen vs., 220–224
    independence of, 295
    as parents, 28, 31, 222–226
    technology accommodation by, 18
    technology use by Net Gen vs., 41–44
    workplace clash of Net Gen and,
        153–155
Baby Bust (*see* Generation X)
Bailey, John, 156
Bakht, Aditi, 160, 165, 303
Bannister, Jeffery, 128
Bantay Usok project, 258
Barnard, Robert, 172–173
Bauerlein, Mark, 3, 5, 98, 117–118, 245,
        289, 306
Bavelier, Daphne, 98, 101–102

Beck, Glenn, 4, 230
Benkler, Yochai, 210
Best Buy, 76, 89, 149–150, 158, 170
The Big Picture Company, 141
Blakemore, Sarah-Jayne, 101
Blinkoff, Robbie, 46
Blogs, 45, 178, 195–196
Bly, Robert, 3, 5, 289
BoingBoing, 200
Bolstad, Rachel, 145
Boomer generation (*see* Baby boomers)
Borde, Keenan, 131
Bowlby, Melissa, 45
boyd, dana, 55, 179, 180
Brain, 97–119
    absorption of information by, 104–106
    adaptation of, 290
    adolescent, 100–101
    and gaming, 101–104
    and multitasking, 106–110
    of Net Geners vs. parents, 29
    post-childhood changes in, 99–100
    and thinking skills, 110–117
Brain Reactions, 201
Brands, 215–216
Brantley-Patterson, Michelle, 140, 146
Brinkman, Amy, 232
Broadcast style, 130, 244, 258–265
Bullying, online, 4, 229–233, 297–298
Burton, Matthew, 154
Burton, Whitney, 270
Bush, George H. W., 248, 266
Bush, George W., 247–248
Buxton, Bill, 173
Buzz Marketing, 201

Canuel, Ron, 143
Car customization, 78
Carr, Nicholas, 116
Casio cameras, 54
Cayley, Briony, 144
Ceniceros, Matt, 41, 304
Center for Academic Integrity, 297
Cheating, 297
Cheese, Peter, 176–177
CIRCLE, 278

Civic action, 11, 37, 288
  move to political activity from, 247–249
  of Net Gen, 61–62, 245–246, 279
Clarke, Victoria, 279
Climate change, 282–284
Clinton, Hillary, 170, 243, 249, 252, 266
Clinton, William, 249, 262
Coca-Cola, 203, 215–216
Cognition, distributed, 114
Cohler, Matt, 64, 69
Colbert Report, 210
Collaboration norm, 35, 89–91, 162–164,
  190–191, 285
Collaborative work systems, 178–180
College enrollment, 123
Collins, Brian, 251
Colombia, rebellion in, 61–62
Coloroso, Barbara, 232–233
Communications, political, 266–267
Communications Decency Act (1996), 234
CompUSA, 204
Computers, 17, 142–144
Concentration, 116–117
Conn, Coco, 19
Consumers, Net Gen, 11, 36–37, 81,
  185–217
  ABCDEs of Marketing to, 212–216
  and decentralization of knowledge,
    195–196
  influences on, 192–201
  listening and responding to, 204–205
  and marketers' penetration of networks,
    201–204
  and network "superusers," 207–208
  norms as guide for, 188–192
  as prosumers, 208–212
  and social network acquaintances,
    198–200
  spending by, 188
  targeting niche communities of, 205–207
  unprecedented influence of, 188
Corriero, Jennifer, 280–281
Coster Ann, 145
Cox, Kelly, 283–286
Creativity, 114
Crime, 32, 222, 298–299
Criticisms of Net Gen, 289–306
  bases of, 304–306
  as bullying, 297–298
  as dishonest, 296–297
  as dumbest generation, 290–293
  as giving up privacy, 294–295
  as having bad work ethic, 299–300
  as having sense of entitlement, 299–300

Criticisms of Net Gen (Cont.):
  as lacking independence, 295–296
  as losing social skills, 293–294
  as narcissistic, 200
  as shallow, 300–302
  as violent, 298–299
Croft, Roy, 149–150
Cronkite, Walter, 265–267
Cross, Rob, 292
C-SPAN, 267
Current TV, 258
Curtis, Greg, 263
Customization norm, 34–35, 77–79, 161,
  189, 285
CYBERsitter, 234–235

Daily Show with Jon Stewart, The, 5, 266–267
Damon, William, 4–5
Darfur campaign, 274–276, 285
Dasilva, Kevin, 117
Daum, 255
Davis, Vicki, 138
De Alwis, Rhadeena, 269–270
Dean, Rob, 176
Dede, Chris, 122, 135–136
Defense Intelligence Agency, 154
Degrees of separation, 194–195
Dell, 191
Dell, Michael, 191
Della Volpe, John, 247, 256
Deloitte, 155, 169, 300
Democracy, 258–265, 268
Democratic parenting style, 220, 225–226
Democrats, Net Gen as, 249–250
Digg, 76, 189–190, 196, 208
Digital brainstorms, 262–263
Digital Divide, 262
DIRECTV, 177
Distributed cognition, 114
Dobrzynski, Rebecca, 107
Doctorow, Cory, 200
Doidge, Norman, 99
Dormia, 210
Douglas, Lawrence, 81
Dove "Campaign for Real Beauty," 80, 200
Dover, Mike, 174, 175
Dreitlein, Janet, 220
Dreitlein, Matthew, 219–220
Dreitlein, William, 220
Dropouts, 123, 126, 291
Drucker, Peter, 154
Dubois, Nick, 138, 303
Dumouchel, Phil, 37
Dunbar, Robin, 193–194

Dunbar's number, 193
Durham, M. Gigi, 4

"Echo" generation, 11, 15–17 (*See also* Net Generation)
Edelman, 205
Education, 11, 121–148
   American divide in, 123–126
   broadcast vs. interactive, 130–133
   for changing information/skills, 127
   collaborative, 91
   computers in, 142–144
   cost of, 31
   focus on student in, 129–130
   individual vs. collaborative, 137–139
   instruction vs. discovery in, 134–136
   mass- vs. individualized, 139–141
   old paradigms in, 127–129
   paradigm for change in, 144–148
   personalized conceptual framework in, 109
   role reversal in, 145
   strategies for teaching, 148
EdVisions, 141
Elrom, Ben, 246, 248, 261, 304
E-mail, 46, 94, 251
Employees, Net Gen, 10–11, 36, 149–183
   clash of boomer employees and, 153–155
   collaborative work systems for, 178–180
   engaging, 176–178
   entitlement attitude of, 151–153
   evolving relationships with, 180–182
   and generational firewall, 169–170
   initiating relationships with, 173–176
   job-hopping by, 169–171
   and Net Gen norms, 160–172
   and new models of high-performance work, 157–159
   talent management for, 172–183
   and War for Talent, 155–157
   and work ethic, 299–300
Endgadget.com, 203
Entertainment norm, 35, 91–93, 165, 191, 285–286
Entitlement, sense of, 151–153, 299–300
Entrepreneurship, 170
Environmental issues, 282–284
E-Petitions (UK), 263
Epstein, Robert, 227, 295
Erickson, Tamara, 162
Ewing, Charles, 32

Facebook, 39–40, 54–56, 62–68, 76
   banned in workplaces, 165

Facebook (*Cont.*):
   customer control of, 211
   Obama's presence on, 253
   political campaign friends on, 252
   as virtual microphone/movie screen, 59
Family, 11, 219–241
   of boomers vs. Net Gen, 220–224
   generational changes in, 31–32
   online threats to, 229–237
   perceived income of, 313
   spending time with, 314
   (*See also* Parenting; Parents)
Family and Work Institute, 238
Farley, Jim, 78
Fede, Colby, 192
FedEx, 210
Felt, Adrienne, 68
Fetherstonhaugh, Allison, 185–186
Fetherstonhaugh, Brian, 185–186, 213
FighttheSmears.com, 254
Film industry, 58–61, 195–196
Financial goals of Net Gen, 301
"Florida beat-down," 230–231, 298
Freedom norm, 34, 74–77, 160–161, 188–189, 284–285
Friedman, Stephen, 275–276
Friedman, Thomas, 27, 282
Friends, 197–198, 252, 314
Furdyk, Michael, 6, 270–271, 280–281

Game-based job training, 177
Gaming and video games, 57–58, 316
   addiction to, 3
   and brain development, 101–104
   and collaboration, 171–172
   multiplayer, 315
   skills used in, 290
   violence incited by, 4, 298
Gap, 213
Gardner, Howard, 139
Gee, James, 103
General Motors (GM), 90
Generation Lap, 28–29, 178–179, 223, 226–227
Generation Me, 83–84, 245 (*See also* Net Generation)
Generation Next, 15–16
Generation X, 14–16
Generation Y, 17 (*See also* Net Generation)
Geraci, John, 23
Gessner, Kevin, 187, 189
Gilbert, Jane, 145
Gillett, Stephen, 171–172
Gillman, Ashley, 279

Gladwell, Malcolm, 196–197
Global climate change, 282–284
Global Peace Exchange, 293
Good Questions program, 131, 132
Goodnight, Jim, 143–144
Google, 48–49, 76, 91–92, 292
Gore, Al, 258–260, 283
Gosman, Fred, 4
Grafman, Jordan, 108–109
Grand Theft Auto IV, 298
Grantham, Charles, 92
Green, C. Shawn, 97–98, 101–102, 105
Green Day, 283
Greenfield, Susan, 109, 110, 114, 290
Greenwood College School (Toronto,
    Canada), 146
Greeson, Michael, 95
Griffiths, Joanna, 279
Gzowski, Peter, 142

Habitat Jam, 262–263
Hais, Michael D., 252–253
Hale, Alyssa, 58
Hallowell, Edward, 3
Hancock, Denis, 181
Hanons, Matt, 61
Hansen, Randall, 157
Harassment, 297–298
Harel, Idit, 19
Harfoush, Rahaf, 44–45, 51–53
Harper, Dennis, 137–138
Harrison, Lee Hecht, 180
Hay, Aaron, 304
Helicopter parents, 31, 227–229, 295–296
Herbst, Danny, 246
Hochwarter, Wayne, 151–152
Honda, 206
Horizon Project, 138
Howard, Jeff, 140–141
Howe, Neil, 227, 229, 279–280, 294
Hughes, Chris, 243–244, 250, 253
Hugo, Victor, 262
Hunka, Steve, 133

IBM, 262, 267
Income, family, 313
An Inconvenient Truth (movie), 283
Independence of Net Gen, 4, 295–296
Infosys Technologies, 95–96, 166
Innocentive network, 258
Innovation norm, 36, 94–96, 168–169, 192,
    286
Instant messaging, 93, 94

Integrity norm, 35, 82–86, 162, 189–190,
    285
Intel, 76
Intellectual property rights, 4, 86,
    296–297
Intelligence of Net Gen, 3, 30–31, 98, 114,
    290–293
Intellipedia, 154
Internet, 17–18
    activism prior to, 273–274
    as communications archive, 266–267
    creating content on, 40, 45
    and creativity, 114
    entertainment on, 92
    as escape for Net Gen, 223–224
    and global youth culture, 23, 27–28
    Net Gen vs. boomer use of, 42
    Net Gen's influence on, 53–54
    parental tracking on, 221, 234–235
    product information on, 189
    revolution in nature of, 40
    self-organizing on, 56–57, 61–62
    skills for searching, 111–112
iPod, 189
iPod Nano, 95, 201
Irwin, Emilee, 279
Itsyournature widget, 284

"Jams," 262–263
Jenkins, Henry, 114, 265
Job recruiting, online, 173–174
Job-hopping, 169–171
Johansson, Scarlett, 253
Johnson, Samuel, 292
Johnson, Steven, 103
Jones, Graham, 167
Jones, Savannah, 303
Joseph, Barry, 136
Just, Marcel, 104
Just-in-time teaching, 131–132

Kanert, Mike, 302
Kay, Alan, 19
Kenalty, Vanessa, 303
Kenninger, Melissa, 147
Kersten, Scot, 158
Kettler, Moritz, 73, 94, 167
Khan, Sarof, 58
Knowles, Zoe, 114
Kong, Cherrie, 134, 145
Kreeda, 58
Kutcher, Matthew, 29–30, 100, 113
Kutcher, Stanley, 29–30, 100, 113

Lazear, Mike, 250
Lcbabieee, 231
Leadership guidelines, 311
Learning, 103, 109, 110 (*See also* Education)
Lee Myung-Bak, 255–256
Lego, 191, 211
Leskovec, Jure, 194–195
Lessig, Lawrence, 45
Leu, Donald, 112, 129, 291
Levine, Mel, 152
Levy, Stephen, 206
Lewin, Nate, 304
Lewis, Erin, 55
Lewitinn, Sarah, 196
Liberal arts education, 142
Lindsay, Julie, 138
LinkedIn, 174–175
Locke, Austin, 28
Logue, Ronald, 156
LonelyGirl15, 205
Lorenz, Edward, 207

Majer, Alan, 56
Malischewski, Charlotte-Anne, 256–257
Managers, guidelines for, 183
Marketface, 213
Marketing to Net Gen, 64–65, 67, 201–204, 212–217 (*See also* Consumers, Net Gen)
Marsden, Paul, 205–206
Marx, Anthony W., 124–125
Mashups, 45, 210
Massachusetts Institute of Technology (MIT), 138–139
Mazur, Eric, 132
McCabe, Don, 297
McCain, John, 252, 266
McCaughey, Martha, 287
McEwan, Bill, 169
McEwan, Matthew, 169
McGraw, Phil (Dr. Phil), 230
McLean, Del, 303
McLeod, Margaret, 144, 145
McLuhan, Marshall, 36, 104, 128, 208
Me Generation, 83–84, 245 (*See also* Net Generation)
Media:
    babies' exposure to, 239
    boomers' vs. Net Geners' use of, 7
    and brain development, 30
    customization of, 79
    multitasking with, 106–110

Media (*Cont.*):
    Net Gen attitude toward, 20–21
    (*See also specific forms, e.g.:* Television)
Meier, Megan, 231, 232
Meier, Tina, 231
Memory, 115
Merry, Mollie, 249
Meyer, David, 107, 109
Michael, Erica, 104
Michalski, Jerry, 41, 103–104
Microsoft, 91, 136
Middle College High School (Memphis, Tennessee), 140–141, 146–147
Middle College National Consortium, 140–141
Milgram, Stanley, 194
Millennials, 17 (*See also* Net Generation)
The Mills Corporation, 191
Mobile phones, 46–51, 70, 95, 191–192, 317
Moglen, Eben, 211
Montgomery, Kathryn, 65, 234, 282
Moore, Geoffrey, 205–206
Morales, Oscar, 62
Morgan, Jesse, 43
Mothers Against Videogame Addiction and Violence (MAVAV), 3, 4
Motorola, 95
Mountain Dew, 211
MTV, 274–275
mtvU, 93, 274–276, 286
Mulder, Adam, 178
Mullenweg, Matt, 170–171
Multiplayer gaming, 53, 57–58, 315
Multitasking, 106–110, 291
Munroe, Bobbi, 303
Murthy, N.R. Narayana, 95–96
Music, 58–61, 86–88, 196, 296, 317
My.barackobama.com, 250, 253
MyDesktop.com, 280
Myers, Matthew, 103
MySpace, 59, 66, 174, 200, 201, 230, 236

Narcissism, 5, 83–84, 300
National Institute for School Leadership, 177
Natural Resources Defense Council (NRDC), 283, 284
Negroponte, Nicholas, 17
Net Generation, 1–3, 9–37
    affinity for technology in, 9–10
    characteristics of, 6–7
    contemporary characterization of, 304–306

Net Generation (*Cont.*):
  criticisms of, 3–5
  demographics of, 15–16
  as distinct generation, 11–14
  fear of, 304–306
  as first global generation, 21–28
  as force for change, 306–310
  and "generation lap," 28–29
  and generational vs. life-stage differences, 29–30
  media diet of, 20–21
  norms of, 34–36 (*See also* Norms of Net Gen)
  in other countries, 156
  in overall population, 318
  as parents, 237–241
  potential of, 309–310
  as smartest generation, 30–31
  technology assimilation by, 18–20
  transformation of modern life by, 10–11, 36–37
  troubling issues for, 34
  values of, 32–34
  world inherited by, 272–273
Network Foundation Technologies, 59
Networks, 201–204, 207–208 (*See also* Social networks)
News sources, 5, 44–45, 267
N-Fluence networks, 89, 187
  as advertising channel, 201–204, 215
  rise of, 192–197
  types of, 197–201
nGenera, 1, 178
NGenophobia, 306, 308–309
Niche communities, targeting, 205–207
Nike, 95, 201
Nilekani, Nandan M., 96
Niscembene, Juan, 271
Njoroge, Kevina Power, 263
No Child Left Behind, 128–129
Norms of Net Gen, 6–7, 73–96
  and activism, 284–287
  collaboration, 89–91
  customization, 89–91
  entertainment, 91–93
  freedom, 74–77
  innovation, 94–96
  integrity, 82–86
  scrutiny, 79–82
  speed, 93–94
  (*See also individual norms*)

Obama, Barack, 75, 170, 243
Obama, Michelle, 254

Obama campaign, 6, 243–244, 250–255
Oke, Jason, 252
One Laptop Per Child campaign, 17
Open Educational Resources (OER) movement, 138
Open family, 233, 237–238, 240–241
OpenCongress.org, 267
O'Reilly Media, 206
O'Shea, Joe, 180, 292–293
Ourstage.com, 58–59

Page, Ellen, 61
Paige, Rod, 143
Papert, Seymour, 19, 134
Parenting:
  generational differences in, 305
  guidelines for, 241
  styles of, 28, 220, 224–226
Parents:
  authority of, 28
  baby boomers as, 28, 222–226, 306–307
  helicopter parents, 31, 227–229, 295–296
  Net Geners as, 237–241
Patterson, Frank, 292–293
Pearson, P. David, 111
Peddie, Caitlin, 279
Personal information, posting, 4, 7, 40–41, 64–70
Pictures, posting, 294–295
Plagiarism, 297
Political activity, 11, 37, 243–268
  and broadcast vs. interactive democracy, 258–265
  and civic engagement, 245–246
  and liberal views of Net Geners, 249–250
  and Obama campaign, 243–244, 250–255
  protests, 255–257
  through entertainment, 93
  traditional, 246–247
  and trust in government, 265–267
PoliticalBase.com, 267
Politicopia.com, 263
Population, 15, 16, 21–28, 33
Pornography, online, 233–236
Potter, Eric, 190, 303
Prensky, Marc, 105, 108, 113, 126, 135
Privacy, 7, 64–70, 294–295
Procter & Gamble, 201, 208
Product design, input to, 89–90, 211 (*See also* prosumers, Net Gen as)
Proenza, Luis M., 127

Progressive Group of Insurance
    Companies, 82
Prosumers, Net Gen as, 90, 208–212
Purohit, Sanjay, 96
Putschoegl, Andy, 18

Quigley, Jim, 155, 157, 169, 177, 300
Quintessential Careers, 157

RAND Reading Study Group, 112
Rasmussen, Chris, 158–159
Ratey, John, 129
Rattray, Ben, 44, 162
Rauf, Feroz, 227
Raymond, Jade, 60
Reading, 109–112, 290–291
Red Bull, 210
Reebok, 276
Ressler, Steve, 165
Rich, Frank, 253
Rin, 49
"River City," 135–136
Rivieri, Salvatore, 63
Rock, Jennifer, 89
Roosendaal, Ton, 60–61
Rosenfeld, Alvin, 223
Rosenkrantz, Brooke, 302
RottenTomatoes.com, 61
Rubadeau, Erik, 119, 146

Salzillo, Alex, 302
Samsung Group, 95
Sarnes, Brittnie, 199
SAS, 143–144
Satris, Stephen, 297
Scanning, 113–114
Schmidt, Eric, 292
Schulze, Richard M., 149
Schwartz, Jonathan, 296–297
Schwartz, Russell, 195–196
Scrutiny norm, 35, 79–82, 161–162, 189,
    285
Seaward, Stephen, 299
Seely Brown, John, 28, 29, 100, 103,
    134–135, 137, 139, 171–172, 179
Segal, Meredith, 252
Seidberg, Effie, 165
Self-organization, 56–57, 61–62
Sexual predators, online, 236–237
Shaw, Jen, 304
Shea, Dan, 278–279
Shenzhen General Talents Market (China),
    168
Sher, Julian, 236

Shim, Karen, 276
Shimberg, Andy, 239
Shimberg, Madison, 239
Shniderman, Adam, 81
Smith, Graham, 303
Sobeys Inc., 169
Social networks, 54–58
    for activism, 271
    consumer influence of, 198–200
    marketers' penetration of, 201–204
    news spread by, 273
    Obama campaign's use of, 250–255
    privacy with, 67–70, 294–295
    (*See also* N-Fluence networks)
Social skills, 293–294
Somers, Patricia, 228
Sony Ericsson, 202–203
Speed norm, 35–36, 93–94, 166–168,
    191–192, 286
Spencer, Gregory, 33
STAND action group, 275
Stealing, 296
Steinfeld, Trudy, 294
Stewart, Jon, 5, 34, 272–273
Straka, Nadine, 279
Strassel, Quinn, 58
Strauss, William, 227, 229, 301
Sturgeon, Tina, 260
Suffolk, John, 263
Sun Microsystems, 296–297
Sunlight Labs, 267
Svengsouk, Jocelyn, 135, 136
Swanson, Christopher, 125–126
Sweeney, Richard, 130
Szymanski, Eva, 279, 302

TakingITGlobal, 6, 271, 281, 282, 284–285
Tang, Anita, 168
Tapscott, Alex, 1–2, 6, 19–20, 43–44,
    56–57, 66, 74–75, 78, 79, 82–83, 111,
    163, 181, 223, 225–226, 235, 237, 304
Tapscott, Ana, 19, 111, 225–226, 235
Tapscott, Nicole (Niki), 1–2, 6, 20, 73–74,
    77, 78, 81, 82, 88, 91, 95, 107–108,
    111, 188, 193, 197–199, 225–226,
    237, 240–241, 279
Tatum, Mike, 267
Technology assimilation, 18–20
Technology use by Net Geners, 9–10, 39–71
    boomers' technology use vs., 41–44
    for civic causes, 61–62
    for conversation, 45
    Facebook, 63–66
    gaming, 57–58

Technology use by Net Geners (*Cont.*):
  influence of, 51–54, 280
  and lack of privacy, 64–70
  mobile phones, 46–51
  for music and movies, 58–61
  for news, 44–45
  and power shift away from authorities,
    62–63
  social networks, 54–57
  TV, 41–44
Technorati, 53
Telepresence, 173
Television, 7, 13–14, 20, 40–44,
    259–260, 290
Terrell, Maria, 131, 132
Thinking skills, 110–117, 119
Thomlinson, Carol Ann, 141
Thompson, David, 146
Thompson, Emma, 269
Thompson, Jody, 76
Tinkham, Katie, 46, 246
Toffler, Alvin, 90, 208
Top Coder Network, 258
Toyota, 78
Transparency, 162, 266, 267, 285
Tremor, 201
Turkle, Sherry, 222
Turnitin.com, 297
Twain, Mark, 282
Twenge, Jean, 5, 83–84, 289, 300, 308
Twitter, 252, 255

Unilever, 80–81
U.S. Army, 174
U.S. Marine Corps, 174
Unruh, Jeremy, 59
Urquhart, Steve, 263

Values of Net Gen, 5, 31–34, 231, 300–302
Vans shoe company, 191
Video games (*see* Gaming and video games)
Violence, 4, 298–299 (*See also* Bullying,
    online)
Virtual town hall meetings, 263
Virtual world sites, 315
Visual information processing, 101–106

Vocalpoint, 208
Volunteerism, 277–278, 288, 301–302
Voting, by Net Gen, 244, 245, 247

Wal-Mart, 205
Watterson, Kim, 232
Web 2.0, 18, 53, 264, 291
Wellington Girls' College (New
    Zealand), 144
Wernham, Richard, 146
Wesch, Michael, 122
Westwell, Martin, 108
Wikipedia, 53, 91, 258
Wikis, 138
will.i.am, 75, 253
Williams, Anthony, 208, 239
Williamson, Daniel, 302
Wind-up Records, 45
Winn, William D., 104–105
Winograd, Morley, 252–253
Wireless Portal (Canada), 258
Wiremedia, 192
Without Tomorrow (band), 59–60
Wolf, Jonathan, 159, 198, 215, 302
wordpress.com, 170
Work ethic, 4–5, 299–300
Workplace issues (*see* Employees, Net Gen)
World Economic Forum, 269
World Wide Web, 17–18
Wright, Jeremiah, 254
Wright, Nate, 275

YouTube, 53–54, 60, 76
  advertising campaigns on, 201
  Baltimore Cop on, 63
  Evolution video, 80
  Florida beat-down on, 230–231
  interactivity of, 92
  as most visited site, 200
  Obama videos on, 252–254
  as permanent searchable record, 266
  A Vision of Students Today, 121–122
Yunan Jin, 270

Zajack, Alex, 303
Zuckerberg, Mark, 6, 39, 54, 55, 64, 67, 243